The Web of Friendship

Frontispiece: The Ferrars' harmony borrowed by King Charles I in 1633 and bearing his annotation in the lower left corner; Houghton Library, Harvard College Library, Vault A 1275.5 F. Cf. the page of the harmony (p. 169) made at the king's request in which Nicholas Ferrar incorporated new and elaborate cross-referencing tools.

The Web of Friendship

Nicholas Ferrar and Little Gidding

Joyce Ransome

James Clarke & Co

James Clarke and Co
P.O. Box 60
Cambridge
CB1 2NT
UK

www.jamesclarke.co
publishing@jamesclarke.co

ISBN: 978 0 227 17348 0

British Library Cataloguing in Publication Data
A record is available from the British Library

First Published, 2011

Contents

List of Illustrations

Acknowledgements

It is indeed a pleasure at the conclusion of a work of scholarship to thank the many people who gave help and encouragement along what has been a lengthy but rewarding way. I am grateful for the unfailing help and courtesy of the staffs of the libraries in which I have worked: Brown University, Harvard University, the University Library, Cambridge, the Bodleian Library, Oxford, and the British Library. Dr David Sykes of Dr Williams's Library kindly gave us access to the Jones MSS despite the alterations that the library was then undergoing. I am grateful also to Mark Priddey, Archives Manager of the Oxfordshire Record Office, for permission to use the estate map of Little Gidding that is in the Annesley Papers.

Investigation of the Little Gidding harmonies, those products of the 'scissors-work' of the women of the household, has incurred its own special debts of gratitude to the institutions and individuals who hold them and who readily gave me permission to see the volumes. First I am indebted to Her Majesty the Queen by whose gracious permission I inspected the Pentateuch harmony in the Royal Library, Windsor. My path to it was eased by Bridget Wright and the Rev. Canon John White of St George's Chapel, to whom I am also indebted for his and Lynette Muir's essential volume on Nicholas Ferrar, *Materials for the Life of Nicholas Ferrar*. In addition to the harmonies in the British Library and the Bodleian, I was fortunate to be able to see the very fragile original harmony in the Houghton Library at Harvard, and I am grateful to William Stoneman for permission to do so. The curator and staff of the Cotsen Children's Library at Princeton made my visit there both pleasant and productive as did the National Trust staff at Ickworth House. I am grateful also to Harriet and Michael Flower for their hospitality during my visit to Princeton. R. Harcourt (SP??) Williams, Librarian of the Cecil Collections at Hatfield House, enabled me to see the sumptuous harmony in that collection. I am most grateful to Lord Normanton and his secretary, Mrs. Valerie Garner, for welcoming my husband and me to Somerley and allowing us to see the singular polyglot harmony in his lordship's library. Catherine Hilliard, Librarian of St. John's College, Oxford, was similarly welcoming and helpful when we visited the college to study Archbishop Laud's Pentateuch harmony. Greg Cowley provided timely help that expedited our access to both of the Oxford harmonies.

Finally I offer thanks to the present owner of the Heming harmony and Nicholas Ferrar's manuscript volume on 'The Duties Common to Man and Woman' for permission to study these books.

Visits to Little Gidding have given an essential sense of place, the setting in which the family lived, even though their manor house has vanished and their church has been altered. To those who welcomed us and furnished us with information from their own experience of community as well as the materials in Ferrar House, especially Rev. Pat Saunders, the late Margaret Smith, Rev. Tony and Judith Hodgson, and Jillian Wilkinson I offer my warmest thanks.

I am grateful to the Master and Fellows of Magdalene College, Cambridge, and especially to Dr Richard Luckett, Keeper of the Old Library, for permission to see and to quote from the Ferrar Papers in the Old Library and to reproduce the portrait of Nicholas Ferrar that is in the college. Mrs. Aude Fitz Simons also provided gracious and timely assistance during our numerous visits to Magdalene. To preserve the fragile original papers I have largely worked from first the microfilm and now the excellent Adam Mathew digital edition that makes the Papers available online. I offer my thanks to William Pidduck of AMDigital for giving access to this essential resource. To Dr Richard Maber I owe thanks both for permission to use material that first appeared in *The Seventeenth Century* and for providing in the Seventeenth-Century Conferences he has organised at Durham, a stimulating forum in which to give these ideas a first trial. Dr Sidney Gottlieb, Editor of *The George Herbert Journal*, has kindly given me permission to use material that first appeared in that journal. I am grateful also to Adrian Brink and Charlie Livingston of the Lutterworth Press not only for their care in editing the text and illustrations but also for their encouragement to an author new to the world of publishing. To John Walsh I am indebted for discussions of voluntary societies in general and in the Church of England in particular. They illuminated for me the significance of Little Gidding as a community. I have benefited also from discussions of family history and structure with Leonore Davidoff. Our paths that had diverged since undergraduate days came together again to help me understand the Ferrars in a larger context. My great friend Elisabeth Gleason has been an admirable guide to the complicated ecclesiastical world of sixteenth-century Italy in which Juan de Valdes and the Italian *spirituali* lived and wrote. Her critical comments have not only saved me from errors but also helped me to understand the context of ideas and examples that were vital to Nicholas Ferrar. To other friends who have read and offered helpful and encouraging comments on earlier drafts I offer thanks: Paul Dyck, Jeremy Gregory, and Tim Harris. Special thanks are due to those generous and intrepid friends who have read the entire script: Margaret Aston, Trevor Cooper, and Andrew Foster. Their comments have clarified my prose, corrected my mistakes, and encouraged me to persevere. Errors that remain are of course solely my responsibility. To Trevor Cooper I am further indebted for his work on Little Gidding church including not only the way worship was conducted in it but also its original architecture before the alterations of 1714.

My greatest debt is to my husband, David Ransome, whose editing of the Ferrar Papers first drew me to Nicholas and his family. Without his help and encouragement I could not have completed this work. The discovery in the Oxfordshire Arichives of the 1626 estate map of Little Gidding, communicated to him by Philip Saunders of the Cambridgeshire Record Office, enabled us to walk the fields and mark how many of the hedgerows and paths remain intact. David has supplied much of the genealogical information, including the Appendix to this volume, that is so crucial to understanding characters and relationships within the family. The Ferrars are an unusually well documented seventeenth-century family and our discussions (including disagreements) about relationships and characters of both family and friends have helped me to sharpen and articulate my own views. He has read numerous drafts, first of articles and then of the complete text, pruning my sentences and correcting my facts. To him I dedicate this book, with love.

Editorial Conventions

For the Ferrars the year began on 25 March and they dated their letters accordingly. In citations of their letters I have retained the day and month given. For those letters written between 1 January and 24 March, however, I have given the year as a double date (1630/31) rather than the single one based on a new year beginning on 1 January.

In quoting from the letters in the Ferrar Papers I have expanded the conventional abbreviations but retained the original spelling as much as possible. Given the difficulty in these manuscript letters, however, of distinguishing a 'v' from a 'u' in words such as 'have', I have generally opted for the 'v' of modern usage. When I have added letters and punctuation that I thought necessary for clarity, I have put these in brackets.

Note on Sources

The sources I have used to create this new and complex picture of Ferrar and the community he formed at Little Gidding are numerous and varied. Some of them are well-known, most notably the materials assembled by John Ferrar and used by Francis Turner, who had completed an 'authorised' but unpublished biography by 1681. Though both the folio volume of John's notes and the manuscript of Turner's biography were eventually lost, they survived long enough for several copyists to make varying extracts that have been preserved and in some cases printed. These biographies have formed the basis of that hagiographic portrait of Nicholas and roseate account of life at Little Gidding that has formed a staple of Anglican historiography from the 1650s up to the most recent (1938) biography of Ferrar by Alan Maycock.[1] The early biographies remain, of course, an important source not only of basic information about the daily life of the family at Gidding but also about their earlier life in London and Nicholas's education, travels and Virginia Company experience.

A manuscript volume now in the Bodleian Library, Oxford, is of special interest because it includes not only one of these biographical extracts but also the notes Turner compiled as he worked on his biography.[2] This rich vein of material has not been used before. It contains not only directions to himself about how to write the life but also extracts from Ferrar's own writings that were available to Turner but that have now vanished. These extracts range from a summary of George Herbert's letters to Ferrar to Ferrar's detailed instructions to pupils on polite behaviour. They provide insight into Ferrar's own spiritual life, though hardly as much as his lost spiritual diary would have done. They also make clear just how closely he supervised Little Gidding's communal life. 'The best minds are like clocks which to goe right need daily winding upp'.[3] As a committed teacher Ferrar conscientiously wound those clocks. He was not only a spiritual director but a managing director as well, whose essential combination of empathy and authority produced willing friends and followers though it is difficult to recapture retrospectively.

From the early biographies one would get no hint of any strains or conflicts at Gidding or any suggestion of a more outward-looking attitude. John Ferrar never mentioned his fractious wife Bathsheba, for example, or the trouble caused by young Edward Collet, who had eventually to be shipped off to the East Indies, or the very existence of the Little Academy. The only tiny hint of voluntarism comes in the form of a mention that only the willing should participate in night vigils. Such episodes as these one can only find in the letters and in the 'Story Books' of the Little Academy. In using the Story Books as sources, however, one must remember that they are fair copies and therefore edited versions, not literal transcriptions, of what was actually said. What surprised me to find in them were the covenants and solemn and sometimes written promises by which the group formally organised and revived itself as a voluntary society. There must, however, have been considerable pressure on members of the younger generation to accept these obligations, for their parents and uncles were also present and participating in the sessions. The buildup of such pressures comes out in Ferrar's account of the Academy's final resurrection when it was reduced to just four members with him as an active participant rather than, as earlier, a supervisory presence. The Academy initially played a significant role in Gidding's development as a community but in the longer run proved more ambitious than most of the members were willing to sustain.

There are besides the Story Books other volumes created within the household that are also significant sources of knowledge about Gidding as a community. These are the biblical harmonies that, like the Little Academy, are another and ultimately more successful example of Ferrar's pedagogy. Studying the actual volumes makes clear the intricacy of the craft work that produced this 'new kind of printing', and the learning and cooperation the work required and the satisfaction it gave its practitioners. That harmony-making went on past the demise of the Little Academy and the death of Ferrar himself suggests a significantly freer atmosphere in the Concordance Room than prevailed within the Academy.

The Ferrar Papers, that archive of family letters in Magdalene College, Cambridge, were not unknown in the twentieth century; Blackstone published some of the letters and Maycock used them in his biography. They had remained in the family and only came to Magdalene from its Master, Peter Peckard (1717-97), whose wife Martha (1729-1805) was a Ferrar. What has made them a new and vital source for me has been the discovery of additional letters, the cataloguing of the whole collection and its availability first on microfilm and now online. The detail that the letters furnish makes possible a much more revealing picture of relationships and family dynamics than was earlier possible. The sustained sequences of letters between Nicholas and Arthur Woodnoth and between Nicholas and Joshua Mapletoft give an unusual depth of insight into these three men and particularly into Nicholas as counsellor and friend. The letters also reveal him as a different style of counsellor with his older Collet nieces.

The letters also round out the picture of both the community and its leader by documenting Ferrar's ongoing involvement in traditional domestic concerns, a necessary corrective to the picture of him as wholly pre-occupied with matters spiritual. The Ferrars, like any seventeenth-century family, needed to manage their resources, maintain their network of friends and family and place in suitable work and marriage the members of the younger generation. Here the letters of Nicholas's sister Susanna Collet supplement the Magdalene material on these worldly concerns, for she was deeply involved in matters concerning her children. She consulted both Arthur Woodnoth and her brother on whom much of the burden of such negotiations fell. The question of how to deal with the delinquent Edward Collet, for example, generated serious disagreement between Nicholas and the Collet parents. The correspondence makes very clear that even had he wished to, Nicholas could not have abandoned the world when he went to Little Gidding.

Nor was the world willing to abandon him and his unusual household. While it is difficult to gauge how much attention outside the circle of friends and family Gidding actually attracted, there must have been enough curious visitors to prompt the family to deveise a standard reception for them. The early biographies of Ferrar describe it, as did Edward Lenton's letter, of either 1633 or early 1634, to Sir Thomas Hetley of nearby Brampton. That letter is the only substantial evidence of an outsider's reaction to Gidding and it tells us much about the nature of the subterranean gossip about the household that clearly circulated in the neighbourhood and beyond.

These are the chief primary sources on which I have relied in this study to bring to life the man Nicholas Ferrar and the community that formed his 'web of friendship'. In interpreting them and placing them in a larger seventeenth-century context I have used secondary studies of gender roles and family structure that have been particularly helpful in understanding a Little Gidding where women outnumbered men and where the education of women was a major concern. They also help to clarify how unusual the family structure of the household was in having a bachelor patriarch and a widowed matriarch at its head yet how conventionally Nicholas and his mother functioned together as leaders of the family. They have also supplied the mercantile and parliamentary context that played a vital part in shaping Ferrar's response to the economic crises that brought the family to Little Gidding. I have also drawn on at least some of the vast literature on the Jacobean and Caroline Church of England in order to understand both his own churchmanship and the theological and liturgical controversies that he strove earnestly to avoid. To this I have added material on the post-Restoration church and especially on the appearance of voluntary societies within that church that gave it a new strength even as it lost its comprehensive character.

Abbreviations

Blackstone	Blackstone, B., ed., *The Ferrar Papers*, Cambridge: Cambridge University Press, 1938
CCEd	*Clergy of the Church of England Database*, http://www.theclergydatabase.org.uk
FP	*The Ferrar Papers*, 1590-1790, David R. Ransome, ed. [in microform, Wakefield, Eng: Microform Academic Publishers, 1992, and online, Marlrough, Wilts: Adam Matthew Publications, 2005, *The Virginia Company Archives*]
Herbert, Works	Herbert, George, *The Complete English Works*, Anne Pasternak Slater, ed., London: Everyman, 1995
M&W	Muir, Lynette R and John White, eds., *Materials for the Life of Nicholas Ferrar*, Leeds: The Leeds Philosophical and Literary Society Ltd, 1996
Maycock	Maycock, A. L., *Nicholas Ferrar of Little Gidding*, Grand Rapids, MI: William B. Eerdmans, 1980 [first published in 1938]
Mayor	Mayor, J. E. B., ed., *Nicholas Ferrar: Two Lives by his Brother John and by Dr Jebb*, Cambridge: Cambridge University Press, 1855
Monotessaron	Ransome, Joyce, 'Monotessaron: The Harmonies of Little Gidding', *The Seventeenth Century* 20:1 (Spring 2005), 22-52
NA	National Archives, Kew (formerly the Public Record Office)

Peckard	Peckard, Peter, *Memoirs of the Life of Mr Nicholas Ferrar*, Cambridge: J. Archdeacon, 1790
S Collet Letters	Letters of Susanna Collet (copied by John Ferrar III); Oxford, Bodleian Library, Ms. Top. Hunts.e.1. This volume was first used, possibly by John Mapletoft *c.* 1655, for 'Some Directions for the Collecting (SP??) of Materialls for the Writeing of the life of Mr Nicholas Ferrar'. A generation later John Ferrar III (1660-1721) SOMETHING the volume and transcribed the letters of his great-aunt, Susanna Ferrar Collet.
Sharland	Sharland, E. Cruwys, ed., *The Story Books of Little Gidding*, London: Seeley and Co., 1899
Turner	Notebook of Francis Turner; Oxford, Bodleian Library, Ms. Rawlinson. D. 2
Venn	John Venn and J. A. Venn, *Alumni Cantabrigiensis*, Part I (to 1751), 4 vols., Cambridge: Cambridge University Press, 1922-54
Williams	Williams, A. M., ed., *Conversations at Little Gidding*: 'On the Retirement of Charles V' 'On the Austere Life', Cambridge: Cambridge University Press, 1970
Wordsworth	Christopher Wordsworth, 'Nicholas Ferrar', *Ecclesiastical Biography* (London: Rivington, 1818), Vol. 4, pp. 73-108

Introduction

When in 1980 Nicholas Ferrar was added to the Church of England's calendar, he was commemorated as 'the Founder of the Little Gidding community'.[1] The twentieth century had indeed seen the establishment of communities, including one at Little Gidding itself, which invoked the Little Gidding example.[2] Basil Blackstone, who in 1938 published a composite of three early biographies of Ferrar along with a number of letters from the Ferrar Papers, there called him a 'seeker after the perfect community'.[3] Clearly the idea of community appealed to many in the twentieth century, including some Anglicans. The Little Gidding they envisioned, however, was still the idealised community portrayed in nineteenth-century novels and in the biographies of Nicholas Ferrar based on the hagiographic notes of Nicholas's brother John. In presenting Ferrar as a creator of community I am not seeking to portray an Anglican saint or to promote a particular version of Anglicanism. I have taken community as a central theme not only because it was central to Ferrar's life but also because it produces a more balanced portrait of the man himself and his family and friends. It brings together both the unusual and strenuous manner of the Ferrars' dedication to God's service that made them different from their contemporaries and the inevitable responsibilities and problems they shared with other families in their seventeenth-century world. Much as they condemned many of its values, they could not escape that world. Instead, through the example of their community life they aspired to instruct it. The theme of community also points up a hitherto unexplored aspect of Gidding's influence on later Anglicanism.

'Community' connotes both a voluntary and a purposeful society, both of which characteristics Ferrar gave to Little Gidding. It is not possible to say from the surviving evidence why or exactly when community assumed such importance for Ferrar though it does reveal what groups influenced his concept of what a community might or should be. The vicissitudes of 1624 from which Nicholas had to extricate the family would have brought those influences together in the move to Gidding. The printed sources, together with the enlarged collection of Ferrar Papers in Magdalene College (now available online), Cambridge, show how he introduced both voluntarism and purpose as he transformed a family-centred household grateful to God for its deliverance from near disaster into a community dedicated to God's service. As bonds within the household strengthened, Ferrar saw new and larger possibilities for that service. He expanded the community to include family and friends outside the immediate household. He sought to strengthen its bonds by introducing new projects for the community that would make it a more active presence capable not merely of rejecting worldly values but of instructing the world, particularly by its example of temperance. Gidding was to become a 'light on a hill' as John Winthrop's Boston was to be a 'city upon a hill'.[4] Little Gidding was thus not a static but an evolving community.

The demands of a community exact a price from its members that they must be willing to pay. One member of the community was clearly unwilling to pay that price: John Ferrar's wife Bathsheba, who was at Gidding not by her own choice but by that of her husband. Her rebellious behaviour throws into relief the remarkable willingness of most of the family to sacrifice individual privacy to a highly regulated communal life and also to embrace the additional projects Ferrar introduced after 1630.

This book has a basically chronological structure as befits both an evolving individual and an evolving community. Mary Woodnoth Ferrar, the family's matriarch, had purchased Little Gidding with her dower money in 1624 to help rescue the family from threatened bankruptcy. Two years later the family had decided to make it their permanent home. Those early years at Gidding, up to 1630, make clear the dual demands that Ferrar faced in establishing an expanded household in a new way of life while also attending to worldly business essential to the family's support.

Chapter one introduces the family and gives an account of the education of Nicholas Ferrar and his experience of various communities both at home and abroad that influenced his concept of the 'perfect community'. The chapter concludes with the crises of the Virginia Company and John Ferrar's brush with bankruptcy in the course of which the family acquired the Gidding property and resolved to leave London for a new life together in the Huntingdonshire countryside.

Chapter two recounts the character of this new and carefully structured life in an unusual household headed not by a married couple (though two couples and their children were there) but by the widowed Mary Ferrar and her bachelor son Nicholas. Governing a group of thirty or more required planning and direction from its leader, Nicholas, but also willing consent from those he led in order to operate smoothly. He was able generally to govern by persuasion rather than by command, thanks not only to his own skill but also to the firm support of his mother and brother. Also crucial for the cohesion of the new household was finding for the younger generation, especially the older Collet nieces, satisfying roles through which they could genuinely contribute to the new household and readily accept their uncle's spiritual direction. To that end he carefully cultivated individual relationships with them and provided them with useful and instructional work, namely the practical task of managing the household and the making of harmonies that combined the four gospel accounts of Christ's life into a continuous and illustrated narrative. Demanding as organising the new household was, however, he could not give his full attention to Little Gidding for he had also to spend considerable time in London tending to necessary family business that included not only matters financial and legal but also the marriage of one Collet nephew and the apprenticeships of two others. The move to Little Gidding, particularly in these early years, was for him no withdrawal from the world.

By 1630 the family was sufficiently settled that Mary Ferrar could write to an old friend in London 'now I begin to live', explaining that her new life in God's service was proving more rewarding than she could have hoped.[5] Nicholas too was by then able to spend most of his time at Gidding and to devote his energies to introducing those new projects that strengthened the household's sense of community and expanded its horizons of service.

Chapters three to six take up in turn these particular projects to which the community turned its attention in the years from 1630 till Ferrar's death in 1637. Chapter three concerns Ferrar's efforts to expand his community into a 'web of friendship', bringing into the network friends and family outside the household. These included his cousin Arthur Woodnoth, his friend who later became his nephew by marriage, Rev. Joshua Mapletoft, and another particularly close friend George Herbert. The counsel he offered to Woodnoth and Mapletoft reveals in unusual depth the nature of these important relationships and of the spiritual direction Ferrar offered. Of a different sort was his counsel to his brother whose wife Bathsheba had no desire either to join the web of friendship or to accept her brother-in-law's spiritual direction. What effect if any her example had on her Collet nieces remains an intriguing but undocumented question.

Chapters four and five together describe an intensification of the community through activities during 1632 that culminated in a great experiment in temperance that the family hoped would set an example for the world to follow. For this experiment they adopted a diet from George

Herbert's translation of Luigi Cornaro's *Treatise on Sobriety* based on measured quantities of solid and liquid food. At the same time the two men were collaborating on a translation of one of Ferrar's favourite authors, Juan de Valdes, and on adding night vigils to the family's daytime devotions. Ferrar with the help of the Collet nieces also prepared for the printer his friend's volume of poems, *The Temple*. In what they called their Little Academy the family prepared themselves for their experiment by a lengthy discussion of the meaning of temperance that they followed by a pledge to follow Cornaro's diet during Christmastide. The result did not live up to their expectations. During the ensuing two years some continued the diet but others drew back. Both the Little Academy and the community's ambitious hopes for leadership were casualties of this tension between the zealous and the lukewarm. When the Little Academy was eventually reconstituted in late 1634 or early 1635 its membership was reduced to a dedicated quartet of the zealous: Mary and Anna Collet, and Nicholas and John Ferrar, a measure of the changes in the household that those two years had brought.

Chapter six recounts a more successful and enduring outreach to a more exalted world than the Ferrars could ever have anticipated. In 1633 King Charles had borrowed the family's gospel harmony and when he had returned it requested that they make first one and then others for him. For his keen royal reader Ferrar developed harmonies with more elaborate formats and different biblical subjects that required the family to master new techniques. The work of making them, as John Ferrar said, kept both hands and minds occupied with what was good and useful.[6] Indeed the family continued to produce harmonies up to 1642 when the king on his way north made his first visit to Gidding and watched the work in progress on a splendid volume for Prince Charles.

Chapter seven traces the legacy of Ferrar and Little Gidding from the initial effort of John Ferrar in 1655 to assemble materials for a biography of his brother to the death in 1721 of Dr John Mapletoft, Nicholas's great-nephew and godson. That legacy is twofold: first, the selections from Francis Turner's unpublished biography of Ferrar that preserved the knowledge of both Ferrar himself and the daily life of Gidding and second, the influence of Gidding's example of community. The network that grew out of the web of friendship included men who became leaders of the post-Restoration Church of England and were active promoters of voluntary societies such as the Society for Promoting Christian Knowledge that addressed what they felt as an urgent need to revive piety, promote education and combat vice. Using Little Gidding's example of unquestioned piety and obvious loyalty, they could reassure those who had feared such groups as subversive of the established church. Acceptance of such societies represented a significant change in a church whose membership after the Toleration Act of 1689 had ceased to be automatic and had become in effect voluntary.

A concluding chapter considers Ferrar as a man and as a spiritual leader. His character was neither simple nor without fault. He was a model of piety, a generous and learned friend, an ingenious and dedicated teacher. Yet he could be at once controlling and self-effacing, open and secretive, wary of spontaneity while valuing voluntarism, a mystic and a micromanager. As a spiritual leader he possessed the authority and persuasive power to convince family and friends to join in his quest for a community that would be not a refuge from the world but an exemplary presence in it.

St Paul admonished the Christians in Rome to 'be not conformed to this world: but be ye transformed. . .that ye may prove what is that good, and acceptable, and perfect, will of God' (Romans 12:2). No one expected that being 'in' the world but not 'of' it would be easy and that message was for Francis Turner the first main point to be learned from Ferrar's life, that 'the mixt [life] is the best & the hardest'. [7]

What follows here is an account of that mixed life as Nicholas Ferrar organised it and his family and friends experienced it.

1

Formative Years:
'the time of his ingathering'

Nicholas Ferrar as the spiritual director of Little Gidding was above all an educator and one whose idea of education spanned a wide spectrum ranging from the spiritual to the academic to the practical. Isaac Walton rightly characterised the household at Gidding as 'a little college'; it was certainly the 'school of religion' that George Herbert's Country Parson desired his household to be.[1] It was also a school of crafts and music, history and geography, household management and of course the standard curriculum of reading, writing, arithmetic and languages. The varied educational programmes he devised for his family inevitably incorporated and adapted methods and materials and experiences from his own education. There were four formative influences on which he drew. The first and most fundamental was the family in which he grew up. The second was his formal schooling up to and including his time at Cambridge. The third comprised his years of Continental travel and the fourth his experience in the business world of London. This opening chapter will consider each of these factors in turn, a sequence that will conclude with the crisis of 1624 in the aftermath of which the family moved to Little Gidding and embarked on their new life together.

The family of the senior Nicholas and his wife Mary Woodnoth Ferrar was but one of many mercantile households in London that maintained a godly establishment of the sort delineated in the numerous conduct books of the late sixteenth and seventeenth centuries.[2] Theirs was not solely a nuclear family of parents and unmarried children but a household family of the conventional patriarchal type led by a husband and wife and including all who dwelt under their roof: servants, apprentices, and other long-term visitors, who might or might not be kin.[3] Within their marriage Nicholas and Mary Ferrar built a close and conventional partnership with each fulfilling their prescribed roles, he as the head and provider and she as the manager of the household and educator of children. She brought to her role not only piety and strength of character but upward mobility through her own gentry family. From that household base they extended their network and maintained contacts with 'friends', whether literally kin or not, through an extensive correspondence.[4]

The family's worldly success was of recent origin. The senior Nicholas Ferrar, head of the family until his death in 1620, had been born in Hertford about 1545, the son of John Ferrar, a linen draper. As a young man he had made his way to London, as did many of his contemporaries who hoped to make their fortunes in England's expanding overseas trade. There he was apprenticed for ten years from Michaelmas 1564 to John Harby, a member of the Skinners' Company and a Merchant Adventurer, and was sworn as a freeman of that Company on 13 December 1574.[5] In a world where partnerships were the standard mode of doing business, personal connections mattered enormously and he proved skillful at building himself a successful network of collaborators. In the 1580s and 1590s he and Erasmus Harby, probably John Harby's nephew,[6] and Thomas Middleton[7] were partners in a sugar refinery in Mincing Lane, London and later moved into the Hamburg trade, establishing a depot at Stade for trading both in grocer's wares and cloth. In 1589 the three also entered upon the very profitable activity of 'reprisall' or privateering and continued it through the 1590s.[8] He also availed himself of Middleton's financial skills.[9] In 1599 the elder Ferrar had added to the Hamburg trade investment in the East India Company. He subsequently joined the Spanish Company in 1604 and the Virginia Company in 1609 along with its later offshoot the Bermuda Company.[10] He remained close to the Middletons throughout these years and left to Thomas and his brother Hugh and to their sister-in-law Anna, probably Robert's widow, each a gold ring of £3 value.[11] In worldly terms, therefore, his was a classic story of mercantile success.

As befitted his wealth and rank, the elder Nicholas was said to have kept 'a good table' and governed his household well. His guest list testified to the breadth of his interests, for he entertained not only business colleagues like the Middletons but also such notable persons as Sir John Hawkins, Sir Francis Drake, and Sir Walter Ralegh.[12] Small wonder that in such surroundings his family acquired a taste for accounts of travel and exploration as well as of history. At the same time his zeal for religion led him to entertain ministers so frequently that the family was said to have been 'never without a clergyman' in the house to conduct morning and evening prayer. One such guest was Augustine Lindsell, a Fellow of

Clare Hall, Cambridge, who became young Nicholas Ferrar's tutor and subsequently his colleague and lifelong friend. Another was Francis White, whom the elder Nicholas brought to London as a lecturer and who went on to become one of Richard Neile's circle at Durham House and eventually Bishop of Ely.[13] Ferrar also provided his parish church, St Benet Sherehog, with seating and repairs to the chancel.[14]

For his religious zeal the Virginia Company offered further scope, this time directly connected to his commercial interests. The settlements on the banks of the James presented opportunities not only to develop trade but also to propagate the gospel, and he responded by giving generously (£300) to provide education for the Indians, a concern shared by his sons John and Nicholas.[15]

Ferrar's wife, Mary Woodnoth Ferrar, brought to the family many gifts of person and character, not least the prestigious status of her family. The Woodnoths were old and established gentry, who had been lords of the manor of Shavington in Cheshire for many generations. Contemporaries remarked that Mary Ferrar had no taste for the mere gossip and frivolous chat in which many women indulged. She must nonetheless have been a skillful and interested hostess at her husband's 'good table', eager to learn from her guests and adventurous enough to want to see for herself a ship lying in the Thames ready to depart for the Indies.[16] Herself a model of personal piety, she admirably fulfilled not only her role as dutiful wife but also the prescribed task of mother and mistress to provide Christian instruction to both children and servants. The Ferrars were a musical family and as members of the household gathered round their mistress, she led them in singing psalms together as they worked. She also heard her children read aloud from the Bible and also from Foxe's *Actes and Monuments* and other worthy volumes. She herself read scripture daily, attended church for prayers on Wednesdays and Fridays, and was said to have heard 12,000 sermons in her lifetime. Contemporaries also noted her feat of memorising the entire Psalter when she was sixty. Augustine Lindsell described her as a woman of few words but those eloquent and full of wisdom and sound judgment.[17] While thus fulfilling her expected role within the conventional patriarchal framework, she nevertheless retained a sense of independence and strength of mind and character. The senior Ferrars, likened to Zechariah and Elizabeth, the parents of John the Baptist, who are 'both righteous before God',[18] thus made an impressive couple and worked together, as the conduct literature prescribed, to create not only a pious but also a lively and happy family. Indeed, the readiness of her children later to join her in building a special household at Little

Gidding must constitute its own testimony to the harmony of the London household in which they had grown up.

Six of the nine children born to Nicholas and Mary survived to adulthood.[19] Susanna, the eldest and only daughter to reach adulthood, received in addition to a basic general education and religious instruction lessons in French and music, becoming a skilled performer on the lute.[20] Her parents had then fulfilled another parental duty by providing for her a good husband. By 1600 she had married John Collet, son of another prosperous London family, who inherited properties in Southwark and, no later than 1606, a lease on property at Bourn, near Cambridge.[21] There they could create their own godly household for themselves and their numerous progeny as well as a 'home-from-home' for Susanna's brothers, especially William and Nicholas during the years they spent in Cambridge. Susanna certainly was her mother's daughter; as we shall see, her numerous letters show her to have been not only literate but articulate and she was unhesitating in offering forceful advice and criticism to her children. Her later interventions in the discussions of the family's 'Little Academy' show her ready to do so with equal vigour face-to-face.

The five Ferrar sons were also carefully instructed in the precepts and practices of piety. Their parents likewise undertook that other duty expounded in the conduct books, providing an education that would set them up in adult life. All the brothers attended the school of Rev. Robert Brooke, a family friend and former London preacher, at Enborne in Berkshire.[22] Thereafter a choice of career for each of them was supposed to take into account not only the family's status and aspirations but also the abilities and preferences of the boys themselves, advice which their father conscientiously followed.[23] Erasmus and William trained as barristers, which called for a year or two at university (Oxford for Erasmus and Cambridge for William) followed by seven or eight years at one of the Inns of Court. Unhappily, neither of these young men lived long enough to contribute to the family's continued prosperity and social ascent, as such a training would have led their parents to hope for and expect. Erasmus died in 1609, too soon to have qualified; William, who was called to the Bar on 19 June 1618, perished in the course of the year following, probably while on his way to Virginia. [24]

Richard, the only one of the adult sons who was to take no part in the life of Little Gidding, was trained like his older brother John as a merchant. Unfortunately he lacked John's steadiness and application and ended up spending much of his adult life running from his creditors and trying to cadge money from his family. His letters to his father from Hamburg in

1617-18, when he was twenty-one or twenty-two, were full of apologies for not writing more often and protestations of gratitude and determination to prove himself a dutiful child and good man. He received under his father's will a £100 legacy as well as forgiveness of his debts, the latter suggestive of the more serious trouble to come.[25] He was still entrusted with family business in 1626, but the following year saw Nicholas trying to arrange for him sanctuary at the Savoy from his creditors. His mother evidently supplied substantial subsidies at various times but by the time she made her will in 1628 she left nothing directly to Richard, stipulating only that his brothers John and Nicholas should do for him as he deserved.[26]

These two sons will in turn assume leadership of the family and become the chief architects of its fortunes and misfortunes and its new direction.

The parental household also included those servants who assembled round their mistress and sang psalms together while they worked and the young men who came as apprentices to Nicholas.[27] Visitors would have included besides the Middletons, Bateman, Raleigh, White and Lindsell, Anthony Wotton and after 1619 those involved in running the Virginia Company: Sir Edwin Sandys, Sir John Danvers, indeed as many of the members as could attend company meetings held in the Ferrars' last London house in St Sithes Lane. There were also those unnamed clerics less notable than White and Lindsell, who took advantage of Ferrar hospitality. There were in addition kin in London: Cousin Arthur Woodnoth as an apprentice and then a qualified goldsmith, his older half-brother John, and the Steads, cousins with whom Susanna Collet kept in contact. The Collets themselves were probably regular visitors and indeed entrusted their eldest child, Mary, to her grandparents for the greater part of her upbringing.[28] Susanna Collet's letters also document her contacts with Collet cousins in Streatham and in Kent.[29] Nicholas and Mary Woodnoth Ferrar thus admirably combined in their household family secular success and spiritual nurture that made it a model for their children and a magnet for their friends and kin. The bonds thus created drew the family together in the face of the later crisis and laid the foundations on which their son would build his 'little college'.

Within that nurturing framework Nicholas, the fourth of the five sons, occupied a special place. Born on 22 February 1593 he had from a very early age shown himself both unusually pious and intellectually able. He was described as 'fair and of bright hair like his mother'.[30] He was also of delicate health,[31] which reinforced his mother's protective instincts and strengthened the bond between them, a bond that would later prove so vital to Little Gidding. He was a model child from her point of view, the embodiment of qualities she admired: easy to teach because eager and quick to learn, bookish but lively-minded and sensitive enough to others' reactions to capture his peers' attention with his story-telling, and almost preternaturally pious.

As a child Nicholas had declared his intention to become a priest, an ambition that doubtless pleased his parents and certainly accorded with his academic ability and early piety.[32] Thomas Middleton, his father's good friend and business partner, took to calling him 'Archbishop of Canterbury' when he was perhaps five or six.[33] For a clerical career a university degree had become increasingly essential, and for this Nicholas received appropriate preparation. Because he advanced so quickly with his Latin and other studies, he was sent off to school at Enborne at the same time as his older brother William.[34] Again he was so successful that his teacher pronounced him ready for Cambridge at the early age of thirteen, a year before William went up. Unlike William and Erasmus, however, Nicholas stayed the full course and took a degree.[35]

Clare Hall had recognised his academic ability by electing him a fellow as soon as he had taken his B.A in 1610. He was, however, the Physick Fellow, which suggests a primary interest not in theology but in medicine, perhaps a result of his own medical problems. He could have stayed in that congenial setting for the rest of his days had he been so inclined and had his health permitted. He had, however, always been subject to 'agues', which the damp of Cambridge worsened. These recurrent fevers finally forced him in 1613 to take what he evidently regarded as a temporary leave of the academic world and embark on a lengthy tour of the Continent as a last resort to restore his health. He had clearly thrived in an academic ambience, which gave him opportunity for both teaching and learning and a model of community he could later adapt to his own 'little college'.

He spent four years travelling from the Netherlands to Hamburg, then south through Germany and across the Alps to Italy and finally to Spain. Like his earlier home life and schooling his time on the Continent was to prove a seminal experience when he came to organise the family's new life at Little Gidding though he could hardly have anticipated such an outcome when he set out. 'The time of his Travell . . . was ye tyme of his Ingathering, to fill his minde, to encrease his stocke wth Wisedome & Virtue'.[36]

Ferrar was only one of many young Englishmen who embarked on a grand tour although most undertook it for the sake of their education rather than their health.[37] As the above direction to Ferrar's potential biographer indicates, the former purpose also figured largely in Ferrar's travels, the more so after the violent seasickness he experienced on the North Sea crossing had vanquished his Cambridge ague and restored him to health.[38]

Portrait of Nicholas Ferrar, attributed to Cornelius Janssen, at Magdalene College, Cambridge.

A perhaps more significant difference between him and many other young travellers was that he journeyed without the company of an older man. He was, to be sure, not a youth of sixteen but a man of twenty and a Master of Arts and Fellow of his Cambridge college. Nevertheless, his tutor at Clare, Augustine Lindsell, had to reassure the parent Ferrars that their son was 'so firmly fixed in his religious principles that there was no fear of his being seduced by any thing that he should hear or see'.[39]

Thanks to the court connections of Dr Robert Scot, the new Master of Clare Hall and the king's Sub-Almoner, Ferrar made the crossing in the entourage of the Princess Elizabeth and her new husband, Frederick, Elector Palatine of the Rhine, whom she had married on St. Valentine's Day, 1613.[40] Having exchanged his scholar's gown for the courtier's garb in which he was presented to the Princess, he departed from London on 10 April leaving a valedictory letter for his family tucked in a window for them to find after he had gone. The party sailed from Margate on the 25th, arriving at Flushing on the 29th. Two days later Ferrar wrote to his brother John that he had decided not to continue with the Princess's party to Heidelberg but to leave them at Utrecht, return to Leyden and then go on to Hamburg.[41] So early a date for such an announcement suggests that Ferrar had concluded almost immediately on arrival, if not earlier en route, that he had no interest in securing a court post at Heidelberg, a possibility others had set enthusiastically before him as an incentive to continue with the princely entourage.

Once free to pursue his own itinerary and interests what did Ferrar choose to investigate that might later shape his plans for Little Gidding? His choices in the first stages of his journey suggested at least some preparatory acquaintance with the various books published to aid travellers. In the Netherlands, his first opportunity to apply such directions, Ferrar put a brief time to good use.[42] Indeed, we have more detailed information about what he did there than we have proportionately for those places where he spent longer time. Those with him remarked on what an assiduous observer he was, always carrying his Dutch-English dictionary with him and keen to learn the language as well as to see the country and meet the people. His wide-ranging interests covered both spiritual and secular aspects of Dutch life.

The spiritual realm offered unique opportunities. The degree of religious toleration in the United Provinces presented an interested visitor with a diversity not readily or perhaps even safely experienced in England. What John Ferrar recorded many years later of his brother's visits to Dutch churches included only those separatist sects of 'Brownists' and 'Anabaptists', more precisely Mennonites, groups that could not worship openly in England, and the even more remarkable Jewish synagogue. If Nicholas singled out from among the Protestants only separatist churches, one must wonder what drew him to them and of course what he learned from this contact. John's omissions in this account of his brother's church visiting are as interesting and frustrating as what he included. He never mentioned the established Reformed churches then in the throes of increasing doctrinal tension between Arminians and Calvinists, tension that would increasingly afflict the Church of England.[43] He might also have discovered that the Reformed churches maintained a two-tiered membership in which only those who had made a public profession of their faith and commitment, a voluntary group within the larger congregation, could partake of communion.[44] Such a distinction, reminiscent not only of Brownists but of the churches established later in Massachusetts Bay colony, would certainly have qualified as 'puritan' if not downright 'separatist' at home. Gathered churches as well as self-selected groups within parish churches were, of course, voluntary societies and this opportunity to observe such groups at first hand may have contributed to the great importance Ferrar was later to attach to both oral and written commitment at Little Gidding. Nevertheless any such voluntarism never for him led to a demand for fundamental church reform let alone a justification for separatism, for he remained wholeheartedly loyal to the Church of England.

There were also significant numbers of Catholics in the Netherlands. Though they were unable to worship as openly as Protestants, their position was far more secure than that of their co-religionists in England.[45] They too would have displayed to Ferrar examples of voluntary societies at work, for among them were the *klopjes*, lay women 'who did not take vows but lived a celibate life in communities'. They and their less numerous male counterparts, the *Klopbroeders*, supplemented a shortage of priests by assisting at services, catechizing, and visiting parishioners.[46] If Ferrar had learned of such groups in Holland, he would have been the better prepared to encounter the numerous societies both clerical and lay that had sprung up in Catholic Italy to combine a collective devotional life with an active ministry among the urban populace.[47]

Visiting churches was not the only form his religious investigations took. He was also said to have set about collecting examples of divine providences and miracles, evidence of God's active intervention in His creation, the sorts of stories he subsequently collected for his family to use.[48] His collection must have included his own subsequent deliverances because his brother John clearly remembered them and passed them on to later biographers.

He investigated matters secular as well: the layout of cities, the nature of government and laws, regional differences among the provinces and their people, defenses, different methods of ship construction, and trade

and commerce. An aspect of civic life that seems to have drawn his particular attention was poor relief, in particular a type of almshouse 'where
young children of both sexes are brought up to learn handicrafts'.[49] These
workshops provided for orphans a kind of group apprenticeship of the sort
that a more prosperous family might arrange individually for its children.
Ferrar also looked at other almshouses set up to employ the disabled and
enable them to support themselves without begging.[50] Perhaps Ferrar's
initial interest in almshouses was largely dutiful, part of what he thought
he ought, as a well-informed traveller and concerned Christian, to take
an interest in. On the other hand these particular projects involved not
just alms but education of a practical sort appropriate to humbler folk,
an interest which Ferrar would continue to pursue on his travels and later
incorporate in distinctive ways at Little Gidding. He left no sign then or
later, however, of interest in systematic plans for universal and practical
education like those put forward by Comenius or Dury or William Petty
and much discussed in the 1640s and 50s.[51]

There was no mention here or subsequently of any book- or print-
buying despite the fact that Ferrar was supposed to have brought home not
only many of the prints the family later used in making biblical harmonies
but also numerous 'worldly' books such as *Orlando* that on his deathbed he
commanded his brother to burn.[52] Certainly the prints, however he acquired
them, that remain at Magdalene College, Cambridge, together with the
illustrated harmonies, point to Ferrar's strong interest in the visual arts. He
of course would not have had to travel to the Netherlands to see such prints
for the Dutch exported quantities of them to England. His strong later
interest in such prints, however, might well have been stimulated during
his travels.[53] Roman Catholic books would obviously have been easier to
buy abroad than in England, and we know from Ferrar's later references
and translations that he possessed a number of these at least some of which
he probably purchased on his travels. Whether, however, he acquired then
or later the particular works we know he had by Lessius, de Sales, Valdes,
Cornaro or Carbone remains uncertain.[54]

After a fortnight or so in Holland he reached Hamburg by late
May, having visited Bremen and Stade on the way.[55] Ferrar there had
introductions to many friends and business associates of his father and
brother, among them John's partner and brother-in-law, Thomas Sheppard,
whose later bankruptcy was to have such profound consequences for the
Ferrars.[56] As in Holland, he set about studying the language, the history,
and the institutions, civil and religious, as well as the trade and commerce
of the place. He also visited nearby Lubeck.[57] Here again are conspicuous

omissions in Ferrar's study of religious institutions that stand in contrast to the careful mention of Anabaptists and Jews in Amsterdam. In his brother's account Ferrar's time in Germany never included in Hamburg or anywhere else attendance at Lutheran churches, or indeed any other churches. As with the Dutch Reformed churches what significance to attach to this omission is difficult to judge; did it represent Ferrar's attitude to Lutheranism or his brother's selective memory?[58] A more prosaic unknown is the duration of Ferrar's stay in Hamburg. In his letter to John of 29 May he reported himself still awaiting company for the journey to Leipzig.[59] If he actually did all he was said to have done in Hamburg, he probably spent at least a week if not longer there.

In Leipzig he planned to stay for six weeks to two months, his first lengthy stop on the journey. A stay of that length allowed him to cultivate in greater depth both his academic and his practical interests in education. In the university he met members of the faculty and engaged tutors with whom to continue his study of German language, history and institutions. One of the skills he was also said to have acquired was 'artificial memory'.[60] Extending the interest in practical training he had shown in the Netherlands, he eagerly cultivated those craftsmen who practiced the wide variety of 'mechanical arts' for which Germany was noted. He persuaded masters of these crafts, painters, weavers, dyers, smiths, architects, and mariners to give him a brief introduction not only to the required skills but also to the technical language that would enable him to discuss work in progress and so acquire a fuller understanding. Sightseeing also figured in his programme in the form of visits to the courts of neighboring princes and dukes, Dresden being the most notable.

The details of his journey between Leipzig and Venice remain uncertain. If he stayed in Leipzig for the full two months he had earlier proposed, he would have left there in early August and crossed the Alps by mid-September, certainly a reasonable precaution to avoid early snowfalls and the general hazards of winter travel.[61] He would therefore have had perhaps six weeks to cover a great deal of ground in Germany, especially if his first stop after Leipzig took him as far east as Prague, as Peckard claimed.[62] He certainly spent time in Augsburg because he claimed to have written to his mother three times from there telling her of his intention to head south to Italy.[63] Augsburg was the traditional starting point for the journey south across the Brenner, which would suggest that he visited the other cities mentioned by Peckard and Jebb (Strasburg, Nuremberg, Ulm, and Speyer) on a circular route that ultimately brought him there.[64] Our sources unfortunately give no hint of Ferrar's response to these cities although with his now-fluent German he could the more readily have pursued those investigations of aspects of their history, government, religion, commerce and education that had interested him in Hamburg and Leipzig.

After a rather strenuous period of travel south from Augsburg, which included the Alpine crossing and the isolation of quarantine, Ferrar reached Italy where he planned a lengthier stay. Venice and its neighbouring university city of Padua were popular and comparatively safe destinations for Protestant Englishmen in Counter-Reformation Italy although the plague in Germany had reduced the numbers of Englishmen and indeed students in general at the time Ferrar arrived.[65] He remained restless, however, and confessed to John early in 1614 that he again had a desire to travel, this time to Vienna. February and March would not have been ideal times for a transalpine journey but at least the danger of plague would have drastically diminished.[66] He evidently went somewhere and for an extended time because his next letter of 1 April reported that he had returned to Venice just three or four days previously and intended to go on to Padua the next day.[67] Unfortunately, as so often with this Continental sojourn, no evidence survives to fill out the story and reveal where he travelled and what he saw.

Back in Padua, particularly if he felt that he had now 'done' Germany, he could proceed to apply himself 'intensely to the study of physic'.[68] Padua was, after all, the pre-eminent university in Europe for the study of medicine and Ferrar held the physic fellowship at Clare. As in Leipzig, Ferrar hired tutors, cultivated members of the medical faculty as well as others in the university, and generally impressed the scholarly community with his learning and acumen though there is no evidence that he ever formally matriculated. As in Leipzig he found himself so inundated with visitors, especially fellow Englishmen eager to speak their native tongue, that he had to take refuge in villages outside the city from time to time to find some peace and quiet.[69] He did, however, make one very close friend, a young Englishman named Garton. Garton had killed a man in a duel in England and had taken refuge in Venice, where his remorse had brought him to the verge of suicide. From this despair Ferrar was able with sympathetic counsel to rescue him, a successful early effort at the kind of spiritual direction he was later to practice with family and friends at Little Gidding.[70] Garton, in turn, was able to reciprocate with help when Ferrar later fell desperately ill in Marseilles. Though Garton never appeared in Ferrar's life once he had finally left Italy, he must have spoken of him or John would not have known of these episodes. Perhaps remembrance of that relationship made some contribution to Ferrar's thoughts, expounded later at Gidding to his cousin Arthur Woodnoth, on a 'web of friendship' and the openness and trust that should exist between friends.[71]

Probably before Garton had appeared on the scene Ferrar near died from an illness in Padua in October 1614. Fortunately for us, the only letter of his from Italy that has survived recounts this story and thus serves as a check on the versions his biographers subsequently offered.[72] The problem, 'my Last dubell sycknes...my old infermetie of Augeu', had confined him to his chamber for twenty-six days and he had been bled four different times for a total of two and a half pounds of blood. He was by then well enough to joke about it, telling John he could be sure after that treatment that 'it was not wylld Bludd that maid me com abrode otherwise I should have now a greater desyer to Returne home'.

John Ferrar's memory, however, offered a version significantly different from his brother's letter. According to John there was no blood-letting. Instead Nicholas valiantly resisted the advice of his learned but of course Catholic Paduan doctors, who maintained that blood-letting offered his only hope of recovery.[73] Only one old physician sided with Nicholas, but his intervention sufficed to delay the proceedings long enough so that the fever broke of its own accord and the treatment became unnecessary. Afterward all the Paduan physicians conceded that had the bleeding taken place it would surely have proved fatal. Whether consciously or not his earliest biographers, his brother and Barnabas Oley, used this version to demonstrate not only that Ferrar's medical knowledge was superior to that of his Catholic doctors but that his resistance to their ministrations made him a champion of Protestantism. His later biographer, Francis Turner, was equally keen for his own political as well as religious purposes in the 1670s to show Ferrar as staunchly anti-Catholic.[74]

Ferrar spent the remainder of 1614 and the following year in Italy, perfecting his Italian and visiting many of its notable cities. His surreptitious April journey to Rome gave his biographers another opportunity to dramatise his Protestantism. He had to make the journey in secret, they averred, to avoid capture by those archetypal Catholic villains, the Jesuits, who were said to be lying in wait for him. A further hazard came in the form of a brush with a Swiss Guard when he failed to kneel as a papal Holy Week procession passed. No other difficulties arose, however, to interfere with his sightseeing and his experience of Holy Week and Easter in the venerable city. Not all encounters with Catholics were dangerous; he visited without incident the shrine at Loreto and proceeded to Malta, where one of the Knights befriended him and even presented him with a small version of the cross that was the order's insignia.[75]

By early 1616, however, Ferrar was ready to leave Italy and launch himself on the next phase of his travels to France and Spain.[76] In Marseilles he went down with a fever worse than the one in Padua and summoned Garton, who arrived just as the fever broke; Garton then stayed with Ferrar as he convalesced first in Marseilles and then back in Venice. Ferrar wrote from there to his family in April telling them of his illness and no doubt reassuring them as to its outcome.[77] When he resumed his journey to Spain, he took with him a handsome rapier that Garton had given him as a parting gift, which he supposedly used when rallying the ship's crew to prepare resistance to pursuing pirates.[78]

Once landed in Spain, Ferrar made his way to Madrid but cut short his Spanish visit and abandoned altogether plans to travel home through France because he experienced a revelation that his family was in difficulties and needed his help. In response he headed on foot, a hazardous journey, directly to San Sebastian, where he was further delayed by contrary winds before at last making port in Dover and hastening to the family home in St. Sithes Lane, London no later than the end of July 1617, rather than in 1618, the usual date given.[79] His parents welcomed him warmly, though his father had not at first recognised the young sword-carrying gallant who suddenly appeared and knelt before him in the garden.

The retrospective portraits of Ferrar as traveller in Italy differ considerably from those of him in Holland and Germany. Though he was said to have visited many cities in Italy and indeed spent far more of his time there than in the north, he was nowhere described as investigating the sort of geographical, cultural, and civic aspects of life to which he was said to have devoted his attention in the north. As suggested earlier, John Ferrar instead distorted situations such as Nicholas's illness in Padua, twisting them into confrontations in which he outwitted the papists or resisted their efforts to convert him. By the 1650s John in his role as defender of his brother from charges of popish sympathies was hardly likely to attribute to him any Catholic influences. He might even have thought it politic to emphasise Nicholas's interest in gathered churches in Holland similar to those Independent churches that flourished in Oliver Cromwell's Commonwealth in the 1650s.

A half-century earlier, John and Nicholas's friend, Sir Edwin Sandys, had sought to protect himself from similar suspicions of popish sympathies by emphasising in his *Europae Speculum* the power and deviousness of the papacy. He had nevertheless also singled out for praise the good provision in Italy of hospitals and 'houses of pietie' for the elderly, the ill and disabled, foundlings, and converted prostitutes, as well as the numerous 'spirituall fraternities & companies' for lay people.[80] Such institutions reflected the intense concern of groups within reformed Catholicism to combine educational and social service with a shared devotional life for their members. If Sandys in 1597 was aware of such movements, it is hard to believe that they escaped the notice or failed to evoke the sympathy of a man like Ferrar, especially when he had already shown interest in such matters during the earlier, Protestant stages of his travels. He and Sandys could indeed have discussed them when they were working closely together in the Virginia Company.

Though John never mentioned such societies, other evidence does demonstrate that Nicholas indeed knew of at least some of the charitable Italian institutions created to care for and to educate children. One of the works he had by 1634 translated but was refused permission to publish was Ludovico Carbone's *Dello Ammaestramento de' Figliuoli nella Dottrina Christiana*, which Ferrar rendered as 'Of the Christian Education of Children'.[81] The original work was published in Venice in 1596 and contained a detailed account of the 'Schools of Christian Doctrine' in which Carbone was an active teacher. These schools represented a major educational effort if Carbone was correct in claiming that there were in Venice some 500 teachers, mostly lay men and women, teaching over 6,000 boys and girls in at least 30 and probably more single-sex schools. Similar schools and the confraternities that ran them existed also in Milan, Bologna, Florence and Rome. The schools met only on Sundays and religious holidays and chiefly attracted children of the lower and sometimes middling ranks, despite Carbone's efforts to persuade better-off parents to send their children also. Along with religious instruction based on traditional doctrinal formularies such as the Lord's Prayer, the Hail Mary, the Ten Commandments and the Seven Sacraments, the schools taught reading and writing as part of a concerted attack on ignorance both spiritual and literary. Their work was certainly akin to what Ferrar could have seen in the Netherlands. Carbone indeed thought himself engaged in a mission to the 'pagans' at home comparable to that of the friars who brought Christianity to the Indians in the New World.[82] He and other advocates of the schools promised that they would provide wise and merciful magistrates and ministers and obedient and industrious citizens to benefit both individuals and society as a whole.

Ferrar was unlikely to have met Carbone's book other than in Italy, probably either in Venice itself or nearby Padua. If he attached sufficient importance to it to want to translate and publish it later in England, he probably also wanted while in Italy to see for himself these schools in operation. There were also other schools to observe, schools run by those new religious groups prominent in the Catholic Reformation: Barnabites, Jesuits, Oratorians, Ursuline nuns. Certainly this translation of Carbone testifies to the attention Ferrar paid to education in Italy. It also supports Mayor's characterization of Ferrar as 'so incomparable a teacher' and his claim that Ferrar owed some of that pedagogical skill to his travels abroad.[83]

Ferrar probably also first encountered during his grand tour the ideas of the Spaniard Juan de Valdes (1500-41) whose book, *One Hundred and Ten Considerations*, he later translated. What Ferrar valued in this work, which stressed the importance of an individual's direct experience of God, sheds significant light on his own spiritual life. I shall consider this point later along with the possible influence of Valdes's example in gathering round him in the 1530s in Naples an informal group of followers who explored in discussion this 'experimental' religion.[84] The practices as well as the writings of Valdes and Carbone thus served to reinforce what Ferrar had seen of committed communities in Holland and in Italy.

The impact of such examples on the life of the family at Little Gidding, however, lay well into the future. Upon his return to England after this time of 'ingathering' abroad, Ferrar neither returned to Cambridge and the academic life nor retreated from worldly affairs. Instead he stayed in London to aid his aging parents, and became as a consequence increasingly involved in the world of business and politics that was the sphere of his father and of his brother John. It was to force on him an education very different from what his family, schooling and travels had earlier provided.

When the elder Nicholas died in 1620, his son John inherited the London house and became the head of the family. It was not, of course, a position he had grown up expecting to assume, since he had been the second son until his older brother Erasmus died in 1609. He had not received the 'gentleman's' education given to Erasmus and later to William. He had instead gone directly from school into the family business.[85] He would there have acquired the business skills necessary to keep accounts and manage the credit and shipping and customs regulations essential to an import/export enterprise. He was then sent to Hamburg to learn German and to practice those skills and to meet his father's associates in what was a long-established centre of the family business. If, as his correspondence suggests, John lacked verbal facility, he was certainly sufficiently skillful in practical matters to use his inherited advantages and connections to develop his own active and successful business life. He took his independent place within the mercantile community when he was made free of the Skinners' Company by patrimony on 26 February 1612/3.[86]

In that same month he married, another important step in establishing his position. As they had done for his older sister Susanna, his parents played their appropriate role in this matter by negotiating his union with the entirely suitable partner of his choice.[87] She was Anne Sheppard, sister of Thomas Sheppard, another young merchant with whom John had become a close friend while they were both in Hamburg. While his father Nicholas arranged terms with Anne's father, John waited impatiently in Hamburg and lamented in a letter to his mother the unhappy situation of his future brother-in-law whose suit for a Miss Middleton had been summarily and unjustly, according to John, rejected by her father.[88] His mother's counsel in a later letter to be patient and trust in God for a favourable outcome for his own suit proved ultimately justified, and John hastened back to London to claim his bride early in 1613. Unfortunately, she died later that same year, perhaps in childbirth, and John erected a fine monument to her in St. Benet Sherehog Church.[89] He remained loyal to Thomas, however, and became his business partner, a fateful alliance as events turned out.

Within two years on Valentine's Day 1615 John married again, this time Bathsheba Owen, daughter of another prosperous merchant family and a Londoner born and bred. When she married John Ferrar, she doubtless expected to live the comfortable life of a prosperous London merchant's wife. That was the world she had grown up in. Her father, Israel Owen, belonged to the Mercer's Company and had been as successful in the mercantile world as old Nicholas Ferrar. Bathsheba could even boast that her mother's father had been an Alderman of London. As he prospered Israel Owen marked his success in the time-honoured way by acquiring a country estate in Bardfield in Essex. If a country property played any part in Bathsheba's vision of her future life, it would probably have been as a signal and an engine of upward social mobility that would complement but not replace her London residence. She would most certainly not have anticipated that its communal life would be dedicated to a religious agenda of her brother-in-law's devising. Indeed, Bathsheba would not have met her brother-in-law Nicholas till his return in 1617. When he decided to remain in London rather than return to Cambridge, Bathsheba would have perceived his importance in the family and his close relationship to his mother. As long as the family stayed in London and John continued to prosper, however, she did not see her brother-in-law as a threat to hers and John's position in the family.

When his father died in 1620, John inherited the family home in which he and Bathsheba already lived. Their first child, Mary, had died young though not before she appeared swaddled on her mother's lap in a family portrait.[90] A son arrived shortly before his grandfather's death and was named, of course, Nicholas. By 1620 John had become a man of consequence: Deputy of the Virginia Company and close associate of the Earl of Southampton and Sir Edwin Sandys, who had taken control of the Company in 1619, and a Member of Parliament in 1621. While Deputy John increasingly concentrated his attentions on Virginia, leaving his partner Thomas Sheppard to handle their other business ventures, particularly the Baltic trade. The godly and prosperous household John had inherited and now headed included his wife and son, his widowed mother, his niece Mary Collet, his unmarried brothers Richard and Nicholas as well as the usual complement of servants, apprentices and visitors. The future for the next generation of Ferrars under John's leadership thus appeared bright and secure.

But within five years the family had abandoned the mercantile world of London and moved to the Huntingdonshire countryside. This dramatic change of course was not, as some earlier historians have claimed, simply the realisation of a longstanding plan on Nicholas's part to remove himself and his family from 'the world'. It was rather a response to two intertwined crises that threatened the family with financial ruin. The disasters struck the family almost simultaneously in 1624 and plunged the brothers into the turbulent and often cutthroat politics of the mid-1620s. Its impact was powerful enough to shift leadership of the family from John to Nicholas and to move Nicholas, with his mother's support, to alter not only his own but the whole family's way of life.

One of these disasters was triggered by a power struggle within the Virginia Company. There had been an apparently amicable change of leadership in 1619. Sir Thomas Smith resigned as Treasurer (Governor) of the Company and Sir Edwin Sandys, backed by the Earl of Southampton and acceptable to the Earl of Warwick, succeeded him. The new Deputy (second in command), whose duty was to implement the policies devised by Sandys, was John Ferrar. Meetings of the company were held thereafter at the Ferrar house in St Sithes Lane and attended with increasing frequency by Nicholas.

The company's leaders, recognising his formidable memory and verbal fluency, began to delegate various tasks to him.[91] John, who lacked his brother's skill with words, may informally have turned over to him the Deputy's official duty to supervise the Secretary who kept the

Court records.[92] In June 1620 Nicholas was appointed one of the sixteen 'committees' (so called because to them the management of the company's operations was committed) and in the following month he was among those chosen to attend the Privy Council regarding the company's petition about tobacco importation.[93] With the suspension in 1621 of the lotteries that had funded the company's activities, the company initiated a series of particular 'magazines' to diversify and develop the colony's economy. Each focused on a specialised project, supplying necessary materials initially from funds put up by subscribers to be supplemented latterly by trading in the finished products. The subscribers to each magazine elected a Treasurer to oversee their venture. Nicholas took charge of two projects: the fur trade with the Indians and the Jamestown glass furnace. His accounts for these ventures were especially commended in 1622 as models of clarity and accuracy.[94] Already in May 1621 he had been added to the company's Council both in recognition of his past efforts and in the (justified) belief that he would be constant in attendance.[95] When he succeeded his brother as Deputy in May 1622,[96] he was thus well versed in the Company's affairs and prepared to play a significant role both in its Courts and no doubt behind the scenes. He was also ready to defend the Company's interests before the Privy Council and later in Parliament.

By this time the initially amicable transfer of power from Smith first to Sandys and then to Southampton had given way to acrimony. The new leadership antagonised Smith when they sought to audit his accounts and he proved unable or unwilling to produce them. Further investigation led the leadership to conclude that he had withheld funds owing to the company, funds that were sorely needed after the suspension of the lotteries. The leaders simultaneously alienated Warwick, who then made common cause with Smith. The shortage of funds was critical because Sandys and Southampton had embarked on ambitious plans for Virginia's development as a colony rather than a trading post. Nicholas took an active part in implementing these plans. Sandys had presented them to a company Court on 7 July 1620 as part of a larger project for reorganizing the company's operations. Recognising the danger of dependence on a single cash crop of tobacco, Sandys advocated a rapid increase in the colony's population and a diversification of its economy. The company accordingly sent women in the hope of giving the colony the greater strength and stability of family life, boys to be apprenticed and others to be servants. Economic diversification included the introduction of ironworks at the falls of the River James and the production of a variety of commodities: wine, silk, oil from the native (to Virginia) walnut trees and from olive trees (imported from Europe), salt, fish, hemp, flax, pitch and tar.[97] The plan was a far-sighted one but required capital and time for its implementation. Neither was forthcoming. The Indian attack on the settlers in March 1622 decimated the colonists and destroyed the ironworks just as it was coming into production, and the preceding suspension of the lotteries put it out of company's power to fund further development or to subsidise continued migration.

In these circumstances the profitable sale of Virginia's cash crop of tobacco, an issue with which Nicholas was already familiar, assumed enormous importance for the future of both Company and colony. The Company was therefore driven, eventually and reluctantly, to accept the proposal of Lionel Cranfield, Earl of Middlesex and Lord Treasurer, for a Tobacco Contract, which would give them a monopoly of the importation and sale of tobacco both from Virginia and from Spain. The terms of the Contract, however, produced contentious debates within the Company, especially over the large salaries to be awarded to Sir Edwin Sandys and John Ferrar for administering the Contract. As the debates grew more acrimonious Nicholas as Deputy found himself charged with attempting to promote the Contract by manipulating discussions, pressuring members and presenting biased and inaccurate records of meetings. Pacifying the disgruntled and keeping the meetings from descending into *ad hominem* attacks were not congenial tasks for a careful, precise and orderly man like Nicholas. Ultimately the factions within the Company led by Warwick and Smith brought their grievances before the king and the Privy Council, charging that the current leadership had grievously mismanaged the Company's affairs by putting their own profit ahead of the colonists' welfare and that the Company's charter should therefore be revoked.[98]

Called upon in October 1623 to surrender the charter, the Company refused. On 4 November therefore, the Crown initiated *quo warranto* proceedings.[99] No peers were named among the defendants, thus Southampton as Treasurer was omitted and Nicholas, as Deputy, headed the list of those indicted. Thereafter he played a leading role in organising the charter's defense. He and his brother made numerous appearances before the Privy Council where on one occasion the exchanges grew so heated that the two Ferrars were charged with contempt of the Council's order and temporarily put under house arrest.[100] When the Privy Council ordered the company to surrender its records, Ferrar saw the importance of retaining copies of the court books, organised a team of copyists and sent the finished copies to the Earl of Southampton for safekeeping.[101]

The company also launched a counterattack on Cranfield, whom it blamed for the collapse of the Tobacco Contract. When Parliament met in February 1624 some 20% of its members, including Ferrar and Sandys, were members of the Virginia Company and its leaders joined eagerly in the campaign against Cranfield.[102] On 28 April Nicholas Ferrar opened the attack, rehearsing 'the Oppressions in matter of Tobacco', and he was followed, as the company had arranged that very morning, by Sir Edwin Sandys speaking on the Tobacco Contract, Lord Cavendish on the fact-finding commission established to investigate the company in 1623, and Sir John Danvers on events since then.[103] The onslaught destroyed Cranfield, but it did not save the company. In May 1624 the company's charter was revoked, a result of political manoeuvring rather than proof of the allegations. Two months later the King issued letters patent returning political control of the colony constitutionally to the crown and *de facto* to Sir Thomas Smith, the previous Treasurer.[104]

Even so the struggle continued. Nicholas drafted an account in which he turned the charges of misgovernment back on Smith and his allies. He reiterated the inadequacy of Smith's accounts and his neglect of Virginia and emphasised the opposition his policies and appointees had aroused among Virginians, the very people Smith's faction claimed to be championing.[105] Within the year 'A Discourse on the Old Company' (1625) was submitted, as requested, to the Privy Council. It is hard to believe Nicholas Ferrar had no hand in it. The opening disclaimer that the respondents had resolved not to meddle further in Virginia's affairs because of the wrongs and injuries inflicted on them by their opponents certainly reflected the attitude of the Ferrars and especially Nicholas. So too did its answer to the Privy Council's questions as to what form of government would be best for Virginia and what form of Tobacco Contract would best protect the royal revenue and not harm the colony. After rehearsing at length all the wrongs and injuries yet again, it concluded that the old Company form and the Tobacco contract it had proposed were best, not a proposal likely to be taken up by the crown.[106] The 'Discourse' was probably presented in April or May 1625. By this time Charles I had succeeded to his father's throne, plague was about to break out in London, and Nicholas Ferrar was preparing to abandon public life.[107]

The events of the past six years had made plain to Ferrar the price and perils of rising to great place by Bacon's 'winding stair'. Even Cranfield, as hard and ruthless a competitor as any, confessed to moments of wanting to withdraw from the contentious and malicious world of politics and business.[108] Deeply pious and with an orderly mind Ferrar was dismayed by the often unpredictable and vindictive politicking and backstabbing he had encountered and probably also by his own readiness to retaliate in kind.[109] His revulsion was reinforced by the prevailing view that trials, whether of body or mind or estate, were God's calls to repentance and reform. [110] He had not come back from the continent intending to become a man of business; he had returned home because he believed his family needed him. Hence when his aging parents had begged him to stay on with them in London rather than return to Cambridge, he had answered such a need and as a result had become steadily more immersed in the affairs of the Virginia Company. Ultimately the effects of those tumultuous years were not wholly negative. If they made Ferrar disillusioned with worldliness and public life, they also equipped him with the administrative and managerial skills he used immediately to deal with an even more direct and catastrophic threat to the Ferrar family and ultimately to shape a quite different ministry to his family.

In that same fateful May of 1624, which saw the charter revoked and Cranfield driven from office, Thomas Sheppard, John Ferrar's trading partner and former brother-in-law, faced bankruptcy when his creditors turned on him and demanded payment.[111] Unlike bankruptcy in a corporation or joint stock company where stockholders could only lose what they had invested in the company, in a partnership each partner was liable to the full extent of his personal resources for obligations incurred by another partner. When Sheppard could not cover his debts himself, therefore, his partner John became liable for them, and the scale of Sheppard's failure threatened to take down John with him.[112] Cash flow was a continual and substantial problem for even the most prosperous of businessmen and a sudden call from many creditors could easily spell ruin. Indeed in malicious hands it could become a powerful and spiteful weapon. John never identified the various creditors who precipitated this crisis or why they chose that particular moment.[113] Given the turbulence of early 1624 we might well wonder whether the attack on Sheppard and thus John Ferrar had any connection with the factional fighting within the Virginia Company or the impeachment proceedings against Cranfield.

There is some evidence that a similar manoeuvre had been launched against Sir Edwin Sandys in November 1623, the month in which the *quo warranto* proceedings against the Virginia Company had begun.[114] Sandys, in a letter to John, explained that he was enclosing a separate letter 'touching the rumors of my debts'. John was to circulate this letter to certain named friends, all colleagues in the Company, and any others John thought appropriate, 'who I trust will control that false rumor when they meet it'.[115] If such tactics had been tried on Sandys, they could certainly also have been directed at Sheppard and John Ferrar and have even included Nicholas to whom Robert Byng had written a month earlier. Byng's assurance that

'I make no question of your iust & vpright dealing with all men' hinted that others might indeed have raised just such a question to create 'the difficulties you are to passe'.[116]

Whether or not the creditors' run on them had any such sinister aspect, it clearly created a seismic upheaval in the world of the Ferrars. John wrote a couple of years later to his cousin, Rev. Theophilus Woodnoth of Linkinhorne in Cornwall an account of the episode that is long on piety but short on details:

> Since we last parted with you God hath shewed unto us Greate troubles and Adversitys but he hath in most unexpected manner turned and refreshed us; I have binne forced to pay above 8 thousand pounds debte since Chrismas was two years which I stood surtity [surety] for without any assurance at all, but gods grate and infinite mersy hath almost myraculously brought me forth of it by my mother buying of littell Gidding in Huntingtonshire which stoode her upon the poynt of 6000 ₶: and hether both shee and her whole family hath repared ever since the beginning of the last summer and I hope we shall soe Continew together having but one purse and one mind as we are but one flesh and blood.[117]

The Ferrar Papers contain no systematic account of how this miraculous deliverance was accomplished. Later notes evidently intended by Rev. Thomas Ferrar for a biography of Nicholas implied that Nicholas managed with some £3,000 available to reschedule payment of the outstanding obligations over a sufficient length of time so that they could eventually be paid off as they came due.[118] A great deal obviously depended on negotiating skill and whatever leverage, financial or familial or political, the parties could bring to bear. How therefore did the purchase of Little Gidding with Mary Ferrar's dower money provide for Nicholas a bargaining chip with John's creditors? It was not a random or fortuitous choice, for Gidding's previous owner was none other than the hapless Thomas Sheppard himself. By this purchase the Ferrars in effect put up money that Nicholas could offer, along with whatever additional funds were available, to Sheppard's creditors to cover John's share of the liability. Most of the creditors evidently accepted Nicholas's terms, preferring certain if perhaps only partial payments to lawsuits that might cost more than they recovered.[119]

One of the creditors, however, proved unwilling to accept a negotiated settlement and his refusal produced ongoing consequences that lasted the remainder of Nicholas's lifetime. The problem began in that same eventful

May of 1624 that saw the Virginia Company charter revoked. One Thomas Barker brought before a group of four commissioners a charge against Sheppard and John Ferrar demanding the return of a shipment of goods that Barker claimed to have sent to the partners. This hearing was not a lawsuit but a kind of informal procedure within the business community to settle disputes. John successfully defended himself by testifying that he had no part in the transaction, a claim Sheppard also attested.[120] Since subsequent documents named only Sheppard, the Commissioners evidently accepted John's argument. That decision, however, was not the end of the Ferrars' involvement for neither John nor Nicholas was prepared to abandon Sheppard.

The ongoing Barker case did not detract from John's sense of his and the family's God-given deliverance. Nevertheless, the fact that it was Nicholas, rather than John himself, who did the negotiating, constituted a tacit if not explicit acknowledgment of his greater verbal and analytical skill as well as his close relationship with his mother. As a consequence of his leadership in this crisis he became the effective head of the family and in subsequent years he continued to manage the family's finances while John assumed a subordinate role. John's willingness to defer to his younger brother in all these matters suggested that the financial debacle had dealt a severe blow to his self-confidence.[121] To compound the damage his deference in turn angered his wife, who periodically vented her wrath on both him and Nicholas, thereby disrupting the harmony of the household.[122]

Clearly the family regarded 1624 as a turning point, as John's account to Theophilus Woodnoth made plain. They had become over the many years they had lived there very much a London family, though Mary Woodnoth would have spent her childhood on her family's Cheshire estate and the Collets had property in Cambridgeshire as well as in Southwark. Now the deal with the Sheppard creditors had left the Ferrars with a country property at Little Gidding. Sheppard himself, for the short time he owned it, had used it purely as a source of rental income and the Ferrars could have done the same. Instead, however, they chose to give up their London property and move to the country. Unlike other merchant families, including the Middletons, the Saltonstalls, and the Owens (Bathsheba's family), who acquired country property for the status and security of income it conferred, the Ferrars took Gidding, admittedly under duress, not to acquire social prestige but to seek godliness. That dramatic change of direction was the work of Nicholas, who had promoted this outcome and convinced his mother, his brother, and his sister to participate with their families in a quite different style of life. Nicholas's task as the leader of this enlarged household was to organise its life so that its members would, as John put it, 'soe Continew together having but one purse and one mind as we are but one flesh and blood'. The pattern he devised drew, as we shall see, upon all the elements of his earlier education, from the godly household in which he grew up and the formal schooling he received to his Continental travels and the years he spent in the world of business and politics in London.

2

The New Household at Little Gidding: 'United not only in Cohabitation but in Hartes'

The ministry to his family that Nicholas Ferrar had taken as his mission required more than a simple exchange of hectic London life for contemplative country retreat. As 'a Father for Care' and 'mayster for instruction',[1] he faced immediately a twofold task: 1) to renovate the house itself, not simply to make it habitable but also to adapt it to provide living quarters for the several families and individuals as well as common rooms for the household's meals and their devotional and instructional activities; 2) to order the household's life in a way that would instruct the minds and promote the spiritual growth of all its members. Vital as these needs were, however, Ferrar could not give them his undivided attention, for he had also to attend to ongoing business arising from the Sheppard crisis as well as the management of the family's reallocated resources and the education of the older Collet sons. Indeed in the first years after the move he had to spend half his time in London, a point that I shall take up in more detail later. Therefore whilst his was the vision and the organising authority and he commanded the loyalty of the family (except that of his sister-in-law Bathsheba), he could not have succeeded without the help of others, notably his brother John, his cousin Arthur Woodnoth, and above all his mother.

In the management of the Little Gidding estate, which was now the family's chief resource, Ferrar incorporated an educational role. Household management, the traditional sphere of women, he delegated to the older Collet nieces. They took it in turn month by month and were responsible for planning the day's work and supervising the servants in its execution. They were also expected to keep accounts accurate to the penny of all expenditures. His years in the Virginia Company had taught their uncle the importance of careful accounting. Tenants delivered provisions (eggs, butter, cheese, meat and bread) but the nieces supervised the dairy and the cows that provided the family's milk as well as the baking of the special manchet bread. This arrangement not only trained the nieces but relieved their mother and grandmother of these tasks. The nieces were also skilled needlewomen and dispensed medical ministrations to the local villagers. Beyond the immediate household, however, Ferrar kept management of the estate to a minimum by leasing its pastures to tenants and keeping only a little land around the house for family use. As the dilapidated state of the house and church testified, such leasing was the pattern previous non-resident owners including Sheppard had followed. The estate yielded an annual income of between £400 and £500 and gave the family maximum freedom from worldly cares the better to devote themselves to God's service.[2]

As the many conduct manuals of the period made plain, a household needed the skills of both a man and a woman for its smooth functioning. Little Gidding had such a partnership but in the unconventional form of a widowed mother and her unmarried son. While seventeenth-century widows certainly headed households and owned property and ran businesses, their households usually comprised only the widow and her unmarried children with perhaps an apprentice or servant.[3] Mary Ferrar, in contrast, lived at Little Gidding not simply with her bachelor son Nicholas, but with two of her married children and their families. The two married men, her son John and her son-in-law John Collet, who had previously headed their own households,[4] were prepared to accept this unconventional pattern of leadership.

The partnership was certainly successful for Mary Ferrar and Nicholas worked closely together and clearly shared a vision of the life they wished to promote. It was an exaggeration to attribute the whole 'Institution and Appointment' of Gidding to Mary Ferrar, but her contribution was substantial.[5] She was a strong personality and Nicholas took care to consult her and heed her wishes. Because she owned the property she participated in at least some of the business transactions that ownership involved. In a practical vein, Nicholas was careful to keep his mother informed of a variety of business matters ranging from housekeeping to checking his brother-in-law's Bourn accounts. These letters, sent while he was absent in London in the years between 1625 and 1629, assume that she knew at least enough about these activities to understand what he was doing and that he thought it important to keep her informed.[6] He also included, on at least one occasion, a religious exhortation warning of the need for self-examination and amendment in the face of 'thees late approaches of Fyre and water' with which God was warning them.[7]

Despite the unusual composition of the household, the partnership of mother and son in fact functioned in a more conventionally patriarchal mode than one might expect because Mary Ferrar was firmly convinced of Nicholas's special wisdom and the value of his vision. Nicholas's assumption of leadership within the household thus depended not only on his own spiritual stature and intellectual competence but also on his mother's affections and her readiness ultimately to defer to him.[8] His brother and brother-in-law and his sister and her older daughters likewise chose to accept his leadership. It is important to remember that at the outset the household, with the notable exception of John's wife, Bathsheba, joined together voluntarily, for voluntarism was to assume increasing significance as the family's collective life developed.

John testified to the importance of his mother's leadership when he called her 'the head in the Body and the Bond and Simont [cement] to hould the whole Body of our Family United not only in Cohabitation but in Hartes.'[9] Her importance to the family he reiterated many years later in a letter to his son in which he referred to 'your Pious Grandmother and devoute Vnkell' as 'the Founders of our Family and p[re]sent state We possess in Gidding'.[10] Recognition of her spiritual gifts as well as her more practical contributions to Little Gidding came not only from members of the family but from an unidentified London friend who told her nephew Arthur Woodnoth that he remembered Mary Ferrar as 'one who had brought a new Religion into the world'.[11]

This task of being the family's 'bond and simont', however, was by no means easy in a three-generational household in which women outnumbered men. John himself would have had particular reason to know this because of the difficulties of keeping his own wife bonded when her antipathy to Nicholas and to the whole Gidding regime grew. Despite her alienation and the confrontations it engendered, however, Bathsheba continued to regard her mother-in-law as her friend, surely a powerful testimony to Mary Ferrar's ability to combine authority with tact. She certainly could and did manage the women of the Little Gidding household as she had earlier managed her London household. In the new setting, moreover, she was able to add for them new educational opportunities, to which she attached special importance.

Before Mary Ferrar could turn her attention to new educational ventures, however, she had to confront some fundamental practical necessities. When she set off for Bourn in early June of 1625 with most of the family, John had been deputed to go on ahead to Gidding while Nicholas stayed

1626 estate map of Little Gidding showing the quadrangular house with its (darker) pond at the back and the garden through which the family processed to the church. The map was made for the Ferrars when they took over the Gidding property; the writing is John Ferrar's.

in London to settle necessary business affairs. If John was the first to see what state the property was in, and there is no evidence that anyone had investigated it prior to the purchase, he must have reported rapidly to his brother on its dismal state. Nevertheless it was to their mother rather than John that Nicholas wrote asking her to prepare an emergency room at Gidding sufficient to house three or four people, for which he sent supplies and asked her to keep a careful inventory of what actually arrived.[12] First John and then Nicholas probably used the room in the early days and perhaps even Mary Ferrar herself was glad to have it available during the extensive renovations the house required.[13]

Mary Ferrar's first priority, however, was not the house but the church, which was not only dilapidated but desecrated by its use as a barn. On her arrival she had been appalled to find that the church was so full of hay she could not even get through the door to give thanks for the family's deliverance.[14] A functioning church was essential to the household's devotional life and as soon as it was minimally fit for use, the rector of nearby Steeple Gidding came with his parishioners to Little Gidding for an afternoon sermon.[15] By 1629 the church had been refurbished with new wainscoting and other furniture, plate, and a service book bound in blue velvet and, as the final touch, Arthur Woodnoth sent down the wall tablets with the Creed, Lord's Prayer, and Ten Commandments.[16]

When that physical restoration was complete, however, Mary Ferrar remained unsatisfied, for the church could not support a resident rector on its small stipend.[17] Though the rectors of Great and Steeple Gidding remained willing helpers, she hoped by making a gift to the church of lands from the estate equivalent to its old glebe to secure its own minister for Little Gidding. The lawsuit necessary to transfer title to the designated parcels of land forced so long a delay that the process was not complete until 1634. Though she died later that year, she was able to attend the special service to celebrate her gift. John Williams, Bishop of Lincoln and Gidding's diocesan as well as an old friend of the Ferrars from the days of the Virginia Company, preached a sermon and the choir of Peterborough Cathedral sang. Williams praised Mrs. Ferrar for her generosity and care for the church, calling her 'an example for all the gentry of England'.[18] Despite her efforts, however, the first resident rector, her granddaughter Joyce's husband Edward Wallis, was not installed until late in the Commonwealth period.[19]

In restoring the house, which had been in as parlous a state as the church, Mary Ferrar found other avenues of local practical charity, one of which was provision of what was described as an almshouse for four poor widows. How quickly it was set up is unclear but as part of the restoration of the house, it would probably have been done sooner rather than later. It was in fact not a separate building, as almshouses generally were, but a private apartment within the big house, probably on the ground floor, that consisted of a large room with four beds plus a kitchen and its own separate entrance through which the widows had access to the grounds and could join the family on their way to the church. They were regarded as part of the household and participated in at least some of the daily prayers.[20]

As the 'bond and simont' of the family Mary Ferrar could take satisfaction in accomplishments both practical and spiritual during these first five years at Little Gidding. In 1630 she looked back on her life before and after the move, expressing her thoughts at some length in a letter to Robert Bateman, whom she had known since he came as a youth to her London household as her husband's first apprentice.[21] God had shown His great mercy toward her, she told him, not only by giving her unusual bodily strength but many other blessings at this, the end of her life. Where she had expected punishment for her sins and destruction from 'the daungers That I was compassed with' she instead had received far richer opportunities to serve Him in a situation free from worldly cares and distractions. 'Now I begin to Live[,] all heertofore was but days consumed in Vanity and yeares in trouble'. She had thought God's service would be much more onerous than it had proved to be. 'The world[']s is an yron Yoake[;] Christ[']s Yoake is easy.' She particularly wanted her friends to understand these her present thoughts because they were now the centre of her life and the most precious thing she could offer them. Whilst Nicholas drafted the version that survives as he probably also formulated the interpretation of the circumstances and purpose that brought the family to Gidding, he and his mother had doubtless already discussed these matters at length and agreed upon the points to be made. Mary Ferrar would surely have felt free to amend any draft and would certainly have written the final letter herself.

Certainly an exchange of letters between her and her granddaughters Mary and Anna confirmed these earlier comments to Bateman on the importance of avoiding vanity and worldly distractions.[22] That lesson her granddaughters absorbed, so they told her, not only from her words but also from her actions. She regarded that message as particularly relevant for women, who were generally thought especially liable to such weakness. One special avenue of godly service that she saw open to her, therefore, was educating these young women to avoid that stereotypical fault. Like her son she too aspired to be 'a mayster for instruction'.

Unlike Nicholas she seldom left Gidding and so could give continuing attention to the spiritual and practical needs of the new and complex household. She could also call upon the practical advice and support of her son John, who probably took charge of the day-to-day operations necessary to repair the house and church and certainly oversaw the renovation of George Herbert's prebendal church at neighbouring Leighton Bromswold. He could also have given a significant lead to others in the household as they put into practice his brother's programme of devotions and readings. The role of her son-in-law John Collet is less clear but suggests that while he was a willing participant in family activities, he also spent much of his time and energy on his own matters of business, including his properties at Bourn and in Southwark.[23] Managing his properties also gave him freedom to leave Gidding as he deemed necessary, a freedom that contrasts with that other in-law, Bathsheba, who resented the wifely duty that required her to follow her husband to Gidding and responded with dramatic efforts to resist and escape. John Collet could leave his children's affairs mostly in his wife's hands although he did intervene at critical moments, as in the case of his miscreant son Edward. It was Susanna who, along with her mother, provided a forceful feminine presence in managing the household and organising the marriages of their children, the apprenticeships of their sons and the education of their daughters at Gidding.

Whereas John Ferrar spent most of his time at Gidding, Nicholas in the five years after 1624 could be only a part-time 'mayster for instruction' because he had to shuttle back and forth to London. He had not only to supervise the family's reorganised business affairs but also subsequently to shelter his brother Richard from his creditors and arrange a marriage and apprenticeships for his Collet nephews. These problems kept him very much involved in worldly affairs. They also strengthened his bond with his cousin Arthur Woodnoth.

Though he was only an occasional visitor at Little Gidding Woodnoth had long been a part of the family circle in London. Mary Ferrar was sister to Arthur's father John, and Arthur and Nicholas were only two years apart in age. Woodnoth came to London from Cheshire as a youth of fourteen to serve an apprenticeship with Richard Keane of the Goldsmiths Company in 1609. Six years later, on 31 March 1615, he was made free of the Company and set up in business for himself.[24] His uncle Nicholas Ferrar probably helped to launch him, for Woodnoth later acknowledged the many benefits the elder Nicholas had bestowed on him and the rest of his family.[25] He was a welcome visitor at the home of his uncle and aunt and after 1617, when the younger Nicholas had returned from the Continent, the cousins would have met frequently. Woodnoth must have heard a good deal about the Virginia Company including the tortuous proceedings to revoke its charter.[26] When that blow had been followed by the Sheppard disaster and the family departed for Little Gidding, Woodnoth was ready with help. He was thus involved from the beginning in this major transformation of the Ferrar family's life. His help began soon after Ferrar had finally left London in July 1625. He reported various monies collected and owed and detailed his efforts, so far unsuccessful, to persuade Thomas Sheppard to come down to Gidding. Woodnoth added that he himself would arrive as soon as possible.[27] His London household at the 'Bunch of Grapes' in Foster Lane subsequently became the family's London base as Nicholas came increasingly to rely on him for managing matters in London.

A detailed reconstruction of these early years is necessary for an understanding not only of Ferrar himself but of the dynamics of the family to whom he had pledged to minister. It was perforce a ministry to worldly as well as spiritual needs and to meet them Ferrar would draw on his business acumen along with his religious insights and pedagogical skills. To the education of the younger generation, his nieces and nephews, he gave particular care. The nephews, with the exception of John's son Nicholas, received their training outside the home, as was customary; for them the goal was independence in the adult world. The nieces on the other hand remained at Gidding where their relationship with their uncle assumed a primary importance. Dealing with these varied demands meant that Ferrar had to shuttle back and forth between Gidding and London.

Business had kept him in London after the rest of the family left in June 1625 but he finally reached Gidding in late July. At that point he could have seen for himself the daunting scale of physical renovation the property would require before the family could properly embark on their new life. He stayed on at Gidding both to escape the plague and to launch the repairs, which he left his brother to supervise in his absence. He journeyed back in early December to London and stayed for most of that month.[28] He probably returned to Gidding sometime during the Christmas season but set out again for London in the course of February 1626, perhaps bringing with him his nephew Nicholas Collet to take up his apprenticeship with Arthur Woodnoth.[29] When the family had decided to make the move to Gidding permanent, they assembled for the last time at their old home in St. Sithes Lane in March and remained there at least until after Nicholas's ordination to the diaconate in Westminster Abbey on Trinity Sunday.[30] He could not, however, then return to Gidding with the family and begin the ministry for which he had sought ordination because he felt a prior duty to remain in town with John until the latter part of July to deal with the ongoing difficulties of the unfortunate Thomas Sheppard.

Although after 1624 John was no longer directly liable, he and Nicholas had continued to gather evidence for Sheppard's defence against charges brought by Thomas Barker.[31] Nicholas suggested that Barker might have secretly altered the Hamburg account books whilst John accused the investigating commissioners of deliberately ignoring evidence of Barker's debts to Sheppard that Richard Ferrar had collected in Hamburg. The brothers also presented a more balanced assessment of Sheppard's resources by including money owed him by Robert Bateman and Robert Middleton and discounting his debts to Mary Ferrar.[32] Their efforts failed to deter Barker, who launched a full-scale lawsuit against Sheppard in the

Court of King's Bench. John and Nicholas, armed with their evidence, met with Sheppard's attorney as he prepared to present the case. They assured Sheppard, who had gone into hiding, that they would hand over his 'greate tr[unk]' to his cousin Sadd and tell anyone who came to Gidding looking for him that they had no idea where he was.[33] When the decision went against him and his hiding place in London was revealed, he was arrested and imprisoned on 2 August.[34] The end of the case, however, was not the end of Barker's litigation nor was it the end of the Ferrars' efforts to provide the imprisoned Sheppard with both advice and financial help.[35] Ferrar arranged to send him money periodically, often via Arthur Woodnoth, the last instance recorded being in August 1636.[36] Certainly this whole frustrating experience of litigation and negotiation gave Ferrar an understandable dislike of lawyers and made him later applaud the Isle of Man for not needing them. Moreover the end of Thomas Sheppard's case was not the end of Ferrar's time in London that year. He had to return yet again by mid-November and remain for a month or more.[37] He would thus have spent more than half of 1626, at least seven months, in London pursuing the legal strategy and business consequences of the settlement he had negotiated in 1624.

The following year the specific problems changed but the London pressures on Ferrar remained and produced a similar pattern of divided time. He was in London in January and back by mid-June at the latest.[38] He remained there till the first week of July, during which time he arranged sales of tobacco, some for the benefit of the Virginia Company's shareholders and some directly for his brother John.[39] While in London he also corresponded with his devoted nieces, Anna and Susanna Collet, a reminder of that other aspect of his ministry that awaited him at Gidding.[40] To this very important relationship with his nieces we shall return presently. Nicholas returned to Gidding later in July but was back in London again by late October. From that point until at least mid-December he had to contend, in addition to any ongoing financial or legal problems connected to the 1624 settlement, with the major task of protecting his brother Richard from his creditors, who were closing in on him.[41] Nicholas was probably thankful to return to Gidding for Christmas and remain there through January.

Another worldly concern in this and subsequent years was the settlement of his nephews. Sometime during 1627 a complication arose in what had earlier appeared to be the very satisfactory apprenticeship of Nicholas Collet to Arthur Woodnoth. It was an advantageous situation for the boy and a generous offer that Woodnoth viewed as an opportunity to repay his uncle Ferrar's kindness to him as a young man.[42] Nicholas Collet, however, was not taking proper advantage of this opportunity, and the normally gentle and patient Woodnoth took his young apprentice to task in a lengthy letter.[43] Young Nicholas made his naturally 'heavy disposition' worse by his idleness and was so unwilling and negligent about doing anything he did not fancy that Woodnoth preferred to do tasks himself rather than try to chivvy Nick into doing them. He furthermore did not take proper care of the clothing Arthur provided him and generally displayed a manner that was unpleasant and discontented. Worst of all from Woodnoth's point of view, Nick appeared indifferent about the most vital obligation of all, namely his duty to God, the very foundation of any future happiness and success.

After this dressing down, however, Woodnoth concluded on a more encouraging note. If Nick would expend sufficient care and study to correct his 'badd humor' and develop his knowledge and dexterity, he could quite sufficiently compensate for any lack of natural talent. Furthermore, the skills required by the goldsmith's craft, though numerous, were complementary and sufficiently varied and interesting that anyone willing to put forth a sustained effort could master them. If Nicholas would work diligently at his drawing and engraving and learn chasing and embossing, he could look forward to a comfortable and profitable life; if not, he could anticipate only disaster 'for he that [is] not good in his owne art is comonly good for nothing'. Happily, Nicholas heeded the advice for in November 1628 his mother wrote to him that Woodnoth had given her a reassuring report of his performance and progress to which she added that:

> altho' I do evidently perceive so much love in him [Woodnoth] towards you as may breed a suspicion of partiality & know such a dearness & tenderness of his Affection towards myself and all your other freinds, as causeth him to make the best of all things, which tends to our Joy and Comfort: yet I trust in Gods mercy that it is not without good & assured hope in himself that he desires to give us this Confidence of your well doing:[44]

A pattern roughly similar to 1627 occurred the following year: Nicholas was in London for February and March, at Gidding probably for Easter (25 March) and on into April, back to London for May and June and perhaps some of July, at Gidding in August for a longer stay there than usual, partly because he was ill in October. He came to London for only a brief visit in December. Though the apprenticeship of Edward Collet gave some hints of problems to come, in 1628 it was the marriages of Edward's brother Thomas and his sister Su Collet that occupied their uncle's time both in London and at Gidding. Su Collet's marriage to her uncle's friend, Rev Joshua Mapletoft, was the first for one of the nieces and will receive detailed consideration presently.

The future of Thomas, the eldest Collet son, had already been decided before the family moved to Little Gidding. He had been admitted to the Middle Temple on 4 June 1619 and therefore remained in London when the family moved to Gidding. He was called to the Bar on 24 November 1626.[45] What concerned the family in 1628 was not his vocation but his marriage. As a result Nicholas spent some of his time in February and March 1628 as the go-between in negotiations for Thomas's marriage to Martha Sherington. Susanna Collet meanwhile, deputed by her husband, informed Thomas of the settlement his parents were prepared to offer to the Sheringtons to match Martha's £800 portion.[46] In addition Susanna also enlisted other family members in and around London to offer him their advice as negotiations proceeded.[47] John Collet ultimately settled on his son enough Southwark property to give him an income acceptable to the Sheringtons and on 3 June 1628 as a final step before the wedding Thomas signed a release of his share in the £1,500 his grandfather Nicholas had left to the Collet children other than Mary, who had received a separate bequest; the marriage took place soon thereafter.[48] To his mother's delight Tom brought his wife from London to live at Gidding and the family gave her a warm welcome.[49]

Subsequently, however, Thomas's aunt Bathsheba (John's discontented wife) had taken it upon herself to write to Martha's mother that Martha was being kept at Gidding against her will. Ferrar countered her accusation in a letter to Martha's mother declaring that Martha was certainly not a prisoner at Gidding and that Bathsheba had written not out of love for Martha but out of 'evill respects', adding that the episode 'shall not breed any displeasure agaynst my sister farrar from whom such like things are ordinary matters. And as ordinarily passed over'. Nicholas asked Mrs. Sherington to get from Martha herself an honest answer to Bathsheba's charge and enclosed a copy of his own letter to Martha with the same request. Martha's responses have not survived but she and Thomas opted, not surprisingly, to return to London in 1630 despite the strenuous disapproval Susanna expressed at this move.[50] Their departure, however, by no means ruptured their ties with the family, for various members including Susanna proved only too willing to call upon Thomas for legal and other assistance. He was particularly involved in the difficulties of his wayward brother Edward.

By 1628 Edward, like his younger brother Nicholas, had been apprenticed in London though to whom and in what craft is not clear. When his first placement had not worked out well, Arthur Woodnoth had evidently found a new master, a Mr. Brown, willing to take him on. Edward had hardly settled in his new place when he contracted a dangerous illness through which his new master and mistress nursed him with great kindness.[51] Edward's anxious mother hoped that, having recovered, he would learn from his past mistakes and would take to his work diligently and faithfully. Unfortunately he did not heed those lessons as his brother Nicholas had done, but resembled instead his profligate uncle Richard.

Signs of the major troubles to come were already showing by January 1630 when his mother asked his brother Nicholas to tell Edward of her dismay at reports of Mr Brown's dissatisfaction with him. The downhill trajectory continued for by April 1631 Woodnoth had to report to her that Edward had in some unspecified but obviously serious way wronged his master, perhaps by helping himself to money. Deciding how to deal with the sinner, whom Arthur Woodnoth had taken into his house, produced tensions and tears at Gidding and revealed John Collet as a more active presence and one prepared to clash with his brother-in-law.[52] Ferrar certainly had his own views on how best to proceed, which he explained at length to Woodnoth and shared with his brother John and niece Mary. But he had initially refrained from offering the Collets any advice so that they could not hold him responsible for any untoward consequences of their choice. Once Susanna had revealed what she (and presumably her husband) wanted for Edward, however, Ferrar felt free to counter with the views he had already set down in his letter to Woodnoth. The Collet parents hoped to find a way to keep Edward in London. Ferrar, however, had concluded that Edward's master or indeed any other master would not take him without his father's offering a substantial bond and that bond would be very much at risk given the unlikelihood of Edward's true repentance and reformation. In those circumstances Ferrar's solution was to send him to either the Somers Islands (Bermuda) or Virginia. Edward had obviously forfeited whatever sympathy his uncle had ever had for him. To this rather hardheaded assessment the Collets responded with tearful passion. Since Susanna had not explicitly rejected such a possibility in her letter and Ferrar had thought the financial hazards of trying to place Edward in London were so self-evidently overwhelming, he at first could scarcely credit that the overseas option could so surprise and agitate the Collets. Susanna soon calmed down; she was more realistic than her husband about their son's character.[53] Ferrar nevertheless took the precaution of spelling out to her in writing that while he would never again propose sending Edward to the Somers Islands or Virginia unless they firmly endorsed the idea, they would post a bond for him at their own risk and should not expect help if it were forfeit. John Collet, however, had gone away from this conference and told John Ferrar, who already knew Nicholas's view, that he strongly opposed sending Edward overseas and would do everything he could to keep him in London. Woodnoth, who would have John Collet with him in London during the negotiations, shared Ferrar's assessment of the alternatives open to the Collets as did other friends, Mr Buckeridge and Mr Straung, whom he consulted as the situation developed. In these circumstances Ferrar firmly counseled the kind-hearted Woodnoth not to allow himself to be co-opted into sharing any of the risk or even continuing to shelter the culprit but to dispatch the whole business as quickly as possible.

Edward was presently removed from Woodnoth's house to that of his brother Thomas, whom their mother charged strictly to prevent Edward from leaving the house except to attend church on Sundays.[54] The situation dragged on into the autumn by which time the Collets had turned for alternative advice to Robert Bateman, the Chamberlain of London, a member of the East India Company and, as old Nicholas's first apprentice, a family friend.[55] Perhaps John Collet, realising he could not keep Edward in London, found advice from Bateman easier to accept than the earlier advice of his brother-in-law. Bateman's intervention would mean, should Edward have to go overseas, that he would go east to the Indies rather than west to the new world. When Susanna again consulted her brother in the latter part of October, it was Nicholas's turn to be awkward. He told her that he did not approve of this plan but would offer no alternative advice because the Collets so obviously favoured the Indies solution, not a particularly gracious response in the circumstances. He did, moreover, feel free to tell his sister that she and her husband were wrong to expect Thomas to maintain Edward without compensation from them.[56] The tone of this exchange suggests considerable tension between the brothers-in-law that Susanna was left to mediate. Edward, however, was not shipped off to the Indies until in January Woodnoth found him among the gamesters at the Temple. Then even John Collet bowed to the inevitable and Edward was very shortly on board a ship bound for the East.[57]

Two younger nephews followed an academic path albeit in somewhat different form. Ferrar Collet was a boy of seven when the family first came to Little Gidding while John Ferrar's son Nicholas was five. The two thus shared a Gidding childhood and a relationship with their uncle different from that of the older Collet brothers. Ferrar presumably began his education at Little Gidding though his later Latin letters probably came from Ashley in Cambridgeshire, suggesting that he by that time had been sent away to school.[58] Offered by his parents a choice of career, he declared his wish to be trained as a scholar so that he could eventually be a teacher.[59] He duly matriculated in 1636 from Peterhouse, Cambridge, was entrusted to the tutelage of Richard Crashaw, a frequent and sympathetic visitor to Little Gidding, took his B.A. and M.A. in due course and was elected a Fellow in 1643. He was probably frequently at Gidding during the time he was at Cambridge and we shall find him then assisting to develop the new forms of harmonies the family produced in those years.[60]

Ferrar's cousin Nicholas, however, received all his schooling at home from his uncle Nicholas, who was said to love him so entirely that he would not permit him to be educated anywhere but at Gidding.[61]. He stammered, a trait that later formed a bond between him and King Charles. Ferrar clearly perceived his nephew's talent for languages and provided instruction not only in the traditional Latin but in modern languages as well. The boy did not emerge as a significant scholar in his own right till after his uncle's death when he assumed leadership in creating the new harmonies of the later 1630s, probably with the collaboration of Ferrar Collet.[62]

Not only the younger generation required Nicholas's attention in 1628. That year Richard Ferrar again needed rescue from the consequences of his precarious finances.[63] By this time, however, Nicholas could leave much of the London end of his problems to Arthur Woodnoth, making only a quick trip to London in late November and early December and returning to Gidding before Christmas.[64]

By 1629 he was able to spend a larger portion of his time in the country though his sister-in-law Bathsheba made his January at Gidding decidedly less than restful.[65] He was in London in February and the first half of March and again in June, November, and December though these visits were easier and briefer thanks to Arthur's assistance, which included keeping an eye on the problematic Edward Collet and the defaulting Richard. Woodnoth tried to persuade Richard that his best hope of help from the family lay in going to Gidding and restoring himself to his mother's good graces.[66] Whatever success Richard enjoyed in that quest was only temporary and he remained a continuing source of vexation for his family.[67]

In 1630 Nicholas had to spend only a month or so (mid-February to mid-March) in London. The most pressing problems generated by the financial crisis of 1624 had been resolved and five of the eldest Collet children (Thomas and Nicholas, Mary, Anna and Susanna) were settled in appropriate paths for their adult life. By that time too Ferrar had brought to conclusion the renovation of house and church and had imposed the pattern on the household's life that his mother declared had enabled her to 'begin to live'.[68] That pattern was Little Gidding's distinctive characteristic and one that would elicit from outsiders both admiration and suspicion.

Ferrar, like St. Benedict centuries earlier, recognised the compelling importance of an orderly and balanced structure for communal life. 'The best minds are like clocks which to goe right need daily winding upp.'[69] Because the family's overriding call was dedication to God's service, Ferrar gave particular importance to an expanded devotional life that went well beyond the simple pattern of daily morning and evening prayer and Sunday worship and catechizing prescribed in the Book of Common Prayer. The Ferrars' enlarged household, which numbered between thirty and forty, made possible as well as desirable a more elaborate programme of devotions than a smaller group could readily sustain. Moreover the life of a group of that size and complexity would certainly proceed in a more edifying and orderly fashion with a clear and full programme that combined devotional and educational as well as practical activities. Such a programme would also be more effective if its members felt a voluntary commitment to its aims. Ferrar clearly sought, as we shall see, to cultivate that attitude.

The household's daily routine centred on a series of devotional exercises in which the entire family participated. Shared activities in turn provided opportunities to draw family members together and in some cases redefine their relationships, points to which I shall return shortly. As a loyal Churchman Ferrar grounded both the family's public and private devotions in the Bible and the Book of Common Prayer. Because the household constituted the whole of the membership of the parish and its titular rector was nonresident, the parish church risked looking like the family's private chapel, an appearance Ferrar perhaps consciously sought to counter particularly after 1629 when royal opposition to such chapels became clear.[70] Prayer Book services were always held in the church, never in the house. As an ordained deacon (though never licensed to preach) Ferrar could lead these daily services of matins and evensong for which the family formally processed to the church. On Sundays, however, the church served a wider parish when others from neighbouring parishes attended a second morning service that included both a sermon and, once a month, communion provided by the rector of Steeple Gidding. For the afternoon evensong on Sunday the family reciprocated by walking the short distance to Steeple Gidding. Ferrar added to these services at least one other connected to special circumstances in the family's life. This was a recitation, again in the church, every weekday of the litany, a practice initiated with special permission on account of the plague epidemic raging in London in 1625 when the family first departed for Gidding.[71] To these Prayer Book services in the church were added prayers at home, individually upon arising and collectively before retiring. Family members, particularly the younger ones, also began the day by coming to the Great Chamber to recite to Ferrar psalms and passages they had memorised.[72]

Reading, as would be appropriate for a household that was a 'school of religion', featured prominently in many of its shared activities. How much of that reading was done by individuals in private is unclear from the accounts that survive. Ferrar himself obviously devoted much of his time when he was at Gidding to study and probably encouraged at least his namesake nephew, whom he educated wholly at home, to do the same. For the most part, however, reading seems to have been very much a social as well as an educational activity and one fundamental to Ferrar's method of interactive instruction for all ages. The younger children took turns reading aloud to the household during dinner and supper. They read works of history and travel or perhaps lives of the saints and of those Protestant martyrs extolled in John Foxe's *Acts and Monuments*. Ferrar chose stories that provided both entertainment and instruction. Afterward the stories were abstracted by an adult and transcribed by the children into a book kept for the purpose. The children were also quizzed on the stories to be sure they had understood and would remember them. As a further reinforcement, after each of the main meals one child recited a story from memory to the assembled household still at table, a task that not only fixed the story in memory but also gave practice and confidence in public speaking.[73] Presumably such collections of stories were available for individual children to consult by way of preparation as well as for pleasure. The women of the family would also have had opportunity during the day for similar consultation and indeed might have read to one another as they sat together in the Great Chamber around old Mary Ferrar. Certainly the social ambience for reading and family devotions for which John Rastrick later yearned was very much present at Little Gidding.[74]

Music was also a part of that ambience; indeed, one of the resident schoolmasters was a musician and Susanna Collet was said to have been a skilled lutenist. The family had an organ in the house and sang hymns before and after meals as well as at devotions and later at meetings of the Little Academy.[75] There were also designated periods of free time; Ferrar was well aware that children especially needed breaks and chances to run about if they were to learn effectively. Nevertheless, time was highly structured and well filled. Ferrar reinforced his metaphor of the mind as clock or watch[76] by providing within the house some sort of timepiece in every room as well as a clock with a sonorous bell to summon particip- ants at the appropriate times. He also placed sundials on three sides of the church tower, each with an appropriate motto.[77] For Ferrar order was essential to 'redeem the time' in the phrase of his twentieth-century admirer T. S. Eliot, and his care in this matter reveals an important trait of his character.

Not all education at Little Gidding was part of the household's devotional programme. Besides their mealtime reading the younger children received conventional instruction in the dovecote that Ferrar had had converted into a schoolhouse. They could hardly have participated in such a literate family life without it. He staffed it with three instructors, one of whom was the music master. The others taught basic reading and writing and arithmetic and for the older boys Latin. The pupils, including not only the family's children but also other children from the neighbourhood and sometimes boarders from farther away, such as Arthur Woodnoth's nephew Ralph and Sir John Danvers's godson,[78] would also have received instruction in proper behaviour. Turner's notes include excerpts from Ferrar's 'Instructions' for pupils and children about deportment that caution them not to make 'foolish & idle motions' with their hands (putting them in pockets, scratching their heads) that testify to Ferrar's attention to detail.[79] On a loftier note and aimed at older pupils (probably the Collet nieces, a propos the controversial 'nuns' of Gidding) was a treatise on virginity and a manuscript volume on 'The Duties of Man and Woman' that concluded with a section on 'Duties Peculiar to Woman' enjoining Pauline obedience to husbands.[80] Clearly Ferrar's fatherly care and masterful instruction extended to every level of learning and behaviour in his household!

The most distinctive element of Little Gidding's daily devotions had also its significant educational role. After the family had returned from matins in the church, they began a series of hourly readings in the Great Chamber, that 'devout Psalmody' which Joshua Mapletoft later called one of 'the particular tessera of our family'.[81] This psalmody probably developed out of Ferrar's practice during his Continental travels of reciting psalms every hour and at appropriate times other offices from the Book of Common Prayer, all of which he knew by heart.[82] There were two characteristics that made this 'Psalmody' of Little Gidding 'particular'. One was the regularity of the family's hourly observances and the other was their use in those exercises of a gospel 'harmony' together with the psalter. Surviving accounts describe these exercises as 'hourly' without being absolutely clear if those 'hours' were literal or canonical. In either case the sessions were conspicuously regular and frequent.[83] The size of the household made possible so intensive a programme because not everyone was expected to be present at every session. Members of the household took turns during the day, which meant that others could get on with other work. Nevertheless their regularity and frequency roused contemporary comment; the sympathetic among Ferrar's contemporaries applauded the hourly readings as evidence of exemplary spiritual fervour while others feared them as the not-very-thin end of the Romish monastic wedge.[84]

The content of the sessions, as opposed to their frequency, excited no such controversy being impeccably biblical if somewhat unusual, for along with the psalms appointed for the day were chapters in a gospel 'harmony'.[85] Harmonies, which Christians had created since the second century, aimed to integrate the texts of the four gospels into a continuous narrative of the life and teachings of Christ. The Reformation, with its intense scrutiny of biblical texts and keen interest in promoting biblical knowledge for clergy and laity alike, had produced on the Continent throughout the sixteenth century and into the seventeenth a renewed burst of attention to this approach from both Protestants and Catholics.[86] The assumption behind these numerous syntheses was that Holy Writ could neither contradict itself nor contain superfluous material. The hope behind them was that an integrated narrative would make the gospel message clearer and easier for preachers to expound and readers to remember and understand. Harmonies thus were preeminently teaching tools and as such would have an obvious appeal to someone entrusted with educating a household.

When Ferrar collected stories and sayings for reading aloud at family mealtimes, he knew that to be memorable, especially for children, these stories had to be not only edifying but also enjoyable and lively.[87] What therefore could seem more appropriate to such a teacher than a gospel harmony that would present the greatest story of all as a continuous and dramatic narrative?

Even without a harmony the household had ample exposure to readings of scripture through the passages prescribed in the Prayer Book's calendar for the daily services of matins and evensong. Following this pattern the family would in church have read through the psalter every month, the New Testament three times in a year and the Old Testament, or most of it, once in the year. During the first year or so at Gidding those same passages of gospels, epistles, and psalms used at matins and evensong were also the hourly readings at home. Ferrar, however, was too perceptive a teacher not to realise that too much repetition risked losing listeners' attention. A variant version would avoid this difficulty. A different story line, however, was not the only device he adopted to make the harmony's narrative more vivid. In July 1627 his niece, Anna Collet, wrote to him in London to thank him 'for our pictur[e]s', a possible indicator that the harmony she and her sisters were already at work on would have illustrations.[88] Even if only the reader could see the pictures in the harmony during the hourly sessions, those involved in making such a volume would, as we shall see, have ample opportunity to match text and picture.

A rapid start on producing a harmony for the family's use suggests that Ferrar was already familiar with such works and indeed probably already had in mind a particular model, that of a Netherlander, Cornelius Jansen. Jansen had divided his harmony, *Concordia Evangelica* (1549) into 150 chapters.[89] From Ferrar's point of view a harmony having the same number of chapters as there were psalms fitted admirably into his reading plan. He could readily apportion each so that it would be read through in a thirty-day month and thus repeated twelve times in the course of the year.[90]

Ferrar could have encountered Jansen during his student days in Cambridge, if the copies now found in many of the college libraries, including that of his own college, Clare, had reached the shelves while he was there. Also possibly present were copies of numerous other harmonies by authors both Catholic and Protestant.[91] On the other hand no copies of Buisson, the other source he subsequently acknowledged, appear on any Cambridge lists that I have seen. Ferrar might, therefore, have discovered that elaborately cross-referenced work only later, perhaps during his travels on the Continent or later still after he had launched the harmonies project at Little Gidding.

If numerous harmonies already existed, why did the Ferrars have to create one for themselves? Language was the problem. Most of the continental harmonies including Jansen's and Buisson's were in Latin, with a few in French or German.[92] While harmonies in these languages would have been accessible to Cambridge dons and undergraduates, they would hardly have served for general family use at Gidding. In 1596 Robert Hill published in English a chapter-by-chapter summary of Jansen's harmony and bound it with his more extensive summary of the whole bible.[93] Hill was at that time a Fellow of St. John's College, Cambridge, but also resident with the family of Sir William Fitzwilliam in Essex. He clearly hoped to reach with his summary harmony a 'popular' audience, godly households such as the one in which he was then living for which the existing harmonies were inaccessible. Hill's subsequent career as a preacher showed him to have been as keen to educate his parishioners as Ferrar was to instruct his family.[94] Hill's book, however, would not have served Ferrar's purpose.[95] What he wanted was the actual words of scripture.

Thus Ferrar in 1625, whether or not he knew of Hill and his summary, could only have obtained the kind of English harmony he wanted by making it himself, that is, by cutting up English bibles and arranging their verses in Jansen's sequence. This necessity, however, Ferrar took not as an obstacle but an opportunity, an ideal shared activity for the entire family that maximised both participation and instruction. Once Ferrar had provided the necessary materials and laid out the order of the passages, everyone capable of using scissors and paste could help. Not only the work itself but also the setting drew the participants together. A special room in the house was set aside for this activity.[96] It probably became for the Collet daughters, who did most of the work, their special domain among the public spaces in the house. It contained, besides the necessary work tables and chairs, two 'great presses' which produced pasted pages so neatly and firmly joined that people who saw them believed them to be 'a new kind of printing'.[97] The room also housed the bindery.[98] As John Ferrar put it,

> the younger sort learned [the gospel passages] without book, and hourly made repetition of some part of them, that so both their hands and minds might be partakers in what was good and useful.[99]

Though the early biographies of Ferrar suggest that everyone, including on occasion the matriarch Mary Woodnoth Ferrar herself,[100] took part, the bulk of the craft work evidently fell to the elder Collet daughters. John Ferrar indeed described the harmonies 'as rarities in their kinds and the handy-work of women (for their manufacture, I mean, and labour of putting together, by way of pasting, &c.)'.[101] Mary, the eldest and in her mid-twenties when the family moved to Gidding, took the lead in this as in various other projects.[102] Anna, Hester, and Margaret were also all at Gidding till 1635.[103] They in turn could have supervised their younger sisters as they became old enough to join in.[104] As George Herbert declared when he wrote to the ladies of Gidding to thank them for the harmony they had given him:

> he most humbly blessed God that he had lived now to see women's scissors brought to so rare a use as to serve at God's altar.[105]

As this gift to George Herbert suggests, once the Ferrars had made and used a harmony in their own household, they wanted to share its benefits with others. Herbert was an obvious choice of recipient for he already enjoyed close links with Ferrar which may have dated back to their time at Cambridge and would subsequently be reinforced by participation in other major family projects. From that modest beginning with the gift to Herbert the harmonies grew in scope and style and audience, coming ultimately to encompass Old Testament as well as New Testament subjects and bringing the family into contact with King Charles himself. These developments, however, belong to a later stage in the family's story.

From the start, as John Ferrar remarked in the passage quoted earlier, making the harmonies drew the individuals of the multi-generational household together and thus served as an especially effective tool for building a sense of community at Little Gidding. Mary Woodnoth Ferrar and her children had already united in cohabitation and heart when they chose to move together to Gidding. Working on the harmonies provided the necessary bonding for the Collet daughters who had had no initial choice but to accompany their parents. Nicholas could then strengthen that sense of community by introducing explicit voluntary commitments into later family activities: the discussion group called the 'Little Academy', night vigils, and the temperance programme of 1632-33.

Those bonds depended not only on joint endeavours but also on the individual relationships that Ferrar developed with his older Collet nieces. These he was building during these years even as he was also concerned with the settlement of their brothers. The education of the Collet daughters took a different form, of course, from that of their brothers and was of more immediate impact on the Gidding household itself. The eight Collet sisters spanned a wide range in age from Mary, born probably in 1601, to little Judith, baptised in 1624.[106] We have for the years Nicholas Ferrar led the Gidding household no substantial record of the youngest nieces, Joyce and Judith Collet and Virginia Ferrar, though they would presumably have received basic instruction in reading, writing and arithmetic and participated in the devotions and readings as soon as they were able. Whether any of the nieces went on to learn Latin or French and whether the younger ones eventually took their turns at managing the household as their older sisters had done is undocumented. All the nieces clearly had ample opportunity and presumably sufficient instruction to share in the household's extensive musical life from a young age. In addition to wielding those 'womens scissors' that created harmonies were related lessons in bookbinding, a craft in which Mary Collet Ferrar in particular became expert.[107] These activities, to which were later added the discussions of the 'Little Academy', could have included the younger girls but chiefly provided ongoing education for the older daughters who had moved beyond formal lessons in the dovecote schoolhouse. Especially for the older nieces the early years at Gidding also posed for each the challenge of building a relationship with her uncle Nicholas in his self-appointed role as her spiritual director. The most extensively documented, those of the three eldest daughters, Mary, Anna and Susanna (Su), create the picture that Ferrar's first biographer described as 'His mayster-piece ye frameing of his Virgin Neices'.[108]

The 'particular psalmody' of the family had already given rise in some quarters of suspicions of popery. These suspicions were reinforced when the two eldest nieces, Mary and Anna, the 'virgin nieces', embraced the celibate life declaring that they had chosen that path as a way they could better serve God.[109] We have, unfortunately, no clear evidence to indicate when or in what circumstances they made that choice or what part their uncle played in it.

For himself he declared, when refusing a highly advantageous offer of marriage, that he was determined never to marry.[110] Because he was so obviously the spiritual director of the household, he could have steered his nieces in that direction by his example if not by explicit words.[111] He certainly supported Mary and Anna in their choice but only after they had explicitly acknowledged it.[112] He was at pains to refute stories circulated about their desire to take formal vows of celibacy, telling Edward Lenton no later than 1634 that he abhorred the idea of such vows.[113] They were quite unnecessary, Ferrar believed, for Christ would provide without any solemn and public declarations the necessary self-control to a committed follower who truly desired a celibate life dedicated to God's service. As mentioned earlier Francis Turner noted in his biographical materials that 'He [NF] wrote a Tract of Virginity' and subsequent comments toward the end of the volume suggest that Turner had this manuscript among his materials and excerpted parts of it that reiterate this point.[114] Virginity is commendable provided it is freely chosen, hence taking vows should not be necessary. Such a choice is a gift of God and He will provide the strength to follow it. That the nieces read this tract is evident in the discussion around the election of Mary Collet Ferrar to be 'Mother' in the place of her grandmother as leader of the Little Academy. Her sister 'Cheerful' produces the tract's argument that while virginity is commendable so too is marriage and motherhood; temperance is just as vital, if not more so, to the married mother as to her celibate sister; the married woman's cares for children and household are as demanding as the virgin's pursuit of sanctity. 'Cheerful' and 'Affectionate' (Margaret and Hester Collet) clearly see themselves as potential wives in contrast to their elder sisters.[115] At the same time another manuscript volume, presumably also aimed at the nieces, on 'Duties Common to Man & Woman' contained a thoroughly Pauline final section on 'Duties Peculiar to Women' that declared women should live not celibate but as wives obedient to their husbands .

Despite his protests and the obvious fact that Little Gidding was a family household and not a cloister, Ferrar nevertheless did value uniformity to an extent that could further support suspicions of popery.[116] Not only were there the frequent and structured household devotions but also the uniformly black clothing that Edward Lenton reported all the family, except Mary in her 'grey friar's gown', wore to church.[117] Ferrar indeed valued clothing that was uniform (but not necessarily black) not only for spiritual but also for economic reasons as an episode in 1631 revealed. He wrote to his mother that he had purchased in London for the nieces' dresses a supply of green wool cloth in sufficient quantity to obtain an advantageous price and had added to it for 'sleeves' not the originally intended lace but black silk, which would not only last longer but also had the additional merit of being out of fashion and thus available at half-price. He assumed that, of course, considerations of fashion were of no consequence and further hoped 'That the likeness in all outward things may be a remembraunce and motive to there Indeauour of perfect Inward Vnity and agreement amongst the sisters – ', not perhaps his most perceptive piece of spiritual direction![118]

Another and more revealing window into these relationships can be found in the correspondence between Ferrar and the three oldest sisters, Mary, Anna, and Susanna (Su), who enjoyed the closest relationships with him. Most of the letters fell within the years from 1626 to 1632, when the family was implementing Ferrar's plan for their collective life at the same time that he was necessarily often absent in London. By far the largest number of surviving letters were from Anna to Nicholas, fifteen as opposed to two from Mary and three from Susanna.[119] Also notable, I think, is the fact that Mary's letters were written only in 1631 and 1632 while the younger sisters were writing in the earlier years. While these facts may merely reflect the vagaries of document survival, I believe they permit of more significant conclusions.

Mary was undoubtedly the eldest granddaughter and almost certainly the eldest grandchild. She was her grandmother's namesake and spent a great deal of her childhood with her grandparents.[120] She was at most only eight years younger than her uncle Nicholas, whom she would have seen both in her parents' house at Bourn when he visited from Cambridge, and at her grandparents' house in St. Sithes Lane during academic vacations. When in 1617 Nicholas returned from his Continental travels and took up permanent residence with his parents, Mary, by now in her late teens, was almost certainly living there with her aging grandparents. That possibility looks the more likely in light of the £500 legacy she received from her grandfather's will in 1620, the only one of his grandchildren specially singled out. If she were indeed in the London household for much, if not all, of those years from 1617 to 1624, she would have lived through stirring times that included the dramatically changing fortunes of the Virginia Company, her uncles' participation in the Parliaments of 1621 and 1624, and the financial debacle that brought the family to Gidding. During those years she would have had daily contact with Nicholas, indeed with both her uncles, as well as opportunity to learn a good deal about both the business and household affairs of the family. Had she and Nicholas in fact discovered during those years a spiritual affinity, the move to Gidding would simply have extended and deepened that already existing bond. Certainly by the time Nicholas wrote the one letter we have from him to her he addressed her as 'sister of my soule' and signed himself 'your brother'.[121] The tone of the letter suggests the openness and mutual trust of two people who knew each other well.

By contrast Anna's and Susanna's first letters to their uncle were rather anxious confessions of sin, assuring him of their hearty repentance and earnestly promising amendment.[122] Both also expressed deep gratitude for the 'kind and fatherly admonitions' he gave them when they had expected and felt they deserved severe castigations. The nature of their sins is not altogether clear. Anna sounds, from her offer to make 'restitution' of £1 10s 8d, as if she had made some foolish expenditure or come up short in her housekeeping accounts. Whatever it was, she felt her repentance was incomplete without this fuller written confession, which she would have sent earlier had not 'Tears and my intemperate affections over ruled my desires'.

All of Anna's letters to her uncle are filled with extravagant expressions not only of gratitude for his gentle fatherly guidance but also of obsequious praise for his wisdom and understanding, displaying in them an emotional, impulsive and dependent personality quite different from Mary's. There is a crescendo from the early remark that 'your Love to mee hath not bine unequall to ye Love of a moste Deare parent'[123] to a letter of 15 June 1629 addressed to 'My Most Deare and Honoured Father' in which she proclaims that 'Bearing ye Name of yr Daughter I esteeme as a Sealle of . . .[blot]. . . Love And that you have benne pleased so to addopte mee yours'.[124] Nicholas replied promptly in a letter addressed to 'My dearest Nan,' in which he mentioned Mary as 'Lately becom my sister alsoe'.[125]

This curious transformation of the relationship of uncle and niece into one of brother and sister included John as well as Nicholas and Hester and probably Margaret as well as Mary and Anna.[126] Mary indeed took to calling herself Mary Collet Ferrar and sometimes simply Mary Ferrar, perhaps to signal this changed sisterly relationship.[127] Anna, however, remained Collet and figured in Nicholas's letters as a 'daughter'. Her letters suggest that her eagerness to claim that role reflected an urgent need to assure herself of a special place in her uncle's affection, a 'special relationship' quite different in tone from that which Mary already enjoyed. While Mary addressed Nicholas as 'Father of my soul', their letters sound much more fraternal than parental. It is hard to imagine Nicholas addressing Mary as 'Myne owne Deare childe' as he did Anna in a very tender and inspirational letter of 1631.[128]

Whilst both sisters chose the celibate life, Anna, unlike Mary, had suitors, including her cousin Arthur Woodnoth, who twice asked permission to make her his wife. On the second occasion a sequence of letters survives that illustrates the somewhat tortuous but not atypical process within the household that Ferrar used to counsel his family and particularly his nieces. Woodnoth had visited Gidding in September but had had to leave sooner than he had intended.[129] Even if he had not by then said anything explicit to Anna, she sensed hints enough to feel misgivings, for soon after he had left she wrote a letter to her uncle reiterating her desire not to marry but asking his counsel about the wisdom of her wish. She however kept the letter for a month and then only turned it over to him via her sister Mary as intermediary.[130] In it she insisted that her reluctance to marry stemmed not from any doubts about Woodnoth's merits but purely from doubts that she could perform her duty to God as she wished to do if she were a married woman. If, however, her parents and relatives insisted, she would of course submit to their better judgment though she declared that to be free from this fear would be worth more to her than an estate of £100 p.a.

Before Ferrar ever received that letter, however, Mary had intervened to apprise her uncle of a new development that had arisen suddenly and unexpectedly.[131] According to Mary, Anna had received a letter from Woodnoth some ten days after Anna had written her still undelivered letter to her uncle. Anna had confided to her sister that Woodnoth's letter had produced in her the same anxious reaction as she had had four years before when she discovered that her family would happily have bestowed her on 'Cosen Arthur' in marriage. Mary must have delivered her own letter to her uncle promptly for Ferrar had already written reassuringly to Anna before he had received from Mary Anna's earlier letter. Anna replied to his letter of reassurance on the very day she entrusted to Mary her earlier letter, offering him fervent thanks for banishing her fears.[132] When Ferrar finally received from Mary Anna's earlier letter, he asked Mary to hold it until the next day at which time he read it in her presence and, without further discussion, directed her to show it only to old Mrs. Ferrar and John Ferrar. She was not by implication to show it to her parents. We have seen Ferrar share an earlier letter about Edward Collet with her and his brother while he waited to learn what the Collets wanted for Edward before offering his own advice. Perhaps he was also remembering the Collets' tearful reaction to his recommendation that Edward be sent to Bermuda or Virginia.[133] If he thought that the Collets still favoured the marriage and feared they would use the letter to pressure Anna, he was in effect sending Mary to enlist from his mother and brother support for her sister's wishes. These letters between nieces and uncle were exchanged between family members living together under the same roof and demonstrate not only Ferrar's concern for Anna's wishes but also a curious combination of written as well as spoken communication and a secretiveness in Ferrar that contrasts with his appeals for candour. Once Anna had furnished him with a written declaration of what she herself wanted, her uncle readily supported her.

Between these two episodes with Woodnoth came another in 1629 involving another suitor, which was only elliptically recounted in a letter from her mother to Nicholas.[134] Susanna particularly emphasised to her brother that she did not want her 'dear Anna' to be given in marriage to any man who did not sincerely love and choose her and she clearly had doubts about this would-be suitor.[135] After the second episode with Woodnoth in 1631, when Anna had made it very clear that she really did not want to marry anybody, the question never again surfaced.

For Mary we have no evidence of any offers of marriage despite the substantial portion her grandfather had left her. That might represent merely a gap in the evidence, but it could also indicate that either her choice or character were so clear as to discourage any suitors. Moreover, she had shown herself thoroughly committed to building the holy household at Gidding, making her grandfather's legacy over to her uncles for that purpose.[136] Her strength of character, articulateness, and ability to lead made her a mainstay of the family's life, but might well have made her look too formidable to many men and at the same time have made her unwilling to exchange her role there for a life of prescribed wifely submission.[137]

The contrast between these two nieces appeared not only in their letters to their uncle and in the presence or absence of suitors but also in their differing roles in the Gidding household. Mary was very much a leader on whom her uncle and grandmother depended in practical as well as spiritual matters. She supervised the village children's Sunday morning recitations of memorised psalms and the preparation and dispensing of medical help to neighbours. She also, with her uncle John, took charge of the family's mealtime readings. This task required ensuring that the collection of stories was maintained, that the household's children took their readings in turn, and that the others remembered and understood what they had heard.[138] Mary was evidently good with children. Not for nothing did she take the name of 'Mother' in the reconstituted Little Academy of 1632 and find herself 'mother' to her own siblings.[139] Her sister Susanna praised her care of Su's little daughter Mary or 'Mall', who was sent to Gidding while her mother was ill, and Arthur Woodnoth had earlier requested that she take a hand in educating his niece.[140] Mary, as the chief bookbinder, was the one who created the harmony now in the Bodleian Library and bound the one presented to the king. She also supplied her brother-in-law, Joshua Mapletoft, with psalters and prayer books for use by his parishioners.[141] She manifestly had managerial, practical and pedagogical skills on which the family came increasingly to rely.

Anna in contrast, while she had her share of work in the household, was not in sole charge of anything except, presumably, her monthly turn at running the household. She assisted Mary with the psalm children and could, like others of the sisters, take temporary charge of dispensing medicines and dressings when Mary was unavailable. In all likelihood she helped with the harmonies and shared in the copying of the Story Books recording the Little Academy's discussions.[142] She comes across as one who was an enthusiastic supporter and assistant rather than a leader, more malleable than her older sister and keen to earn her uncle's approval.

If Mary and Anna as the 'virgin nieces' had their special place in the Gidding household and in the affection of their uncle, what about their next sister, Susanna, or Su as the family often addressed her? Her confessional letter to her uncle came almost a year later than Anna's and her 'sin' apparently involved not bad bookkeeping but refusing to obey her parents. Her deliverance, Ferrar told her firmly, could come only from a resolute determination to follow their advice entirely. Such submissive obedience, assisted by God's mercy, 'shall rectify the error and prevent the daunger which overmuch presumption of your owne iudgement hath heretofore bred'.[143] Ferrar tempered his condemnation of the sin with praise for 'the fruites of Piety and vertue growing on to greate maturity in you' that increased his natural affection for her. She had in her own letter thanked him for his fatherly and loving admonitions, in much the same style as Anna professed her gratitude for kindness where she had deserved stern rebuke.

In what way had Su manifested this 'presumption'? Perhaps she had rejected her parents' (and probably also uncle's) plan to marry her to Joshua Mapletoft. We know that Anna refused her cousin Arthur Woodnoth's first offer of marriage sometime during this year; perhaps Su also had rejected the widowed Mapletoft. If that were the case, she did the following year yield to her elders' wishes. She had been seriously ill during the interval, which might have contributed to her change of mind.[144] Certainly her mother thought very highly of Mapletoft.[145] Her subsequent praise of him suggests that she might well have been very angry at Su's initial refusal, the more so if she were anxious not to see her follow her older sisters' examples. Indeed, when she wrote to Su soon after the marriage, she called her 'the first of my Branches that are transplanted into a new ground' and hoped that she would be 'a leading Xample to the rest [of her sisters]'.[146]

Once the marriage had taken place in October 1628 and Su had left Gidding for Mapletoft's parish of Margaretting in Essex, the family certainly rallied round to support her. She was probably homesick as well as overwhelmed at finding herself not only immediately a stepmother to little Anne Mapletoft but shortly on the way to becoming a mother herself. She had difficult pregnancies, which must have made more stressful the adjustment to married life in a strange place several days' journey from Gidding. Her sisters took turns visiting her in the course of that first year. Anna came in January, Margaret was there in May and June, and Hester arrived with her mother, who came in August and September for the birth of Mary. They all came presumably not simply to give practical help but to boost Su's morale whenever she felt overwhelmed and homesick.

In addition to the visitors and letters from her mother came a stream of letters apparently from Su's sisters but drafted for them by their uncle. The first letter, sent within a month of the marriage, came ostensibly from Hester but read like her uncle. Having received an 'affectionate and loving report' about Su from her new husband, Hester declared herself more pleased to hear of Su's inward grace than of the outward comforts of her new home. Not only would this growth in grace bring Su greater love from her husband in Margaretting but also from her family in Gidding.[147] Ferrar's readiness to provide such encouragement suggests that he felt some responsibility for Su as well as for his friend Joshua. That would not be surprising, of course, if he had played a significant part in promoting the marriage, particularly had he done so despite Su's initial objections. And had Su shown herself less than submissive once, she might do so again; hence the praise for her increase in grace and, in a subsequent letter this time signed by Mary, admonitions to submit herself to God's will and not lament her separation from her family.[148] Between these two letters had come a couple from Anna and another from Hester, again all drafted by Nicholas.[149] The control he exercised over the content of the messages Su received illustrates the commanding as well as the encouraging style in which he acted as spiritual leader.

Ferrar wheeled the family support system into action again in January 1630, this time in response to a letter from Arthur Woodnoth. Woodnoth had visited the Mapletofts at Margaretting and attended one of their 'feasts' in the church, a meal preceded by a service of prayer and praise. To Mapletoft's remark that there had been more food than necessary at the feast Su had explained that fewer guests had come than she had expected but that such a surplus would not happen again. At the next such feast Su replied respectfully to her husband's inquiry whether she would be serving rabbits that she would omit them if he wished. Woodnoth professed himself much impressed by this submissive response, which confirmed his high opinion of Su as 'one, if not the cheif of those, I had mett with, who were redy to imbrace others, & relinquish ther own opinions'.[150]

Such a change from her earlier sin of 'presumption' Nicholas obviously wanted to reinforce, again with letters he drafted for others in the family, this time sister Mary and uncle John, to send. Both of these letters repeated Woodnoth's very words, quoted above, in their praises of Su's humility and evident growth in grace and virtue.[151] The next month Su developed a fever and became seriously ill. Nicholas himself paid a visit to Margaretting in late February to bolster the recovering patient with his presence and good advice, for which Su wrote to thank him.[152] He followed up this visit with a congratulatory letter to Su on her second wedding anniversary, wishing her joy of the occasion that had given her such a fine husband and her family such a worthy kinsman.[153] It must have been a relief to the family to see Su adjusting to married life in what they firmly believed was the appropriate manner. If she had trouble at first assuming the submissiveness of a dutiful wife, she eventually did so, for we hear no more of the sort of admonitions she received in the early years. Ferrar may have had a special relationship as spiritual director to his virgin nieces Mary and Anna, but he was no less concerned to support his married niece Su. Marriage to a clergyman was obviously highly acceptable to the family and three other of the nieces (Margaret, Joyce, and Judith) followed this pattern.

Ferrar's role as a 'Father for care' thus included both unusual and conventional aspects. He had to juggle worldly and practical demands against his aspirations for a household dedicated to God's service. He had to manage the family's worldly resources whilst he extended the conventional worship prescribed in the Prayer Book with hourly readings from the gospel harmony he had first to devise and then teach his nieces to make. His careful provision for the education of his nieces and nephews included not only their spiritual formation but their worldly vocations. He was not concerned, however, with just his immediate household; he hoped to enlist others in his orbit of service, as we shall see in the following chapter.

3

Enlarging the Community:
The 'Web of Friendship'

The preceding chapter focused on the establishment of the distinctive household at Little Gidding itself, a process that took place not in isolation but in
company with worldly demands to which Nicholas Ferrar himself as well
as other family members, especially cousin Arthur Woodnoth in London,
had to respond. While he certainly assumed the role of spiritual director for
the household, Ferrar did not limit that role to those living at Gidding. He
also looked beyond the immediate household, seeking to bind Woodnoth and
others who were united 'in heart' though not 'in cohabitation' with the family
at Gidding into what he called a 'Web of Friendship'. 'Friends' in seventeenth
century terms might or might not be kin and Ferrar's 'Web' included both.
Many were members of what was essentially a Cambridge clerical circle:
Robert Mapletoft, Joshua's brother, Augustine Lindsell, Richard Crashaw,
Barnabas Oley, Francis Dee, Timothy Thurscross, Edmund Duncon, Paul
Glisson, and John Ramsay, who became one of the family when he married
Margaret Collet in 1636. They not only corresponded with Ferrar and helped
him in both academic and business matters but also visited Gidding and
participated in the family's daily life. Such a network offered Ferrar a way to
enlarge the circle of participants in many of the household's shared activities
and make it a model of 'the communion of saints', an ideal by which 'I
have cheifly indeavored to fix my Affections'.[1] Ferrar's large hopes and
high standards for friendship come across most clearly in a letter of 1630
to Woodnoth, who was both kin and friend.[2] True friends must share freely
their hopes, fears and plans in the confidence that each loved and accepted
the other completely and generously. Only on that basis could they give real
help and support to each other and become 'that Webb of freindshyp which
I hope might. . .proue a patterne In an adge that needs patternes'. How he

translated that noble but general ideal into individual counsel for particular friends is the subject this chapter will explore.

Woodnoth was by no means the only non-resident friend with whom Ferrar communed at this level and to whom he offered support and counsel. Joshua Mapletoft and George Herbert were also major participants in his 'web of friendship' and all three were friends in turn with one another as well as with Ferrar. So too were those in that Cambridge clerical circle mentioned above. While letters to and from members of this latter group, who visited Gidding and knew the family, appear among the Ferrar Papers, it is Ferrar's extensive correspondence with Woodnoth and with Joshua Mapletoft that reveals most clearly the style and content of his spiritual direction. It provides also, of course, a measure of the man himself.

Three major topics emerge from this body of correspondence: calling or vocation, sickness and health, and marriage. Settling the young Collets in an appropriate calling was, as we have seen, an essential aspect of parenting in which Ferrar played a part. Woodnoth's case, however, entailed different hazards, the risks and responsibilities an older, established man faced in deciding to make a radical change in his vocation. Sickness and health, perennial concerns for anyone in seventeenth-century England, were of particular interest to Ferrar not only personally in the light of his own bouts of serious illness but also intellectually as the Physic Fellow at Clare Hall and student of medicine at Padua and spiritually as an interpreter of their role as special providences of God. He thus had a range of counsel both practical and spiritual to offer to Joshua Mapletoft in his protracted and painful illness. Marriage was, of course, a relationship fundamental to family and status and one governed by conventional gender roles based on scriptural rules. Though he himself never married, Ferrar dispensed advice on this matter to family and friends, including Woodnoth and his niece Anna Collet. Most dramatically, however, he had to contend with his brother John's unhappy wife Bathsheba who was deeply antipathetic to him and to the life he had established for the household at Gidding. In all of these instances Ferrar provided practical advice while insisting that voluntary commitment and decisive action based on honest self-knowledge were essential for carrying it out.

Arthur Woodnoth, unlike George Herbert and Joshua Mapletoft, was not a university graduate or a clergyman and he was acutely aware of what he believed were his cousin's superior spiritual gifts. He therefore remained deferential, addressing Ferrar as 'Sir' or 'Reverent Sir' in contrast to Ferrar's 'My dearest Cosen'.[3] On the other hand, we do also have at least a few examples of Ferrar unburdening himself to Woodnoth and receiving

counsel as well as reproofs from him. These suggest a greater measure of
equality in their relationship than might at first appear. In the years up to
1630, as we have seen, their weekly correspondence centred mainly on
family business, and such matters continued to occupy them in subsequent
years. At the beginning of that year, however, Woodnoth introduced a new
topic when he wrote to Ferrar that he would the next day set off on a
journey with Sir John Danvers.[4] Subsequent letters make clear that it was
a journey into Wiltshire designed to acquaint Woodnoth with Sir John's
business affairs, the start in fact of his employment by Danvers as his agent
or steward. It was a big step, a major change of direction for Woodnoth,
and one over which he suffered fears and anxieties that he shared with
Ferrar, sometimes readily and other times reluctantly. His reluctance Ferrar
sought to counter with appeals for the openness essential to true friendship.
Certainly both the revelations and the reticences in their correspondence
on the Danvers problem provided over the next couple of years the single
sharpest test of both their friendship and Ferrar's pastoral skills. It also
involved those other friends in the web, Joshua Mapletoft and George
Herbert.

Why did Woodnoth decide at age 34 to exchange a successful career
as a goldsmith for a post as Danvers' steward? His stated reason was that
he wanted a new vocation that would 'cheifly tend to gods Glory, and be a
meanes, & way, more directly tending to wards heaven'. He implied that
Ferrar had suggested the move as an answer to this need.[5] Ferrar and Sir
John had certainly worked together in the Virginia Company, particularly in
the last desperate struggle to prevent the Crown's resumption of the charter.
Woodnoth, who also attended Company meetings,[6] could himself have met
Danvers there as he might also have encountered George Herbert, Danvers'
stepson and also a shareholder in the Company. Danvers had a reputation
for extravagance, being a particularly lavish spender on gardens.[7] He had
a house in Chelsea and through his second wife, Elizabeth Dauntsey, had
acquired property in Wiltshire. No doubt he needed a knowledgeable and
strong-minded agent to keep his finances under control and his creditors
at bay. Danvers would have had ample opportunity to observe Ferrar's
skills in managing the Virginia Company and perhaps also to discover the
confidence Sir Edwin Sandys placed in Ferrar's financial acumen.[8] He
might in consequence himself have elicited Ferrar's advice on such matters.
In such a situation Ferrar could have suggested his cousin as a suitable
steward, particularly if he knew that Woodnoth was looking for a change.
Woodnoth offered no further explanation for his dissatisfaction with his
craft than that he desired greater opportunities than it provided to do good

Letter (FP 712: c. 1 March 1629/30) from Arthur Woodnoth to Nicholas Ferrar on implementing his decision to work for Sir John Danvers and his proposal to hand over as a consequence his goldsmith's shop to Ned and Nicholas Collet.

and serve God.[9] As he got a clearer understanding of what the Danvers position entailed, however, Woodnoth became increasingly uncertain that he was either capable of performing it or desirous of commiting himself to it. He became a man who could not decide what he wanted and in his uncertainty he turned to Ferrar for counsel.

Initially, however, in January 1630, Woodnoth sounded eager to take up the post. Indeed, his account to Ferrar of his Wiltshire experience suggested that he found life with the Dauntseys at Lavington rather a heady experience and was gratified to be taken into the confidence not only of Danvers but also of Sir John Dauntsey, Danvers' wife's grandfather.[10] He also reported that on the journey back to London Danvers had questioned him at some length about the Ferrar family and their Gidding household and pronounced himself much impressed with what Woodnoth told him. On the strength of this first venture, therefore, Woodnoth sounded pleased with the prospects and ready to commit himself to Danvers more firmly. Danvers presumably offered an acceptable level of pay for this responsible job but never either at first or in the lengthy subsequent discussions was it ever mentioned.

About a month later, however, the first problem surfaced, a practical one, namely, how with his new and demanding commitment should Woodnoth deal with his present responsibilities, his goldsmith's shop and his apprentices and servants. He favoured a proposal to put his business and house in the hands of 'Ned', probably Edward Collet, and his younger brother Nicholas, who was then Woodnoth's apprentice. This he thought preferable to the alternative of placing the apprentices elsewhere and giving up the business. He generously supposed that they would respond to such an opportunity with extra diligence. It is a somewhat surprising proposal for there is no evidence that Ned was trained as a goldsmith though Woodnoth spoke of him as being more able at that point than Nicholas. Nor is there anything except in a letter from Ned's mother that mentions Ned's master's dissatisfaction with him or the flaws in his character that caused the family much anguish.[11] Perhaps an unacknowledged but appealing advantage of this first option was that Woodnoth would retain his London base and business and have available an avenue of retreat should the Danvers position prove unsatisfactory.[12] Both possibilities that Woodnoth presented, however, implied that he would devote full time to the Danvers post.

To these practical options Ferrar replied within the week with practical criticism. He calculated the costs and profits of both alternatives and concluded that Woodnoth's favoured option would give him too paltry an income to keep up his reputation as he moved amongst the Danvers circle.

Letter (FP 714; 9 March 1629/30) from Nicholas Ferrar to Arthur Woodnoth replying with practical criticism of Woodnoth's plan to put Ned and Nicholas Collet in charge of his goldsmith's shop.

If Danvers was not offering him adequate compensation, and there is no mention of any in the correspondence, a small income would indeed have been a handicap. More serious than the financial consequences, however, were those likely to arise from discontent generated by Woodnoth's proposed way of sharing the profits between the senior apprentice (Ned?) and his junior, Nicholas Collet, and the latter's reaction to a sudden absence of authoritative supervision. The result, Ferrar admonished, would be discord and disrepute for Woodnoth, who would find himself uncomfortably dependent on those who had been his servants while simultaneously diminished in the eyes of those in his new circle. To drive home his point Ferrar quoted two general maxims the gist of which was that anyone undertaking significant employment or service to a person of rank should have at the same time no business of his own and only a minimum of anyone else's besides his employer's. Woodnoth's work for Danvers, in other words, required a total commitment incompatible with this first option. Ferrar therefore thought the second plan, giving up the house and shop and apprentices, a better one even if it meant a smaller return for Woodnoth. He then held out a third possibility, that Woodnoth offer Ned the opportunity to buy out the business and take sole charge, an offer that should please Ned's family. Nicholas Collet would then finish out his apprenticeship elsewhere. In this initial stage, therefore, Woodnoth clearly wanted the Danvers post, but with it perhaps a sort of safety net in the form of a residual interest in his old place. Ferrar interpreted Woodnoth's protestations of concern for his dependents as hedging and had no hesitation in offering trenchant criticism and analysis. He made clear his view that his cousin would do better, from a practical point of view, to make a full commitment to the Danvers job and abandon his goldsmith's shop, rather than attempt to combine the two however loosely.[13] Commitment would subsequently in Ferrar's counsel assume not simply a practical importance but also a moral one and emerge as the core of Woodnoth's difficulty.

About a month later a letter from Ferrar to Nicholas Collet suggested that Woodnoth had indeed opted for full commitment to Danvers. The letter contained important instructions about disposing of materials that Ferrar had earlier left at Woodnoth's London house, a move that suggested Ferrar anticipated that the house would soon be unavailable as a repository for family records. These materials included 'bookes and writings and Deeds wheron our whole Estate doth almost depende' as well as a certain white hamper that young Collet was to seal up and let absolutely no one open without Ferrar's written permission.[14] Perhaps

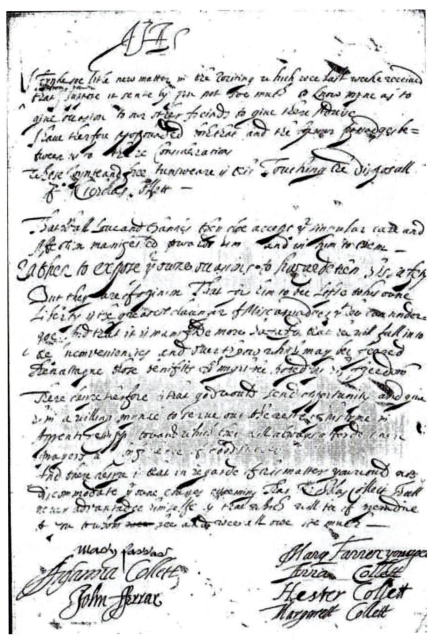

Letter (FP 720; 3 May 1630) from Nicholas Ferrar to Arthur Woodnoth containing
this enclosure signed by Ferrars and Collets urging that Nicholas Collet finish out his
apprenticeship because he was not yet ready to work unsupervised.

that mysterious hamper contained those frivolous and worldly books such as *Orlando* that Ferrar on his deathbed ordered his brother to burn.

Meanwhile Woodnoth had begun to have more fundamental qualms about his situation. A week after Ferrar had written to his nephew about the materials in Woodnoth's house, Ferrar wrote to Woodnoth in Wiltshire what was to prove the first of many letters in a different vein from his March letter of practical advice. The important decision now had become not what was best for Woodnoth's dependents but for Woodnoth himself, who had become uncertain that he really wanted to abandon his trade for service to Danvers. Ferrar encouraged him to stick to his earlier resolves, concentrate on the immediate tasks to hand, and not be disconcerted by the 'discomposure which a sudden cessation of buisiness breeds in your mynde'.[15] He followed this up a couple of weeks later with another letter, accompanied by a statement signed by his mother and the Collet parents and sisters essentially vetoing Woodnoth's idea of putting his business into the hands of his apprentices.[16] In the light of that verdict from the family at Gidding he reiterated his earlier advice that Woodnoth needed to make for himself a clear choice between continuing as a goldsmith or taking up service to Danvers and then act decisively to implement that choice. Yet for all his continued protestations that he would not tell Woodnoth what to choose because Woodnoth must make this decision for himself, Ferrar had presented the choices open to him in a way that precluded the option of combining the two jobs.

The trouble was, as nearly two years of subsequent correspondence would demonstrate, Woodnoth was not sure enough of what he really wanted to make the stark choice that Ferrar insisted was necessary. Perhaps greater knowledge of Danvers' circumstances and character had begun to generate those doubts he later expressed to George Herbert as well as to Ferrar about his chances of success in the job. In that case his hope that serving Danvers would open to him greater opportunities to do good and serve God would have dimmed and the security of his old trade looked more appealing. Ferrar certainly recognised Woodnoth's ambivalence and offered himself as a sounding board to help Woodnoth discover his real wishes and take his own decision. He could do that, however, only if Woodnoth were open with him, hence Ferrar's repeated pleas for trust and candour. His counsel now to Woodnoth was an even stronger statement about the importance of commitment than he had made previously, declaring that an individual could effectively pursue a course of action only if he had deliberately and voluntarily chosen it. He was in effect trying to nudge Woodnoth to make a choice, a device to which he had recourse not only with Woodnoth but also with others. Whether he was right to see the situation in these terms is now, of course, impossible to know though George Herbert, as his later intervention will show, concurred in this assessment.

Ferrar's advice was not, however, easy for either of the friends to follow and Woodnoth's 'discomposure' continued for at least another year and a half. In late July Ferrar wrote anxiously about the great agitation he sensed in Woodnoth's latest letter.[17] He feared Woodnoth was only telling him what he thought Ferrar wanted to hear and begged him instead to write spontaneously whatever was on his mind. Only if he would do that could Ferrar hope to help him confront his real anxieties and hopes. As a perceptive counselor Ferrar sensed the discrepancy between Woodnoth's surface words and underlying emotions and felt frustrated at being unable to reach him at a level that he thought would really help. He also feared that in his agitated state Woodnoth might abruptly cease to waver and rashly adopt a decision he would subsequently regret. His next letter therefore counseled against any hasty moves and, by way of encouragement, enclosed thoughts from friends, probably others of the family at Gidding, intended at least to show Woodnoth their concern and willingness to help in any way they could.[18]

A few days later Woodnoth, perhaps bolstered by Ferrar's own readiness to admit to what he saw as his own weakness and failure,[19] wrote to him that during the past week he had enjoyed 'such a right frame of mind' that he could think more clearly about the Danvers situation. He had, as a result, decided that he could in fact continue his shop himself and still have sufficient time for Danvers' affairs.[20] That was, of course, not a choice that Ferrar thought was valid. A lengthy silence from Woodnoth ensued during which Ferrar marked time but stayed in touch, filling his own letters with an assortment of family news or on another occasion mention of a work now in hand in which he hoped Woodnoth would participate.[21] By the end of October, when nearly two months had passed, Ferrar had become very anxious at Woodnoth's long silence and worried that he was upset and withdrawing from that trusting candour essential to the communion of saints.[22]

When Woodnoth finally did write, he confirmed Ferrar's fears that he had indeed been in a troubled frame of mind for which he could not discover any specific cause but which, with God's help, he had finally overcome. Nevertheless he was still unable to come to an unequivocal decision about his work for Danvers and set out for Ferrar some of the hazards he could foresee. Danvers had not yet decided whether to live at his Chelsea house or move to Wiltshire to the house he would presently inherit from Sir John Dauntsey. Either alternative would require great financial care and restraint of a sort that Woodnoth by this time probably doubted he could persuade Danvers to accept. If Woodnoth already knew he had had difficulty being strict enough with his apprentices, he might justifiably have quailed at the prospect of trying to keep someone of superior rank like Danvers in line. At the same time he hesitated to offend Danvers whom he believed would not be happy if Woodnoth decided to leave his employ. He added a further complication when he admitted to a fear that 'weakness of sight' might prevent him from carrying on his trade and so make that option problematical. He was obviously still a man torn by uncertainties, as Ferrar had perceived some six months earlier.[23]

Ferrar replied with two letters in rapid succession in the first of which he confessed that he did not know what to suggest but again counseled, as he had many times before, against hasty action and for frank and open communication. 'As for your own Judgment it is now I am afrayde like a troubled water that cannot clearely represent the Imadges of things which it receiveth'.[24] The next day he decided that despite having no clear answer to offer he must say more even at the risk of appearing presumptuous. Why he felt a need to risk this 'presumption' he went on to explain:

> it is on my parte necessary to offer what I thinke needefull least wilfull forbearance of the excercise of Love and Carefulness should grow indeed into Carelessness and Coldness as it hath don towards to many neere unto mee.[25]

What did he mean by this rather surprising statement? He had carefully said earlier that he would not tell his cousin what to do but would rather help him to discover for himself what he really wanted to do – within the options as Ferrar defined them. He could only do that effectively if Woodnoth trusted him enough to be completely open with him, and he hoped now to promote that openness by offering explicit assurances of his own love for his cousin and his appreciation for Woodnoth's friendship and kindness and worthiness. His hopes and assurances, however, came accompanied by a warning that Woodnoth had also not been sufficiently open with God. The failure of his efforts and prayers so far was a sign, according to Ferrar, that he was not properly submissive and had not conformed to God's will for him, a situation especially dangerous if compounded by self-will and obstinacy. Since Woodnoth had initially seen this change of calling as an opportunity to serve God better, his decision about it must involve his seeking not only to know his own mind but also to understand and submit to God's will for him in this matter. A suggestion that his own self-will and obstinacy were compounding his difficulties could hardly have been easy for Woodnoth to accept. Not surprisingly Joshua Mapletoft, visiting Woodnoth in London soon after the arrival of Ferrar's letter, saw evidence of its effect. Mapletoft added his own assurances of esteem to reinforce Ferrar's when he wrote after his visit to thank Woodnoth for the love he had shown him, adding that he only said such things to those who truly touched him. Since he had left London, he had been thinking of Woodnoth and was worried about his 'discomposure' of mind. He promised to keep Woodnoth in his prayers and to render any help he could give.[26]

Was Ferrar, however, in justifying his 'presumption' to Woodnoth also offering a more general insight into his own character? He generally made a point of waiting to be asked before offering advice. He was certainly capable of detachment as, for example, in the cool but courteous reception he accorded to casual and curious visitors to Gidding.[27] He could also be ruthless as he was in his defence of the Virginia Company and in his attacks on Sir Thomas Smith and Lord Treasurer Cranfield. But except for his sister-in-law Bathsheba, his family and friends never spoke of him as cold and uncaring. Quite the reverse were the accounts of his ability to persuade, to put himself in another's place and tailor his comments accordingly, to use carrots rather than sticks to teach.[28] Who then were those 'many neere unto mee' toward whom he had turned cold and careless? Some candidates suggest themselves: those black sheep of the family, Edward Collet and Richard Ferrar, perhaps also his brother-in-law John Collet, or John Gabbet whom he was happy to send away from Gidding.[29] Unfortunately no unambiguous answers emerge clearly from the documents but the self-criticism is relevant to any general assessment of Ferrar's character.

At the close of the eventful year of 1630, Woodnoth was again in Wiltshire with Danvers, summoned by the probably terminal illness of Sir John Dauntsey. On his death Danvers would inherit the Lavington estate and probably have to confront that decision about his Chelsea house that had worried Woodnoth earlier. When he wrote, Ferrar did not address this point but only urged Woodnoth not to put his own estate at risk in trying to help others or to be too definite with his advice to anyone else about how to arrange his life.[30] Woodnoth continued to work for Danvers though without further discussion of the problem for some ten months. It had perhaps been superseded by the more pressing crisis with Edward Collet in which Woodnoth was deeply involved.

When the Danvers issue reappeared in the following October still unresolved, it had acquired a further dimension. In the autumn of 1631,

Woodnoth apparently contemplated marriage, for he reported to Ferrar that on his visit to George Herbert he had asked Herbert explicitly whether he could continue working for Sir John Danvers 'if I shold inclyne to maridg'.[31] The hand he sought was that of his cousin Anna Collet, who had consistently expressed her desire to remain single.[32] We have seen how her uncle supported her in that resolve though all we know of Woodnoth's side of the story is that in the wake of his visit to Gidding in Septemjber Anna became anxious about his possible intentions and then professed not to understand his subsequent letter to her.[33] Entirely absent from surviving records is whatever counsel Ferrar offered to Woodnoth.

Did he act the part of a true friend to Woodnoth in this matter of his marriage? It is hard to imagine that Woodnoth had said nothing about his hopes at least during that visit to Gidding, if not earlier. Had Ferrar voiced strong reservations it is equally hard to imagine Woodnoth persevering by letter after he had left Gidding. Yet Ferrar knew that Anna wished to remain unmarried; she had rejected Woodnoth's earlier suit in 1627. Why then did he not tactfully discourage Woodnoth's hopes and thereby save him from greater disappointment? Perhaps he did make some veiled attempt that would account for the ambiguity in Woodnoth's letter to Anna, but he clearly had not intervened preventively. In this instance Ferrar did not act with the candour he had professed to be essential to true friendship and had pleaded that Woodnoth would use with him.

Though Woodnoth in 1631 was clear about his marriage hopes but disappointed in their outcome, he remained a prey to uncertainty about his position with Sir John Danvers. Danvers, for his part, demonstrated his high regard for the household at Gidding by sending his godson there for his education.[34] For Woodnoth, however, matters were not so straightforward. Though he had declared the previous year that he thought he could provide the services Danvers required while still maintaining his goldsmith's shop, his subsequent bouts of agitation and anxiety suggest that he was having second thoughts. Perhaps he had consulted Ferrar on the matter during his Gidding visit in September for Ferrar was now prepared to call for a second opinion by way of further counsel. To that end he had given Woodnoth a letter on the subject to take to their mutual friend and Danvers' stepson George Herbert in Bemerton.[35]

When he handed over Ferrar's letter, he hastened to explain to an initially puzzled Herbert that it concerned himself and his uncertainties about the Danvers position. When he there raised with Herbert the question of combining marriage with work for Danvers, he could not have known the outcome of his hopes to marry Anna Collet.[36] The crux of his dilemma, however, was not the question of marriage but what he described to Herbert as 'the Vnsatisfiedness of both those courses betwixt w[hi]ch I hanged in suspence the one being too strayte to fill my desyres and the other too difficult for me to effect.' Interestingly, Herbert's first reaction was that if Woodnoth came to live and work with him, he would give him complete information about his estate and power to employ its resources as he thought best, implying by contrast that Danvers had not done so. After listening further to Woodnoth's recital in general terms of his hopes and fears, Herbert surprised him with a specific comment to the effect that he and Ferrar were making too much of the title of 'a Divine' when Woodnoth could be a ministering angel to Danvers without literally being a minister. What exactly prompted this rather oracular pronouncement is not clear, but it is certainly at best an ambiguous hint that ordination had ever figured in any of Woodnoth's plans. Nor does it square with Herbert's previous remarks about his providing Woodnoth with information and power to utilise his estate's resources were Woodnoth working for him. Woodnoth indeed was, as he continued in his report to Ferrar, concluding that his trade was more important to him than he had previously reckoned. Although he wondered whether God accounted this his lawful calling, he found his inclination to return to it reinforced through prayer and also through his conviction that it promoted his own wellbeing by requiring physical labor and engendering humility of mind. His trade evidently had come to look increasingly appealing as he increasingly feared that work for Danvers, whatever its potential for doing good, would have only limited success.

Having had time to think over both Ferrar's letter and Woodnoth's explanation, Herbert offered his own written advice. Unlike Ferrar, he was quite prepared to tell Woodnoth what he thought he ought to do. Herbert had no doubt that service to Sir John represented a higher opportunity of doing good than did work in Woodnoth's trade.[37] Hence, having made that good choice Woodnoth should stick to it and not show himself changeable and inconstant. On this point Herbert was echoing Ferrar's earlier counsel as he did also by casting the problem as an either/ or choice between Danvers and his trade. Herbert never mentioned as an alternative a combination of the two and indeed noted that Woodnoth had no need to work at his trade to support either himself or his kin. Furthermore, if dissatisfaction with his trade derived from the very nature of the work while dissatisfaction with Danvers' service derived simply from his lack of success, he should put his trust in God Who was the source of all success and risk the Danvers situation. In addition, Herbert clearly thought Woodnoth underrated what he had accomplished for

Danvers thus far. If his influence on Sir John had been more in the nature of negative restraint than positive inclination, that was nonetheless helpful and acceptable to God for its good intentions even when unsuccessful. 'For any scruple of leaving your trade, throw it away'. For Herbert service to Danvers was without doubt a higher work and as such commendable in God's eyes. Herbert's advice certainly did not mesh with Woodnoth's growing inclination to return to his trade, a conflict that probably explains why Woodnoth felt reluctant about sending on some subsequent letters of Ferrar's to Herbert.[38] At that point Woodnoth could only resignedly declare his hope that the matter would finally be finished satisfactorily.

In January and February 1632 there was a lull during which Woodnoth received from Herbert a little notebook of directions about another project which he then managed to send on to Ferrar despite being laid up by a couple of bouts of illness.[39] By March, however, Woodnoth had recovered and was again wrestling with the Danvers problem and his inability to make up his mind. Herbert had applauded the virtue of constancy, adding that changeableness did not become a man. Taking up that theme Woodnoth acknowledged to Ferrar the truth of St. James's condemnation of the double-minded man as unstable in all his ways.[40] Whilst he claimed that he was not trying to excuse himself from this error with which Ferrar too had taxed him, he did plead extenuating circumstances in the form of a life-long 'natural' weakness that made such choices especially difficult for him. To compensate for this weakness he declared himself prepared, when he could not make his own decision, to accept others' direction. He had, however, resolved that his best choice lay in pursuing 'A quiett Life in laborious and humble courses'. These had been in the past the circumstances in which he had best experienced God's grace and found himself readiest to submit to God's will; therefore a 'low estate' would be his best situation for the future. If, then, Ferrar would reassess for him their earlier conclusions about the Danvers position, he hoped he could quickly resolve the whole question. In doing so, however, he would have to 'have respect to Mr Harbert'. That comment suggested that Woodnoth was on the brink of rejecting Herbert's advice and deciding instead to stick to his trade and abandon Danvers. But he still wanted Ferrar's reassessment before taking a firm decision.

Ferrar, however, did not respond sympathetically. Instead of reassessing the situation he criticised Woodnoth's claim that his inconstancy was simply a natural and constitutional weakness. How could Woodnoth then be sure, Ferrar asked, that his desire to do good was not equally 'natural' and if so, what had become of God and His grace? In any case, even natural wisdom without grace should enable a man to perceive and pursue his own best interests without equivocation. Arguments from 'nature', therefore, were no justification for indecision or for opting out by putting the burden of choice on someone else.[41] After rehearsing again the scriptural condemnations of inconstancy and his certainty that grace was surely rooted in Woodnoth's heart and would triumph over any 'natural' temptations to vacillate, Ferrar thrust the decision back to Woodnoth with the advice to 'Setle yourselfe one way or other and I have a stronge assurance That by Gods mercy you shall by your good Conversation glorify God—'. He added that if Woodnoth were to concentrate on the aim of providing temporal benefits to others, then he would be likely also to find assurance of his own salvation and promote the salvation of others.[42] He could not tell Woodnoth what to do but was sure that God would enable him to carry out whatever decision he made for himself. Ferrar had evidently diagnosed Woodnoth's primary need as full commitment to whichever course he chose, the commitment being more important than the particular course. He was presumably speaking both about his own experience of making just such a commitment to his ministry to his family and about the sort of commitment he asked of family members to various projects like temperance and night vigils. While this attitude might seem to place undue emphasis on free will in the work of salvation, it should be balanced against his 'assurance' about Woodnoth that God's mercy was the (antecedent) enabling force behind his 'good Conversation' that would glorify God and benefit others. He hoped they could continue the discussion face to face if Woodnoth came to Gidding at Easter.[43]

Whatever course Ferrar privately thought Woodnoth ought to choose, he steadfastly refused to let Woodnoth off the hook by making the decision for him. Although there are no explicit declarations of a choice finally made, the disappearance of Danvers from Woodnoth's correspondence points to his eventual decision to return to his trade. He continued also to participate in the work of restoring Leighton Bromswold and to attend to a range of family business affairs. In October he nursed Nicholas Collet, who had remained his apprentice, through a nearly fatal illness, writing daily letters to Gidding during the crisis days. His next great spiritual exercise within the web of friendship was not the resolution of an individual problem but his participation in a programme of temperance that he shared not only with Ferrar but with the whole family as well as the Mapletofts and George Herbert.

In this matter of Woodnoth and Sir John Danvers Ferrar very much took the lead, Woodnoth often entreating his guidance and counsel in the tones of a supplicant. He saw his cousin as a man of superior spiritual gifts, a particularly striking example of which he experienced during an illness whose cure he believed was a powerful demonstration of the efficacy of Ferrar's prayers.[44] At the very time he reckoned word of his illness and his request for Ferrar's prayers had reached Gidding 'Health began to com from my God to me'. Specifically, the medicines which physicians had administered earlier without success suddenly began to work, 'As if God had lockt upp the remedy under that ward which nothing but faythfull & devout Prayers could open'. He was not telling Ferrar this to compliment him, he hastened to add, but only to ask that he continue to pray for him.

Sometimes, however, the positions were reversed. In August 1630 Ferrar poured out a lament to Woodnoth, whose turn it then was to offer comfort and encouragement. Ferrar was upset by what he saw as his own mishandling of three young people who had been sent to live and learn at Gidding. Ralph Woodnoth, Arthur's nephew, had returned home at his mother's request. Though her letter to Ferrar bore no hint of dissatisfaction behind this request, he for his part thought it not in Ralph's best interests.[45] Dorothy, whose relationship, if any, to the family was never explained, had at the same time persuaded Ferrar to agree to her making an unspecified journey, permission he subsequently concluded had been a great mistake. Dorothy's father apparently thought so too, for he had come to Gidding to prevent her from going.[46] The most awkward individual was another young man, a Danvers connection, named John Gabbet, who had to be removed from the household. Subsequent letters lamented Gabbet's misdeeds and described his tearful and repentant departure from Gidding. Perhaps he had also led Ralph astray while they were there together, for Woodnoth spoke of Ralph's being in 'great danger'.[47]

Ferrar had taken all this turmoil as a personal failure, telling Woodnoth that he wanted to warn as many people as he could about his mistakes.

> oh what a mass of Guilt more heavy then a whole myne of Leade hath this one parte of Misgovernance brought uppon mee which now soe sore presseth mee that That uppon this grounde cheifely (perhapps) am I often moued to disavow the farther gouernment of any [other] then those that god hath already tyed unto mee – Whilst I fynde not the couradge in myselfe to enforce weaker affections to there good or to restrayne them from there harme – But I trouble you perhapps to much with myne owne Infirmities and Temptations[48]

This was certainly not the response of one grown cold and withdrawn toward these young people but rather of one who blamed himself for lacking courage to discipline them, a fault that Woodnoth had also acknowledged in himself. Woodnoth rushed to respond sympathetically to Ferrar's lament and to assure him that he should on no account succumb to a temptation to withdraw from his efforts at 'governance' outside the family circle. He must persevere in the confidence that God who sent this temptation would also enable him to bear and conquer it.[49] This was a significant exchange, particularly with Ferrar's perhaps surprising confession that he found himself lacking courage to impose necessary discipline on others. He did not often unburden himself so revealingly or acknowledge how hard he took what he saw as his personal failings. That he should do so to Woodnoth was a measure of the depth of their friendship and surely also a measure of that trust he held up as essential to the web of friendship.

When therefore Arthur Woodnoth decided in midlife to make a major career change that he believed offered him opportunity for higher service to God, he set in motion a lengthy and complex sequence of events that revealed how Nicholas Ferrar translated his ideal of friendship into concrete counseling. Having encountered problems in the new career, Woodnoth found himself caught between his old and his new careers unable to give his wholehearted commitment to either. Nor could he successfully combine the two. As we have seen, both Ferrar and Herbert, whose help Ferrar enlisted, pressed on him the necessity of a clear choice, which he eventually made but not without much anxiety and soul-searching. While ministering to Woodnoth in this struggle Ferrar had occasion incidentally to counsel his niece Anna Collet on the subject of marriage as well as to receive from his cousin in turn sympathy and encouragement when he was stricken over a failure of his own. The emphasis on deliberate and decisive choice and commitment in Ferrar's counsel, so apparent here, also characterised the counsel he offered to others and, as we shall see, played a vital part in his ambitious projects for his household and his web of friendship.

They also had a part to play in the diagnosis and treatment of illness, that ever present reality of seventeenth-century life, on which Ferrar was called to counsel friends and family, most notably Joshua Mapletoft. Mapletoft had been friend before he became family. The two men had known each other since their undergraduate days at Cambridge. Ferrar matriculated at Clare Hall in 1607, Mapletoft in 1609. They had both subsequently been elected Fellows of the college. They had thus shared an experience that neither John Ferrar nor Arthur Woodnoth had had, and one that conferred not only intellectual training but also special status. They were equals in a world to which the others had never had access. They addressed each other in their letters as 'Frend' in contrast to Woodnoth's 'Reverent Sir' to

Ferrar. That difference, however, was no bar to close friendship among all three. Both Ferrar and Mapletoft stayed with Woodnoth when they were in London and corresponded regularly. Mapletoft, of course, became a relative as well as a friend when he married as his second wife Susanna Collet in 1628. The family welcomed him warmly and unreservedly into their midst. The Mapletofts were frequent visitors to Little Gidding, as the Ferrars were to Margaretting, and their daughter Mary (Mall), who eventually emigrated to Virginia, lived from a very early age in the Ferrar household and was brought up by her aunt, Mary Collet Ferrar.[50] In their prayer for Susanna's recovery from a dangerous illness in 1631 the Ferrars offered thanks to God for Mapletoft, who had

> bee Come our Brother As truly in harte as in Name. . . .. That in so difficulte Hazardous and unusiull way As we by thy appoyntment have undertaken Thou hast furnished us with such a guide Help and Companion as thou hast made him Abell to bee.[51]

As that glowing testimonial indicates, Mapletoft sympathised whole-heartedly with the 'difficulte Hazardous and unusiull' way of life the family had established at Gidding. He and his wife participated in the family's activities as much as they could as nonresidents. He corresponded with his sisters-in-law as well as with Ferrar himself, sending to Mary in November 1631 his thanks for papers she had sent, which he protested showed that whatever project they described was already on a proper course and needed no further advice from him. He added, however, his prayer that performance would measure up to promise.[52]

Over the years Mapletoft had discussed with Ferrar not only specifics of diet but general questions of the nature of illness, its physical causes and its spiritual significance. Ferrar, of course, had been the Physic Fellow at Clare and had studied medicine at Padua so that he could offer medical as well as spiritual diagnosis and treatment. These issues assumed a compelling urgency in the second half of 1634 when Mapletoft suffered a long, painful and nearly fatal illness. To him in his affliction Ferrar offered advice and counsel as he had earlier done to Woodnoth in his indecision about Danvers. Ferrar's initial medical advice to Mapletoft, however, began with an account of illnesses suffered by his brother John, niece Mary, and himself. Their afflictions were quite different one from the other, and he was careful to distinguish their different causes. John's 'languishment' during the first week of Christmas arose from 'oppression of mind', very possibly a result of his recurrent marital problems. Mary, however, had brought her illness on herself by 'too much boldeness in her

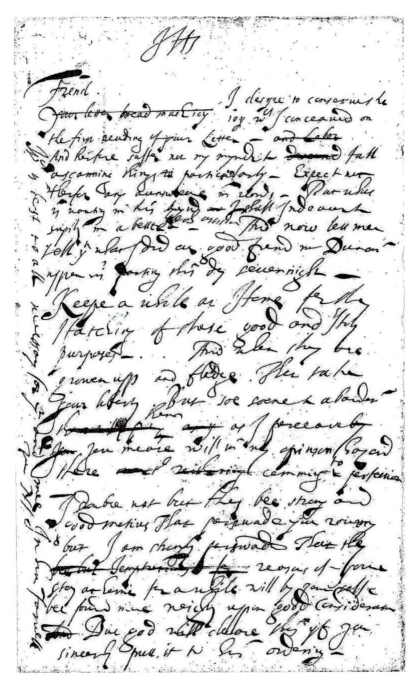

Letter (FP 993 23 March 1634/5) from Nicholas Ferrar to Joshua Mapletoft on his recovery from illness. An example of Ferrar's draft letters.

diett'.[53] Ferrar himself suffered from what he diagnosed as 'a spice of the scurvy' the symptoms of which were a sore mouth, great pain in his thighs when he moved them and red spots all over his legs. Lack of exercise contributed to the problem but so too did 'much also which I have endured this winter more then ever I did in my Lyfe', a clear recognition of the effects of stress. He had indeed experienced a turbulent several months, which had included two major battles between brother John and his wife, Bathsheba, a serious misunderstanding with Woodnoth over the terms of publication for Herbert's *The Temple*, and yet another plea for money from his improvident brother Richard.[54] His ability to continue his studies despite these troubles he interpreted as a clear endorsement from God of the model of temperance he was following, 'For without Moderation in my diett I had questionless been utterly unable for the performance of any thing and outright sick yf not deade'. What he needed was simply some exercise. With that added to his moderate diet he hoped he would quickly recover 'without the helpe of any Phisique which I am very much afrayde to deale with'. For Ferrar temperance was not simply a path to virtue through self-denial, though that was always part of its value, but also the key to maintaining health and a medicine far more effective than conventional physic. Nevertheless Robert Mapletoft, when he had news from Joshua of Ferrar's illness, sounded a note of caution, hoping that Ferrar was availing himself not only of prayer but also of those other means of cure God had provided, namely the physicians and their prescriptions, even 'those who are lesse skilfull and able [than Ferrar himself]'.[55]

Ferrar had long believed that temperance in diet was key to his own wellbeing and during 1633 had made it a major project for the family and others in the 'web of friendship'.[56] Not surprisingly therefore he invoked it not only to understand his own and Mary's illnesses but also to diagnose Mapletoft's, which he attributed to overeating and lack of exercise. The remedy he prescribed was a light diet, time for rest and quiet, at least two hours of strenuous exercise (walking would not suffice unless it was so swift as to amount to running), and less time spent in study. He reinforced this advice not to overdo on study with the revealing comment that knowledge was not so valuable that one should put one's life at risk to acquire it. If, however, 'Grace Lyfe and Salvation' rather than simply academic knowledge were at stake, then, but only then, could one justify sacrificing health for study. Since that was not Mapletoft's situation, he could safely, once he was fit again, concentrate a much larger proportion of his time on the practical aspects of his pastoral work. He should not be put off by the possibility of catching a cold in the process, as had happened earlier, because such ailments would cause little harm without 'ill matter in the body to worke on'. Mapletoft's brother Robert, Ferrar reminded him, had had a cold during most of Christmas that had caused him no serious inconvenience.[57] When called upon to advise as a physician, therefore, Ferrar clearly prescribed his temperate diet as part of a larger, balanced regime of work, rest and exercise that he firmly believed would, in most cases, obviate the need for the more drastic courses of physic common in his day. He preferred preventive medicine to radical intervention. As his later advice to Mapletoft will show, he remained at the same time firmly convinced that illness came from God as a warning to us of sins and errors to be discovered and forsaken and that a proper cure would not come without joining spiritual medication to any physical remedies. In a similar vein he had earlier told Woodnoth that a failure to submit and conform himself to God's will was contributing to his inability to resolve his situation with Danvers.[58]

During the summer of 1634 Mapletoft showed the first symptoms of that grave illness which nearly carried him off during the following winter and put the whole diet question into a much more radical context. It sounded at first like a bad cold with sore throat and laryngitis; the previous Sunday Mapletoft reported himself as barely able to speak enough to help administer communion. Pills prescribed by the doctor had helped. He worried, however, about some of his friends 'who seriously impute my infirmity to the strictnesse of my dyet contrary to reason as I understand but they will not be so satisfyed'. The doctor, at least, approved of his 'spare dyett' only requiring that he substitute French barley for rice and take occasional doses of vinegar of squills (sea onions whose extract had diuretic and expectorant qualities). He sought Ferrar's further advice about diet and exercise as well as the prayers of him and others of the family.

> If it may stand with the good pleasure of my God my desire is
> to enioy proportionable health and strength to my businesse in
> this regular dyett that the Businesse of Temperance may not be
> preiudiced with others by my example.[59]

The family had hoped that their example might preach the good news of temperance to a wider audience. Mapletoft too saw himself as an exemplar of temperance and worried lest his illness diminish the force of his example and so damage the cause. In a similar vein his brother Robert advised Ferrar himself to use the means prescribed by his physicians lest, by falling ill, he bring Lessius's teaching on temperance into disrepute.[60]

The hopeful tone of Mapletoft's August letter gave way in September to a foreboding sufficient to prompt him to write at length to Ferrar detailed

directions for the care of his wife and children should he die. By the end
of the month he had decided to take the advice of his friends and go up to
London to seek better treatment for what had now become a very painful
mouth ulcer. He moved into Arthur Woodnoth's house in Foster Lane,
London, and remained there until the following March.[61]

At first he showed improvement[62] but nonetheless resolved, as he
told both Ferrar brothers, particularly to seek the meaning of this illness,
coming as he knew it did from the hand of God, and to study how best
to use it to improve the health of soul as well as body. He acknowledged
their good advice not to rush his convalescence and promised to submit
absolutely to his physician's advice and not interject his own wishes and
opinions. He was, however, looking forward to resuming his ministry
and asked the Ferrars to let their mutual friend, Edmund Duncon, know
that Mapletoft, following Duncon's example, had begun the practice of
monthly communion at Margaretting.[63]

Mapletoft's hopes for a speedy recovery and return to his parish and
the innovations he had just introduced suffered a setback only a week of
so after that hopeful letter. Its cause remained uncertain though Mapletoft
himself thought one possibility was 'Leaving off my Dyett drink last
week'. The seriousness and stubbornness of the illness, however, drove
the patient and his friends to raise questions not merely about specific
points of diet but larger issues of the relation of diet to other aspects of
treatment including the medications prescribed by physicians. Ferrar,
as we have seen, had ambivalent feelings about these ministrations and
hoped that temperance would largely eliminate a need for them. He had to
acknowledge, however, that physic was indeed a means provided by God,
which He expected people to use and he encouraged Mapletoft's resolve to
follow his physician's advice precisely. He was equally convinced, as was
Mapletoft himself, of the importance of seeking a disease's spiritual cause,
and as the illness dragged on his letters to Mapletoft increasingly featured
pastoral counsel directed to that end.

Only a week after receiving Mapletoft's letter recounting the setback,
Ferrar wrote him a very detailed analysis of his situation, again emphasising
that his advice had been explicitly requested.

> Since you so Importunately and seriously desyre it I shall sincerely
> give you my opinion and Counsell[.] That part of Holliness
> which God intends to make you partake of especially by this
> Chastizement [is] Temperance in diett[.] Unto which besyds the
> common obligation of All Christians you were straightly bound

by many particulars and Resolutions promises and other strong
engagements which cast an undefeasable obligation on you –
Unto the dischardge therof God calls you uppon penalty of highest
Loss[,] The Abatement of Grace on your soule – wherfore obey
him readily or else yf hee Love you as tenderly as I hope looke
for noe health in your flesh nor rest in your Bones – [64]

When the request came he clearly pulled no punches in his diagnosis.
Mapletoft had bound himself by solemn promises to follow a temperate
diet and he had not properly fulfilled this obligation.[65] God had therefore
sent this illness to recall Mapletoft to those promises lest worse befall him.
Unlike Woodnoth who could not make a choice and commit himself to it,
Mapletoft had committed himself to temperance and then failed to perform.
In both cases Ferrar's counsel reflected the primary importance he attached
to voluntary choice and commitment as essential to a genuine sense of
community. He would repeat and elaborate this advice at subsequent points
in the course of Mapletoft's illness. On one occasion he did so indirectly
through Robert Mapletoft, who had gone to London to be with his brother.
Ferrar urged Robert to

Lett your soule bee a faithfull midwife unto his. . . . That you
should counsell and lead him into a particular determination of
his good resolutions in every kynd. . . . Generall Intendements
of Reformation are commonly the more unsound by how
much they seeme the more fervent and if said in a mans owne
Aprehension[.] the true proof what we meane is by bynding our
selves in particulars and yf we cannot goe through every branch
lett us make an entrance at Least by imposing a necessity of
doing some one or twoe and god shall carry us on to perfection.[66]

Here again, as with his and Woodnoth's weekly resolutions the previous
year,[67] we have Ferrar's methodical approach to spiritual instruction and his
insistence on formal commitment achieved not through passionate but vague
avowals but through small (but no less binding for that), specific steps.

Whether in response to Robert's spiritual midwifery or Ferrar's earlier
letter, Mapletoft wrote a penitential letter addressed to 'My Deare Brethren'
but intended to include Mary and Anna Collet as well as Nicholas and
John Ferrar. He acknowledged the need for his 'Deare Brother' (possibly
Robert but more likely Ferrar) to reprove him and 'I must therfore plead
guilty to the inditement' but he then confessed not to the intemperance with
which Ferrar had taxed him but to pride, impatience, and unthankfulness.
News of the death of his and Ferrar's friend and former tutor, Augustine

Lindsell, had aggravated these feelings already roused by his illness and its uncertain course and by his wife's recent illness. He could now take some comfort from the fact that God had vouchsafed to heal her and prayed that his present sufferings would act as God's 'means' to heal his own soul of these faults. That he could endure what must have been grievous pain, discouragement and anxiety with as little impatience and unthankfulness as his letters display speaks volumes, at least to a modern reader, for the quality of his character and his faith as well as the support he drew from the prayers of his friends and family. They would have made belief in the communion of saints a very present reality.

December brought a crisis sufficiently grave to prompt Woodnoth to send to Ferrar an account of Mapletoft's estate should the worst befall. His doctor, however, tried a new treatment, which healed the ulcer to the point where in January Mapletoft could return home to Margaretting. This optimism proved unfounded, alas; the ulcer reopened in early February and he had to return to London.[68] There followed another agonising month, which provoked further efforts by Ferrar to help Mapletoft recognise what God was telling him through this illness and how therefore he should respond. He reiterated his earlier advice

> that you should reduce your good resolutions to some partic-
> ularities and those such as might bee of Cost in performance. . . .
> Adding now onely That you should well ponder Davids word
> in the 38th spalme and the 107. Where hee atributes sickness to
> mans folly.

Mapletoft had already confessed to those provocative sins of pride, impatience, and unthankfulness (though not intemperance). But discovering and acknowledging his fault and begging God for forgiveness were not enough. He must equally firmly commit himself to specific and appropriately painful actions. In a covering letter to Woodnoth accompanying the above to Mapletoft, Ferrar rephrased this essential point, declaring that he was hopeful of a cure for Mapletoft.

> If hee could once fynd and resolve uppon a firme performance
> of that which god calleth him unto by meanes of this Infirmity[.]
> I shall therfore pray and desyre you and all other frends to ioyne
> with mee That this secrett may bee revealed unto him wherin as
> I beleiv consisteth his health and lyfe

Whatever physical factors contributed to illness, and Ferrar refers on various occasions to the prevailing theory of bodily humors, he was convinced that beneath these lay some key and quite specific spiritual message from God. A healing response to this call demanded not just penitent words but 'firme performance'. He offered the same essential advice to Woodnoth when he too became ill during this anxious time for Mapletoft.[69]

As he had done earlier, Mapletoft accepted Ferrar's diagnosis and counsel including the need for particular actions and ones that cost an individual some pain and effort to perform. Everyone, he declared, 'in these last and evill dayes wherin we live' applauded virtue and piety in general as long as it made no concrete demands or required any sacrifices. He had in fact in this last crisis become sure of the three sins for which God was punishing him with an illness peculiarly appropriate to those transgressions. For his pride he had been afflicted by a disease with particularly loathsome manifestations; for his impatience he had been scourged with a series of relapses, and for his intemperance both of diet and speech (rather than his earlier 'unthankfulness') he suffered in his mouth, the organ by which he had committed both those faults. By now he even bore on his arm 'the very badge of intemperance,' the mark left by a bleeding done to remove any remaining ill humors and prevent a relapse. He promised in future to 'mortify the evill lusts and affections' of these sins, which he knew would certainly cost him much pain and effort because his 'depraved nature' found pride, impatience, and intemperance so attractive. After this breast-beating and promise of amendment, Mapletoft could, with heartfelt thanks to God, go on to report that his sore had completely healed and he would shortly return home.[70]

Subsequent correspondence up to August 1635 showed him back at his priestly duties in Margaretting, reporting the successful start of monthly communions and requesting psalm books in order to encourage his parishioners in that favorite Ferrar devotional exercise of memorising psalms.[71] He and Ferrar both received bequests of books from the estate of Augustine Lindsell. In his last letter to Ferrar Mapletoft was anticipating the latter's visit to Margaretting.[72] There was no mention of illness or other problems, but just over a month later he was dead.[73] There survives no letter in the family's correspondence reporting the death and indicating whether it resulted from a recurrence of his earlier illness or a new one altogether. The next we hear of him, at least in the Ferrar Papers, is a November letter from Ferrar to his brother Robert about dealing with the income and status of some Southwark leases that were part of Joshua's estate, leases that had probably come to him as Su's marriage portion.[74]

When the preventive and curative effects of temperance and physic proved inadequate to effect a cure, therefore, Ferrar looked for a spiritual fault responsible for this divine chastisement. Such an attitude was commonplace in his time. What was distinctive in his counsel to Mapletoft was first of all the moral weight he attached to Mapletoft's formal commitment to temperance. Second was his insistence that the spiritual remedy for a lapse from that commitment lay in 'particulars' rather than 'Generall Intendements of Reformation'. As with his admonitions to Woodnoth about commitment to a decision, when Ferrar talked of seeking 'perfection', he was careful to acknowledge that without God's grace no human effort could earn salvation. To labour for perfection entailed, however, the effort of voluntary and formal commitment to appropriate goals followed by some specific and concrete steps for their attainment of the sort he advised for Woodnoth as well as Mapletoft. Such a model of the Christian life embodied Ferrar's strongly felt need for order and method in the pursuit of holiness. It provided also the sort of example he clearly saw as the most effective teacher for 'an adge that needs patterns'.[75]

His 'epistolary friendship' with George Herbert, the most notable of his correspondents and one whom he considered his 'brother', would probably have furnished another such example had not these letters almost wholly vanished. He certainly turned to him for help with Woodnoth, as we have seen. Some letters about Leighton Bromswold also survive but the advice for which Herbert thanks Ferrar was practical and had to do specifically with funding and implementing that project. There is, however, also in Francis Turner's seventeenth-century manuscript a summary of Herbert's letters to him, letters to which Turner presumably had access. It is only one side of the correspondence but Herbert's comments, as Turner reported them, certainly bespeak that openness and depth that Ferrar believed must characterise true friendship. They also reveal both his understanding of Ferrar's aims and his familiarity with the life of Gidding.

> Mr Herbert writes to Mr NF letters of great affection, much commendation, free and Xtian Counsell. That they would proceed in their well begun devotions & Exercises humbly, Thankfully, Constantly, to inflame their hearts every day more & more with the love of God & his holy & sweet word & sacrament. To attend to the great Christian duty of Mortification & reall, true, humble contempt of the world: not to be frighted with the suspitions, slanders & scornes which worldly persons would throw uppon Them. To read often the Lives of the S[ain]ts, and Martyrs in all Ages. To have ever in their Minds the 11th to the Hebr[ews], that cloud of Witnesses & noble Army of Martyrs, Virgins, S[ain] ts. Looking unto our sweetest Jesus, the Author & Finisher

Letter (FP 1004: 2 November 1635) from Nicholas Ferrar to Robert Mapletoft about settling his now-deceased brother's estate: see p. 105. The Letter is an example of Ferrar's fair hand in contrast to drafts such as FP 993.

of our Faith & finally to have a very Constant due regard & Circumspection to their health. [76]

Ferrar presumably offered comparable 'free and Xtian Counsell' to Herbert in return though we cannot know in detail what specific counsel he offered other than what can be gleaned from their collaborative publications of Lessius and Valdes and Herbert's suggestion of night vigils at Gidding.[77] Turner's summary suggests that it included those topics that have also figured in his counsel to Mapletoft, mortification, temperance and health. If Ferrar counseled Herbert in his fatal illness, however, the letters have vanished leaving only the family's prayer for Herbert's recovery and Ferrar's sending Edmund Duncon to visit the dying Herbert at Bemerton.[78]

Did these themes of choice and commitment carry over into Ferrar's counsel on marriage? In the case of Anna Collet he defended her choice of and commitment to celibacy once she had made her wishes clear. Unfortunately, what he said, if anything, to her suitor Woodnoth went unrecorded. Anna's sister Mary had, so far as is known, no suitors and so no problem in remaining single. All the other Collet daughters married and their uncle played an active role in arranging such of those unions that took place during his lifetime. He certainly took pains to supply sustained support for Su Collet in her marriage to his friend Mapletoft. Marriage counselling became much thornier, however, when his brother John sought his help in dealing with the outbursts of his discontented wife Bathsheba. The first of these involved her effort to go behind the family's back to inform Martha Sherington Collet's mother that her daughter, young Thomas Collet's bride, was being kept at Gidding against her will.[79] Details of subsequent episodes will appear presently in the context of later family activities.[80] Did his counsel to his brother in these rather different circumstances have elements in common with his advice to Woodnoth and Mapletoft?

Husbands and wives were supposed to be each other's best friends but John and Bathsheba's relationship patently did not partake of that openness, love and trust essential to true friendship. As their relationship deteriorated John certainly invited his brother to intervene and welcomed his help as Woodnoth, Mapletoft and Anna Collet had done. Bathsheba in contrast had no desire to consult her brother-in-law or hear his advice though she was forced to do so on several occasions. Ferrar thus confronted here a limitation he had not faced in these other instances. In the Sherington case he certainly imposed penitential steps on his brother by requiring him to deliver and read to Mrs. Sherington his own and Martha's letters denying that she was 'captive' at Gidding. His letter took a dismissive attitude to Bathsheba; whether he also addressed her directly on the subject and in that tone is unknown. In later comments he suggested that Bathsheba would resist any proposal from him or John or their sister Susanna, even were it something she would otherwise have wanted to do. Only her mother-in-law might have limited leverage in such situations. Quarrels over the upbringing of her two younger children became particularly heated, eventually leading Bathsheba to lash out at Nicholas for encouraging John to put their son into breeches despite her objections that he was too young. Nicholas denied any such role, saying he would even have supported her had he known of her views. Nevertheless the commitment he insisted on from both of them in all these episodes was recognition of patriarchal authority; about this there could ultimately be no choice though accommodation within that framework was both possible and desirable. Scripture ordained that wives should obey their husbands and recognise their authority over the family and the pair of them must accept what was plainly God's will.[81] John was a wise and loving father and entitled to the final say over the raising of his children. Bathsheba's defiance was a danger both to herself and to her children and she must stop being 'contentious'. In subsequent quarrels over property rights he reiterated this message in yet starker form, culminating in Bathsheba's outraged recounting to her brother of Nicholas's statement to her that a wife had no power over anything while her husband lived: 'the Cote of[f] my Backe is not myne owne but my husbands he Saith'.[82] Nicholas was vehement that John must not under any circumstances abdicate this God-given authority. Having made his choice in marriage he must commit himself to fulfilling the husband's ordained role. That was the 'firme performance' God required of him as He had required decision and commitment from Mapletoft and Woodnoth in their different circumstances.

The disruptions generated by the contentious Bathsheba could only have made clearer by contrast the importance of voluntary choice and commitment in creating the community that Nicholas Ferrar wanted for his 'web of friendship'. As a spiritual director we have seen that he deemed such choice and commitment essential to finding one's true vocation, to restoring bodily health, and to maintaining a harmonious marriage. A proper choice required both knowledge of oneself and discernment of God's will, just as commitment required firmness of purpose assisted by His grace. A community thus gathered would have strength not only to undertake further service to its own members but also to reach out to a wider sphere. For such service Ferrar believed Little Gidding was ready.

4

Voluntarism and the Wider Mission: A Light Upon a Hill, could not be hid[1]

After 1630, the year in which Mary Ferrar, then in her mid-seventies, had declared that 'now I begin to live', Nicholas too found himself free to turn his attention and that of his household in new directions. We have seen how in those preceding years his ministry to the family had drawn the household more closely together in a now firmly established routine. By 1630 he had also begun developing a 'web of friendship' that extended his ministry to those outside the household. It was a significant step in his search for the 'perfect community'. This larger community could engage with the wider world in ways that would not only strengthen the bonds within the group but also make its activities and values known and emulated. Little Gidding would thereby provide a kind of collective 'exemplary life' for a world the family believed was very much in need of such an example. Realising that success in such an ambitious ministry depended on participants who embraced its particular projects voluntarily, Ferrar insisted on explicit promises, often in writing, from those taking part. Willing members of the household and of the web of friendship thereby made themselves a committed and purposeful community. Their example was certainly known to contemporaries but more relevant to later 'voluntary Anglicans' who in the late seventeenth and early eighteenth centuries formed societies to promote piety, reform manners and provide religious instruction at home and abroad.[2]

One of Ferrar's earliest efforts to reach to a wider audience centred round the gospel harmony now in the Bodleian Library at Oxford. A note at the end declared that Mary [Collet] Ferrar had completed it on 3 December 1631.[3] The family clearly valued the harmony that played so important a part in their daily devotions and by presenting one to George Herbert in the previous October demonstrated a wish to make such a treasure available to others.[4] This subsequent Bodleian harmony, though it displayed greater skill in its craftsmanship, differed significantly from the earliest surviving volume the family had made, probably in 1630, for its own use.[5] Were it not for the handwritten page numbers, chapter headings and linking phrases,[6] the Bodleian volume's pages of pasted text neatly enclosed in double red lines would have been sufficiently uniform and skilfully done to demonstrate why contemporaries called it 'a new kind of printing'. It also had clearer indications in the margins of the gospel sources for particular verses and passages. These would enable a reader not only to follow the continuous narrative but also to follow the text of an individual gospel. Even more significant than these improvements in cross-referencing, however, was the absence of pictures, the most striking difference between the Bodleian Harmony and all the other surviving harmonies.

A letter to Arthur Woodnoth in January 1632 suggests the explanation for this harmony's changed format. In the latter part of 1631, when Mary Collet Ferrar was completing her harmony, she and Ferrar appear to have hoped to produce a publishable version. What the January letter to Woodnoth revealed was their discovery that someone else had got in ahead of them:

> Touching the Concordance reason persuades us to beare the same affections to him that hath don it as wee would have desyred from others – Wee Honnour wee Love him wee pray god it may prove to his owne as undoubtedly it will to the Benefitt of Gods Church in which regard Relligion enforceth us to reioyce in it And to bless God That it is Don and not onely to be content but glad That it comes forth from better hands then our[s] bee shall Any kynde of [^toole] Instrument murmure agaynst the workman or it[s] fellow Instrument because another is rather imployed then it selfe –
>
> Our greate Master hath made choyse of another to bring this worke to light with ['by' in margin] his blessing he knows whats best to his owne service and wee are assured That it is likewyse best for our good
>
> Hee hath not taken the Worke out of our hands but onely the Publication of it – hee hath not deprived us of what wee have don but hee hath restrayned us from what wee desyred – Honnour and profit The last perhaps neither very Comely nor Certayne The first assuredly very perillous – Well blessed bee his holy name

for that hee hath given and that hee hath taken away. But though in this regard our purposes are frustrated yett not in respect of that which we first began and cheifely aymed at that is our owne Good and furtherance in true good – to which it may bee others workes will not soe much enduce as our own.[7]

In the six weeks after Mary had finished her book the Ferrars had apparently learned of the imminent publication of Johan Hiud's *The Storie of Stories*.[8] It had received its imprimatur in November 1631 from William Haywood, one of Laud's chaplains, and was published in 1632.[9] Like that of the Ferrars it blended into a continuous narrative without additional commentary the gospel accounts of Christ's life. If Ferrar and his niece had regarded their 1631 harmony as a potential printer's dummy, that hope would explain the greater care to indicate source gospels and to provide bridging phrases to help a reader follow the text of a single gospel as well as the composite narrative. It would also have signaled their apparent willingness to sacrifice illustrations for the sake of this wider circulation. Reaching a larger audience was evidently more important than including pictures that would significantly have increased the book's cost. The poignant disappointment expressed in the letter provides a measure of the importance they had attached to this project.

Ferrar may have given up too quickly on a possible printed version of his harmony. With his Cambridge connections he could have approached Thomas and John Buck, the printers to the university, who had begun publishing bibles in Cambridge in 1629.[10] Certainly it was Thomas Buck with another partner, Roger Daniel, who published in 1633 George Herbert's *The Temple*, for which Ferrar provided the anonymous preface. The following year Daniel published Ferrar's translation of Leonard Lessius's *Hygiasticon*. That same year Buck and Daniel also published an unillustrated harmony, *Monotessaron* by Henry Garthwait, which suggests that Ferrar might indeed have persuaded them to publish his harmony had he persevered. Instead he apparently abandoned his hopes of being the one to bring to 'Gods Church' the benefits he acknowledged would come from Hiud's work. That he had aspired to do so, however, points to a developing sense of Little Gidding's mission that was soon to receive further expression. But at that immediate moment in January he could only comfort Woodnoth, and no doubt himself and Mary as well, with the notion that they had been spared the temptations of honour and profit while retaining the benefits that came from doing the work themselves.[11]

Several other of these outwardly directed activities involved George

Herbert, whom Ferrar regarded as a brother and very much a member of his 'web of friendship'. The Ferrars gave Herbert a gospel harmony, supervised the reconstruction of Herbert's prebendal church at Leighton Bromswold and of course arranged for the posthumous publication of *The Temple*.[12] Herbert for his part suggested to Ferrar a new form of devotional exercise, night vigils, to add to the family's established pattern. The two men also collaborated on two publications that Ferrar hoped would bring the light of Little Gidding to the world. These were Juan de Valdes's *One Hundred and Ten Considerations* and Luigi Cornaro's *Treatise on Temperance and Sobriety*. The Cornaro, which Herbert translated, was published in 1634 bound with Ferrar's translation of Leonard Lessius's *Hygiasticon*. The Valdes was not published till 1638, when both Ferrar and Herbert were dead, but its message and the reasons Ferrar and Herbert offered to justify its presentation to an English readership shed interesting light on the theological views and pastoral purposes of the two friends. Moreover, juxtaposing those publications with activities at Little Gidding demonstrates the way Ferrar used Herbert's contributions to strengthen the household's bonds of community and inspire its hope of becoming a 'pattern for an adge that needs patterns'.[13] Their friendship clearly played a key role in their personal lives although we have only a later summary of Herbert's counsel to Ferrar and nothing of Ferrar's counsel to him comparable to what Ferrar offered to Arthur Woodnoth and Joshua Mapletoft. Their relationship also differed in scope from others in his Web of Friendship in offering not simply personal counsel but also 'pious works' both practical and literary to minister to a wider world.[14]

Whether or when Herbert and Ferrar actually met is a point on which many have speculated but with little evidence on which to draw. So too is the nature of their 'epistolary friendship', since their letters have largely vanished. There survives, however, in Francis Turner's seventeenth-century manuscript materials for a biography of Ferrar that summary of Herbert's 'free and Xtian Counsell' to Ferrar[15] (quoted earlier, pp. 149-50) which revealed his knowledge of his friend's aims and the life of his household. Herbert's poetry testifies to the way his devotions inflamed his own heart just as his *The Country Parson* indicates the way he translated that experience into practical exercises. In his counsel to Ferrar, moreover, he proposed particular ways to enhance that devotional flame at Little Gidding when he invited Ferrar, probably in the spring of 1632, to add night vigils to Little Gidding's 'well begun devotions and exercises'.[16] His suggestion probably fell on prepared ground for Turner's notes include several comments from

Ferrar on the value of such vigils in which Ferrar called 'Night-watching or keeping Vigils...ye fairest & loveliest of all bodily exercises & perfections whatsoever'.[17] Not surprisingly, then, Ferrar took up the suggestion, and the vigils, once launched, became a 'pious work' that attracted considerable contemporary comment, some of it admiring, some notably hostile.[18] As well as these vigils for the family Ferrar maintained his own individual vigils. These provide insight into his own spirituality as well as its link with Valdes that I shall consider presently.

The men and women who participated in the Gidding vigils on any given night met from nine until one in concurrent but separate groups; the house was large enough to provide an 'oratory' for each group on different sides of the quadrangular structure. At these sessions those present recited antiphonally the psalms and sometimes sang them with a soft organ accompaniment. To minimise risks to health, especially among the young, each participant could attend only once in a week. When Ferrar took his own turn at these vigils, he too took care to observe this limit when his young nephews joined him. He clearly shared Herbert's concern that exercises of meditation and mortification should not imperil the health of participants though he excepted himself from such limitations.

These vigils not only expanded the household's devotional framework; they also included that element of voluntarism that we shall see Ferrar adopt for other 'pious works' introduced during this time. He had, for example, sought explicit consent in writing from participants in the discussion group the family called its 'Little Academy'. In presenting the idea of night vigils to the household he therefore carefully stressed that no stigma should attach to those who chose not to join in, implying an acknowledgment that while only the willing would be effective participants, the lukewarm might find it hard to say 'no'.[19] Who actually chose to take part and who to opt out is never revealed, but no doubt his Collet nieces would have found it difficult to turn down such an invitation. Nor is it clear how Ferrar would have responded to anyone who had once agreed to participate but subsequently wanted to opt out. His criticisms of Arthur Woodnoth's 'double-mindedness' about working for Sir John Danvers or his view of the binding nature of Joshua Mapletoft's promise of temperance, however, suggest that Ferrar would have taken a strong line against such backsliding.[20] At least he clearly recognised the necessity of such voluntary commitment while at the same time showing some awareness of the subtler forms of coercion that some might feel he exercised. Awareness, however, was one thing while successful handling of the problem in a situation where he enjoyed great honour and authority was another and one challenging to evaluate in retrospect.

While the family's vigils took place in the earlier half of the night and consisted simply of psalmody, Ferrar maintained his own personal vigils that began when the others retired at one o'clock. The importance he attached to vigils and meditation testifies to a spirituality that was 'mystical and devotional rather than theological'.[21] This approach, which he shared with his 'brother Herbert', was fundamental not only to his own inner life and to his ministry to his family but also to his efforts, with Herbert's collaboration, to extend that ministry to a wider audience. Had the spiritual diary in which he set down 'Thots or Reflexions upon his Conduct in the Day' survived, it would have provided a more extensive and coherent record of his inner life.[22] This volume's disappearance has left us with only fragmentary glimpses of the experiences that shaped his spiritual pilgrimage. One such fragment is his brother's retrospective account of the precocious six-year-old's religious encounter in the garden of the family's London home. Stricken by doubt of God's existence and care, he had prostrated himself there, wrestled with his doubts and ultimately received an assurance of God's presence that remained with him for the rest of his life.[23] At Gidding he gave the psalms special prominence not only for his own intensive individual meditation but also for collective recitation and for the instruction of the local children. 'I will tell you a Mystery not to be understood but by practise. . . . [Those who] dive into ye secrett are amazed at the strange mixture of joy & grief in ye Psalms'.[24] He presumably hoped the family's psalm-centred devotions would provide the practice that would enable them to make such a dive. In addition to the psalms he and the family knew the meditative work of St Francis de Sales[25] and probably John Cosin's *Devotions,* which comprised scriptural passages along with excerpts from patristic writings and passages from the *Book of Common Prayer.* Lancelot Andrewes's *Manual of Private Devotions* was not published till 1648, eleven years after Ferrar's death, but his brother John was one of its early purchasers.[26] Without Ferrar's library, which has also disappeared, we can have only an imperfect idea of what else he knew of 'the church's mystical repast'.[27] Turner, however, in his notes on Ferrar reported that every day Ferrar wrote a meditation or two on that day's lessons or psalms and that his 'Beloved Authors' included Epictetus, Seneca, and Antoninus as well as the Divine Considerations of Valdes. His library included 'Many bookes of Instructio[n] and practique Devotio[n] in French, Spanish & Italian'.[28]

Did he also use that little book of meditative poetry that Edmund

Duncon brought to Little Gidding from Bemerton in March 1633? In leaving the decision to publish it to Ferrar, Herbert perhaps knew from their correspondence or at least sensed that Ferrar too could say that he had had 'many spiritual conflicts that had passed betwixt God and my soul'?[29] Beyond the approval implicit in publishing the poems with a laudatory preface, however, Ferrar never indicated what, if any, use he made of them in his own spiritual life. All we can document of his response to *The Temple* is the brief preface and the business problems involved in its publication. On the other hand the nieces who produced the fair copy obviously had opportunity for careful reading, and it is hard to imagine that they never talked of it within the family circle.[30] Their brother-in-law Joshua Mapletoft wrote from Essex appreciative comments to Ferrar and complained of the shortage of available copies.[31] Ferrar's sister Susanna Collet sent copies to her scapegrace son Edward in the East Indies in hopes that he would take its message to heart.[32]

There exists, however, in an unlikely place a passage that gives some flavour of Ferrar's inner life that he might have shared with Herbert in their lost correspondence. In his account of the final revival of the Little Academy he digressed from the main story into an exalted outburst extolling 'real [as opposed to sensual and earthly] Wealth, Glorie & Delight':

> the streames of them oftimes arise like spring tydes in their Pride, not only filling the banks of the soul & spirit brim-full, but so richly falling on the Lower Faculties of the mind & the very lowest of the Body, as the Enioyment of the best of that, which this world can afford, would be of annoyance, & the vttermost of pleasures, that the sences could take of, disgust, whilst these spiritual raptures are in the Flowing-course & Tide. But wee are mounted to a high straine not to be apprehended by any other Arguments then of Experiment.

It has the ring of personal experience if not of poetic talent, evidence of a heart inflamed.[33]

That concluding note that only 'Experiment' can apprehend such spiritual raptures perhaps helps to explain his decision to translate a book by his 'beloved author', the sixteenth-century Spaniard Juan de Valdes (d. 1541), 'a Marrano, a humanist Illuminist. . . an Evangelical Spiritualist with a strong sense of the imminent Second Advent.'[34] Valdes's heterodox views had forced him to flee his native land to escape the Inquisition, bringing him first to Rome and by 1535 to Naples. The former imperial courtier became spiritual director to Giulia Gonzaga as well as the friend of Gasparo Contarini and Reginald Pole, Bernardino Ochino and Peter Martyr Vermigli, the group of reforming Catholics known as the *spirituali*. As the name would suggest, these reformers laid particular emphasis on that transforming experience of grace by which an individual could know himself called by God and possessed of redemptive faith. Valdes held a view of justification by faith close to and indeed influenced by contemporary Protestant reformers as well as by the *Alumbrados* of his native Spain.[35] His book offered not a method for meditation like Loyola's *Spiritual Exercises*, but a message on which to meditate and a message, furthermore, that Ferrar thought not only matched his own inner experience but was one that his contemporaries needed to hear.

How and when did Ferrar encounter Valdes? If, as Turner noted, Valdes was one of Ferrar's 'beloved authors', he presumably had at some point acquired the copy of the Italian version of the *One Hundred Ten Considerations* from which he made his translation. This he could have done either during the three years he spent in Italy (1614-16) or perhaps in one of the Imperial cities he visited earlier in his travels. Perhaps he had before departing from Cambridge already learned of the book from Augustine Lindsell, his tutor and lifelong friend, who possessed a copy of the 1563 French translation that Ferrar acquired after Lindsell's death. By 1632 Lindsell would likely have known that Valdes was one of Ferrar's favourite authors though there is no evidence that he knew of the translation project.[36] Other Gidding friends, notably Edmund and John Duncon, also knew of Valdes though when and how they encountered him, whether independently or through Ferrar or Lindsell, is unrecorded. Valdes's message thus clearly attracted not only Ferrar but also several of his friends, most of whom were numbered among the 'Laudians' in the Caroline church. The significance of this attraction is a point to which I shall return.

It was in the summer of 1632, when Herbert had suggested night vigils for Little Gidding, that Ferrar sent to Herbert his translation of Valdes for comment and presumably for advice as to the wisdom of publishing it. His choice of Herbert as commentator testified not only to their spiritual kinship but also to his confidence that his friend would give the work a favourable and judicious reading, as of course he did. Had Herbert already discovered for himself Valdes's book in either its Italian original or its French translation or learned of it either from Ferrar or from some other source?[37] If so, and they had previously discussed this 'beloved author', Ferrar would have had at least some idea of Herbert's response to the book, as he probably knew that of Lindsell and Edmund Duncon. If on the other hand Herbert did not already know Valdes, his comments would at once provide Ferrar an opportunity to share with his 'brother' a work he treasured and also get the reaction of someone encountering it for the first time. The latter point might prove especially helpful in anticipating possible problems with official censorship.

Ferrar, who preferred anonymity, published this book as well as *Hygiasticon* without revealing himself as the translator. Nor did he put his name to the preface of *The Temple*. Yet in the *One Hundred and Ten Considerations* he identified Herbert and included in the book his recommendation to publish it. He did not, however, explicitly identify Herbert as the writer of the notes that he inserted immediately after his own anonymous preface. These points raise interesting questions about the nature of their collaboration. Did Ferrar intend to leave the reader to infer that the translator was also the author of the notes? Herbert's letter, which refers to notes he returned along with the translated text, appears only some seventeen pages after the notes have ended. A reader could be forgiven for failing to make the connection. Did Herbert know that Ferrar would use his notes to answer those 'dubious and offensive places' that Ferrar's preface acknowledged were 'stumbling blocks'? If he did know, would he too, like Ferrar, have welcomed anonymity or wanted his authorship known? He certainly recommended publication but perhaps harboured more reservations about particular ideas than he admitted to Ferrar or than we can document today. Answers to these questions are speculative at best and complicated by the fact that Herbert died only five months after he returned the notes and translation to Ferrar and no evidence survives to show that Ferrar consulted with Herbert on the manuscript's final form during that brief period. Immediately after his death, of course, Ferrar had the manuscript of *The Temple* to deal with and did so with a speed that suggests that for the next several months it took precedence over other projects such as Valdes. The question remains, however, as to what Ferrar intended by the placement and anonymity of Herbert's notes and how much Herbert knew and approved of those intentions.

Not surprisingly for one who declared that only 'Experiment' could apprehend real spiritual raptures, Ferrar singled out Valdes's 'experimentall and practical divinity' as particularly valuable for its treatment of the doctrines of justification and mortification. These were hardly neglected topics in the Church of England in 1632 although church authorities endeavoured to suppress their predestinarian aspects as too controversial. What was distinctive about Valdes's treatment of them? His message was characterised by a pastoral hopefulness that gave readers positive encouragement to persevere in their pursuit of redemptive faith while recognising that such faith could only come as God's gift.[38] During Valdes's lifetime he and other *spirituali* still hoped to find a formulation of the doctrine of justification acceptable to both Protestants and Catholics, one that would reunite the church and spare them the choice between heresy and obedience. Such hopes for unity did not survive the failure of the Colloquy of Regensburg in 1540, the establishment that same year of the Roman Inquisition, and the subsequent pronouncements on justification by the Council of Trent in 1545. Valdes, however, had developed his 'experimentall divinity' with its emphasis on justification by faith within a still fluid and hopeful context and could assert that through an 'experience' of the Holy Spirit an individual knew that by faith he was incorporated in Christ and justified by His merits alone. Valdes asserted his understanding of justification in a voice at least nominally Catholic but acceptable, as Ferrar pointed out in his preface, to earlier French and Italian Protestants and, Ferrar evidently hoped, now acceptable to those in England who sought to promote Christian unity, or at the very least a less antagonistic view of the Roman church.[39]

Valdes was careful to point out that while no amount of 'natural' mortification or other good works could oblige God to give this gift, actions could nevertheless serve to keep one 'wakeful' or prepared to receive when God chose to give. He gave particular emphasis to what he called 'pretending', i.e. claiming, that one had justifying faith and was incorporated in Christ as Christ was incorporated in him. Such 'pretending', however, must at the same time include acknowledgement that it was God who bestowed this faith. With such a stance Valdes could reconcile divine omnipotence with human agency. He was optimistic that after a period of 'pretending':

> in a short time [the Christian] shall finde himselfe much comfort-
> able [conformable?] to the image of God, & unto that of Iesus
> Christ our Lord.[40]

Or in the Prayer Book's words, 'very members incorporate in the mystical body of thy Son'. By way of further encouragement he declared that having difficulty in believing would produce a more authentic faith. He was also at pains to point out that real faith did not have to come in the dramatic form of St Paul's experience on the Damascus Road but could be a gradual process.[41] The crucial question underlying this 'pretending' was, of course, how one could know that the faith to which one 'pretended' was genuine. Valdes discussed this point at length and proposed a very subjective answer, summed up (in Consideration 57) by the statement that 'the Christian businesse is not *knowledge* but *experience*'. Through an 'experience' of the Holy Spirit an individual knew that by faith he was incorporated in Christ and justified by His merits alone.

> to all them, who know, and feele themselves incorporated in the death of Christ, and in the resurrection of Christ, it appertaines to fix their eyes upon this so high perfection, to pretend to obtaine it, and in effect to procure it.[42]

Faced with such a method of authentication one could understand why Calvin thought Valdes had 'an anabaptist spirit' despite Valdes's criticism of sectaries.[43] Herbert's commentaries make it plain that he too was well aware of this hazard, which he countered chiefly by reiterating that Valdes did not give sufficient weight to scripture. Valdes's assertion that scripture, like images, was only a starting point in Christian formation, an 'alphabet' for beginners that would eventually give way to direct instruction by the Holy Spirit was plainly described by Herbert as a dangerous invitation to 'enthusiasm'.[44] Ferrar in contrast did not single out this or any other specific stumbling block for explicit comment, contenting himself with the simple statement in his anonymous preface that Valdes had lived where scripture was not valued so that it was only surprising that he revered it as much as he did. Did Ferrar not perceive the dangers to which Valdes's 'experimentall' approach could lead and indeed in the past had led? Perhaps he regarded Valdes's denunciation of sectaries as sufficient. One can only speculate, for he did not explain how he himself understood Valdes's meaning. But Ferrar's lack of concern for the dangers of 'enthusiasm' is hard to credit in someone as careful as Ferrar was to keep himself and his household under control, someone whose preferred method of dealing with conflicts was to ask the parties to put their views in writing even when they were together under one roof.[45] Or did he, along with other of his friends who knew Valdes's work, think that the Laudian church was strong enough to prevent such disastrous interpretations of the Holy Spirit's instruction? He was said toward the end of his life to have premonitions of difficult times to come.[46] Fortunately he did not live to see future events fulfill Herbert's warning about the dangers of 'enthusiasm'.

Valdes's very individualistic and subjective approach, moreover, left little scope not only for scripture as ultimate authority but also for the institutional church and its sacraments as channels of grace. While he acknowledged (Consideration 6) the importance of baptism in removing 'natural' (original) sin, he also (Consideration 3) pronounced dismissively on 'ceremonies to co[n]serve the health of their soules' that sons of God observe only for the sake of outward conformity with the sons of Adam rather than out of any need for them. Without explicitly abandoning or attacking the larger institutional church Valdes had in effect quietly shifted his hopes for spiritual renewal to smaller, more intimate groups within it, groups indeed not unlike Little Gidding.[47] Yet while Ferrar clearly valued community and voluntary commitment within his godly household, he also valued the 'ceremonies' and sacraments of the established church as did his Laudian friends. He made clear in 'The Duties Common to Man and Woman' that sacraments together with prayer and patience in affliction were essential parts of the primary duty of loving God, and he included elaborate instruction on the proper preparation for and reception of communion.[48] Herbert too in such poems as 'The British Church' and 'The Holy Communion' as well as in his prose treatise *The Country Parson* expressed the importance he attached to church and sacraments. Ferrar and Herbert were perhaps readier to overlook Valde's dismissive attitude toward 'ceremonies' because of the overriding importance they attached to his delineation of the 'experimental' workings of grace within the individual. It is hard to imagine that either Ferrar or Herbert was unaware of this significant omission in Valdes's book even if Herbert in his comments on 'enthusiasm' failed to add church and sacraments to scripture as necessary counters to excesses of enthusiasm.

Ferrar and Herbert evidently felt more confident of their handling of the doctrinal stumbling blocks in Valdes's book than did the Cambridge censors, who refused to publish either it or another of Ferrar's translations, Ludovico Carbone's much more practical book on catechizing children.[49] Though the grounds of the censors' objections have not survived, they would likely have reinforced any reservations Herbert might have had. When the *One Hundred and Ten Considerations* was finally published in the year after Ferrar's death, it was done in Oxford rather than London or Cambridge and Thomas Jackson, President of Corpus Christi College, Oxford, provided the necessary approval and expressed his confidence that the preface and Herbert's comments provided adequate safeguards for any unprejudiced reader.[50]

What then did Ferrar and Herbert see as the pastoral value of Valdes's 'experimental and practical divinity' for the England of 1632? Not surely a polemical argument to support one or the other side in the Calvinist/ Arminian debate. Ferrar, as Oley pointed out, was 'very modest in points of controversy' and in any case Valdes's message was too ambiguous for that.[51] While for example his individualistic and experiential vision of redemption had much in common with Calvinist conversion, his 'pretending' allowed also an Arminian role for human will. Not ambiguous, however, was the contrast between the rather dismissive attitude of Valdes toward ceremonies and sacraments and the almost antinomian aspects of his 'anabaptist spirit' and the importance Ferrar and his friends, to say nothing of Archbishop Laud, attached to the sacramental and liturgical 'beauty of holiness'.[52] Perhaps doctrinal consistency under whatever label is not a helpful measure of the 'practicall divinity' of either Ferrar or Herbert or indeed many of their contemporaries.

Were there besides the publication of Valdes other indicators of the message Ferrar and Herbert hoped to convey to their contemporaries in 1632? If in *The Country Parson* Herbert, writing at this same time, envisioned a *via media* that allowed considerable local autonomy to the parish and to the parson to adapt the canons of the church to local needs and sensibilities, he was advocating a 'dexterity' at odds with the Laudian campaign for greater uniformity across the national church.[53] Certainly his emphasis on community within the parish and the parson's role in implementing it would have echoed his 'brother' Ferrar's concern to build his parish/household of Little Gidding into a committed community. Not only through parish autonomy and community, however, did Herbert's vision of a *via media* express itself but also in the very structure of his rebuilt prebendal church of Leighton Bromswold where the pulpit and reading desk were placed at equal height to emphasise the equal importance of prayer and preaching. Ferrar also incorporated this unusual arrangement into the church at Gidding, indeed might have been the first to adopt it when he restored and remodeled the derelict church in the late 1620s. It was an architectural setting that fitted peculiarly well with Herbert's description of Gidding's devotions and exercises as inflaming hearts with love of God's 'holy and sweet word and sacraments'.[54]

While both men accepted the importance of 'the beauty of holiness', they evidently sought a mode of worship that balanced ritual with preaching, a mediating alternative to the extremes of Laudian stress on liturgy over preaching and puritan insistence on the primacy of preaching.[55] In this context Valdes's book provided a reminder that what really mattered was an inward transformation to which both the teaching of sermons and the grace of sacraments could contribute. Herbert's argument that Valdes's work should be published for its expression of 'the intent of the gospel in the acceptation of Christs righteousness' and for his 'observation of the working of Gods kingdom within us' could equally apply to his own poetry. The great appeal of *The Temple*, also an account of inner experience told in a way that attracted people of as different theological views as King Charles and Richard Baxter, served

Exterior of the church at Little Gidding, altered in 1714 by removal of the west tower, which is shown on the estate map (p. 53).

just such a purpose and could only have reinforced Ferrar's hope that Valdes would have a similar appeal. Indeed, the very absence of discussion of such controversial issues as predestination and election, ecclesiastical authority, liturgy and sacraments would have been an advantage in reaching a wider audience. Certainly such a hope had animated Arthur Golding when he translated in 1573 a work entitled *Beneficio di Cristo* that had been revised by Marcantonio Flaminio, a member of Valdes's circle in Naples.[56]

In this little book is that benefit, which commeth by Christ crucified, to the Christians, truly and comfortably handled: which benefit if all Christians did truly understand and faithfully embrace, this division would vanish away, and in Christ the Christians should become one. To this end reade this booke, and much good in Christ may it doe to all them which doe reade it.[57]

Interestingly, yet another publication of Golding's translation of the *Beneficio,* this one with a possible family connection to Ferrar, appeared in that same year that the *One Hundred and Ten Considerations* was finally published. Its printer was John Legat, who was probably a cousin by marriage of both Ferrar and Joshua Mapletoft.[58] Ferrar and Herbert could, like Golding, have hoped that Valdes's treatment of justification as the 'benefit of Christ' might in their own day bring Christians together by offering a basis sufficiently flexible to counter the polarisation made worse by the Laudian pursuit of uniformity.

Was there another irenic hope behind Ferrar's desire to offer Valdes's work to an English readership? As Anthony Milton has so clearly demonstrated, Arminians like Lindsell were seeking during these years not only to portray the Church of Rome as a true though flawed church but also to hold out some hope for reconciliation with the Church of England. In that context Ferrar might have hoped that older and even heretical Roman Catholic voices such as Valdes and the author of the *Beneficio* might be useful.

If Ferrar and Herbert thought that Valdes's handling of justification offered a basis on which Christians could unite, what of mortification, another point in Valdes's divinity that Ferrar recommended? While it of course could not earn justification, it could express sanctification and received practical implementation as well as theoretical discussion at both Little Gidding and Bemerton. Temperance as an exercise in mortification was a topic that concerned both men, and a practice that Ferrar particularly hoped would make Little Gidding a light upon a hill. The next chapter will recount in detail the family's effort in which they took as their guide another collaborative effort, a volume entitled *Hygiasticon* that combined Ferrar's translation of Leonard Lessius's volume of that name and Herbert's translation of Luigi Cornaro's *A Treatise of Temperance and Sobriety.*

Besides the translations of Valdes, Cornaro, and Lessius, the collaboration between Herbert and Ferrar also gave the world after Herbert's death his poetic record of spiritual conflict and consummation. The reception accorded to *The Temple* by readers across the theological spectrum would have reinforced for Ferrar his and Herbert's hope that Valdes too could encourage a pattern of piety transcending doctrinal partisanship. Neither of them lived

Interior of the church at Little Gidding as restored by William Hopkinson in 1853.

to see its publication in 1638 or to be disappointed in that irenic hope. By that time events were moving toward confrontation rather than accommodation in both the religious and political spheres. Nevertheless Valdes's message had evidently enjoyed a reception sufficient to prompt Edmund Duncon, who had brought Herbert's manuscript to Gidding in 1633, to publish in 1646 a new edition of Valdes in a slightly shortened format. If at the end of the first civil war, when he had been turned out of his livings, he might have hoped that a message that emphasised inward piety rather than doctrinal correctness would heal the divisions opened up in that conflict. If he had such hopes, however, he was to be disappointed, for there were already signs of the dangers of that 'enthusiasm' that Herbert had warned might come out of Valdes's reliance on direct instruction by the Holy Spirit.

How Ferrar applied Valdes's ideas in his own life is but one aspect of this intriguing but necessarily inconclusive question of his interpretation of the Spaniard's ideas. How he presented them to the rest of the family is unfortunately no clearer. Before seeking publication he may have tried them out in the household, perhaps read sections aloud within the family circle. He presumably would have stressed those points he praised in his introduction to the *One Hundred and Ten Considerations:* the importance of the inner experience of justification that must precede true piety as well as the value of mortification, particularly connecting that point to temperance in diet. Having found a satisfactory response to Valdes's 'experimentall Divinity' at Gidding and encouragement from Herbert, he presumably hoped that bringing its message to a wider audience, with suitable precautions, would stimulate and deepen his contemporaries' spiritual lives and so counteract the evils of 'our corrupt age'. In the spirit of Arthur Golding's earlier irenic wish that the 'Benefits of Christ' expounded in his translation of the *Beneficio* might end divisions among Christians, Ferrar might have entertained hopes that Valdes likewise would speak to both sides of an increasingly polarised Church of England and end divisive controversy.[59]

If Ferrar made no specific reference to Valdes's scriptural translations and commentaries, he gave also no sign of acquaintance with Valdes's catechetical works, though they would have fitted so readily with his own interest in education. Nor is there any indication that Ferrar knew of the group that Valdes gathered round him in Naples. He must, however, have known of some of its individual members: Giulia Gonzaga through Valdes's dedicatory epistle to her at the end of the *One Hundred and Ten Considerations* and Bernardino Ochino and Peter Martyr Vermigli because of their significant roles in the Edwardian reformation. Had Ferrar known that Valdes had gathered around him an informal community that included those three among others, he could have seen in it a model for his own leadership of Little Gidding, an example of the Holy Spirit working not only to justify and mortify individuals but also to build a sense of community that could reach out to the world.[60]

Yet Ferrar would not have required that particular model to encourage within his own household a comparable group that the family called The Little Academy. It was clearly an educational enterprise well suited to a household that was a 'school of religion'.[61] Moreover the sessions of this group, like the collected letters and documents in the Ferrar Papers, afford us an intimate look at the family in action, providing us with insight not only into the purposes but also the dynamics of the family's life together at Little Gidding. Most importantly, the Academy's discussions laid the groundwork, as we shall see, for one of the family's major projects, their missionary programme of temperance.

The matriarch, Mary Woodnoth Ferrar, was credited with organising the group, initially for the further education of her granddaughters. The daily circle of women gathered round her chair of a morning or afternoon in the Great Chamber must have generated a certain informal level of discussion. It was only the little children who were to be seen and not heard. Perhaps this pattern suggested to her a way readily to transform and extend an informal and thoroughly conventional female activity into a more formal and structured educational device.[62] Whatever the source of inspiration, the result was the Little Academy, whose first session took place in February 1631. It was her special project and one for which she held high hopes. It was also one for which she needed and received substantial help from Nicholas, whose enthusiasm for education matched her own and who took very seriously his role as counsellor to his nieces. He might in turn have found inspiration not only from Valdes but from another influential spiritual director of women, St. Francis de Sales, whose instructional 'Conversations' with the nuns of the Visitation had recently been published.[63] Could the Little Academy also have been modelled after Plato's Academy and did it take its name from it? There is no explicit evidence to prove a conscious imitation. Nevertheless that the socratic dialogue was frequently utilised as a method of instruction would suggest that at least for some of the participants it was a form of learning known about and followed. At the same time the participants were hardly exponents of rationalism except within a carefully circumscribed Christian framework, such as that which operated in the household of Sir Thomas More that Erasmus described as a Christian version of Plato's Academy.[64]

The granddaughters for whose benefit the Academy was intended were the 'Mayden Sisters', daughters of Susanna Ferrar Collet and nieces of Nicholas and John: Mary, Anna, Hester and Margaret, to whose ranks their younger sisters, Elizabeth, Joyce, and Judith were presently added when they were adjudged ready to participate. The young women were not, however, left without the guidance of older generations both male and female. Grandmother Mary, mother Susanna and father John Collet, and uncle John Ferrar were regular participants, and visitors to the household were also welcomed though as listeners rather than active participants. Su

Mapletoft, at that time the only married and therefore non-resident sister, was made an honourary member. At their grandmother's direction, her sisters sent her the first bound volume of the group's discussions so that she could share, at least belatedly, in the project.[65]

Ferrar himself almost never intervened in the actual discussions, at least as they are recorded in the 'Story Books'. He was initially given the title of 'Visitor', indicative of a supervisory role that extended from the preparatory stage of providing many of the stories and suggesting themes that tied them together to the final recording of the discussions for collection into book form.[66] The sisters' claims that they were presenting their stories in the way in which they themselves had learned them suggests that he had a tutorial role in their preparation if not in the actual discussions. Their question and answer method produced conversations that resembled a sort of socratic dialogue or perhaps a catechizing session by George Herbert's 'Country Parson'. It very probably reflected their uncle's teaching style, which clearly aimed not simply at rote memorisation but at active understanding.[67] How much in turn he actually intervened to shape the final written records is unclear. He was said to know shorthand and could have kept notes of the conversations for later transcription either by himself or by the nieces with his supervision. It is hard to imagine that the man who recorded minutes of the Virginia Company and drafted letters for members of the family would not have maintained at least supervisory control of this important educational venture.

At their initial meeting in February 1631 the group offered an account of their purposes. The better to imitate those saints whose names they bore the 'Mayden Sisters' had covenanted with close relatives (Founder, Guardian, Visitor) to perform various religious exercises. Fearful that as they performed these exercises they might come to feel distaste for them in the way that sweet liquors can become sour if they are put into sour containers, they determined to combine their devotions with the study of wisdom, especially concerning those things appropriate to their 'Condition and Sex'. How did they propose to go about this study of wisdom? They had concluded that ignorance of the truth constituted the greatest hindrance to sincere seekers after virtue and 'perfection', the latter being a term Ferrar used frequently. The members of the Little Academy were not seeking 'perfection' through the individual route of contemplation as in traditional mysticism but rather through the active and collective pursuit of virtue through discussion. The truth that they needed for this purpose was knowledge of what in fact was true virtue and they acknowledged that the only place to seek that truth was in scripture. Consequently they would bring to bear 'true and right reason' on scripture to discover this truth and in the light of that discovery judge the true value of any action or idea. They would in that way avoid the mistakes of judgment that would come with uncritical acceptance of worldly standards, those conventional customs and traditional wisdom handed down 'from our Fathers'. They were not, of course, trained philosophers and did not proceed by abstract logical propositions. They were justified Christians and as such were committed to pursuing perfection as a consequence of that justification.[68] Their raw material was to be, for the most part, stories of human lives, of saints and secular rulers, whose actions they could compare with scriptural and worldly standards of virtue and so discover the truth that would bring them closer to perfection. In this way they would study wisdom, not with unaided human 'right reason' but always with God's help, an entirely orthodox combination of reason and faith applied to the understanding of revelation. To achieve their aim, therefore, the signers of the Academy's covenant agreed to regular meetings to confer upon subjects that would either inform the understanding or excite the affections and so assist them in the better pursuit of those virtues and duties appropriate to their present and future lives.[69]

The Academy's professed aim to judge actions and aims only by scriptural standards would certainly have had Mary Ferrar's approval and have readily translated into considerations of whether worldly goods or success could provide human happiness. The 'Mayden Sisters', as they discussed such questions, might have worn those identical gowns of green wool with unfashionable silk trim that their uncle hoped would promote harmony among them.[70] As a further teaching device each of the active participants took (or was given) a name. For the older generation these were straightforward: Mary Ferrar was the Founder, Nicholas Ferrar the Visitor, John Ferrar the Guardian, Susanna Collet the Moderator, and her husband (the only touch of irony here) the Resolved. In the younger generation Mary Collet as leader was simply the Chief. For the younger sisters, however, the names had their own teaching function, being virtues each of the girls were supposed particularly to try to cultivate: Patient, Cheerful, Affectionate, Obedient, Submiss.[71]

There is no contemporary identification of which sister received which name; we can only speculate on the basis of other evidence of their characters. The attempt, however, affords insight into the relationships among the sisters themselves as well into how the parental generation saw these young women. Anna, given as we have seen to emotional outbursts, seems the most likely candidate for the Patient. Attaching the names to the other sisters is rather more uncertain. If, at the first meeting of the group, the sisters were called upon to speak in order of seniority, then Hester would have been the Cheerful and Margaret the Affectionate. A possible indication that Hester needed to cultivate cheerfulness appears in her mother's letter of October 1629. She there told Su Mapletoft that she was content for Hester to stay longer to help Su after the birth of her child, 'but we much fear least the Return of her Usual Indisposition might cause both greife and trouble instead of comfort to you'.[72] Though that 'indisposition' could have been some recurrent physical ailment, it could also have been a tendency to melancholy. In that case she would have been not only more trouble than help for post-partum Su but also a candidate for the nickname of 'Cheerful'. Cheerful was also the rather strident advocate in Advent 1632 of a more austere observance of the Christmas season, delivering a denunciation of 'good cheer' worthy of one inclined to a darker view. Two years later, when Hester wished to marry Francis Kestian, her mother voiced concern over whether Hester really could cope with life on less money and comforts than she was used to. Hester evidently felt confident that she could, for the marriage took place sometime in the next six months.[73] Whether Hester's optimism reflected a genuine effort to deserve her nickname or just a complacent assumption that the name automatically bestowed the quality we can only guess.[74]

The evidence we have for Margaret could be made to fit either the Cheerful or the Affectionate designations though I think the latter is more likely. Like Hester she too visited Su at Margaretting in 1629. While she was there, her sisters sent her a letter Ferrar had drafted for them.[75] They thanked Margaret for the good counsel and example expressed in her letter to them, which has not survived. They added that they rejoiced that she was so happy at Margaretting, a kind of happiness they (or Ferrar on their behalf!) described as perhaps not lesser but merely different from the happiness they had at Gidding. If her elders thought that Margaret sounded happier absent from Gidding than present, they could take that as a sign of insufficient affection for the family and its way of life. When her turn came to marry, however, she unlike Hester did follow her sister Su in the family's approved course of marrying a clergyman, John Ramsay, who was also a friend of Ferrar. Either Elizabeth or Joyce could have been the 'Submiss' to whom her mother delivered a lengthy reproof of her wish to become servant to a gentlewoman.[76] They must both have shown a rebellious streak if the one who was not 'Submiss' became the 'Obedient'. Judith, who would have been only seven when the Academy began, would presumably not have been old enough to participate except perhaps to sing a song to the group and so did not acquire a nickname.[77]

About a fortnight after the original meeting of the Academy Ferrar complained to Arthur Woodnoth that he could not get his sister and the others (presumably her daughters) 'to sett Downe there Ends and desyres'. His complaint shows the importance he attached to written commitment to particular projects and purposes.[78] He clearly wanted such a commitment to the Academy from its participants at the outset and proposed to take a tough line if they continued reluctant. He would accuse them, he wrote, of hesitating because of guilty consciences, which arose from the fact that their avowed ambition for honour sprang chiefly from vanity as did their desire to wield authority without the constant effort required to justify it. He also would accuse them of being impatient of contempt, though what exactly he meant by that was not clear because the letter at that point is too torn and blotched to decipher further. Perhaps he did not have to resort to such stern spiritual reproof but if he did he could only have undermined the 'voluntary' nature of their consent. Subsequent difficulties that resulted in lapses and revivals of the Academy suggest that that might indeed have been the case. Nevertheless he evidently got the written statements he wanted, for in the first of the Academy's story books the sisters spoke of having 'entered into a joynt Covenant betweene themselves and some other of neerest Blood' to prevent their abandoning the worthy project on which they had promised to embark.[79] The Little Academy thus became a voluntary society constituted by covenant.

Despite all the emphasis on the sisters' role in the group, however, members of the parental generation were also active participants. The Academy was by no means a youth group but very much an intergenerational assembly. Indeed, one of the interesting aspects of the group's development was the changing relationship between the generations within it. In earlier meetings the generational hierarchy was scarcely concealed below the surface, and the daughters tended to defer to their parents and uncle. In the discussion of Charles V, for example, Mary Collet Ferrar declared herself unfit to act as instructor to her uncle John and suggested he appoint instead one of her sisters to debate the issue with her.[80] At the same time the older generation proved ready enough in the course of that same discussion to argue strongly among themselves, John Ferrar taking issue with his sister over the harshness with which she scolded her daughter's wish to become a gentlewoman's servant. There were subsequent confessional moments and reproofs of faults but these were neither so extended as in that instance nor without any reply from the accused party. As the group worked together this imbalance gave way to a much more egalitarian style such as we can see in the Christmas 1631 discussion of patience. This change was probably furthered by the elevation of Mary Collet Ferrar to a new leadership role in the reconstituted group of 1632 and the new sense of mission that seemed to pervade the group.[81] John Ferrar and Susanna Collet, by the same token, seemed more willing and able to participate as equals while their nieces/ daughters were readier to propound their own views and argue their cases. In the discussion of temperance indeed the two elders tried to tone down the militant Hester's denunciations of feasting and 'carnal excess'.

Their initial aim to judge worldly activities purely by scriptural standards gradually narrowed its focus from this broad purpose to the specific goal of establishing the nature and value of temperance. By Easter 1631 they were resolving to present sadder and more solemn stories to counter the seasonal temptation to excessive cheer and lightheartedness that spring encouraged. They wished to promote 'moderate and temperate enjoyment of their outward Comforts'.[82] Thereafter came Mary Collet Ferrar's lengthy examination of Charles V's renunciation of the world, evidence of her clear leadership within the group and probably also of her close relationship with Nicholas. This developing theme of renunciation and the vanity of worldly goods, exemplified by Charles V, thus led readily into considerations of temperance and how best to pursue it. When in the summer of 1631 her discourse ended, however, the group held no more recorded meetings until Christmas time.

As that traditional time of feasting and good cheer approached old Mrs. Ferrar proposed a plan to translate the group's earlier talk about renunciation and temperance into action. The Academy should resume its meetings with the specific purpose of substituting for the traditional Christmas pastimes such as card-playing and neighbourly visiting the more spiritual entertainment of 'storying' appropriate to the season. Members of the group declared she had set them a hard task but they evidently tackled it with enthusiasm.[83] Certainly the readings at dinner and supper, those regular features of the household's routine, would have furnished everyone with at least some store from which to draw a contribution to such sessions. Temperance as such was not, however, the focus of their attention. They took their subjects instead from the feast days of the Christmas season: forgiveness of enemies on St. Stephen's Day, tales of heroic child-martyrs on Holy Innocents Day and, when the group decided to extend the sessions beyond the first of January, the virtues represented by the names given to each of the participants, e.g. Patience.

At some point after the Christmas season had finished the Little Academy again ceased its meetings, this time for a longer period than before. This lapse occasioned in retrospect considerable soul-searching among its leaders, but in the immediate weeks after the Christmas season they could take satisfaction in presenting to their grandmother the bound volume recording their proceedings.[84] She expressed her approval and in turn requested that the book be sent on to Su Mapletoft at Margaretting so that she would know she was included in the group.[85]

In July while Ferrar was in London, his nieces wrote to him in a rather exalted tone of the great designs God had chosen him to undertake and them to assist.[86] Two possibilities for these 'great designs' suggest themselves, both of which indeed came to pass later in 1632. One possible great design could have been the night vigils discussed earlier in this chapter. Another might have been an effort to revive the Academy led by Mary Collet Ferrar, with her uncle's and grandmother's encouragement.[87] This was, of course, the summer in the course of which Herbert, who knew of and encouraged both designs, received Ferrar's translation of Valdes and in turn sent to the family his translation of Cornaro's treatise, which presented a practical programme for implementing one aspect of that doctrine of mortification Ferrar had valued in Valdes.

The efforts to publish a gospel harmony and a translation of Valdes testified to Ferrar's growing sense of a mission that his household and members of his Web of Friendship could undertake empowered by their willingness to covenant themselves for this purpose. The Little Academy, reconstituted under Mary Collet Ferrar's leadership, furnished an instrument by which to launch a campaign for temperance. Through it the participants could educate and encourage each other as well as the rest of the family in a style of temperance that could in turn supply a 'pattern' much needed by their benighted age. Academy participants had clearly become mindful of such a possibility when during Advent of 1632 they not only discussed but also demonstrated in their collective life the feasibility and value of temperance. Through this project particularly Ferrar hoped that Little Gidding, like the Boston of his contemporary John Winthrop, would be for his contemporaries a 'City Set Upon a Hill'.

5

Temperance and Tensions: 'Frayltie & Fears'

'And though wee may not preach by words,. . .yet wee may preach by our Actions. . . .Our example may perhaps hearten on some others.'[1]

Earlier attempts to preach by words in the form of a publishable gospel harmony and a translation of Valdes had disappointed the hopes that Nicholas Ferrar had invested in them. He had not, however, lost his ambitious aim to make Little Gidding 'a Light on a Hill', a pattern for an age he was convinced needed such patterns. He had a message for his contemporaries and an instrument to hand by which to convey it. Temperance was the message and the Little Academy, reconstituted in October 1632 under Mary Collet Ferrar's leadership, provided the means of clarifying the message and mobilising the participants to become the hoped-for preaching example. A detailed consideration of this temperance project will reveal not only the specific diet that was prescribed but also the essential role of voluntarism that all concerned acknowledged was essential for effective action. Formal and written consent, Mary Collet Ferrar declared, was vital because it would 'more solemnly oblige them, who agree[,] & more seriously & plainly represent their true condition and Estate to them, who shall refuse this subscription'.[2] Gone was her uncle's earlier concern that no stigma should attach to those who declined to participate in night vigils. Not surprisingly, this uncompromising attitude subsequently produced tensions within the family and brought the Little Academy to an unhappy end, not before, however, their example had been celebrated anonymously in print. These tensions were further complicated by the actions of that thoroughly unwilling and disgruntled member of the household, John's unhappy wife Bathsheba, who would have been a very unlikely participant either in the temperance enterprise or any other of the special projects.

That temperance should be the focus of this effort was no accident. It had long been vital, as we have seen, to both George Herbert and Ferrar and a significant part of their collaborative efforts in 1632. Ferrar defined temperance as simply eating 'only to necessity of nature and conveniency of employment, so as we may the better perform that which God calls us to the performance of'.[3] Readings about holy men of the early church and their austerities that his tutor Augustine Lindsell had recommended were an early inspiration reinforced by the advice of Dr William Butler, an eminent Cambridge physician as well as a Fellow of Clare and a personal friend, who told him that he could only hope to preserve his health 'through a spare diet, and great temperance all your life long'.[4] George Herbert too had suffered from repeated illness and believed he owed his recovery to a rigorously spare diet, perhaps that very diet he had discovered in Luigi Cornaro's little treatise on the subject.[5] He also included advice in *The Country Parson* on proper diet and the superiority of herbal remedies to 'physick'.[6] Since both men felt that they owed their lives to their practice of temperance, it was not surprising that they wished to persuade a wider audience of its value both spiritual and physical by providing both spiritual and practical advice on its pursuit.[7] For that purpose Ferrar emphasised as especially important Valdes's doctrine of mortification and Herbert sent his translation of Cornaro's treatise to Little Gidding.

Herbert's translation was a seed that fell upon prepared ground, for some in the Little Gidding household had already experimented with a restricted diet.[8] Cornaro provided a systematic programme that the family could readily implement once they were committed to doing so. Reinforcement came soon after when the group encountered *Hygiasticon*, a work by the Belgian Jesuit Leonard Lessius. Lessius knew Cornaro's book, indeed published it together with his own very much longer and more systematic treatment of what for Cornaro was an autobiographical exercise. When and how Ferrar first discovered Lessius is unknown. The book was published in Louvain in 1613, the year Ferrar began his Continental travels, and he could have acquired a copy during his travels. In that case he would already have known of Cornaro's book before Herbert sent his translation. It is also possible, however, that Herbert made the initial discovery of both authors if his copy of Cornaro came from *Hygiasticon*. Whatever the sequence of discovery between Herbert and Ferrar, the family, once aware of Lessius, called for a translation of his book as well and Ferrar responded readily to their request. From these works the family took their model of a temperate diet. What did Cornaro and Lessius there prescribe as temperate?

Luigi Cornaro (1468-1566), a Venetian nobleman whose 98-year lifespan was itself eloquent testimony to the efficacy of his version of temperance, developed his dietary routine out of medical necessity rather than religious vocation. As a young man he had indulged himself in the rich diet and lavish lifestyle possible for one of his rank. By the time he had reached 40 he had suffered for some 5 years with gout, abdominal pains, and continual fever and thirst. His physicians had told him during those 5 years that he should eat bland foods and in small quantities but he had ignored that unpalatable advice. Finally, however, when they confronted him with the stark alternatives of temperance or death, he set about implementing the former by experimenting with a variety of foods to establish which ones and in what quantities best suited him. In a very short time he found himself quite well and resolved to adhere to this routine for the rest of his life. What he presented in his book was not a list of approved and forbidden food and drink. He was clear that everyone must discover these specifics for himself because each individual's needs and reactions varied. What he did insist on were quantities, which were to be measured very precisely. He allowed himself daily twelve ounces of 'meat' (bread, eggs, flesh, and broth) and fourteen ounces of drink.[9] Only once, when he was about seventy-eight, he allowed friends to talk him into increases of two ounces in each category. He promptly fell ill and only recovered when he reverted to his original quantities. Nor was change of diet alone sufficient; temperance also required avoiding excesses of temperature, sexual activity, and strong emotions such as hatred and melancholy. He concluded with an enthusiastic account of the vigorous life he continued, at eighty-three, to live, enjoying the company of friends and grandchildren, supervising improvements on his estates, interesting himself in books, art, and architecture.[10]

Unlike the layman Cornaro, the Jesuit Lessius in *Hygiasticon* emphasised not only the medical but also the religious value of temperance, both as a general Christian virtue and also as a special benefit to priests that would enable them better to perform their priestly office. Otherwise, however, he followed Cornaro's recommendations very closely though the tone of his book is rather more impersonal and sober and it is longer. He elaborated seven rules for establishing appropriate amounts of food and drink for a temperate diet appropriate to different kinds of work, concluding that Cornaro's twelve and fourteen ounce portions of meat and drink were best for those of a sedentary life.[11] He also recommended exercise as part of a balanced regimen of temperance and offered as examples shadow-boxing while holding small weights in each hand or tossing and catching a bar or stool for a quarter to half an hour before meals. 'These are Exercises, which many grave & worthy men, even Cardinalls themselves, do use (and that not undecently) in their Chambers'.[12]

If this was the pattern that the Ferrars were following during Christmas 1632, they had indeed set themselves a hard task to compensate with their stories for such meagre rations.[13] Before the Little Academy could even begin to consider such a project, however, it had to be rescued from the moribund condition into which it had fallen by the summer of 1632. If its revival were the 'great design' about which Ferrar and his nieces wrote in July, then several more months had to elapse before they formally attempted it. When the meeting for reconstitution finally took place on St. Luke's Day (18 October), there was certainly considerable though general talk of sins to repent and difficulties to overcome both within the family circle and in the outside world.[14] The initial covenant of 1631 with which the Little Academy had launched its first series of meetings had by the beginning of 1632 clearly broken down and required renewal. Maintaining momentum in a voluntary society was patently not an easy task even in as well ordered a household as Little Gidding. John Ferrar in his character as 'Guardian' made an eloquent plea to 'rise again in our hopes, in our resolutions, in our endeavours. . . . And let us doe it together by bonds of mutual Promise, of mutual encouragement, and of mutual Assistance'.[15]

A fortnight later on All Saints' Day came a change of leadership when the group unanimously chose Mary Collet Ferrar to take her grandmother's place with the name no longer of 'Chief' but now of 'Mother'.[16] She proved an effective leader. The Academy's participants had during the previous Christmas season accepted old Mrs. Ferrar's proposal that they forego the usual holiday games and entertainments in favour of edifying stories.[17] Now her granddaughter took this idea further when she explicitly declared her intention of making story-telling 'serve for Christmas Cheere. . . . It must bee a very sober table that a virgin sitts at the head of, and simple cakes that are of her providing.' Her sister, 'Cheerful' (probably Hester), immediately applauded this resolve and announced that 'There's no doubt, then, but my Law will gett passage when it comes to the question.'[18] She would have to wait, however, until Advent was well underway to put her question to the group.

During the third week of Advent, which in 1632 would have been 16-22 December, Hester requested a special meeting of the Academy with the plea that 'Necessitie' would brook no further delay. Mary agreed arguing that unless Hester's case for a different kind of Christmas carried the day the family would have to start making their conventional 'Christmas provisions'. Hester promptly dubbed such provisions 'Carnal Excesses & spiritual preiudices, that corrupt the Body, defile the soul, & wast the Estate.'[19] There followed a lengthy and vigorous debate spelling out how conventional 'good cheer' wrought these disastrous effects and should therefore not be part of the Christian life at Christmas or indeed any other time. This session differed from the usual story-telling pattern of the Academy for the group kept to the impersonal topic and attacked in analytic fashion questions such as the meaning of the biblical phrase 'being given to wine'.[20]

At the outset Mary, echoing her uncle's stress on practical, incremental steps in the pursuit of 'perfection' through temperance, suggested that the participants concentrate on a single goal, to increase God's grace within themselves, and to demonstrate how temperance would promote that goal. The group took it in turn to make an explicit verbal commitment to that goal, a step that all agreed was important because 'everyone, whom it concernes, should actually express their Agreements in the Foundation, before wee goe forward with the Building'.[21] Achieving that agreement Mary Collet Ferrar declared merited 'a Red Letter in our Calendar' and should promptly be followed up by confirmation in writing.[22] Thus the group constituted itself a voluntary society with a mission to preach by action and example.

Hester then proceeded to make her case for temperance and against 'good cheer', an argument in more general terms than the specific programmes of Cornaro and Lessius. She prefaced it with an apology that she was only repeating ideas taught her by others (her uncle Nicholas almost certainly). Mary, however, assured her that she had every right to call this knowledge her own 'Since you have made it trebly your own by understanding, by Assent, & by so Learning it, as you are able to communicate it to others.'[23] Indeed, a little later, when Margaret offered herself as a devil's advocate to present arguments against temperance that Hester could rebut, Hester accepted with particular alacrity because, she declared, that was the way she herself had been taught.[24] Mary put as a question to Hester, 'And how then can it be, that there should be such an opposition & overthrow of Wisdome & vertue by Satietie & Good Cheere'. That question framed the entire remainder of the discussion in which the rest of the group joined.[25] Advocates of that good cheer produced by feasting and drinking claimed it promoted friendship, facilitated business, and inspired poetry and other arts. As Hester and her companions examined these claims, however, they concluded that indulging in more than moderate amounts of food and drink had just the opposite effects. It impaired the judgment in business affairs, made the mind dull and lethargic because all bodily energies were directed to digestion rather than thought, and worst of all it encouraged lust, which when frustrated took the form of slander and backbiting, the very opposite of friendship. As a first step the group discussed what constituted 'food' and 'drink'. Wine and 'Dainties', particularly spices, savories and sweets (these latter categories included lemons and oranges, raisins and candied fruits) came under intensive scrutiny. They concluded that none of them were properly 'drink' or 'food' because they neither quenched thirst nor provided nourishment. Wine therefore should rather be classified as a medicine, following St. Paul's dictum of taking a little wine for thy stomach's sake, and used as sparingly as medicine would be. John Ferrar, as Guardian, did offer here a little demur, declaring 'It is a pleasant Medicine, if it be a Medicine'.[26] Dainties, having no biblical sanction for their consumption even in modest quantities, could be abandoned altogether though no one said so in this record of the proceedings. The family did, however, explicitly agree to cut out those 'superfluous excesses of Christmas cheare', spices and fruit.[27]

The group then moved to consider in some detail those intangible but certainly no less evil consequences of gluttony and excesses of wine, namely slander and backbiting. Folk who committed such sins, they concluded, might be motivated sometimes by straightforward malice but other times by a desire to curry favor with one person through attacks on others. Still worse than the aggressors were those who listened to such attacks with relish and paraded this behaviour as a virtue because they could claim to be comforters of victims. One could legitimately reveal another's faults, the members of the Academy concluded, only if one were motivated by a sincere desire to reform them or to prevent them from causing harm.[28] John Ferrar announced his resolve on this point neither to tell tales about others nor listen to them, an audience being essential to a slanderer. Those who were eager listeners to such gossip were as culpable as the speakers and responsible for many evils including rebellious children, conspiring servants and insubordinate wives, the latter an evil of which John himself had vivid experience.[29] Arthur Woodnoth also reiterated this point a month or so later when he resolved in January 1633 to close his ears to slanders.[30]

Hester, an energetic and forthright activist in this matter, had early in the discussion urged her companions to stop merely talking about notable people who renounced worldly pleasures and start following their good

examples. To this summons Mary added that the group could preach by
actions where they could not preach by sermons:

> '& perhaps that Real kind of Instruction [that] hath in all Ages
> beene the most forcible, is in this the most Necessarie. Where
> there are many Masters but few guides. A Dearth of Patterns in
> an exuberance of Rules'.[31]

Here was a mission statement for their voluntary society that John
Ferrar seconded in the hope that the family's example would 'in the end
spred abroad'.[32]

By the time these sessions had ended and Christmas had actually arrived,
the pattern for the new, temperate mode of celebration at Gidding was in
place. If the Mapletofts' later comments are any indication, it was based
on the Cornaro measured diet.[33] After its intense and analytical Advent
dicussion, the Little Academy returned to its more usual storying format.
Mary opened the first Christmastide session with comments to Hester about
the hard task they faced, 'double to that which was last yeare enjoyned'.
Substituting stories for games was only exchanging one mental pleasure
for another; using them to compensate for short and plain rations was of a
different order of magnitude. They agreed, however, that the right attitude
could make even the plainest fare seem ambrosial, particularly when good
stories provided 'dainties' for the mind. Hester's choice of story, taken from
'Mr. Fox[e]', might seem somewhat ambivalent here, being an account with
much grisly detail of the grilling of St. Laurence! Her remark that ' "St.
Laurence is rost meat for our soules to feed on" ' suggests the basis for her
choice.[34] The Ferrars' Christmas menus were, as Mary reported, of limited
and measured quantity and simplest quality: 'two dishes, and those but plaine
ones neither, Mutton and Veale (for I heare of no others provisions)'.[35]

While Mary and Hester took the lead in convincing the members of
the Little Academy to adopt this strenuous pattern of temperance, Ferrar
strove to widen the circle of participants to include those in his Web of
Friendship. During the Advent week when the Academy's discussions
were taking place, he wrote to Arthur Woodnoth in terms aimed to inspire
his cousin to become a partner in the 'great design'.

> 'lett us sett our designe and desyres where they cannot fayle
> else double will bee our misery to consume our selves not onely
> in coruptible things but in meere trifles. . . . Lett us vindicate
> ourselves from this misery and begin to live indeed – every
> hower otherwise bestowed is Lost if not worse. – Lett it bee
> therfore yf you will an agreement to this purpose between you

and mee thus[,] since the whole frame of what wee intend is to much to bee sett doune at once and requires much Length of tyme perhapps[,] that wee will at least every weeke present each other with some peice that wee have finished. . .one conclusion at least and communicate each with other[.] I tell you what by Gods grace wee have already established[,] to cutt of[f] all the superfluous excesses belonging to Christmas cheere spice fruite – And to pass the festivall with sobriety as belongs to a spiritual good tyme – This wee thanke God [we have] agreed and concluded and shall be I hope shortly ratifyde after the strongest manner Pr[a]y for us that wee may goe on stedfast in this good [work] & increasing in others'[36]

The passage makes clear Ferrar's pastoral and pedagogical methods that his niece Mary had also employed with the Little Academy: participants must take active responsibility for decisions and follow a systematic programme of practicable steps to pursue their goal. They were not to express their enthusiasm in wild flights of emotion and overambitious austerities. He was subsequently to advise a similar step-by-step approach to Joshua Mapletoft during his desperate illness.[37] It was a style not unlike that of St. Francis de Sales with his 'affections and resolutions' and 'little nosegays of devotion' designed to recall a morning's meditation to mind during the remainder of the day.[38]

The approach certainly worked with Arthur Woodnoth, who responded promptly in a letter dated 22 December: 'By Gods Grace I will Endeavor to Turne away or Close my Eyes from all Corporall objects the vision whereof may indispose my soule from Spirituall'.[39] His surviving letters from January 1633 through March continue to present 'resolutions' which include eschewing 'unproffitable discourse', closing his eyes to 'Dazzling obiects' and his ears to 'the sullferr of Evill & slanderous reports', avoiding wasted time by identifying a purpose in all his actions, not wanting more of this world's goods than would help him in the next, stepping toward temperance by not satisfying any appetites in ways contrary to God's will.[40] The earlier of these resolutions with their echo of the Academy's lengthy delineation of the evils of slander and backbiting promoted by 'good cheer' suggest that Ferrar had kept Woodnoth informed of the Academy's discussions. Woodnoth also referred in early January to a letter from Joshua Mapletoft to Nicholas that contained 'the weight of so many excellent rules & resolutions'.[41] Given Mapletoft's later comment about Psalmody and Temperance and his requests for advice and detailed accounts of his and

Su's diet, that letter could very well have been his and his wife's response to a letter similar to the one Ferrar sent to Woodnoth telling of the Academy's resolutions and discussions. The Mapletofts, despite some delay and initial reservations from Joshua, certainly took up the invitation to participate.

Although they doubtless already knew of the family's temperance discussions and austere Christmas at the end of 1632, their surviving direct comments on matters of diet only begin in the following October. Susanna wrote on the 3rd to her sister Mary, first thanking her for the wonderful care she was taking of Susanna's daughter, who had evidently stayed on at Gidding. She then went on to declare herself in better health than she had ever been since coming to Margaretting, a benefit she attributed to 'my dyet which I find doth agree with my body both for quallity & quant[it]ye much better than that I used before.'[42] A week later came Joshua's long letter to Ferrar, which included his remark that psalmody and temperance were characteristic features of the family's life.[43] He also enclosed a detailed account of his and Susanna's diet for a month for Ferrar's comment and advice, adding that they would set about following it as soon as they had his reply. Joshua added at another point a list of seven relevant questions covering such matters as appropriate quantities for both himself and his wife, proper proportions to maintain between solid and liquid food, whether those proportions should vary when he travelled as opposed to when he was at home and studying, whether rice eaten on its own was permissible without limit 'unto moderate Satiety' and when gingerbread should be taken at breakfast. Such a range of queries and especially the concern for quantities suggests that the Mapletofts were proposing to follow the Cornaro/Lessius pattern. At the end of the month he added a further request for advice on any modifications Susanna should make to her diet if, as she suspected, she were pregnant.[44]

Despite these detailed questions about quantities and the month's sample diet he had sent to Ferrar in the previous October, he wrote in the following March to his sisters-in-law Mary and Anna that he as yet was

> rather indeed a well wisher to those that be Temperate then an observer of Temperance wherof my necessity of the helpe of physick att so unseasonable a time is evidence sufficient to convince me.

He remained convinced of the value of temperance, a conviction strengthened by Mary and Anna's testimony both of its value to soul and body and of the ease with which they had been able to follow the strict diet; his remarks here echo T.S.'s preface to *Hygiasticon*.[45] What has hindered him thus far has been 'so many occasions to call me abroad as I could not hitherto intende the taking of a iust tryall as now ere long I hope I shall'.[46] His wife's subsequent letter to her sisters indicated that the family at Gidding had celebrated a second austere Christmas in 1633. She had been with them for the holiday but confessed that she had not since leaving Gidding eaten by weight or drunk by measure. She hoped, nevertheless, that she had approximated the appropriate quantities reasonably closely. Although she was pregnant she still maintained a routine of one proper meal at noon and simply a 'posset' at supper, which does not sound overly generous in the circumstances. She thanked her sisters for their good advice and a 'token', perhaps a copy of *Hygiasticon*.[47]

Joshua's brother Robert in Cambridge had also taken up Ferrar's invitation to participate. His situation as a Fellow resident in his college (Pembroke) presented special problems with diet. After his visit to Gidding sometime in February or early March 1634, he described his difficulties in observing the diet during Lent. The food served in college during this season of fasting was 'lighter of digestion and less nutritive' and he had often had to take more than the prescribed fourteen ounces in order to 'give satisfaction to a good stomack (such as mine is)'. He hoped in the coming week to get greater certainty and control over quantity and was cheered to find that fish, which he had not eaten for three years, he could now readily tolerate. The regimen clearly took a toll on his energy level, however, for he remarked that 'I am full of what I might write, but already weary with writing this litle'. He also continued to have difficulty with early rising; he had been dismayed to find himself sleeping eight or nine hours at a stretch when he had hoped to rise at three and get on with memorisation of the Epistles. He concluded his letter with the hope that he would see Ferrar about 14 April when their mutual friends, Rev. Timothy Thurscross and his wife, and Rev. Edward [sic: should be Edmund] Duncon proposed to set out for Gidding and he evidently planned to join them there.[48]

The day after Robert wrote thus of his trials Ferrar drafted a letter to Joshua in Margaretting in which he rejoiced to hear that Joshua was coming to Gidding. In response to Joshua's confession to Mary and Anna Collet that he had not yet made a proper trial of the temperance diet Ferrar took great care to assure him that the choice was his. Despite his obvious wish for Joshua's participation and his certainty that God would provide Joshua sufficient strength for the task, he would not want him to undertake greater hazards than he was willing to risk.

> But yf you bee other ways perswaded or not willing to run the
> perrils and Incumbrances that n[e]cessarily will attend it[,]
> For without suffering you cannot bee that Instrument of soe

much good to me and other[s,] I shall by Gods grace[,] without abatement of Love or empeachment of the excercise of this duty to you ward[,] . . . free you from any farther intermedling[49]

Ferrar was here reiterating earlier comments on the importance of free choice for effective participation in spiritual and educational projects. At the same time he was not above putting pressure on Joshua with such a loaded statement of his position that made opting out look like moral and spiritual cowardice. Perhaps, however, Ferrar knew Joshua well enough to sense that a 'challenge' such as this was the only way to bolster his courage sufficiently for him to take a plunge he wanted but feared to attempt. Subsequent letters suggest that he did indeed enlist in the ranks of the temperate. During the summer, however, he showed the first symptoms of that grave illness which nearly carried him off during the following winter and which called forth from Ferrar, as we have seen earlier, not merely counsel on physical matters of diet but on larger questions of spiritual health.[50]

Committed members of the family, including the Mapletofts, thus continued to follow the prescribed regimen through 1633 while Ferrar was preparing *Hygiasticon* for the press. As was his wont he did not put his name either to the book's preface or to the translation itself, but there can be no doubt that he was 'T.S.', the putative author of the preface. In it he described a family (unnamed) that had tried the diet and had found it both easy and beneficial.[51] He also took care, as he had done with Valdes, to acknowledge that while both Cornaro and Lessius were Roman Catholics, this fact in no way invalidated their views on temperance. In addition to this preface various of his friends added laudatory poems to the published volume, testimony to the wider circle whose support Ferrar hoped to enlist. Among the named contributors were Richard Crashaw, Peter Gunning, Barnabas Oley, and J[probably John] Jackson, an excerpt from whose work *Ecclesiastes* (1628) was later incorporated into the Pentateuch Harmony made for Prince Charles in 1641-2.[52] There was also a poem, attributed to 'S.J.', in the 'echo' format used by George Herbert. Whether, however, any of them also attempted to follow Lessius's and Cornaro's regimen is not indicated.

How many in the family persevered during this time and how rigorously they kept to the prescribed amounts of food and drink we do not know though Su Mapletoft's comment on measured quantities suggests that at least some of them made a conscientious effort to do so.[53] How beneficial the diet proved to be over the longer term is questionable in light of Ferrar's letter of January 1633/4 reporting to Joshua Mapletoft that Mary had suffered 'discomposure' as a result of excessive dieting and he himself had been ill with a 'scurvy'.[54] His mother eventually decided that the family's 'mortifications' were excessive and a threat particularly to her son Nicholas's life and health. For her he dutifully modified his austerities until her death in late spring of 1634, but to friends who echoed his mother's concern he insisted that a return to conventional patterns of living would be the death of him.[55]

Although he and some others, including the Mapletofts, continued to follow the measured diet while *Hygiasticon* was in preparation during 1633, the zeal of others had faltered after the Little Academy held its final Christmastide session on Holy Innocents Day (28 December 1632). The meeting closed with a proposal from the leader, Mary Collet Ferrar, that the group should conclude its meeting with the season's customary gift giving. The request evidently took the group by surprise, but Mary declared herself confident that every member of the group could find in their memorised 'store' an appropriate story to offer as a gift that would be both beneficial and useful. Each participant had a particular 'store' from which to draw: Hester's (Cheerful) was Temperance, she having been the initiator of the Advent discussion of this topic; Anna's (Patient) was Sobriety; Margaret's (Affectionate) was Industry; Susanna Collet's (Moderator) was Education; John Ferrar's (Guardian) was Charity. The recipient of the first round of gifts was to be 'our good cozen and Guest', who had accepted the group's 'frugal entertainment' and thoroughly approved of temperance. Who this might be becomes clearer, though still ambiguous, only with added clues from the later account.

Since the cousin and guest was described as approving and practicing temperance, Hester was the obvious one to produce a story on this topic out of her 'store'. Her offering concerned a holy man in Alexandria, who had striven through much mortification to attain purity of heart. He reproved a priest whom he saw coming out of a tavern but the priest pointed out to him that the purity of heart that the priest had and that Jesus required did not consist in the doing or abstaining from particular actions. The holy man was then horrified to realise that despite all his mortifications he had not himself attained to such purity. Mention of taverns led to further accounts from John Ferrar of the evils of taverns and examples of dreadful things done under the influence of drink. Susanna Collet picked up the tavern theme from there and, as befitted one whose 'store' was education, offered to the cousin and guest a preliminary gift in the form of a precept to her son, probably Ferrar Collet then aged 15. She commanded him never to go into a tavern and to say to any who tried to persuade him that his mother had forbidden it. With that firm injunction the session somewhat abruptly ended leaving most of the promised gifts to the cousin and guest undelivered and the Little Academy on the verge of collapse.

What we know of what happened from that time until the revival of a much-altered version of the Little Academy at least two years later depends on a rather enigmatic and anonymous account of the sort Ferrar favoured. Whether this penchant for anonymity and ambiguity that he had revealed earlier reflected modesty or tact or some darker or more devious urge for secrecy or control is impossible to say, but it was clearly a recurrent characteristic of his personality. Whatever his motives for anonymity, only he could have written an account that gave in revealing detail the impact of the temperance programme on the family and on the relationships among its individual members.

As soon as that final session had finished and the 'cousin and guest' (also described as a 'young man') had received the first of his gifts, he proceeded to apply Susanna's precept to himself by seeking out his own mother to request that she lay on him the same prohibition about entering a tavern. His mother was described as a 'grave matron . . . addicted to piety' who had memorised the entire psalter after she was sixty. Mary Woodnoth Ferrar was noted for such characteristics and must be the most plausible candidate for the mother in this account. And if she was the mother, then Ferrar became the likeliest candidate for the 'cousin and guest' and the 'young man' who received the earlier gift despite the fact that he was at that point forty years old and the head of the Gidding household.[56]

As the story moved on, this 'young man' became first the 'Practitioner' and later the 'Compositor'. Once he had taken his vow about taverns, the narrator of this introductory passage (sometimes lapsing into the first person but more usually writing about the Practitioner in the third person) proceeded to extol the benefits of temperance in the pursuit of 'perfection', one of Ferrar's favourite themes. Though the final outcome of the family's experiment and example was beyond human knowledge, the Practitioner, its leader, had already received from his 'Regular Diet' health, wisdom, and honour and those who did likewise could anticipate similar benefits. From lesser virtues like temperance that were, with divine help, within human powers, one could move toward 'perfection' and the redemption that is not within our power and is the highest reward of all.[57] God's rewards were not only certain but appropriate to a man's wishes and expectations because God would adjust those wishes and expectations to match the reward He provided. The Practitioner's reward moved beyond health, wisdom and honour to the mystical experience of 'real Wealth, Glorie & Delight' whilst 'these spiritual raptures are in the Flowing-course & Tide', a reward indeed appropriate to the translator of Valdes.[58]

Although the Practitioner's rewards made members of the Little Academy want to resume their sessions, their initial attempts never succeeded though the Practitioner would not reveal why they failed. Nearly two years elapsed before wishes finally culminated in a decision to implement this revival as a gift to the Practitioner because of his kindness and service to a 'Common Friend and Brother'. The narrative's chronology, however, is far from clear, which makes it difficult to determine what this service was and to whom it was given. An interval of nearly two years would place this action in the autumn of 1634 at which time Ferrar was indeed providing counsel and comfort to Joshua Mapletoft in his worsening illness. But if, as the account implies, the decision to revive the group as a present to the Practitioner preceded the death of Mary Woodnoth Ferrar in April 1634, then Ferrar's earlier service would more plausibly have been the posthumous publication of *The Temple* and Hygiasticon for his friend and brother George Herbert. That timing, however, would have placed the decision considerably earlier than the 'nearly two years' specified. More probably there were two different decisions, one before and one after Mary Ferrar's death, the latter occurring in late 1634 or possibly early 1635. The first, in late 1633 or early 1634, had rapidly stalled because of unspecified 'inconquerable difficulties' that the Practitioner, now in his role as 'Compositor', would have had to address. They included those difficulties, which included 'the Rectification of those Affections, which were most disordered amongst themselues'.[59]

Clearly the household during this two-year period had experienced considerable turbulence. The effort to practice temperance and set an example to the world had proved costly to family harmony. A letter of Susanna Collet points to possible issues, not all of which directly involved temperance, which might have produced disordered affections. It also suggests how the Compositor set about the work of rectification.

> To my Brother Nicholas, caused upon some speeches about his inditing of Letters, for divers in the house, and also for some Exceptions taken for saying somewhat about the stories & other things.
>
> As you desire a free, so I make no doubt but a briefe declaration will give you satisfaction in those two things wherein you require an Answer. . . . [First, she has no problem with his

drafting of letters for others and has been grateful for his help
when she requested it].... For the matter of storying [the Little
Academy's practice], I have accounted the most part of them to
be delivered by way of Relation of the Actions & opinions of
good & Virtuous men and women, and such as for the Substance
ought to be taken for patterns of Imitation, and so for all other
passages that are intermingled with them & do heartily desire
that whatever is contain[e]d in them, that is the will or command
of God, that we in our own particular should do, we may both
consent & conform unto in all points: For any corporal Exercise
there is none imposed, nor as I conceive, expected from Me, but
what I both may & do willingly performe & therefore I shall not
need to say any more to that.[60]

Ferrar here resorted to that favourite device we have seen him use earlier
of asking people to put down their views in writing. Susanna evidently
felt secure in her position in the family and prepared to be frank with her
brother; Ferrar was probably not likely to try to pressure his much older
sister. Others, not surprisingly, did not share that sense of security though
no other letters comparable to hers survive. Clearly there had been criticism
of Ferrar's practice of composing letters for others to sign, as we have seen
him do earlier for his nieces to send their sister in Margaretting. Who the
critics were and what were the grounds of their objections unfortunately
remain hidden. Some, though not Susanna Collet, also evidently had felt
pressured to do more by way of 'corporal exercises' than they wished.
These exercises probably reflected the zeal of at least some in the Little
Academy to promote the Cornaro diet. Mary Collet Ferrar's earlier
comment that the refusal to sign up to the plan would show the unwilling
'their condition & Estate' suggests the possibility that the enthusiasts had
taxed the backsliders with unflattering views of their 'true condition'.[61] The
tensions implied in these comments could well have been strong enough
to persist and influence, as Margaret Aston has postulated, their choice of
martyrdoms from Foxe's print to incorporate into a composite picture for
King Charles's harmony of 1635.[62]

Another heartfelt but more mysterious letter, also undated but written in
her own hand during a difficult time, came from his mother to Nicholas:

My good sone it greveth me that ther should be any deaffarence
betw[e]ne you and me I pray god it maye no longer be so for it
brynges no comfort to me but the contrary I bese[e]ch you doo
not think that it is for want of my love to your persone nor dislyk

of your Iud[g]ment but myne owne wekenes and want of true
understanding what god requires of me. . .let this suffyes that I
doo pourpous and entend by godes assistance not only to consent
but to lyke of such orders as you shaule set downe tendying to
the good of this fammyly in generaull and I will by godes healpe
doo what is in my powr to mantayne them and if I fayll it shaul
no[t] be of porpouse nor willingly but of wekness
     Your weke and unworthy mother   Mary farrar[63]

What this difference was one can only speculate. Perhaps since his
mother was said to have regarded her son's vigils and austerities as
excessive and asked him to moderate them, that issue or the effect that
vigils and dieting were having on others in the family might have prompted
her remarks.[64] What the letter does make entirely clear, however, is that
ultimately she was prepared to defer to her son.

There were other difficulties that would probably have contributed
to 'disordered affections' during 1633 and early 1634. A letter from
Arthur Woodnoth to Ferrar in August 1633 wished him success with an
unspecified but difficult project he was then working on.[65] John Ferrar
became involved in ongoing and no doubt costly litigation over the will
of Timothy Sheppard, Thomas's brother.[66] The most dramatic cases of
'disordered affections', however, involved Ferrar's uncharacteristic but
vehement quarrel with cousin Arthur over the publication of *The Temple*
and two heated and less readily resolved quarrels between John and his
wife Bathsheba, about which John sought Nicholas's advice.[67]

Bathsheba had caused trouble on previous occasions. First had come
her letter to the mother of Martha, Thomas Collet's young wife, claiming
that Martha was being kept at Little Gidding against her will.[68] Next
she tried a different tactic, namely escape to London where she still had
resident relatives. She went up with her husband to London in 1630 and
again in March 1631, probably for John Junior's birth. By June John had
returned to the country but she lingered in town, a separation that caused
anxiety to the family. Nicholas, himself now in London, cast about for
a way to get her and her child back to Gidding. One possibility was to
enlist the help of his sister Susanna, who was in Essex helping at her
daughter's confinement. The snag with proposing that the two sisters-in-
law return to Gidding together, Ferrar acknowledged, was that Bathsheba
might have to be asked to delay her departure to accommodate Susanna,
and such a request would 'prove matter of evill Consequence every way'.
Even if Bathsheba wanted nothing so much as an excuse to remain in

London, he implied, the mere fact that the family had requested it would make her resist.[69]

By July she was still there and Susanna tried to take a hand directly. She sent one of her sons to call on Bathsheba and suggest that the two of them travel back together, to which Bathsheba had replied that she had not yet fixed a date for her return but feared it would be too soon for Susanna safely to leave her daughter and the new infant. Undaunted by what would seem a pretty transparent evasion, Susanna protested that her daughter was recovering so well that she could leave anytime. Bathsheba had only to let her know the date she had chosen in time for Susanna to get up to London and join her.[70] No further exchanges reveal how the manoeuvring progressed, but a hint from another source suggested that Bathsheba was still delaying her departure in October.[71] Not only were the two sisters-in-law not close; Bathsheba was also not open to suggestions from anyone else in the family except possibly her mother-in-law.

Another of Bathsheba's lines of resistance was keeping as much control as possible over her two younger children's upbringing. Although her elder son, Nicholas, was already 'lost' to his uncle's influence, at least little Virginia and John could still be 'hers'. Such efforts, not surprisingly, produced some of the sharpest conflicts with her husband. In September 1633 they had a heated quarrel in the wake of which Nicholas advised John to confess to God (though not apparently directly to Bathsheba herself) his sin of using 'Lofty or bitter language' and promise amendment in future. Bathsheba for her part must acknowledge John's God-given authority over the children's upbringing as well as his patience in the face of her attacks. She was hardly likely to find that advice palatable, particularly coming from Nicholas. One night a couple of months later she staged a more dramatic scene in which she refused to sleep in the conjugal bed and insisted she would instead sleep on a bed in her child's nursery. She objected to the 'undecent' hours at which the servants came into their room, probably to wake John for prayers, and more prosaically to the coldness of the room itself. John's immediate efforts to remedy these complaints failed to satisfy her for she never did return to their bed that night. They must presently have patched up some sort of truce, for sleeping separately defied every accepted convention and expectation of marriage.[72]

In the face of such domestic turbulence it was small wonder that Ferrar reported to Joshua Mapletoft early in 1634 that niece Mary and brother John and he himself had been ill and that he had had more to bear in recent weeks than ever before. Without his temperate diet, he averred, he would never have managed to sustain his work as he had successfully done.[73]

Letter (FP 940: undated) from Mary Ferrar to her son Nicholas. It is transcribed in full on pp. 148-9.

Balancing these negative events was an unexpected and very positive event that went unmentioned in family letters. In the summer of 1633 King Charles asked to borrow the family's harmony. This marked the start of what was to become a hugely significant and rewarding project for the family but also one very demanding of their time and effort.

If, however, 'disordered affections' had prevented the resumption of the Little Academy before Mary Ferrar's death, her passing produced still greater disturbances in 'the essential parts of this institution' that left 'one half of the remaining society. . .disabled for the prosecution of the Business'.[74] What these problems were the narrator, no doubt Nicholas himself here speaking in the first person, again declined to say other than to attribute them to 'our Demeritts' and to 'Frayltie and Fears & other misapprehensions'. For his own part, however, he acknowledged his share of guilt and asked pardon of any who were put off the work through his errors and offered any help he could give to reconcile them to participation. These 'errors' might well have involved the issues Susanna Collet's letter to her brother had addressed: pressures to emulate those 'Actions & opinions of good and Virtuous men and women' related in Little Academy storying and to pursue 'corporal exercises' more arduously than some were willing to do.

According to Nicholas's narrative, old Mary Ferrar, who particularly cherished the idea of the Little Academy, had been much distressed toward the end of her life to see discord within the family strong enough to derail attempts to resume the Academy.[75] When even greater tensions after her death caused another move for revival to collapse, those who had opposed revival began to experience a change of heart. They came to see the Academy not as a burden and an encroachment on 'liberty of carnal Affections'[76] but as a major motivator of virtuous actions. That changed attitude found powerful reinforcement from a written plea for the resumption of the group found after her death among Mary Ferrar's papers. That message proved a turning point, declared the narrator, for then the resumption could be presented as a duty to fulfill her command rather than a 'voluntary choise'.[77] Clearly voluntarism had reached a limit for some of the family, who would respond, at least to calls for study groups, only to a command from beyond the grave. That command was what produced, nearly two years after the last session had ended, not only the successful decision to revive the Academy but the will and authority to implement it.

Once the group had accepted that 'command' basis for reconstituting a 'society' they could then deal with the remaining problems. The most serious of these was a lack of committed resident participants, the result of those disturbances following the death of Mary Ferrar that the narrator claimed had 'disabled' half the potential membership. Who were these earlier participants who could or would no longer be available? They were most probably members of the Collet family. Hester had married Francis Kestian and was living in London by June 1635.[78] Her mother's letter to her in that month revealed a marital problem with another of her children that vexed Susanna greatly. Hester's brother Nicholas had informally engaged himself to marry his cousin Jane Smith, and Susanna strongly opposed cousin marriages.[79] Nicholas was, as his mother feared, too far committed and not at all desirous of backing down; the marriage took place on 11 April 1636. Margaret meanwhile in 1635 had rejected a proposed marriage to an unidentified man, an act that her uncle Nicholas viewed as 'that greate Error of hers'. When Susanna wrote to Nicholas in 1636 about another marriage proposal for Margaret, Nicholas refused to offer any advice. He was not sure, he said, that Margaret had sufficiently repented of her earlier error, and he had resolved in that case not to 'meddle' in her marriage arrangements. Nevertheless, he said that he would feel obliged to be entirely frank and open with his friend Mr. [John] Ramsay (evidently the new suitor) about Margaret herself and the family's situation in general in the same way that he had been with Joshua Mapletoft when he had married Su Collet. If he and Ramsay indeed had such a talk, it promoted rather than deterred the marriage. Nor did Ramsay's being in Holy Orders provoke Margaret to disdain him. They were married before 25 March 1636 when they signed the bonds that constituted the family's settlement on them.[80]

The Collet parents, especially Susanna, were of course deeply involved in these marriage negotiations. The tone of Nicholas's answer to his sister about Ramsay suggests there were tensions between him and the Collets though the marriage nevertheless went ahead. How much time the senior Collets spent at Little Gidding after 1635 is difficult to ascertain. In that year Susanna wrote to her daughter Hester after which there was a gap of ten years in her letter book, and in the Ferrar Papers only one letter from her in London to Nicholas in January 1636.[81] With two daughters newly married she might well have spent considerable time visiting them in their new homes, as she did when Su had married Joshua Mapletoft. When the Little Academy was finally revived, also probably in 1635, John Collet had proposed an addition to the group's formal agreement stating that they should always translate their words and advice into actions. If this rather enigmatic comment was offered as a criticism of previous behaviour, it was additional evidence of family tensions, especially since the group was said initially to have been taken aback at his intervention though they eventually approved of it. Having offered his resolution, however, he did not sign the agreement and took no part in the subsequent discussions.[82] He had never been a notable contributor to earlier discussions of the Academy. Susanna's absence from the new group was the more striking in light of her active participation earlier.

Earlier plans for revival had included Su Mapletoft, again as an absentee. She was provided with a new nickname; no longer the 'Goodwife' of the earlier dialogues, she would now be the 'Well-Married' and was therefore presumably still at Margaretting. After Joshua's death in September 1635, she returned with her children to Little Gidding, but there is no reference to her in the proceedings of the new group.[83] The four participants who signed the 'Common Agreements and Resolutions of the Societie' had probably done so before that September and her reappearance at Gidding.

The signers included only three of the earlier Academy participants with Nicholas as a fourth. Although any others who agreed to abide by the group's rules could attend, the recorded discussions in fact included no contributions from any but the four signers. They styled themselves 'The Register' [Nicholas], 'The Repeater' [John], 'The Learner [probably Anna], and 'The Apprentice' [probably Mary].[84] Readers, who could only have been family members or close friends able to access the manuscript volume, were admonished not to try to figure out who these individuals were. In an interesting comment on the earlier purpose that had governed the choice of names for participants the account stated that the old names were deliberately discarded because they had in fact not shown themselves to be spurs to strive for the virtues named but rather invitations to complacency and pride, as if the individuals had already acquired them.

Though the impetus to reviving the Academy was said to have come as a posthumous command from Mary Ferrar, the 'Common Agreements & Resolutions of the Societie' show that the participants intended the new group to be a voluntary society. The signers' promises of participation they regarded as solemn obligations second only to baptismal vows, hence the importance of the 'public' gesture of committing them to writing.[85] In the agreement they promised, in John Collet's words, to put into action rather than simply into words any advice they gave to themselves or to others as to 'the attainment of Perfection, Giuing Example by Action of that w[hi]ch wee giue Counsel of by words'.[86] They still aspired to a preaching mission.

With these binding commitments not only to talk about but to act upon their contributions to the group's discussions and with the adoption of new names (perhaps a kind of baptism as well as disguise since these promises were given nearly the force of baptismal vows) they were ready to begin their sessions. The Register opened the proceedings with a call to honour their outstanding debts, which turned out to mean completing the gifts promised at the last meeting to the cousin and guest. Nicholas, having progressed from cousin and guest to Practitioner and Compositor, was now as Register in effect requesting the gifts long owing to him in his initial role.

The Learner was the first to offer a story drawn from the wardrobe of apparel and household furnishings of which she had charge. Because in the earlier (1632) session Patient (Anna) was said to have charge of the 'wardrobe of sobriety', she looks the likelier candidate to have been the Learner. Her story provided the title given to the whole dialogue, for the garment she produced from her wardrobe was a winding sheet. No one doubted the value of keeping people mindful of death; Christians were not alone in displaying such reminders. John, however, questioned whether such a *memento mori* could have a proper public role as opposed to one of private contemplation at home. His comment offered Anna opportunity to cite the women of the Isle of Man, who were said to wear their winding sheets as an outer garment whenever they appeared in public.

Mention of the Isle of Man brought in Nicholas, who seized the opportunity to launch a lengthy digression on the supposed virtues of the Manx way of life, in the course of which he announced that were he free to choose he would be inclined to go and live there. The source of his utopian picture was John Speed, who in turn took his account from William Camden's *Britannia*.[87] What appealed to Nicholas first and foremost was that lawsuits were kept to a minimum and quickly resolved with no charge for legal services. On that point John added that anyone who had had experience of lawsuits in England, as we know he certainly had had, would reckon this 'a high point of Happiness' as long as justice was carefully executed. Not only was there no 'malignitie of Lawing' but no robbery, theft or licentious living either because effective 'Rule & Ciuil Discipline' allowed everyone to live in peace and security. Moreover, religion was followed with greater sincerity than in most other places, though of course not as perfectly as it should be. People reverenced and respected their ministers and attended divine service 'without Diuision in the Church, or innovation in the Common-wealth'. Nor were there any beggars; the poor were taken care of so that they did not need to beg from door to door. As Nicholas exclaimed with evident fervour, 'Neither Lawyers, nor Beggars, nor Malefactors, where will you find mee such another state?' To which virtues was added, of course, the wearing of their winding sheets by the women of Man.[88]

Mary, as the chief bookbinder at Little Gidding, was the likeliest Apprentice, for she was the one who could be said to have a trade. In the wake of Nicholas's utopian vision of the Isle of Man, she reverted to the winding sheet theme with her own story about Emperor Maximilian I, who always had his coffin carried about with him, and his father Frederick III, who declared that the most important subject a man could contemplate was the making of a happy departure out of this world. Mary, of course, had led the earlier discussion of Charles V and she must have regarded Imperial history as her special preserve for at one point her sister reproached her for presuming to be 'an Emperors Scholler'.[89] She was hardly alone in her interest and knowledge, however, as the rest of the group joined in the discussion. The remainder of the dialogue thus became a series of accounts of various emperors and kings who demonstrated during their reigns that humility and piety were far superior in value and effectiveness to aggression and confrontation. The participants drew material from de Thou, Pasquier, Baronius and de Serres and their comments ranged from the Crusades and the value or lack of it of religious wars to the piety of the Normans before the battle of Hastings that enabled them to triumph. Edifying deathbed scenes of King Conrad I of Franconia (d. 918) and Emperor/Saint Henry II (d. 1024) and his equally saintly wife Kunegunde (d. 1033 or 1039)[90] brought the group back to the Winding Sheet theme from which they tended to digress into another favourite theme with stories of those in positions of power who denounced worldliness. King Charles I earned particular praise 'as he seemes no lesse a Prince in the Church then in the Realme', and 'the good Estate both of Church & Common wealth, as farre as reason can conceiue wholly depend on his safetie & welfare & is maintained in the Flourishing Condition, which wee enioy, chiefly by his Pietie and iustice'.[91] These were, of course, the years during which the family was producing elaborate Harmonies for the king. They were also the years during which England had flourished because the king had wisely avoided entanglement in the Thirty Years War on the Continent.

This session, which must have taken considerable time to complete, marked the last such recorded meeting of these discussion groups that had formed so significant a part of the Little Gidding educational programme. The diminished numbers involved in this last effort signaled not only the actual or imminent departure of some of those previously resident at Gidding but also suggested in the praise accorded to King Charles the new preoccupation with the rewarding but also demanding task of creating Harmonies.

While she was hardly likely to have been among the potential Little Academy participants, Bathsheba certainly added her own disruptive tactics to whatever difficulties others' 'Demeritts' created. In 1635 or 1636, when her mother-in-law was no longer there to calm her, came another crisis, this time over John's decision to put young John, now five or six, into breeches, a sign that he was past the dresses of babyhood and the predominant influence of women.[92] Bathsheba strongly objected, insisting that he was as yet too young for this step. She accused Nicholas of encouraging John to make this move despite her entreaties to delay it. By this stage she was ready to see his diabolical hand behind anything to which she objected.[93] He said nothing at the time in answer to her tirade but later composed a letter, which he then tried to read to her with John present. It was a device he favoured but not one suited to Bathsheba, who wanted a chance to vent her anger, not to cool it with a written analysis. She was too worked up to register Nicholas's avowal that he would have supported her had he been given any inkling of her strong objections. Any good that that might have done, however, would doubtless have vanished when he then reiterated the scriptural injunctions to wifely obedience and insisted that John was a wise and loving father and she had no right to hinder his plans. Not only would her defiance risk damage to the children, he told her, but bring 'Greife and discontent to your selfe which in this and all other regards ariseth meerely from your being Contentious and not obeying the Truth'. For John, Nicholas could only counsel prayer and patience, advising him to make whatever concessions he appropriately could but on no account to abdicate the authority that was legitimately his.[94]

Her festering discontent reached a dramatic climax in the last year of Nicholas's life. The first outburst she directed not only at Nicholas but also at Mary Collet Ferrar. From John's apologetic letter to his brother we learn that it revolved around a plan, to which Bathsheba objected strenuously, to alter rooms in the Little Gidding house. She apparently believed that John had rights in the house that he could have exercised to block the proposal. From her point of view his failure to do so was yet another galling display of his deference to Nicholas. John's response confirmed her interpretation, for he asked Nicholas to make very clear to Bathsheba what she had long known but conveniently chosen to ignore, namely that their mother had left the estate to Nicholas for life and only thereafter to John. In Nicholas's lifetime John was there only on sufferance and wholly dependent on Nicholas's generosity, a situation with which he, John, was fully satisfied.[95]

After such a reminder one can hardly wonder that Bathsheba subsequently reacted even more strongly to what she regarded as a denial of her rights in the old London house, which may have been part of her marriage settlement. She believed that her widowed mother-in-law, whom she had always regarded as her friend, had intended to protect Bathsheba's rights and that she had instructed John and Nicholas accordingly. Now, three years after her death the two of them were pressuring Bathsheba to accept some sort of substitute arrangement that she regarded as a betrayal of her interests and their mother's trust. Her anger comes across clearly in a letter to her brother Henry in London describing the confrontation and asking advice from him and their cousin, Mr. Smith.

> Then Saith Nicholas we will haue Some of our descires though we Can not haue all Whether mr Smith or Shee will or noe For Saith hee She nor mr Smith hath nothing to doe with it while my husband liveth For Saith Nicholas may not a man doe with his owne what he listeth without asking his wifes good will for what power hath the wife of any thinge whilest her husband doth Liue not the Cote of[f] my Backe is not myne owne but my husbands he Saith. . .pray beeseich mr Smith him to write me a letter in private what I shall doe to with stand them For my husband hath taken a great Spleane against me because I did not give Consent to there doing without asking your leaue Soe how I shall live wth him heare after god knows

There is no certainty that the letter reached its intended recipients. The copy in the Ferrar Papers is in the handwriting of John, who intercepted it from the servants to whom Bathsheba had entrusted it. If, having made his copy, John then sent the letter on, we do not know nor do we know if either Henry or Cousin Smith responded. Help was at hand, however, from another source, the Grim Reaper himself, for Bathsheba went on to report, not without a certain satisfaction, that Nicholas had fallen ill. Six months later his life ended and so did her disruptions. However much Bathsheba was or was not responsible for disaffection and difficulties during these years (and they could hardly have been due to her alone), her unwilling presence at Gidding surely served as a reminder of how important consent was in the building of a successful engine of example and reform.

The missionary zeal with which Nicholas Ferrar and the family had started out in the early 1630s thus had had to confront disaffection within its own ranks as well as the realities of a world unprepared to heed its message or follow its example. The Ferrars did provide an example though not in the form they had envisioned. The pattern that later generations indeed admired and adapted did not have temperance as its end but voluntarism as its means. The possibilities of the voluntary society as an instrument for the revival of piety and the reformation of manners remained for those who knew of Little Gidding to rediscover and implement in subsequent generations.

6

Harmonies Royal:
'Rarities in their Kind'[1]

While disappointment and discord from time to time hampered the Ferrars' efforts to practice and promote their programme of temperance, an earlier disappointment turned quite unexpectedly into a dazzling opportunity to reach a far more exalted audience than they could ever have anticipated. This transformation involved the gospel harmonies* they had first created for use in the family's devotions. They had subsequently hoped, as we have seen, to put out a published harmony and thereby widen its circle of influence but had abandoned that hope when Johan Hiud in 1632 published a version of his own.

Following this disappointment over publication the family continued to make harmonies as demonstrated in a letter from Arthur Woodnoth

---

* There are thirteen complete harmonies. Nine of these are harmonies of the four gospels and include those in Harvard's Houghton Library (*c.* 1630), in the Bodleian Library at Oxford (1631), in the British Library the Royal Harmony made for King Charles I (1635), in Princeton in the Cotsen Library (1635), in the British Library the harmony that had belonged to the Collet family (1637), in Hatfield House the harmony belonging to Lord Salisbury (1637), in Somerley the harmony belonging to Lord Normanton (1640), at Ickworth that belonging earlier to the Hervey family and now to the National Trust (1640), and in private possession one belonging earlier to the Heming family (1640). There are in addition the harmony made of Kings and Chronicles at the request of Charles I in the British Library (1637), a volume of Acts and Revelation also in the British Library that is not in fact a harmony of those books but simply an illustrated version, made for the king probably *c.* 1638, a harmony of the Pentateuch presented to Archbishop Laud in the library of St John's College, Oxford (1640) and another Pentateuch harmony made for Prince Charles and now in the Royal Library, Windsor (1642). There are in addition a partial plan for the harmony of Kings and Chronicles (FP 1057) and a bundle of materials for another Pentateuch harmony (FP 1892a) both in the Ferrar Papers at Magdalene College, Cambridge.

to Ferrar in the following April.[2] Woodnoth there explained that he was sending some 'letters or characters' that might be useful and also a pot of printer's ink and a leather ball with which to apply it to the letters. He supplied directions for doing this and then applying the letters to the prepared paper. Such stamped letters could have substituted neatly for the handwritten marginal indicators of source gospels and were used in later harmonies. Given the importance John Ferrar attached to keeping 'hands and minds' active in 'what was good and useful', it is not surprising that the work continued though perhaps at a diminished pace.[3]

Even if family members continued making harmonies, however, they were by the end of 1632 chiefly occupied with that experiment in temperance that we have considered in the previous chapter. While the more committed of the Ferrars were continuing this regime in the summer of 1633, King Charles undertook at last a journey to Scotland for his long-postponed coronation as King of Scots. It proved a fateful journey for the Ferrars, for on the way north he stayed with the Earl of Westmoreland at Apethorpe and, learning that Little Gidding was nearby, the king dispatched a courtier with a royal request to borrow their harmony, about which 'rare jewel' he had heard.

His request indicates that by this time Gidding harmonies were known in court circles. How had this happened? We know that friends and family who over the years came to visit Gidding often participated in the daily devotions and perhaps even watched the nieces at work on the harmonies. Clerical friends with court connections like John Cosin and Francis White might have seen this for themselves, or, failing that, have heard from their friends in Ferrar's network enthusiastic descriptions of the harmonies. They as royal chaplains had access to both Archbishop Laud and the king to whom they could have passed on accounts of these unusual books. The king might possibly have heard of them earlier from Bishop John Williams, Little Gidding's diocesan and another longtime Ferrar family friend, though by 1633 Williams no longer enjoyed royal favour.[4] George Herbert, who had received a harmony in October 1631 and was a kinsman of the courtier Earl of Pembroke, was a more likely source. Had Herbert brought his harmony from Bemerton to show to the Pembrokes at Wilton, for example,[5] Pembroke, who shared the king's interest in painting, might well have spoken of it to the king and reminded him of it while he was with him on the progress to Scotland.[6]

Despite the family's protestations that the harmony they were using (now at Harvard) was not worthy of a royal reader, the king's messenger insisted that his master would take no denial of his request and they duly handed over the book. Having kept it for some months and not only studied it but carefully annotated it, Charles eventually agreed to return it but only on condition that the family make one for him. It was this royal request that transformed the earlier disappointment into a dazzling opportunity. It had an impact on the family and on the making of harmonies comparable to the impact of Cornaro and Lessius on the practice of temperance and of Herbert on the introduction of night vigils.

To measure and compare that impact requires consideration in some detail of the role that the making of harmonies played in the Gidding household and how it differed from other family projects. Unlike temperance and night vigils it did not represent an addition to but rather an outgrowth and intensification of established practice; making and using a harmony had been among the earliest collective tasks that Ferrar initiated as part of the regular household routine. Moreover, whilst it played a significant role in fostering education, co-operation and a sense of community among the nieces, there was no suggestion then or later that participants should give oral or written consent in order to take part as they did in the Little Academy or the temperance diet or the night vigils. Perhaps willingness could safely be assumed because the older nieces at that early stage of the household's establishment would have welcomed the opportunity it offered not only for the pleasure of the work itself but for the approval of their uncle. The cutting and pasting had, of course, to be carefully and accurately done, but the work offered a social setting with some flexibility in times of starting and stopping and so put less immediate pressure on its participants in the midst of what was otherwise a highly structured day. Moreover, the putting together of words and pictures involved a variety of tasks for both hands and minds and offered at least some scope for individual initiative and collective consultation. In contrast the Little Academy was more formally focused and structured, requiring its participants to prepare information, then present and discuss their own and others' contributions. They had also as an added pressure to try to live up to the names they had been given. The lapses the Academy suffered and the difficulties of reviving it suggest that at least some of its participants found these demands hard to sustain. By the same token the nightly vigils and the temperate diet demanded 'mortification', real physical sacrifices in the form of going without sleep or food. At least until the king's request for a harmony reached them, members of the family might well have seen 'scissors work' on the harmonies as a more relaxed and flexible aspect of their life together than their more strenuous projects to provide 'patterns' for their age.

When he returned the borrowed harmony, the king claimed to have read it daily and his marginal notes lend credence to that claim. He also expressed a 'great good liking of it in all kinds',[7] perhaps a sign of his particular approval of the Ferrars' ability to combine text and pictures. Such a response to what was after all a very basic harmony for family use inspired the pedagogue in Ferrar to create for the king an expanded version whose combination of full scriptural text correlated with carefully selected and arranged pictures he could study in a variety of ways. Pictures in bibles, of course, were controversial for some of the king's subjects who saw such graven images as idolatrous. After a virtual disappearance of pictures in editions of the Geneva Bible of the later sixteenth and early seventeenth centuries, however, they were enjoying, with the support of a king and archbishop sympathetic to the visual arts, a revival in volumes of the new Authorised Version in the late 1620s and 1630s.[8] The prints in these bibles, however, unlike those in the Ferrar harmonies, were 'optional extras', separate sheets selected by the purchaser and interleaved with the pages of text at the time of binding rather than integrated with the text at the time of printing. The Ferrars, assembling their harmonies by hand out of verses cut from previously printed bibles, could more effectively integrate text and pictures on their pages. Indeed they could combine images to create new pictures as they did with Foxe's martyrs; they could also include more pictures than the biblical text strictly justified.[9] Their technique allowed them the freedom to indulge their own as well as their monarch's enthusiasm for pictures. They could produce only a very limited number of books but that, of course, was not a problem in the royal context where quality rather than quantity was paramount.

Whilst the Ferrars' cut-and-paste technique allowed a closer co-ordination of picture with text than interleaving, there remained three problems critical for harmonising the texts themselves. One of these was chronology, establishing a unified time sequence for the new narrative of Christ's life compiled out of four different stories each with its own timeline. Another was reconciling variations in accounts of the same episode in the four gospel sources. The third was the need to retain every word of Holy Writ while avoiding a redundancy that would hinder the narrative flow. The king's request for a gospel harmony stimulated Ferrar to address all these problems in new ways that clarified and cross-referenced the text. The result of this new approach was not simply a more skilfully made and costly replica of the one King Charles had borrowed. Instead Ferrar produced an illustrated harmony with a new format that would, as its introductory 'Advertizement' declared, enable the king even to devise his own syntheses out of variations in the gospel versions, surely an appealing prospect for his keen royal reader.

Ferrar adapted some of the new tools he added to the old harmony format from Jansen's and Buisson's Latin harmonies, a debt he acknowledged. He also, however, borrowed from Hiud's and Henry Garthwait's English ones without any explicit acknowledgment.[10] Robert Mapletoft, whom we have already encountered as a participant in the temperance diet and as bearer of Ferrar's counsel to his ailing brother Joshua, had procured Garthwait's book at Ferrar's request and sent it to him soon after it appeared.[11] That book was not the only additional source Ferrar wished to consult, for he also set Mapletoft as well as Edward Wallis, another Cambridge friend, to searching college libraries for other harmonies, though if he made use of any information they supplied, he never acknowledged it. That he made the request, however, remains a measure of the system and seriousness he brought to the making of a new style of harmony for the king.[12]

These new tools enabled him to enlarge the scope of the king's harmony and address the three harmonising problems of chronology, variant versions of gospel stories and the need to combine a composite narrative with retaining every word of gospel text. Having mastered them himself he had then to explain these new techniques to those family members responsible for the actual scissors work, lessons that would have enlarged their understanding but at the same time made their task more complex and demanding. The need for speed produced additional pressure. Though there was no explicit timetable the family would not have wished to keep the king waiting for his book any longer than necessary.

The splendid volume they produced (now in the British Library) bears the date 1635 and was presented to the king by Archbishop Laud and Dr John Cosin in May 1636.[13] It was the most notable of a cluster of harmonies the Ferrars made between 1635 and 1637 but was singular in utilising the most complete array of Ferrar's new tools. The family clearly spared no pains or expense to produce a book worthy of its recipient.[14] For visual enhancement there were in addition to abundant illustrations gilding, coloured inks, and a handsome binding.[15] The illustrations also introduced a greater emphasis on typology, as the title page promised.[16]. This linking of Old Testament figures and stories with New Testament episodes from the life of Christ was a long established way of portraying Christ as the fulfillment of earlier prophecies. Ferrar evidently wanted to add this dimension to the harmony and the theme continued in later harmonies. Ferrar added an elaborate title page and a lengthy 'Advertizement' to explain his new methods and terminology.

A handwritten table of contents headed 'Order of Chapters' listed the standard Jansenian 150 chapters, which were both numbered and titled, with those source gospels included in each chapter indicated in different coloured inks. The corresponding chapter headings within the text were also handwritten and their titles showed occasional minor variations from those given in the 'Order of Chapters'.[17]

Two of the new devices, the 'Comparison' and 'Composition', dealt specifically with those episodes within a given Chapter that appeared in more than one gospel in variant forms. Both testified to Ferrar's pedagogical care to encourage the active reading the king had demonstrated in his earlier annotations. The 'Comparison' set out in parallel columns each gospel's version of a particular episode to facilitate comparison whilst the 'Composition' created a synthesis, which within its continuous text also bore small printed letters (M/Mr/L/J) indicating the particular gospel sources taken from the 'Comparison's columns. As the 'Advertizement' explained, this format would invite a reader to make his own comparisons and create his own compositions.

The 'Collection', the third component of Ferrar's new format, provided in its 'Context' and 'Supplement' a larger synthesis, 'the whole EVANGELICAL HISTORIE'.[18] It presented the essential narrative in the 'Context' with those relevant passages not included in it added in the 'Supplement' in a different typeface. A reader could either follow a continuous synoptic story by reading the black letter passages of the 'Context' or read any individual gospel by following the passages in either 'Context' or 'Supplement' marked by the letter indicating that gospel. Besides the A/B/C/D markers (for Matthew, Mark, Luke, and John respectively) in different coloured inks were linking phrases to show the reader how to move between 'Context' and 'Supplement' to follow a single gospel. For this elaborate system of Collection, Comparison and Composition, together with explanatory 'Annotations' added at various points to the text Ferrar acknowledged his debt to Buisson, 'the Kings Professor of Diuinitie at Doway', who had devised it about 1570. He used it to transform the king's harmony from a source book for reading aloud to a book for an individual reader and serious student, a substantial leap beyond the beginnings discernible in the Bodleian harmony.

Other harmonies made during these years continued this pattern in modified form. They include the harmony now in the Cotsen Children's Library at Princeton, another in the British Library (the volume that eventually passed from John Collet (d. 1713) to the descendants of Joshua Mapletoft)[19] and a third at Hatfield House.[20] The bibles cut up to provide the components for the royal harmony left the family with a considerable supply of printed text that the nieces, now familiar with their uncle's new approach, could turn into additional harmonies. How much any of them grasped of the possibilities of that new approach or attempted to use it to make their own syntheses of variant episodes is a tantalising point on which only conjecture is possible. Mary Collet Ferrar, involved as she had earlier been in the publication project and in the binding and preservation of later harmonies, was the likeliest to have explored the possibilities to any depth.

Whilst the three volumes that were made contemporaneously with or shortly after the king's harmony no longer included separate 'Comparison' and 'Composition' sections, they did retain the key organisational features of 'Context' and 'Supplement' set in different typefaces. They contained also the 'Advertizement' that explained how to take advantage of the versatility which the new structure made possible and a title page that provided a brief methodological summary in itself:

> The Actions Doctrine and other Passadges Touching Our Lorde and Saviour Jesus Christ as they are related by the Foure Evangelists Reduced into one Complete Body of History wherein that which is Severally Related by Them is Digested into Order and that which is Joyntly by All or any of them is Extracted into one cleare Context by way of Collection Yett soe as whatever is Omitted in the Context is Inserted by way of Supplement in another Point in such Manner as all the Foure Evangelists may be Reade Severally from First to Last.

In place of the omitted 'Comparison' and 'Composition' was simply an explanation of how the 'Context' and 'Supplement' layout would enable the reader to follow either the continuous narrative of the basic 'Evangelicall harmony' or read a single gospel. In these volumes Ferrar aimed to retain the flexibility of the king's harmony though economizing by omitting the additional comparative apparatus.

In all these harmonies, including that of the king there was an extraordinary and puzzling change to the text that only Ferrar himself could have presumed to make. He took the material that Jansen and Ferrar himself in the first two Little Gidding harmonies had included in a single chapter numbered 44 and entitled 'The Leaper [*i.e.* Leper] Cleansed' and divided it into two widely separated chapters. This curious rearrangement, which added a chapter to the total, produced as a consequence a mismatch between the chapters as listed in the table of contents and the actual numbering and headings of chapters in the text.[21] This change became the more striking and also the more entrenched because the chapter lists in the three other volumes in this group were printed in contrast to the handwritten one in the king's book. At some point in 1635 Ferrar had evidently decided that the arrangement of chapters was sufficiently fixed to justify a printed version, yet, very curiously, during that same period he changed the text in a way that made the new printed version incorrect. Surviving documents offered no comment on this contradictory situation. Perhaps it reflected the stresses within the family that also impeded efforts to revive the Little Academy, but that possibility remains entirely conjectural. Whatever the reason, the Ferrars resorted, instead of a reprinting, to various more or less awkward interpolations to correct the discrepancy.[22]

For whom then were these new model harmonies intended? Royal patronage offered access to a promising audience of the wealthy and powerful whose acquisition of a harmony would not only fulfill the Ferrars' missionary hopes but also perhaps replenish their purse. They of course presented their harmonies to the king as gifts, but they were expensive presents and the family might well have hoped to recoup their costs by selling other harmonies to some of the courtiers and churchmen who saw and admired the royal volumes. Lord Wharton fulfilled those hopes when, having seen the royal harmony of Kings and Chronicles, he asked to have a less costly one made for him. That he chose this harmony of political/historical books is interesting, for while Wharton shared the king's interest in art, he most definitely did not share his ecclesiastical and political views.[23] John Ferrar, writing in 1641 to Isaac Basire, declared that while the king's harmony of Kings and Chronicles had cost the family over £100, Lord Wharton had readily handed over the £37 they had requested for his.[24] If the 'Kings-Concordance', as John labeled it, cost over £100 to produce, the earlier and more elaborate gospel harmony for the king must have set them back considerably more. The three harmonies incorporating many of the features developed for the king's book, therefore, might well have been made in hope of recovering some of that cost.

The Cotsen harmony, the only specifically dated one of this group (1635), probably fulfilled this hope, for it contains an extensive statement of its provenance and its early possession by the Cotton family, one branch of which lived nearby at Steeple Gidding.[25] The Collet harmony, tentatively dated 1636, remained within the family; its bookplate bears the name of 'Johannes Collet' (f. [A]), son of Thomas Collet. Thomas's sister Mary Collet Ferrar bound the book herself and was said to have been its original possessor. Whether she was the original possessor in the sense that the book was intended for her from the start, however, we cannot be sure. The family might have hoped initially to offer it to a patron who unfortunately never appeared. Did Mary then take it over by default and bind it for herself in orange vellum rather than the grander morocco or velvet of presentation copies? She presumably took it with her when she went in 1658 to live with her brother Thomas in Highgate.[26] At or perhaps even before her death in 1680 she gave it to his son John Collet, who in turn bequeathed it in 1713 to his cousin Elizabeth Kestian, who by January 1716 had left it to another cousin, Dr John Mapletoft, in whose family it remained till it was acquired by the British Museum in 1894.[27] By that time it had become a family treasure but had perhaps been prepared in the hope of finding an outside purchaser like the Cottons or Lord Wharton.

The handsome volume now at Hatfield House is bound in purple velvet and dated 1640. It certainly looks sufficiently elegant for royal presentation, but the claim that it was made for Prince James in 1640 is purely conjectural and if true would hardly have helped replenish the family coffers. The prince was indeed present in 1640 when his brother received a polyglot harmony from young Nicholas Ferrar and was said then to have begged for a harmony of his own.[28] This could have been the one James eventually received but that it was specifically made for him in 1640 is doubtful. With its Context and Supplement format it is much more like the earlier Cotsen and Collet harmonies than those other harmonies that bear a 1640 date. It could have been made several years earlier along with the Cotsen and Collet harmonies and either left unbound until 1640 or given its velvet binding earlier in hopes of attracting a generous patron.[29] If James did indeed receive the book, we have no idea what happened to it in the turbulent years after 1640 before the Cecils acquired it at the beginning of the eighteenth century.

Another group of three gospel harmonies, all bearing the date 1640 were completed after the death of Ferrar in 1637. One of these was the work of Nicholas Ferrar III and will receive separate consideration later. Another, now at Ickworth, contains the statement that it was made by 12-year-old Virginia Ferrar.[30] Like Lord Wharton's volume, it came into the hands of an eminent family though no record documents how it moved from the Ferrars to the 'Thomas iermine' whose name appears on the final folio of the book.[31] The Herveys, its subsequent owners, in turn must have acquired it before Isabella Hervey's death in 1665 because the names of Thomas and Isabella appear at the bottom of an early page.[32] The third of the volumes descended within the family from the Solomon Mapletofts (Judith Collet) to the Hemings.[33]

By the time the family came to make the Ickworth and Heming harmonies they followed a significantly simpler format than those they had made in the middle of the decade. It may well represent the absence of Nicholas's guiding hand and the different interests of his nephew Nicholas, who took over leadership of the work. The makers of these 1640 harmonies have jettisoned not only the separate 'Comparison' and 'Composition' sections of the king's book but also the 'Supplement' and 'Context', which in the earlier three continued to furnish a reader with reasonably accessible material for comparisons. Instead these later volumes presented simply 'one Compleat body of History wherein that which is severally related by all of them is digested into Order'. They reverted in effect to the single text that we find in the Harvard and Bodleian versions. The simplification might thus also signify that these harmonies were intended for family use, perhaps primarily for reading aloud, as the earliest harmonies had been.

The simplified format might also reflect new demands on the family's time and skill that required them to add to the familiar task of making gospel harmonies the more demanding one of creating harmonies of other biblical texts. When Laud and Cosin presented the king's gospel harmony to him in May 1636, Charles had wondered aloud whether the Ferrars would make him a harmony of the books of Kings and Chronicles.[34] He read them frequently, he declared, and had found difficulties in reconciling some passages. He would like a harmony of them that would provide, like the gospel harmony, both a continuous narrative and a way to read each book separately.[35] As Ferrar's account of the last revival of the Little Academy lamented, the numbers available for participation in that project and presumably others as well had dropped substantially.[36] The king's request, tantamount to a command, meant that Ferrar must accomplish this task with a reduced number of experienced scissors-wielders.

If the king's first request had produced a new and complex format for his gospel harmony, this second required the application of that model to an entirely new subject. I have found no precedents for such a harmony comparable to the numerous gospel harmonies that had been available to Ferrar as models for the earlier project. In any case, the king obviously liked the format Ferrar had developed of a continuous narrative that also preserved the identity of its component parts. Hence Ferrar had to start by devising his own 'Collection' for these texts. Fortunately, he could by this time enlist the help of his nephews, John's son Nicholas and Ferrar Collet, now in their late teens, for this task was altogether more intellectually demanding than the 'scissors' work of the womenfolk. Certainly the draft preserved in the Ferrar Papers, which was clearly the guide for the finished

Chapter XV (Christ's Fast and Temptation) from the harmony made for King Charles showing the 'Comparison', 'Composition' and 'Collection', the latter with its two different typefaces for the 'Context' and 'Supplement'. Copyright The British Library Board: Shelfmark C.23.e.4..

work, looks like a co-operative effort and is written in several different hands.[37] It included an introductory apology for any shortcomings, errors, omissions and unexplained transpositions of passages, the reasons for which an informed reader would readily understand. The strength of these disclaimers along with mention of limitations of space and time that had restricted the scope of the referencing system suggests that Ferrar was very conscious that he had had to do a rushed job.

What passages in this complex history of turbulence, rebellion and invasion King Charles found difficult to reconcile we could wish he had specified, as we could also wish to know what attracted Lord Wharton to this subject. The books were harmonised in a 'Context' narrative in Roman letters, accompanied by a 'Supplement' in black letter of passages not included in the basic narrative, with marginal capitals to indicate sources of the text passages. Such an arrangement fulfilled the king's request and supplied the necessary cross-references by means of three 'Tables', the first listing the titles of the 203 chapters, the second showing which passages appeared in Kings alone, which in Chronicles alone and which in both Kings and Chronicles, and the third showing where every chapter of all of the texts could be found in the collected work. The finished volume in the British Library[38] followed the draft carefully and included the three tables and directions for reading the book either as a continuous narrative or in its several components. It also contained the draft's apology for its manifold imperfections, it having not attained

> the measure of that Perfection which is requisite for things intended to the service & satisfaction of Great & Excellent DIGNITIES & especially of SUPREME MAJESTIE.

As that deferential note suggests, the Ferrars' position as harmony-makers to the king linked them increasingly not only to Charles's spiritual life but also and more controversially to his and his archbishop's ecclesiastical policies, a connection that would leave Little Gidding vulnerable to attack when 'Schism, Faction, and Jealousie [did] kindle that Fire, which destroyed both Church and State'.[39]

As the king's and Laud's attempt to force a new Prayer Book on the Scottish church set that fire alight, the Ferrars, whether by royal request or on their own prescient initiative, created a version of the book of Acts and the Apocalypse.[40] Though it was yet another new subject, this volume was not a 'harmony' at all but simply illustrated texts of these two books. Mary and Anna Collet could in all likelihood have done such 'handy work of women' without learned oversight. Its handsome binding and large and well-arranged prints suggest that it too was destined for the king though the only indirect evidence is Robert Woodforde's report of having seen in the king's bedchamber in 1638 volumes of the four gospels and of the Acts and the Apocalypse.[41] Some of the prints in this volume were part of a series of illustrations of Acts that created a stir in Scotland in 1638 and of which Walter Balcanquall the following year claimed, not altogether plausibly, that the king was ignorant.[42]

In addition to harmonising Kings and Chronicles, Ferrar himself, though under considerable stress from domestic difficulties that included his own illness as well as Bathsheba's outbursts, nevertheless launched yet another different type of harmony that he did not live to see in finished form. This was a harmony of the Pentateuch, 'The Whole Law of God. . .' in a quite different format from those of the gospels and Kings and Chronicles. Gone were 'Context' and 'Supplement' and the need to include every single biblical word or indeed to construct any narrative at all. This was a topical rather than a historical harmony and the 'law' contained in the books was 'Methodically Distributed into Three great Classes Morall Ceremoniall & Polyticall'. This was not an original classification for these categories formed the traditional framework for discussions of the applicability of the Mosaic laws to a Christian society, including of course the vexed question of what constituted idolatry. Within this familiar framework Ferrar applied his harmonising technique to organise (and illustrate) within those three classes the texts fundamental to such debates. An unbound set of red-ruled folio pages, with their bits of heading, text, and pictures, some pasted in, more lying loose, exists in the Ferrar Papers [1852]. Its ruled pages certainly have a sufficiently unfinished look to qualify as the draft version John Ferrar said had been made in his brother's lifetime, despite the presence with them of an obviously later title page bearing the date 1641.[43] Archbishop Laud received a finished volume that followed this pattern and was bound in the gold-tooled velvet of presentation copies. It was probably a gift given to him when he brought young Nicholas and his father to the king and the Prince of Wales in 1940 for the presentation of their polyglot harmonies.[44] More of the cuttings and pictures have fallen out than is the case with most of the other harmonies, evidence perhaps of the greater haste involved when several projects were underway at once.

Why did the elder Nicholas choose this subject? Did it seem a logical outgrowth of the 'History of the Israelites'? Could a section on 'Ceremoniall Law' have reflected concern with the deepening discord aroused by Laud's efforts to enforce ritual conformity? Certainly among its seventy-four headings was one entitled 'Of the Preists and their Vestements For Glory and for Beauty'.[45] Would relating points of 'Politicall Law' back to the 'Moral Law' of the Ten Commandments have shed light on 'idolatry' as well as the duties of subjects to their rulers? Did Archbishop Laud request the subject or did Ferrar himself choose it because he thought it of particular value and interest to Laud? Answers to such questions can only be conjectural, but whatever the reasons behind the initial choice of subject and recipient, the family subsequently made another on a far grander scale and for a royal recipient. Perhaps Prince Charles had seen Laud's volume at the presentations in 1640 and expressed a wish to have one like it.[46] Without such a royal wish it is difficult to explain why, in difficult circumstances, the family took on the task of preparing another volume far more elaborate than the one prepared for Laud.[47] Perhaps for John Ferrar it was both a testament of loyalty and a way in those turbulent times to keep hands and minds occupied. The king was shown the work in progress when, accompanied by Prince Charles and the Palsgrave, he made his first visit to Gidding in March 1642 on his way north to rally his supporters for the looming civil war.[48]

This grand royal Pentateuch followed generally the pattern of the 1640 volume and the draft version in the Ferrar Papers in dividing the 'Whole Law' into 'Moral', 'Ceremonial', and 'Political' sections. There were, however, some significant differences, the most interesting of which was a much greater emphasis on typology than in Laud's volume. Typology had also been part of the gospel harmonies. Here, however, in addition to the juxtaposition of appropriate Old and New Testament passages, there were also lengthy manuscript sections copied from the works of Thomas Jackson.[49] The final section taken from Jackson dealt with more recent persecutions of the Jews in western Europe, claiming that these were all part of the divine plan and foretold in the Mosaic prophecies.[50] Perhaps this topic especially interested Ferrar Collet, now at Peterhouse or was a tribute to the recently deceased Jackson, who had authorised the belated publication of Nicholas Ferrar's translation of Valdes. We have no other evidence besides these excerpts, however, that the Ferrars even in those turbulent times linked typology to predictions of the apocalypse.

After Ferrar's death in December 1637 his nephew Nicholas, whom he had groomed for leadership of Little Gidding, had taken increasing charge of harmony-making though his father, as his manuscript interpolations and correspondence document, continued to play an active role. In these years the family produced the two 1640 gospel harmonies in the new truncated format.[51] A third gospel harmony with that same date, however, reflected the different interests of the younger Nicholas, interests that his uncle had carefully cultivated. He created it for the Prince of Wales to fulfill an earlier promise to make him a harmony of his own. He presented it in person to the prince in 1640. It represented a bridge between the format of the earlier royal harmony and young Nicholas's later polyglot works, which were not harmonies at all but parallel translations. It was an elaborate four-language harmony that revived some of the comparative apparatus used in the king's gospel harmony of 1635, evidence of his understanding of his uncle's methods and purposes. The work is entitled, doubly appropriately, *Monotessaron*, and presents the texts of the four gospels in four languages: Latin, French, English, and Italian.[52] It is a handsome volume, its green velvet binding with gold tooling appropriate for royalty and its parallel columns in the four languages matching verse for verse, a format that offers both spiritual instruction and a language tutorial. The text in these columns provided a continuous narrative labelled the 'Collection' though it was not divided, as were 'Collections' in earlier harmonies, into a 'Context' and 'Supplement'. Source gospels were indicated in coloured letters with chapter numbers added. At the bottom of most pages, in a larger Roman typeface, was the 'Composition' in Latin. In it every word of every gospel was woven into a continuous history, with small letters within the running text to indicate the sources of passages.[53] This elaborate system of letters revived the apparatus borrowed from Jansen and Buisson to provide an equivalent to the 'Comparison' and 'Composition' unique to the royal harmony of 1635. Young Nicholas also incorporated headings like those used earlier in the Collet and Hatfield harmonies to group the narrative chapters by specified years of Christ's ministry. He even added in manuscript an explanation of the discrepancy between Mark's and Luke's versions of Christ's instructions to his apostles when he sent them out to preach.[54]

It was a handsome gift to the prince but its presentation also gave young Nicholas the opportunity personally to offer to the king a gift that demonstrated the new direction in which he proposed to turn the family's book-making efforts. His gift set out plans for two other polyglot volumes of the New Testament, one in eight languages and the other in twenty-four with interlineal translations into either Latin or English.[55] These two volumes were not harmonies in the sense of collations but rather prospectuses for future works of parallel translation. The eight-language volume declared on its title page that it would be aimed at those who wished to learn the languages, or for foreigners who wanted to learn English. Other great polyglot bibles such as the one made for the King of France did not include 'modern' languages. Young Nicholas, adding an imperial touch, justified their inclusion because the king for whom the works were intended ruled a realm whose subjects spoke more languages than did those of any other contemporary ruler. He even included translations into the Indian languages of Virginia and New England, suggesting more than a mere gesture in the direction of his father's continuing interest in North America. His premature death cut short these grand plans though his father, writing to Isaac Basire to ask help in getting bibles in exotic tongues, seems still to have cherished hopes of carrying on the work, probably with the help of his nephew Ferrar Collet.[56]

Nephew Nicholas clearly deserved his title as 'The Linguist of Little Gidding'.[57] How much his language training owed to his uncle's tutelage was, of course, never spelled out, but the claim in his epitaph that he had 'scarcely a teacher, scarcely needed one,' must be something of an exaggeration.[58] As a delicate child he had been educated at home by his uncle, who perhaps knew of the growing interest in and knowledge of Near Eastern languages that promised new insight into ancient biblical scripts. He might in consequence have steered his nephew in a direction that not only fitted his talents but was also intellectually fashionable and patronised by Archbishop Laud.[59] Had young Nicholas lived and especially had he been able to take up the king's offer to send him to university, he would probably have been increasingly drawn into these polyglot bible projects. The result would have been books of a sort quite different from the earlier harmonies, ones that might well not have included pictures and ones to which the women of the household could have contributed little. If the 'proufe book' is any measure, they would have had a pedagogical emphasis different from his uncle's and they would not have provided the sort of work for 'hearts and minds' that the earlier harmonies had done. Whether and for how long the household could have carried on making the simpler harmonies in the 1640 format alongside the new polyglot bibles is uncertain though John Ferrar's letters to Basire soliciting orders and polyglot materials suggests that he was trying to do so. Although King Charles's visit in 1642 found the family at work on the grand Pentateuch volume for Prince Charles, it was a diminished household from which several scissors-wielders had already departed and others were to follow. Not surprisingly, therefore, that Pentateuch volume was the last example of their 'new kind of printing' that the Ferrars could offer to their appreciative but increasingly beleaguered royal patron.

7

Nicholas Posthumous

Ferrar's health declined in the course of 1637, probably hastened by the austerities of diet and vigils that he had long maintained.[1] As Bathsheba reported, not without a certain Schadenfreude indicative of her attitude to the temperance diet,

> Now Nicholas is very Sick[ly] Faulen upon it and they all thinke
> he will dye For he hath soe Starved him selfe with Lussions
> [Lessius] that he hath wasted his Inward parts within[.] he Can
> not Speake ever Since Saturday.[2]

The family, however, described his death in terms reminiscent of those traditional accounts of the deaths of saints that they had read many times over. He had been ill during the spring, as Bathsheba had reported, but had recovered sufficiently to travel to London and visit Bishop Williams in the Tower.[3] During November, however, he grew weaker and took to his bed. He counselled his grieving family, admonishing them to continue in 'the good old way' he had taught them. His brother he instructed to make a fire on the place in front of the church that he had stipulated should be his grave and burn those worldly books such as *Orlando* that he had earlier collected, a personal 'bonfire of the vanities'. He had sufficient strength at the end of November to write out a denunciation of all such books as 'full of idolatry' and liable to arouse readers to 'filthy lusts, as, woe is me, I have proved in myself'; he begged God's forgiveness for this sin.[4] Then on 4 December, with the family and the local clergy kneeling round his bed in prayer, Nicholas died, at what was the very hour (1 a.m.) he had always risen to begin his vigils. In the family's eyes, 'he ended the Sabbath here upon earth to begin the everlasting [one] in heaven'.[5] His sanctity was further attested in the eyes of his devoted family by the fact that his body did not decay and his right hand, so active in God's service, was not stiffened by rigor mortis.

Ferrar had clearly hoped that Little Gidding's service to God would make it a 'light on a hill' and that his 'web of friendship' would provide a 'patterne for an adge that needs patternes'. He enjoyed mixed success in his lifetime. Though hardly a powerful beacon within the Caroline church, Little Gidding and its leader did shine sufficiently to attract the attention of at least some contemporaries. Those within the circle of friends and family of course had direct knowledge and could communicate a glowing picture of the household to their own friends and families, as the king within a loftier circle could praise the harmonies for the light they shed on biblical texts. At the other extreme were those who suspected Gidding as a place not of light but of darkness and mystery. When Nicholas on his deathbed had ordered the burning of his books of worldly plays and poems, villagers, seeing a fire near the house and knowing that Nicholas was dying, spread the rumour that he could not die before he had burnt his conjuring books.[6] Between those extremes were those whose curiosity and perhaps apprehension were piqued by rumours of crypto-Catholic practices and a sense that the family might be hiding something when they chose not to participate in the usual style of country-house entertaining.

The family had a strategy for dealing politely but firmly with those who dropped in hoping to discover what went on behind the household's closed doors. Edward Lenton was one such visitor. He came in either 1633 or early 1634 at the behest of Sir Thomas Hetley of nearby Brampton whose suspicions had been aroused by what he had heard about Gidding.[7] Lenton received the usual light refreshments, met not only Nicholas but also his mother and brother, and attended a service in the church after which Nicholas answered questions about his views on Catholicism and his churchmanship.[8] Though Lenton then murmured about leaving, he actually hoped he would be invited to stay for dinner. Nicholas instead took him at his word, ordered his horse brought for him and politely saw him on his way. Uninvited guests saw only a selection of the household's activities. Privacy had its price, however, as the family discovered when Lenton's letter was distorted and published in 1641 as *The Arminian Nunnery*.

If Ferrar and Little Gidding had detractors as well as admirers during the years preceding the civil war, who and what shaped and preserved the memory of them that was taken up in different ways by those who came later? Ferrar's published translations, despite some problems with the censors, enjoyed a circulation in the public sphere sufficient to justify reprinting. *Hygiasticon* had appeared first at the beginning of 1634 and enjoyed another printing later that year and a further edition two years after that.[9] Its message of temperance must therefore have found interested readers though one is left to wonder how many of them recognised the anonymous family cited in T. S.'s preface or themselves attempted to follow the prescribed dietary regimen. Indeed the book was again reprinted in 1678, suggesting a renewed concern over excesses of public and private indulgence. This time it had a new title page renaming it *The Temperate Man* but it otherwise retained the original format and anonymity.[10] Most seventeenth-century books on temperance simply focused on the evils of drunkenness, but there must have been at least a small audience for Gidding's different and more comprehensive approach. The translation of Valdes too enjoyed a second edition, as we have seen, but apart from that there is no evidence to show what part its emphasis on the importance of inward experience and mortification might have played in promoting contemporary piety. Ferrar's translations therefore did beam a light but one of only limited strength from the hill of Gidding to the wider world. The volume that enjoyed sustained success was one for which he played only the role of midwife, his brother Herbert's poetic masterpiece, *The Temple*.

The harmonies with their 'new kind of printing' were a unique medium and the king's interest and praise provided a strong endorsement of this aspect of the family's pattern of piety. Unfortunately the technique could produce only a small number of volumes, a serious limitation on its ability to provide a significantly wider circulation for this special beam of Gidding's light.

The translations and the harmonies by themselves could tell only a limited part of the Gidding story. More important were the biographical materials John Ferrar collected that described Ferrar's education, travels and public career in London as well as his piety and the exemplary devotional life of the family at Little Gidding. While vital to preserving details of the household's daily life, however, these materials enshrined an uncritical vision of both Nicholas and Little Gidding predicated on the assumption that the move to Gidding represented a withdrawal from the world. The family correspondence, now in Magdalene College, Cambridge, contained ample evidence of the extent to which Ferrar's ministry to the family required him to give time and energy to addressing their worldly needs, but historians did not begin to use this evidence until the twentieth century, and then still within a hagiographic context. As a result the Ferrars were detached from their seventeenth-century context and the complexity and tensions of Ferrar's 'mixt life' that Francis Turner had called the best but the hardest tended to disappear in a hagiographic haze.

Also missing in the biographical materials was the significance of Gidding as a community with its self-conscious voluntarism and aspiration to become a 'light on a hill'. Evidence of these characteristics could be found not only in the Little Academy's Story Books but also in the experience of some who had known Gidding and recollected it as a religious society. Memories of this aspect of Gidding circulated among a number of churchmen who became active in those voluntary societies that sought to promote piety, education and public morality in the late seventeenth- and eighteenth-century church. How much influence the example of Little Gidding had on the members of these voluntary societies is impossible to ascertain with certainty. It remains largely in the realm of the possible and probable; surviving sources provide no explicit comments to confirm that influence. Nevertheless a reconstruction of the networks that connected such men to each other and provided contacts through which information about Gidding could flow suggests a significant link between the community of Little Gidding and these later developments among 'voluntary Anglicans'.[11] Both these aspects, the biographical and the organisational, are part of the posthumous legacy of Nicholas Ferrar to a detailed consideration of which I shall now turn.

After Ferrar's death in 1637 the subsequent turmoil of civil war disrupted, at least temporarily, the household he had created. By the 1650s, however, the family's situation had stabilised sufficiently to allow John Ferrar to launch his efforts to preserve the memory of his brother and promote the example of Little Gidding.[12] He compiled biographical materials about his brother for an unnamed 'Historian', probably Barnabas Oley.[13] Oley had already included some biographical material about Ferrar in his preface to George Herbert's 'The Country Parson', published as *The Remains of That Sweet Singer* in 1652. A 1655 set of 'Directions', a framework for arranging the material, proposed that Ferrar's life should be divided into eight chronological sections within each of which the appropriate details were to be placed.[14] The 'Directions' would appear to be the work of the 'Historian' rather than John Ferrar himself because they advised the recipients, probably John together with his sister Susanna and niece Mary, that by 'rubbing up your memory's & by Conference together' they could supply the historian with material appropriate to each of the sections. A postscript, evidently John's response, then rehearsed how well qualified the 'Historian' was for the task 'because you so well know all that happened in the time after my mothers Death here at Gidding [May 1634], by your often & frequent good company that we were so happy then to enjoy.' The 'Historian' and other visitors close to the family had shared the family's life, listened to the readings at mealtimes and on winter evenings, watched the Collet daughters at work on a harmony, and participated in the household's devotions, including their night vigils, thus furnishing themselves with memories, which they could share with others in later years.[15] With the restoration of the Church of England after 1660, surviving friends could the more readily resume and enlarge these informal circles of 'conference together' and through them maintain and publicise the memory of Little Gidding's distinctive and exemplary piety.

When after 1660 Barnabas Oley was restored to his living and his Clare fellowship and made a prebendary of Worcester, he was well placed both to emulate Ferrar's pedagogical example and to disseminate his memories of Gidding in the clerical and academic circles in which he moved. As vicar of Great Gransden he built there a new vicarage big enough to house a group of boarding students and in addition he provided a separate schoolhouse for the village children that included twelve free places, an arrangement possibly reminiscent of Little Gidding's 'psalm children'.[16] While Oley never completed a formal biography of Ferrar,[17] he maintained, more importantly for the subsequent influence of Little Gidding, contacts that eventually produced a new historian to complete the task.

Among those contacts was Mary Collet Ferrar, whose close relationship with Nicholas and active leadership within the household equipped her to play a significant part in preserving the story of Gidding. After her uncle John had died in 1657 his son John Ferrar Jr. had inherited Gidding. At the instigation of his wife and her brother-in-law the Reverend Basil Berridge, he had more or less forced Mary to leave Gidding,[18] She had moved to Highgate to live with her brother Thomas and took with her papers and books that were hers, often books she had herself bound such as the harmony she later bequeathed to John Collet. The significance of these materials as a source of information about Gidding for later generations I shall consider presently. She was a capable woman and deeply committed to Little Gidding, having been, as we have seen, the leader of the Little Academy and a dedicated exemplar of the temperance diet.[19] She had been especially close to her uncle Nicholas, who addressed her in a letter as 'sister of my soul'[20] and she built her own considerable 'web of friendship' through which she maintained contact with Oley and others as well as with her siblings and their children. She could thus continue to 'rub up' her own and their memories of Gidding and of her uncle until her death in 1680.

Her will stands as evidence of those contacts and of her importance as a channel for preserving and transmitting those memories.[21] Oley received a mourning ring worth £1 as did Oley's former pupil at Clare, Peter Gunning. Whether Gunning had actually visited Gidding in the 1630s is not certain though her gift suggests it as a reasonable possibility, particularly since Gunning had contributed, along with Oley and Richard

Crashaw, a laudatory poem to the preface of *Hygiasticon*. His poem suggests that at the very least he knew of the family's efforts, whether or not he himself had ever tried the prescribed diet. Moreover, he did emphasise the importance of fasting in his later writing and preaching. In the later 1650s Gunning acquired prominence among royalists by ministering to a congregation in London using the proscribed Book of Common Prayer. As a consequence, after the Restoration Gunning's ecclesiastical career flourished. He became the Regius Professor of Divinity and Master of St. John's College, Cambridge, then a bishop, first of Chichester and subsequently of Ely.[22] He clearly wielded authority in the Restoration church. Gunning had other Gidding connections besides Oley and Crashaw, notably Isaac Basire and Timothy Thurscross. In a letter of 1667 to Isaac Basire, who was staying with Richard Busby at Westminster School, Gunning sent greetings not only to Basire but also to Busby and Thurscross and others of 'that good society there'.[23] Basire, like Thurscross and Gunning, had connections with Gidding that went back to the 1630s; he was the one to whom John Ferrar had written in 1641 asking for his help in seeking orders for new harmonies.[24] Clearly that circle around Busby at Westminster had links to the Gidding 'web of friendship'.

Gunning's successor as Regius Professor, Joseph Beaumont, also had Ferrar connections. He was a friend not only of Richard Crashaw, a frequent visitor to Gidding in the 1630s and one who spoke of Mary Collet Ferrar as his 'mother', but also of her much younger brother Ferrar Collet, who was like Beaumont a Fellow of Peterhouse.[25] Given Mary Ferrar's affectionate remembrance that Crashaw relayed to Beaumont in his 1644 letter, her bequest to Beaumont of a £1 ring is not surprising. In the 1650s he had even supplied John Ferrar with 'Verses on Silkworms' to bolster John's promotional efforts for Virginia.[26] Mary Collet Ferrar's bequest suggests that she had remained in touch with Beaumont after the Restoration when he went on to become Master first of Jesus College and then of Peterhouse and finally Regius Professor.[27] Such a sustained relationship also points to the virtual certainty that Beaumont, along with Crashaw and Oley and perhaps Gunning, had spent time with her and the family at Gidding and had met Nicholas Ferrar.

Gunning's successor at St. John's, whom he had brought to the college in 1666, was Francis Turner. This connection brought Turner into the Ferrar circle but was not his only link to the group. He also knew Isaac Basire, who wrote to congratulate him on his election as Master of St. John's in succession to Gunning.[28] Oley, who lived until 1684, perhaps turned over to Turner either directly or via Gunning the biographical materials or copies of them that he and John Ferrar had assembled. Though Turner was too young to have had direct contact with Little Gidding during Ferrar's lifetime, he had clearly come to know Mary Collet Ferrar for to him also she bequeathed a £1 ring, an acknowledgment in effect of his role as the new 'Historian'.[29] Assisted by whatever active help she and others in the Gidding circle gave him, Turner completed during her lifetime the first full biography of Nicholas Ferrar.[30]

Gunning, Oley, Beaumont and Basire were members of that circle from whom Turner could seek information; they were also leaders in the Restoration church who had connections to wider clerical and academic circles. Turner had also known Thomas Ken since the two had been schoolboys at Winchester and he turned to Ken for information while he was at work on the biography.[31] Ken had his own source of knowledge about Little Gidding for he was brother-in-law to Isaac Walton who included in his biography of George Herbert material on the Ferrars said to have come from Arthur Woodnoth. Both Turner, who had succeeded Gunning as Bishop of Ely in 1684, and Ken, who had become Bishop of Bath and Wells in 1685, refused after the Glorious Revolution to take the new oath to William and Mary and as Nonjurors lost their bishoprics. While Turner unlike Ken did not thereafter renounce political action but took some part in Jacobite plotting, both men nevertheless had opportunity in their compulsory retirement to circulate word of Little Gidding among their fellow Nonjurors. It was therefore not surprising that Nonjurors like Thomas Baker and Thomas Hearne, with their High Church views and antiquarian interests, became copiers not only of Turner's completed biography of Ferrar but leading custodians of the materials that were its source.

As he worked on the biography, what was the essential message Turner wanted the book to convey to readers in the late 1670s and why did it fail of publication? Its account of the piety of Ferrar himself was of course the centrepiece of the biographical materials. The family's elaborate pattern of devotions with hourly readings at home and processions to the church, obeisances to the altar, and monthly communion would, he hoped, inspire his readers to emulate at least the spirit if not the elaborate detail of Gidding piety. That pattern, however, by raising the question of how 'Catholic' was Ferrar and how 'monastic' his household, introduced the spectre of popery, as indeed it had done during Ferrar's lifetime.[32] In considering this question, Turner would also have encountered in the 1655 'Directions' to Ferrar's biographer, a marginal note with the enigmatic comment 'NB. His Observa[ci]ons abroad were especially of a regular & religi[ou]s monasterys. this designe was ever in his Mind'.[33] Why did Turner ignore this part of the 'Directions', including in his account of Ferrar's time on the Continent virtually no reference to monasteries while devoting considerable attention to his valiant resistance to Catholic attempts to convert him? The answer to this question lies in the political situation in England during the years from 1677 to 1680 when Turner was writing. The time of Titus Oates's Popish Plot and the attendant Whig effort to exclude the king's Catholic brother James from the succession would hardly have been the moment to present Ferrar as an admirer of Catholic monasteries or to suggest that he had taken them as models for Little Gidding. Turner could only hold up Ferrar's piety and his community as examples and use them as a defence of the Church of England if he could credibly detach them from any appearance of sympathy with Rome. [34]

When the biography was complete, Turner showed it to his friend Henry Dodwell, who already enjoyed well-established anti-papal credentials.[35] He discussed with Dodwell the pros and cons of publishing it and the 'just and innocent Arts that might be used to secure it against 'our mischievous Politicians.' Clearly they had anticipated in 1679-80 that appearances of popery would diminish the effectiveness of the Ferrar example, for in a letter to Turner dated 16 April 1681 Dodwell explained that during their earlier discussion he had felt unable to decide if conditions were right for publication or if publication would instead simply amount to casting pearls before swine. Now, however, he declared himself in favour of it provided Turner took certain precautions. His changed attitude reflected the changed political situation; the dissolution of the Oxford Parliament in March had signaled the beginning of the end of the Whig campaign for Exclusion and the start of a Tory reaction in favour of the crown. In these transformed circumstances Dodwell recognised the propaganda value of the Ferrar biography for the Tory cause provided that Turner presented it in a way that 'the Vulgar' would not find 'obnoxious'. Such a presentation required, Dodwell claimed, not only emphasis on Ferrar's zeal against popery but also a recommendation from a popular person known to be an outspoken critic of the abuses of the Roman church. With such 'just and innocent Arts' Turner could make Ferrar's example not only a stimulus to piety but a weapon to counter the Whig attack on 'popish' bishops and bolster the Tory portrayal of that attack as '41 again'.

Dodwell's counsel, however, came too late. Turner had already become actively involved in other political efforts on behalf of James and the Ferrar project languished unpublished and ended up in the receptive but excluded hands of the Nonjurors. One of Dodwell's suggestions, however, hinted at another interpretation and application that others could give to Little Gidding's example. He recommended the prominent preacher Dr Anthony Horneck, a well-known opponent of popery, as one whom Turner might approach for a recommendation of the Ferrar biography. If Turner knew Horneck at least well enough to approach him for this purpose, their meeting would have brought him together with the leader of the newly formed 'religious societies' in London, the first of the voluntary societies to emerge within the late seventeenth-century Church of England.[36] Could Little Gidding have provided a model for these more broadly based religious societies?

Some twenty years earlier Rev. Timothy Thurscross of Kirkby Moorside in Yorkshire, whom we have already encountered as a friend of Basire and Gunning as well as the Ferrars, had spoken of Gidding in terms suggestive of a voluntary society of the sort Horneck had established. Having spent time at Gidding he knew at first hand Nicholas and John Ferrar as well as their niece Mary Collet Ferrar. So impressed had he been by those visits that in 1638, inspired, as he said, by Nicholas Ferrar's renunciation of worldly place, he had finally resigned his living as Vicar of Kirkby Moorside and his Archdeaconry of Cleveland.[37] Another of Thurscross's friends, to whom he passed on knowledge about Gidding, was Dr John Worthington, the Master during the 1650s of Jesus College, Cambridge.[38] Worthington had been ejected from the Mastership in 1660 to make way for a royalist in need of reward. He declared in the wake of that displacement his inclination to 'a life of devotional retirement, about w[hi]ch I did love to talk with worthy Mr. Thristcross, who knew Mr. Ferrar & Little Gidding, wishing there had been an encrease of religious societies.'[39]

Religious societies were not the only kinds of voluntary societies developing in Restoration England nor were Thurscross and Worthington alone among churchmen in the 1660s in calling, despite the fears reflected in the Clarendon Code and the Conventicle Act of 1664, for such collective action to revive piety and charity.[40] Richard Allestree, author of a best-selling work of popular piety, *The Whole Duty of Man*, published a call in 1667 for 'combinations, and publick Confederacies in Vertue, to ballance and counterpoise those of Vice' as the means to combat the decay of piety in England.[41] While Worthington's wish for 'devotional retirement' proved only temporary, his interest in religious societies continued and took the more activist turn Allestree was to advocate in 1667. He had accepted in 1666 his friend William Brereton's invitation to become the preacher at Holmes Chapel, Cheshire, in the hopes of advancing the work. Both of these men had been friends of Samuel Hartlib, another enthusiast for

'Christian societies',[42] who had also briefly corresponded with John Ferrar, though about the cultivation of silkworms rather than religious societies.[43] The Cheshire move, alas, produced no prospect of religious societies and Worthington's stay there was brief.[44] His interest in Little Gidding, however, continued for in the following year he told his friend Dr Nathaniel Ingelo that he had hopes of bringing 'her that hath Mr. Ferrar's MSS. to a readiness, to communicate some of them for the public good.'[45] Such hopes suggest that by that time both Thurscross and Worthington were in close enough contact with Mary Collet Ferrar to have seen at least some of these papers and perhaps also to have discussed with her their hopes for religious societies. As the leader of the Little Academy and the senior surviving member of the family after 1657, Mary Collet Ferrar was in a position to encourage such hopes as she could also encourage the biographical efforts of Oley and Turner. Turner indeed included comments on Thurscross in his manuscript that suggested an acquaintance with him.[46]

In 1670 Thurscross renewed his efforts to persuade Worthington to undertake the preparing of a substantially larger body of Ferrar's papers for the press. Worthington was an obvious choice for the task since he had earlier produced a carefully edited collection of the works of the eschatologist Joseph Mede. Thurscross apparently hoped he would do the same for Nicholas Ferrar and also felt sufficiently confident that Mary Collet Ferrar would be willing to entrust the task to Worthington. Worthington, however, declined on the grounds that he had not the time in his present circumstances to do the job properly, especially since he knew that the papers were numerous and the need for editing considerable.[47] His comments to Ingelo about editing suggest that by that time he had indeed had a chance to examine the papers in some detail and study their contents. Had he undertaken this editorial task the finished work might have offered a different perspective on Ferrar and Little Gidding, one especially relevant to Worthington's interest in religious societies.[48]

The papers in question were educational materials rather than biographical notes and so of particular interest to one concerned about encouraging religious societies. His talk of piecing together missing parts by comparing different partial versions and checking quoted stories against their original sources describes very well the dialogues of the Little Academy, which existed in a number of partial versions and consisted of stories retold by the participants. The material that Worthington's son passed along to Thomas Hearne for publication, copies of the originals that John Collet later inherited from his aunt, confirms that Worthington was indeed looking at the Little Academy conversations. These provided not only the stories but also the procedures and covenants by which the participants constituted themselves as a society.[49] If Thurscross and Worthington were looking for a model for the religious societies they hoped to set up, the Little Academy with its 'joynt Covenant' by which the participants initiated the group in 1631 and its individual pledges to pursue temperance during Christmastide 1632 could have provided one.[50] This covenant theme was certainly picked up by another contemporary, John Hacket, in the account of Gidding he incorporated into his biography of his patron and Gidding's diocesan John Williams. Hacket there described the family members' first gathering at Gidding as 'purposing and covenanting between themselves to live in as strict a way, according to the Gospel of Christ, as good rules could chalk out, and human infirmity undergo.'[51]

Had Worthington and Thurscross lived longer (both died in 1671) they would have seen their hope for an increase in religious societies fulfilled. Such groups began to appear in London from about 1678 under the initial leadership of none other than Rev. Anthony Homeck, that same staunch anti-papist whom Henry Dodwell had suggested that Francis Turner approach for a recommendation of his life of Ferrar.[52] Turner therefore was probably aware of Horneck's initiative and also of Timothy Thurscross's view of Little Gidding as a religious society. The groups Horneck and others organised were voluntary societies of young men drawn from different parishes who as a condition of membership had promised to observe the 'Orders' of the society and had presented to the group, orally or in writing, 'a solemn account of their sense of spiritual things'.[53] They met regularly together, first in homes and later in parish churches, under the direction of an orthodox and pious minister. Their meetings included bible reading, prayers (but only those in the Prayer Book) and discussion as well as projects to promote practical piety and distribute charity. As they grew stronger in numbers they arranged their own special services and lectures in various parish churches. They were nevertheless faithful in attending regular parish worship, regularly taking communion, and making every effort to allay suspicion of separatism. Such societies, based as they were on explicit consent to the group's rules and dedicated to promoting piety and charity, resembled Nicholas Ferrar's Little Academy and fulfilled the hopes of Thurscross and Worthington. They certainly answered the call of the anonymous author of *The Country-Parson's Advice to his Parishioners* (1680) to the 'good men of this Church' to join 'into Fraternities, or friendly Societies' as the best means of 'restoring our decaying Christianity to its Primitive Life and Vigour and . . . supporting . . . our tottering, and sinking Church'.[54] Not everyone, of course, took so sanguine a view as Gilbert

Burnet, who in his later History carefully differentiated these new societies
that were 'of the church' from those earlier ones that had flourished 'only
among puritans and dissenters'.[55] These religious societies for the most part
successfully rebutted fears of schism by their orthodoxy and conformity, as
Little Gidding had done earlier.[56] They offered a means to address the need
perceived by many for the moral reformation of their corrupt society and
the need for the continuing activism of individuals, both clerical and lay, in
pursuit of social and individual redemption.[57]

While neither the Country Parson nor any other books or sermons
publicly attributed influence to Little Gidding, the continuing and over-
lapping networks that had developed out of Ferrar's original 'web of
friendship' make such a connection likely. Mary Collet Ferrar, living on
until 1680, again proved a significant link for she counted within her own
network not only Thurscross, Worthington and Turner but other younger
friends who later became active participants in and promoters of these
groups. One of them was Edward Fowler, later Bishop of Gloucester but
in the 1670s and 80s a vicar in London, first at All Hallows, Bread Street,
and later in 1681 at St Giles, Cripplegate.[58] Though he was quite prepared
to assail radical separatists like John Bunyan and the Quakers, he had
friendships, indeed family connections, with more orthodox Dissenters
and the voluntarism they had adopted, whether from conviction or
necessity, after 1662. He sought to win them back to the established
church through persuasion rather then persecution, and during the Tory
reaction of the 1680s he was attacked and temporarily suspended from
St Giles for his readiness to admit to communion and to his vestry those
who also attended Nonconformist meetings.[59] As a conscientious pastor
he welcomed the new religious societies and supported the work of
his curate at St Giles, William Smythies, who, like Horneck, promoted
and preached to such groups. Fowler not only defended Smythies from
critics but also offered the use of his church to one such group.[60] After
the Revolution Fowler became an equally enthusiastic advocate of the
Societies for the Reformation of Manners, groups that had developed
out of the religious societies. The efforts of these societies to enforce the
laws and root out vice Fowler, like fellow supporters, saw as a necessary
and appropriate offering of thanks to God for the nation's deliverance
from the threat of popery. Advocates of these societies felt a particular
urgency because failure to reform risked, they believed, the vengeance
of divine wrath. In like manner Fowler took up the cause of reform
through education when he joined in 1699 the newly founded Society for
Promoting Christian Knowledge, becoming the first bishop to be added

to the Society's membership.[61] He clearly was an activist who saw these voluntary societies as significant instruments for 'reformation' in several aspects.[62]

Who brought Fowler into the Little Gidding network? John Worthington, for one, knew him not just as friend but as family, for Fowler was related to Worthington's wife.[63] Worthington made Fowler his executor and entrusted him with responsibility not only for his children but for his papers and other possessions which probably reflected his interest in voluntary societies in general and Little Gidding in particular. In addition Worthington might also have introduced Fowler to Mary Collet Ferrar, a contact which he could then have cultivated once he had come to London from Bedfordshire in 1673. Fowler had another link to her through her friend Anne Grigg, a relative of John Locke, a friend of John Worthington and later of Francis Turner and Turner's friend, Thomas Ken.[64] Not surprisingly, therefore, Fowler too received from Mary Collet Ferrar a £1 mourning ring.

Fowler had another Ferrar contact, a man who was his exact contemporary and uniquely placed to inform a circle of friends about Little Gidding. He was Dr John Mapletoft, who had lived at Gidding as a child and moreover was Nicholas Ferrar's godson as well as his great-nephew.[65] He was the son of Susanna Collet, Mary's sister, and Rev. Joshua Mapletoft, Nicholas Ferrar's close friend since their days together at Clare Hall. After his father had died in 1635, his mother had taken him and his brother and sister back to Gidding; he was then four years old. Young John probably remained at Gidding until at least 1643 when his uncle Robert Mapletoft took charge of his nephew's education. He sent him first to Westminster School whose headmaster, Richard Busby, he knew and then to Trinity College, Cambridge.[66]

Robert Mapletoft was himself another significant individual in the clerical and academic circles of the Restoration church who had direct experience of Gidding during Nicholas Ferrar's lifetime. He had sent Garthwait's harmony to Ferrar and taken part in the search of college libraries for other harmonies. He had also seen *Hygiasticon* through the press and tried to follow Cornaro's diet, despite his reputation for keeping a 'good table'. He had presided at Ferrar's funeral and preached the sermon now lost. Not surprisingly, he had friends in Gidding circles; Timothy Thurscross considered him a possible nominee to succeed him at Kirkby Moorside.[67] Richard Busby sent news of him as well as of Thurscross and John Ferrar to Isaac Basire in 1647. He also knew Mark Frank, a colleague at Pembroke, who had written the Latin epitaph for young Nicholas Ferrar after his untimely death in 1640.[68] Following his ejection in 1644 from his fellowship at Pembroke College, Cambridge, Mapletoft spent time in the royalist household of Sir Robert Shirley that also sheltered Gilbert Sheldon, the future Archbishop of Canterbury. He subsequently ministered to an illicit Prayer Book congregation in Lincoln. After the Restoration Mapletoft received the degree D.D. and the office of Subdean of Lincoln, then followed his friend Mark Frank as the Master of Pembroke in succession to, and finally became Dean of Ely. These latter posts he held until his death in 1677.[69] He was clearly another significant link in the Gidding network with his own memories to share not only with his nephews but also with collegiate and clerical colleagues.

While John Mapletoft was at Cambridge, first as a student and then as a Fellow of Trinity, he furnished his great-uncle John Ferrar with information about silkworms and an abstract of an essay on the silk trade.[70] He left England in 1658 to travel abroad first as tutor to the son of the Earl of Northumberland and later independently to study medicine. With an M.D. from Cambridge (1667) in hand Mapletoft prospered as a physician in London, becoming a member of the Royal Society in 1676 and Professor of Physic at Gresham College from 1675 to 1679. He moved in that influential circle of natural philosophers that included his old schoolfellow John Locke with whom he carried on an extensive correspondence during these years, particularly when one or other of them was out of the country. Locke also knew Mapletoft's cousin John Collet as Mapletoft likewise knew Locke's cousin and his aunt Mary's friend, Anne Grigg.[71] Mapletoft married in 1679 and resigned his Gresham Professorship in order to take up the study of divinity to which he had always been attracted. He was ordained in 1683 and installed in London as vicar of St Lawrence Jewry in 1686.[72] Like Fowler he was an active and conscientious pastor, particularly concerned to promote the education and practical piety of those not only within but also outside his flock.

His childhood at Little Gidding as well as his membership in Gresham College and the Royal Society gave him favourable experiences of societies in general and religious societies in particular. His friend Locke further reinforced and expanded this message with a contractual concept of society and government that saw the whole church as a voluntary society.[73] It is hardly surprising, therefore, to find Mapletoft as an active participant in the several different kinds of societies that appeared from the 1680s onwards, both those devoted to inward piety and those directed to social needs. By 1689-90 his parish of St. Lawrence Jewry could host a well-established religious society.[74] Furthermore by 1698 the society supported at the church a lecture every first Sunday in the month.[75] Mapletoft, like

Fowler, also became an active advocate of the Societies for the Reformation of Manners as they pursued in the 1690s their campaign to enforce the laws against vice.

Mapletoft became a member of the Society for Promoting Christian Knowledge in the same month (July 1699) that Edward Fowler was enrolled. He was a far more active member than Fowler, who by that time had been installed as Bishop of Gloucester. Mapletoft regularly attended the Society's meetings and contributed generously to its funds. He also distributed to his parishioners various of the Society's tracts, including his own *A Perswasive to Lay-Conformity* that he presented to the Dissenters among them. He counted among his many friends Robert Nelson, a layman and Nonjuror and author of a work on the fasts and festivals of the church. When in 1699 Nelson came out of his voluntary retirement as a Nonjuror, Mapletoft was presumably one of those instrumental in drawing him into the voluntary work of the whole range of societies, particularly the newly formed SPCK.[76] As a friend not only of Mapletoft but also of Thomas Ken, Nelson had ample opportunity to learn from them of Little Gidding though he made no explicit reference to it in his call for the establishment of homes for 'decayed gentlemen' and houses for both men and women to which they could repair for periods of prayer and meditation.[77]

The SPCK also adopted other methods besides distributing tracts for promoting Christian knowledge, notably the establishment of so-called 'Charity Schools' designed to instruct poor youngsters not only in religion but also in reading and writing and other skills that would make them good servants or apprentices.[78] Mapletoft was an early and generous supporter of such schools as well as of parochial libraries and the publication of religious tracts for distribution both in England and the colonies. His cousin John Collet, who in his will called Mapletoft his 'good friend & kinsman', also gave generous support to a charity school in Southwark, where the Collets had property.[79] Mapletoft also possessed among his family papers a manuscript copy of his godfather's unpublished translation of Ludovico Carbone's treatise on the education of children, a description of Venetian Sunday schools.[80] If he were familiar with its contents and especially if he discussed it with others in the SPCK, he could have made it an instrument to encourage the work of the charity schools.

Another of the Society's promotional efforts in which Mapletoft played a part was its decision to set up corresponding members in the country. Mapletoft recruited his cousin, Rev. Hugh Mapletoft of Huntingdon, for this post. Hugh accepted, though he reported pessimistically that there was very little interest or enthusiasm for the work in his area, the very area of course that included Little Gidding.[81] John Mapletoft also became a charter member of the Society for the Propagation of the Gospel in Foreign Parts, an appropriate endeavour in light of the family's earlier efforts to promote religion in Virginia.[82] Indeed he not only joined existing societies but also proposed to launch a new one. In a sermon to listeners who included the Lord Mayor and Aldermen of London he proposed that a group of rich men should band together to form a society that would provide centralised oversight of the collection and distribution of charity in the City.[83] Clearly he found voluntary societies a congenial and appropriate way to tackle social problems.

When Mapletoft died in 1721 (in his ninety-first year), he was not only an activist in the voluntary societies but also the possessor of a substantial collection of those family papers that have been instrumental in preserving knowledge of Little Gidding. While there can be no certainty about how much he actually studied these papers, the sheer extent of his collection indicates at the very least a strong interest in and loyalty to his family.[84] What he had were educational materials rather than biographical ones and included a gospel harmony,[85] several versions of the various dialogues of the Little Academy about which Mapletoft could also have heard from his aunt Mary Collet Ferrar, collections of stories for children, a copybook by John Collet (probably Mapletoft's cousin rather than his grandfather), and other collections of sayings and stories as well as two versions of Nicholas Ferrar's unpublished translation of Carbone, copies of his translations of Valdesso and Lessius and his preface to *The Temple*. [86] Mapletoft's publication in 1707 of a volume of *Select Proverbs* suggests that he knew and might as a boy have memorised at least some of the various collections of such material that his godfather carefully assembled for the family's and especially the children's, edification.[87]

Mapletoft's published sermons also hint at his Gidding experience in arguments for the importance of attendance not simply at weekly or thrice-weekly church services but daily morning and evening prayer.[88] He recurred to this theme in a later work, *The Principles and Duties of the Christian Religion* (1710), a copy of which he presented as a valedictory gift to every household in his parish. His friend Robert Nelson's nineteenth-century biographer acknowledged as much when he attributed Mapletoft's 'own earnestness in religion . . . in part, to his early education in the family of his great uncle and godfather, Nicholas Farrar [sic] at Gidding'.[89] Yet ultimately we can only infer from his writings, his actions and his possessions how much Little Gidding meant to him, how he presented it to others, and therefore how it influenced him and other participants in voluntary societies. He is more likely to have made such points explicitly when talking informally about Gidding with his friends and colleagues in the several societies, who would have constituted a sympathetic and even inquisitive audience. In such conversations what would he have singled out as memorable and significant aspects of life at Gidding? Did he characterise it with Thurscross and Worthington as a 'religious society', with Walton as a 'little college', or with his SPCK friend Sir George Wheler, for whom the 'Protestant Monastery' of his book's title was a godly household?[90] Or perhaps with something of all three, for they all designated communities with a devotional rule and an educational purpose.

The acceptability of voluntary societies within the Church of England represented a significant change to which those like Mapletoft with knowledge of Little Gidding contributed. Although before and especially after the Restoration voluntary societies flourished in other spheres (science, history, music) in Britain's 'associational world', in the Church such societies had to overcome what Bishop Burnet called their earlier association with 'puritans and Dissenters'. It was only from the later 1660s onward that churchmen, increasingly alarmed at the moral and spiritual decay of society and the church's inability to combat these evils, began to see voluntary societies as an acceptable source of the needed initiatives and practical actions. These circumstances presented opportunities for those leaders in the Church who had knowledge of Nicholas Ferrar and Little Gidding to appeal to their example as a model for such societies, to make it, as Ferrar had hoped, a pattern for an age that needed such patterns. We know that Francis Turner discussed the Gidding example with Henry Dodwell and possibly also with Anthony Horneck; did others in the network do the same? They could have reassured their colleagues that a prototypical voluntary society like Little Gidding, far from posing a threat to the Church, provided a bulwark for its defence whether against charges of popery or of a lack of 'heart' religion. Ferrar had made a carefully controlled voluntarism at Little Gidding an eminently successful method for promoting a piety that aspired to be for the world a 'light upon a hill'. That reassuring image of Little Gidding as a ministering society that was very much 'of the church' could serve to authenticate voluntary societies for Anglicans as a source of strength rather than schism and to make them instruments that supplied much of the vitality of late seventeenth and early eighteenth-century religious life,[91]

The Ferrars did not call themselves a 'community', but the last revival of its Little Academy did call itself a 'society' constituted by the formal agreement its members signed. Contemporaries recognised the household's collective and self-conscious identity whether as Thurscross's 'religious society', as an 'Arminian Nunnery', as Isaac Walton's 'little college' or as the Historian's 'Light on a Hill'. The upheavals of the civil war and commonwealth years spelled the end of the 'good old way' that Ferrar on his deathbed had exhorted the family to continue. Nevertheless, as this concluding chapter has shown, what he and members of the Little Academy hoped would be a pattern for their own times did live on to provide patterns for subsequent ages. In the years after the death of John Mapletoft there were both societies and biographies and even novels that preserved and appealed to memories of Little Gidding. They ranged from John Wesley's Methodists and those Nonjurors whom J.F.M. Carter credited with preserving 'the story of our Catholic ancestry'[92] to nineteenth-century novels with Mary Collet Ferrar as the exemplar of Gidding's piety and in the twentieth century not only biographies of Ferrar but also actual communities at Gidding.

Clearly Ferrar's ideal of dedication to God's service based on a highly structured life revolving around public and private worship aroused antagonism and fear among some of his contemporaries because of its resemblance to a monastery. By the early eighteenth century, however, Thomas Hearne could use 'The Protestant Monastery' as a positive label in contrast to 'that libel' as John Ferrar had called *The Arminian Nunnery*. Indeed Samuel Wesley, an active supporter of the various societies, had earlier attributed the successes of the Church of Rome to the societies that flourished within her and had declared it admirable if 'we had among us some places wherein those who were piously disposed might have the liberty for a time of a voluntary retirement, once practiced by Mr. Ferrar'.[93] A positive acceptance of a previously controversial term, accompanied by calls for places of shelter or retreat for spiritual refreshment and coupled with the new enthusiasm for voluntary societies to combat disastrously declining standards of public and private piety and morality, reflected the extent to which 'voluntary Anglicans' had become prepared to accommodate communities within a church that was established but no longer national. That change in turn prepared the way not only for the later establishment of Anglican convents and monasteries but ultimately for the 1980 commemoration of Nicholas Ferrar as 'Founder of the Little Gidding Community'.

Conclusion

Francis Turner, like John Ferrar before him and others after him, saw Nicholas Ferrar as an example and bulwark for the Church of England. He called Ferrar 'a most Burning and Shining Light' possessed of wisdom, humility, patience, charity, temperance, and industry together with a quick wit, firm memory and deep judgment, an assessment for which John Ferrar had doubtless supplied evidence.[1] A new perspective modifies this adulatory appraisal, not by denying him those qualities but by making them less absolute. He was undoubtedly temperate and industrious, charitable in alms-giving and in giving emotional support to friends and family members, humble in his sense of himself as a sinner, wise and patient in his pedagogy. Yet he could also judge harshly his brother Richard, and his nephew Edward Collet and press too zealously his programme of temperance. He was undoubtedly temperate and industrious, charitable in alms-giving and in giving emotional support to friends and family members, humble in his sense of himself as a sinner, wise and patient in his pedagogy. That he could be at once a mystic and a man of business points up a complexity, even ambiguity, in his character and attitudes that the earlier hagiographic picture had lacked.

Ferrar's industry Turner called 'heroical', although the twenty-first century would more likely regard it as workaholic. So strenuous were its daytime demands, explained Turner, that Ferrar needed the nights to recover not just physically but spiritually, hence the importance not only of rest, of which he in fact gave himself little, but also of his meditative vigils.[2] According to his friend Timothy Thurscross, Ferrar imposed such a punishing schedule on himself not simply because his duties required it but also because he had found through his own experience that such constant effort afforded special protection against despair over one's sins and doubt of God's willingness to forgive them.[3] If he needed such protection, he must sometimes have lost that assurance of God's presence that he received as a young boy when he wrestled with doubt in the garden of the family home. His outburst to Arthur Woodnoth over what he saw as his mistakes in handling John Gabbit testified to a keen sense of his own sinfulness that made him judge himself very harshly.[4] He professed to welcome the failure of his hope to publish a gospel harmony and to take refuge in anonymity in what he did publish at least in part because he feared the corrupting effect of ambition and success, a lesson he had earlier learnt from his London experience. If he was to that extent driven by a sense of sin and fear of failure, it is not surprising that he needed meditation to restore his balance and that the psalms with their range of emotion had particular appeal.

Meditation recurs frequently as a theme in Turner's notes that often read as if he were drawing on the now vanished spiritual diary and meditations that we know Ferrar wrote. Whether Ferrar there recorded other mystical outbursts comparable to the passage he included in the preface to 'The Winding Sheet' Turner has not told us. He did, however, record Ferrar's comment on the kind of 'madness' often attributed to those who entered so deeply into prayer as to seem to be beside themselves. This was not, Ferrar declared, the 'Enthusiastique Spirit' but the height of wisdom and discretion, the 'practical experiment' without which understanding of divine mysteries could not come.[5] It was not a surprising attitude in one for whom Valdes was a beloved author. It reflected also his own hope that such 'experiment' would remind Christians of the fundamentals of the faith that united them and so help to heal their divisions. Whilst no further evidence survives to reveal the nature of his encounters with God (Herbert would have been the likeliest to recipient of such accounts), the inner strength that he got from them would have been an important source of his spiritual authority among his family and friends. Arthur Woodnoth, despite his criticism of his cousin's readiness to put too great a value on set forms of prayer, was firmly convinced of the special power of Nicholas's own prayers, and he was probably not alone in that view.[6]

Since meditation was so vital for Ferrar he was careful to instruct his family in ways to practice it, making the psalms that were central to his own meditations also the focus of the family's night vigils as well as their other daytime devotions. The psalms were not, of course, the only form of prayer familiar to a family steeped in the Book of Common Prayer. Besides daily morning and evening prayer there was the daily recitation of the litany with its plea for mercy and its thanks for deliverance. Through prayer, Ferrar emphasised, one made God a partner in all aspects of one's daily life. One did not invite God into one's life, however, through spontaneous prayer with its risk of inappropriate words and wandering thoughts. In the 'Duties

Common to Man and Woman' he made it clear that he regarded that as a hazardous practice for all but the most experienced practitioners. Instead he recommended particularly the prayer 'Prevent us, O Lord, in all our doings with thy most gracious favour' and other shorter responses from the Book of Common Prayer as appropriate ways to refer one's works and hopes to God and enlist His help.[7] Accounts of church services as they occur in the biographies, in Lenton's letter and in the gossip circulating in the neighbourhood indicate that he followed the Prayer Book rubric but adopted many of the Laudian 'innovations'. Whilst he certainly had his own convictions in these matters, he had no desire to take part in the arguments over liturgy and theology that roiled the Church of England in the 1630s.

If Ferrar was driven by a sense of sin, he was also driven by a passion for order and regularity reflected in the monastic appearance of the family's life, the clocks he placed throughout the house and his metaphorical concern to wind up the clocks that were family members' minds, his efforts to minimise personal conflicts and emotional confrontations such as those with Bathsheba by putting the issues in writing, and his negative attitude toward spontaneous prayer. Had he lacked the essential element of personal magnetism and perceptiveness that he evidently had his leadership would have risked becoming as oppressively rigid and controlling for others as it was for Bathsheba. He could depend also, however, on his mother's firm conviction of his wisdom and judgment to reinforce his authority and perhaps to moderate its impact. Indeed his own account of the reasons for the difficulties in reviving the Little Academy in 1633-4 acknowledged her importance but also the limitations of her power as well as his own to effect the revival she wanted.

He was driven too by a deep concern for his family that made him return prematurely from his Continental travels, stay with his parents in London rather than return to Cambridge, and finally resolve his brother's financial difficulties and bring the family to Gidding. As head of the family he continued to bear the burden of financial responsibility necessary to provide income and also opportunity for the younger generation although he could delegate some of it to his brother and his cousin Arthur Woodnoth. Turner noted Ferrar's belief, surely an argument for the 'mixt life', that a man was not entitled to pursue his own salvation at the cost of abandoning the responsibilities toward others that came with his station.[8] If Ferrar had been genuinely tempted to move to the Isle of Man, he declared it would have been possible only if he were convinced that all the family were securely settled.[9] That conviction clearly never came. He coupled this sense of responsibility for those entrusted to his care with a conviction that true friendship must rest on openness and unconditional acceptance of one another. Within that context, as he appealed to Arthur Woodnoth, a friend should use that openness not to impose his own solutions but rather to help the other make his own decisions and commitments. It was a noble ideal but hardly easy to realise particularly where, as was especially the case with the Collet nieces, relationships were not between equals.

Relationships with women, his mother, sister, sister-in-law and nieces were vitally important at Little Gidding. He was entirely conventional in his patriarchal and Pauline assumptions but so were the rest of the family as far as the evidence allows us to judge. Theory was one thing, however, and practice another. Telling Bathsheba that not even the clothes on her back were her own was legally sound if not helpful in the circumstances. Other occasions, however, showed him more accommodating and suggest the flexibility that generally prevailed to temper the rigidities of the prevailing assumptions. He advised his brother to be as accommodating to his wife's wishes as possible without forfeiting his ultimate patriarchal authority, but he could be sternly disapproving of his niece Margaret's initial refusal to accept (his?) proposal to marry a clergyman while applauding her sister Susanna's public willingness to follow her husband's wishes.[10]

Turner gave the same idealised view of the family as he did of Nicholas himself. For him they were 'the other parts of the Family [that were] as little Sparkes Ascending in greater flames' and 'The Fairest flowers in this garden of the land for piety'.[11] Ferrar made them so, Turner claimed, by teaching them that they would best attain their private happiness by pursuing the good of the group rather than their individual desires. Could Ferrar look back at the end of his life and find that his instruction and example had indeed produced the community for which he had searched and striven?

In late 1637 on his deathbed he counseled his grieving family to continue in 'the good old way', echoing the prophet Jeremiah's call to his people to 'ask for the old paths, where is the good way, and walk therein'.[12] What for him at the end of his life was that 'good old way'? Not surprisingly it included loyalty to the Church of England and to scripture and what he had taught them out of those sources. Loyalty to the Church presumably implied continuing the services of its Prayer Book though that was left unsaid. For scripture he singled out as especially important the harmonies, their creation and use, as the activity that he specifically urged them to continue. 'Leave not the thoughts of them though I be gone.' For the younger children he supplemented that advice by adding that they should continue to study the books of precepts he had assembled for them as well as to keep their concordance and psalms in memory.[13] Ultimately it was this first project, the harmonies, rather than the more ambitious but divisive later ones on which he centred his hopes for the future of the community he had created. Its appeal to both hands and minds and its ability to bring in the younger members of the family as they grew up contributed to the willingness with which family members continued the work at least through 1642. Later family members who inherited harmonies (Collets and Mapletofts) clearly valued them and made every effort to keep them in the family. As they were important to Ferrar as a teaching and devotional tool so they proved especially effective in creating the community he sought. It was not a 'perfect' community, but its example has lasted long after his death.

Appendix:
The Ferrar and Collet Families

David R. Ransome

Few of the birthdays and dates of death of the Ferrars, Collets and Mapletofts in the early seventeenth century are exactly known to us, and only one Ferrar birthday: in the 1650s John Ferrar recorded his brother Nicholas's birth on 22 February 1593. In some other cases we have the baptismal date; and since baptism in the late sixteenth and early seventeenth centuries usually occurred shortly after birth, we can be reasonably sure of those individuals' ages. Unfortunately we lack such dates for some of Nicholas Ferrar's siblings and most of his Collet nephews and nieces.

Old Nicholas Ferrar, the family patriarch, died on 1 April 1620.[1] A few days before his death, in making his will, he adopted a contemporary convention, instructing his executor to provide mourning gowns for 75 poor men, unusually adding 'which is my age'. Old Nicholas was thus born in 1544 or 1545. His wife, Mary Woodnoth, was some ten years younger. If she was born c.1554, she would have been 24 when she married, a typical age for a woman of her rank at that time, with her first child born in 1579 and her last, Richard, when she was about 42. She died in the early spring of 1634 – her death was known at Aldborough, Yorkshire by 12 May – and Edward Lenton had recently reckoned her 80 years old. Her birth cannot be computed exactly but the evidence suggests that our estimate cannot be far wrong.

The Ferrar parents moved more than once in their married life, drifting westwards through London as they prospered. Five of their children were christened in the parish church of St Gabriel Fenchurch, the last [Erasmus] in 1586. The family then moved to Mark Lane in the parish of St Mary Stayning, where Nicholas was baptised on 28 February 1593. At some point thereafter, but certainly by 1609, they moved again, to St Sithes Lane in the parish of St Benet Sherehog. Both these parishes were burned over in

1666, and their registers perished. We therefore do not know in what years the younger John, William and Richard were born. Indeed the elder John gave an incorrect lead to later historians when he described his brother Nicholas as his parents' 'third son', forgetting that William who had died long before in 1619 was almost certainly older than Nicholas, since they had both gone up to Cambridge in 1607, and it was Nicholas, not William, who was precocious. It is thus possible to suggest only approximate birth years for John, William and Richard.

John and his second wife Bathsheba had at least four children: Mary, Nicholas, Virginia and John. Their parents had married on St. Valentine's Day 1615, a date made fashionable two years earlier when the Princess Elizabeth had married the Elector Palatine. Mary is the baby in the swaddling bands held by her mother in a portrait unlikely to have been painted later than 1618, but is not mentioned in her grandfather's will made in March 1620. Her brother Nicholas was, however. His epitaph dates his death: 19 May 1640. He was in his twenty-first year. Virginia, according to her father in the mid-1650s, was born on Christmas Eve 'the year after he came to Gidding.'[2] The family came in 1625, escaping the plague in London, but it was in 1626 that they made Gidding their sole residence. Since John annotated the gospel harmony now at Ickworth with the statement that it had been made by Virginia in 1640 when she was twelve years old, it would seem that in retrospect he regarded 1626 as the date of the family's move to Gidding. The last child, John, was, I believed until recently, born in June 1630. My attention has now been drawn, however, to a passage in Williams (p.112) in which John and Bathsheba's Nicholas is termed in early 1631 his father's only son. Bathsheba visited London in both 1630 and 1631, each year returning reluctantly to rural Huntingdonshire. Since it was common for a woman to return to her own family to give birth, either of these visits could have been the occasion of John's birth. A letter to the family from Lady Sandys [FP 818] refers to Bathsheba and her little one, the newborn John.[3] The later year therefore is the more probable date.

The Collets also present problems. Not even the number of the Collet children is certainly known. On the memorial plaque removed from Susanna Collet's tombstone and now in the church at Little Gidding, she is said to have been the mother of eight sons and eight daughters, but there is contemporary record of only seven sons. 'William' is not named until the eighteenth century. Disappointingly, when Thomas Collet, the eldest son, made a declaration to the heralds at their visitation of Middlesex in 1663-64, he named only twelve of the children, in two separate sequences, of five sons and seven daughters, omitting Anna, Edward, John I and 'William'.

The five youngest children (Joyce, John, Ferrar, John II and Judith) were baptised in 1615-24 at Bourn in Cambridgeshire where their father had inherited the lease of a college farm. Susanna Ferrar had married John Collet by 1600; thus ten and perhaps eleven children were born between then and 1614. Thomas states that the daughters arrived in the following order: Mary, Su[sanna], Hester, Margaret (Peg), Elizabeth, Joyce and Judith; the sons in the sequence: Thomas, Nicholas, Richard, Ferrar and John II. Visiting Gidding in old Mrs Ferrar's lifetime, Edward Lenton reckoned Mary and Anna respectively 32 and 30, making his visit more likely to have occurred in 1633 than in the more generally cited 1634.

A further clue to the children's ages can be gained from the sequence in which the boys left home. Thomas was enrolled at the Middle Temple in 1619, admitted to the bar in 1626, and married two years later. John II, baptised in 1621, was apprenticed to his older brother Nicholas in 1635. Nick himself had been apprenticed in 1626 and was made free of the Goldsmiths Company in 1634. Ned, it is clear, was older than Nick. When Nick was apprenticed, Ned was shortly to move to his second master in London. The reason is not specified, but a letter to him from his mother hints that he had been at fault. Nevertheless in March 1630 when Nick's master, Arthur Woodnoth, was thinking of changing careers, he thought of turning his business over to Ned and Nick, with Ned taking the more responsible part and overseeing the new boy that would have to be taken on.[4] The sequence of Collet sons will therefore have been: Thomas, Edward, Nicholas, Richard, John I, Ferrar, and John II, with 'William' perhaps needing to be inserted at some point before John (I).

Any attempt to offer a single sequence of Collet children must be to some extent speculative, especially if 'William' is to be included. It seems almost inevitable that there was at least one pair of twins, perhaps two if 'William' was a weakling twin who died at birth. The following order with approximate dates of birth is suggested, only the birth years of the youngest five being certain: Mary (c.1600-1680), Thomas (c.1602-1675) & Anna (c.1602-1638/9), Su[sanna] (c.1603-1657), Hester (c.1605, fl.1646), Margaret (Peg) (c.1607-?1692)[5], Edward (c.1609, fl.1646, d. by 1680, perhaps by 1664), Elizabeth (c.1610-1651), Nicholas (c.1612-1688), Richard (c.1613-1668), Joyce (1615-1692), John I (1616-c.1619), Ferrar (1618-1679), John II (1621-1669?) and Judith (1624-60).

Notes

Note on Sources

1 For an excellent and extended discussion of this topic see Kate E. Riley, 'The Good Old Way Revisited: The Ferrar Family of Little Gidding c. 1625-1637', unpubl. Ph.D. dissertation, University of Western Australia, 2007, pp. 22-39 [hereafter, Riley, 'Good Old Way'].

2 M&W have made this the backbone of their composite version of the biographical materials based on John Ferrar's notes. They have assumed, however, that the notes that follow the biographical extract were not Turner's and therefore not relevant. I discuss this topic in more detail in the final chapter, pp. 279-82.

3 Turner, f 106r.

Introduction

1 The esssentials of this lengthy process are succinctly summarised in Richard Symonds, *Alternative Saints: The Post-Reformation British People Commemorated by the Church of England*, New York: St. Martin's, 1988, pp. 6 and 77-88.

2 The Oratory of the Good Shepherd, founded in 1913; www.ogs.net and the community founded by Tony and Judith Hodgson in 1970 at Gidding; www.littlegiddingchurch.org. See Tony Hodgson, *Little Gidding Then and Now*, Cambridge: Grove Books, 2010.

3 Blackstone, p. 5.

4 The biblical source is Matthew 5:14. The phrase was applied to Little Gidding in the 'Directions to the Historian', M&W, p. 39. Winthrop's much-quoted use of this image occurred in his sermon 'A Modell of Christian Charity' delivered to his fellow passengers aboard the *Arbella* bound for Boston in 1630; *Winthrop Papers*, II, pp. 282-95, quoted in Darret B. Rutman, *Winsthrop's Boston: A Portrait of a Puritan Town, 1630-1649*, Chapel Hill, NC: University of North Carolina Press for the Institute of Early American History and Culture, 1965, p, 4.

5 FP 729 (5 July 1630).

6 Mayor, p. 115.

7 Turner, f.125r.

1

Formative Years: 'the time of his ingathering'

1   Isaac Walton, 'Life of Herbert', p. 377 [hereafter Walton, Herbert] and
     George Herbert, 'The Country Parson', p. 211 in Herbert, Works.
2   Among the vast literature of this sort I have consulted the following: William
     Perkins, *Christian Oeconomie, or, A short survey of the right manner of erecting
     and ordering a familie according to the Scriptures*, London: Felix Kyngston,
     1609. T.[homas] G.[Gainsford], *The Rich Cabinet Furnished with Varietie
     of Excellent descriptions. . .*, London: Printed by I[ohn] B[eale] for Roger
     Iackson, 1616. William Hinde, *A Faithfull Remonstrance of the Holy Life and
     Happy Death, of Iohn Bruen of Bruen-Stapleford, in the County of Chester,
     Esquire*, London: Printed by R. B. for Philemon Stephens, and Christopher
     Meredith, 1645. [John Duncon], *The Returnes of Spiritual Comfort and
     Grief in a Devout Soul* [Lettice, Lady Falkland], London: Richard Royston,
     1648. Thomas Taylor, *The Pilgrims Profession. Or a Sermon Preached at the
     Funerall of M^{ris} Mary Gunter*, London: Printed by I.D. for Io: Bartlet, 1622.
     William Gouge, *Of Domesticall Dvties*, London: Printed by Iohn Haviland
     for William Bladen, 1622. Iohn Dod and Robert Cleuer, *A Godly Forme of
     Houshold Gouernment*, London: Printed by the Asssignes of Thomas Man,
     for Iohn Clarke, 1630. D[aniel] Cawdrey, *Family Reformation Promoted*,
     London: Printed by T.G. for John Wright, 1656. Harbot[tle] Grimston, *A
     Christian New-Years Gift: or Exhortations to the Chief Duties of a Christian*,
     n.p.: Roger Daniel, 1644. Samuel Clark, *The Lives of Sundry Eminent Persons
     in This Later Age*, London: Thomas Simmons, 1683. Richard Bernard,
     *Iosvahs Godly Resolution. . . touching houshold gouernment for well ordering
     a familie*, London: Iohn Legatt, 1612.
3   On family structure I have found particularly helpful Amy Froide's 'Marital
     Status as a Category of Difference: Singlewomen and Widows in Early
     Modern England', in *Singlewomen in the European Past, 1250-1800*, Judith M
     Bennett and Amy M Froide, eds., (Philadelphia: University of Pennsylvania
     Press, 1999), pp. 236-69, [hereafter Froide, *Singlewomen*] and Naomi
     Tadmor's *Family & Friends in Eighteenth-Century England: Household,
     Kinship, and Patronage*, (Cambridge: Cambridge University Press, 2001).
4   As Ralph Houlbrooke has pointed out, in England, individuals could exercise
     a measure of choice over which kinship relationships to cultivate within the
     generally accepted patriarchal hierarchy. The Ferrars certainly exercised a
     wide choice; Houlbrooke, *The English Family 1450-1700*, Chap. 3, esp p. 58.
5   Guildhall of London MS 30719/1: Skinners' Company, Apprentices and
     Freedoms book, 1496-1602, ff. 124v, 162r [numbers taken from the foot
     of the page]. Nicholas would have been about twenty when he entered his
     apprenticeship. I am indebted for much of this information about Nicholas
     Senior's business career to D.R. Ransome, 'John Ferrar of Little Gidding',

Records of Huntingdonshire, Vol 3 No 8 (2000), 16-17 [hereafter, Ransome, 'John Ferrar'].

6   *Ibid.*, f. 219. Erasmus was the son of William Harby of Canons Ashby, Northants and began his ten-year apprenticeship to John at Pentecost 1561; he would therefore have overlapped for some seven years with Nicholas.

7   Thomas Middleton was officially a member of the Grocers' Company, having been apprenticed to Ferdinando Poyntz, but membership in a particular livery company constituted no restriction on the subsequent scope of a merchant's trading activities; William Dodd, 'Mr Myddelton the Merchant of Tower Street', *Elizabethan Government and Society*, eds. S. T. Bindoff, J. Hurstfield, and C. H. Williams, (London: University of London, Athlone Press, 1961), pp. 250-51.[hereafter Dodd, 'Mr Myddelton'].

8   *Ibid.*, pp. 257-58. Also Kenneth R. Andrews, *Elizabethan Privateering . . .*, (Cambridge: Cambridge University Press, 1964), pp. 114, 116, 184-5, 197, 208, and 268. The Ferrar Papers (FP 3) include a 1590 list of supplies for such a ship.

9   He placed £20 with Middleton for his daughter, who was also Middleton's godchild. This was probably Susanna, the eldest surviving daughter, who about this time was preparing to marry John Collet. For this aspect of Middleton's activities see Dodd, 'Mr Myddelton', pp. 261-64.

10   Theodore K. Rabb, *Enterprise and Empire: Merchant and Gentry Investment in the Expansion of England, 1575-1630*, (Cambridge: Harvard University Press), 1967, p. 290.

11   Mayor, p. 342. It was probably one of these Middletons who turned down John's fellow merchant, Thomas Sheppard, as a suitor for his daughter; see below, pp. 46-7.

12   M&W, p. 42. How often such men actually came is of course not specified, but they were not likely to have been the regular visitors that the Middletons and Harbys were.

13   Nicholas Senior was said to have been chiefly responsible for bringing White to London as a lecturer, a significant opportunity for a cleric to advance his career. *Ibid.*, p. 42. See also Peter Peckard's biography of the younger Nicholas in Wordsworth, pp. 78-9, where he identifies this parish church as St. Benet Sherehog. Timothy Wadkins, however, places White as a lecturer at St. Paul's with no reference to his connection to Nicholas Ferrar; 'White, Francis (1563/4-1638)', Oxford Dictionary of National Biography, Oxford University Press, 2004 [accessed 19 Oct 2004: http://www.oxforddnb.com/view/29239] White could, of course, have held more than one lectureship. White preached the sermon at the elder Nicholas's funeral in 1620 and remained a friend of the family until his death as Bishop of Ely in 1638. Supporting lecturers has generally been considered a 'puritan' activity, e.g. the work of the Feoffees for Impropriations. We have no other evidence of the elder Nicholas's theological views but the choice of White would certainly imply Arminian sympathies as might the church furnishings had we more detailed information about them.

14   Peckard reported the refurbishment of the church (p. 10), quoted in Mayor, p. 66. The family gradually moved westwards as Nicholas prospered: from the parish of St. Gabriel, Fenchurch Street to Mark Lane in the parish of St. Mary Stayning and finally to St Sithes Lane in the parish of St. Benet Sherehog; Ransome, 'John Ferrar', p. 17.

15   As late as 1636 the younger Nicholas was arranging support for 'my Indian' then in London: FP 1014 (2 April). Both John and Nicholas also supported a school on Bermuda; Mayor, p. 205; E. Mansfield Forbes, 'Nicholas Ferrar: America and Little Gidding', *Clare College, 1326-1926*, Vol II, Cambridge: Cambridge University Press, 1930, p. 460 [hereafter cited as Forbes, 'Ferrar'].

16   She was one of a group of merchants and their wives, the men presumably having shares in the voyage, who came down to see the ship off, 3-5 April 1582; *An Elizabethan in 1582: The Diary of Richard Maddox, Fellow of All Souls*, Hakluyt Society, 2nd Series, No. 147 (1976), p. 102.

17   M&W, p. 41; Wordsworth, pp. 76-8.

18   Luke 1:6, cited in Mayor, p. 166.

19   Joyce (bapt. 22 Oct 1584) was alive when NF was born in 1593, but thereafter is unrecorded; Mayor, p. 303. Riley, 'The Good Old Way', p. vi.

20   S Collett Letters (28 Aug 1600); letter to Elizabeth Banderlo (SP??), who had taught her French. Susanna was by then married for she signed herself Susanna Collet.

21   On the Collet properties in Southwark, see below, pp. XX (paper 66) and XX (paper 279). That the Collets were at Bourn by 1606 is documented by letters addressed to John Collet at Bourn and dated 31 Oct and 13 Nov 1606; FP 9 and 10. For visits by Nicholas see M&W, p. 96. William wrote from Bourn to his mother in London; FP 21 (*c.* 1609)

22   M&W, pp. 43-4.

23   Peckard, p, 10, suggested that the boys themselves had at least some say in these decisions.

24   H. A. C. Sturges, *Register of Admissions to the Honourable Society of the Middle Temple*, (London: Butterworth & Co, 1949), Vol. I (1501-1781), pp. 81 and 95. Erasmus had been admitted to the Middle Temple on 20 March 1603/4, when he would have been 17 or 18. Those actually called to the Bar normally had been admitted 7-8 years before. William, for example, had been admitted 10 May 1610, eight years before he qualified. Erasmus thus died well before he would have completed his training; FP 2212 (Rev. Thomas Ferrar's notes on the life of Nicholas). He is said to have died at Bourn 29 May 1609, a date supported by a memorial plaque in Bourn church. William was recorded as the third son of Nicholas Ferrar, which leaves unclear his position in the birth order because although Erasmus had died previously, we do not know if the record took that fact into account. Nicholas is called the third son in FP 2214. That William was older than Nicholas is more convincingly attested by the fact that precocious Nicholas was deemed ready to go off to school when William went; M&W, p. 43.

25 Ransome, 'John Ferrar', 16.

26 Mayor, pp. 338-9.

27 Robert Bateman had become Nicholas Ferrar's first apprentice in 1581 and remained a close friend of the family; Guildhall of London MS 30719/1, Skinners' Company, 'Apprentices and Freedoms Book 1496-1602', f. 365.

28 The elder Nicholas in his will (1620) left his granddaughter Mary Collet £500 adding that he had brought her up from her cradle; Mayor, p. 342.

29 S Collet Letters include correspondence with 'Cosens' Stead, Rebecca Parkes, M. Brocas, as well as numerous letters to 'kinswoman' Lady Bodley.

30 M&W, p. 42.

31 Mayor; John's version (p. 12) refers to his 'tender constitution, which was delicate' and in Dr Jebb's version he 'was inclined to aguish distempers from his Infancy' (p. 166).

32 He is supposed to have told his mother that he wanted not lace bands but plain ones 'as Mr Anthony Wotton [a regular visitor to the household] wears; for I will be a preacher as he is'; Mayor, p. 354.

33 M&W, p. 43. Middleton also dubbed brother William, destined for the law, 'Lord Chancellor.' See also FP 2209.

34 M&W, p. 43.

35 Nicholas took his BA in 1609-10 but his matriculation is not given. It could have come in 1606 if he was thirteen but no later than 1607, no later and possibly before William matriculated at Easter 1607. William moved to the Middle Temple in 1610 without taking a degree; Venn, Part I, vol. 2, p. 134.

36 'Some Directions for ye Collecting of materials for ye writing of the life of Mr Nicholas Ferrar', reverse in the book of S Collet Letters and printed in M&W, pp. 37-40, from the version in Turner. For a more detailed account of these travels see my article, 'Prelude to Piety: Nicholas Ferrar's Grand Tour', *The Seventeenth Century*, Vol. XVIII, No. 1 (Spring 2003), 1-24.

37 Two excellent accounts of these travellers, which I have used extensively, are John Stoye, *English Travellers Aboard, 1604-1667,* Revised Edition, New Haven and London: Yale University Press, 1989 [hereafter cited as Stoye] and, Jonathan Woolfson, *Padua and the Tudors*, New York: Penguin, 1985 [hereafter cited as Woolfson].

38 Dr Butler of Clare Hall had predicted such an outcome from this rather drastic homeopathic remedy; Mayor, pp. 180-82.

39 Peckard, p. 40. His parents, who had known Lindsell for some years, accepted these assurances and gave their permission for him to make the trip unaccompanied, though of course he set off as one of a group.

40 The marriage with a Protestant prince was very popular in England, unlike the Spanish marriage proposed for her brother Charles, and Valentine's Day became a fashionable wedding date; Bathsheba Owen chose that date for her marriage to John Ferrar in 1615 and her younger sister also chose that day in 1616; Register of St. Olave, Hart Street.

41   FP 2212, s.16. We do not have the actual letter but only this summary
     made much later by Rev. Thomas Ferrar (1663-1739), Nicholas's great-
     nephew, which was cited subsequently by Peckard. All the biographies
     include comment that this choice meant Nicholas rejected the possibility of
     employment as her secretary at the Princess's court.

42   FP 2212, s.15 (21 May NS). The change to New Style dating means that
     this letter would have borne the date 11 May in England and a subsequent
     letter of 29 May announcing NF's safe arrival in Hamburg would have been
     written on the 19th. He thus spent only a fortnight or so in Holland.

43   T. M. MacDonogh, in his *Brief Memoirs of Nicholas Ferrar, M.A.* (London:
     James Nisbet, 1837), a work based on the lost manuscript life by Francis
     Turner, claims that 'he acquainted himself exactly with the doctrine of
     their church' (p. 20). This must refer to the established Reformed Church
     because the Brownists and Anabaptists are specifically mentioned in
     addition.

44   A. T. Van Deursen, *Plain Lives in a Golden Age* (Cambridge: Cambridge
     University Press, 1991), pp. 233n, 243-44, 262-67; Benedict, Philip,
     Christ's Churches Purely Reformed: A Social History of Calvinism, (New
     Haven and London: Yale University Press, 2002), pp. 194-5 and 199-
     201. The Reformed church was unlike the national Church of England to
     which everyone was assumed automatically to belong. Those who were not
     'members' but attended services were called 'adherents of the reformed
     religion'. Nevertheless anyone was entitled to marry in the church, have
     their children baptised, and be buried in the church or churchyard. Preachers
     sought to bring as many as possible to choose full membership but church
     councils remained rigorous in admitting candidates.

45   R. Po-chia Hsia, *The World of Catholic Renewal: 1540-1770* (Cambridge:
     Cambridge University Press, 1998), pp. 84-88. In the United Provinces they
     could secure a modicum of toleration by paying appropriate fines to the
     authorities.

46   van Deursen, *Plain Lives*, pp. 283-85, 301. In Haarlem the *klopjes* ran a
     sewing school for girls that was so successful that the Protestant regents
     sent their own daughters there. The Haarlem curriculum included verses
     and prayers as well as '"pious, educational games."' There are of course
     suggestive resemblances here to the Little Academy and especially to the
     maiden sisters, Mary and Anna Collet, but no documented connection.

47   For a detailed discussion of these communities see Richard L. DeMolen,
     ed., *Religious Orders of the Catholic Reformation*, (New York: Fordham
     University Press, 1994).

48   A conspicuous example was the account of Nicholas's own miraculous
     deliverance from being swept down an Alpine mountainside by the protruding
     load of timber on the back of a donkey; M&W, 51.

49   Peckard, pp.42-44. Nicholas sought detailed information about these and
     generously rewarded those attendants who supplied it to him. What Nicholas

saw would presumably have resembled the one which the city of Rotterdam established in 1614 by granting to one Daniel de Meijer a sixteen-year contract to set up a weaving shop into which he would receive twenty orphans each year. Though the children worked their first four years without pay, only an already well-established and prosperous craftsman was reckoned able to bear the initial cost in wasted materials as well as maintenance for the children. Theoretically the master should eventually benefit from the increased skill and productivity of these apprentices, always assuming that he was actually exerting himself to train them more than minimally; van Deursen, *Plain Lives*, pp.127-29. Fynes Moryson also looked at almshouses in Amsterdam; *Itinerary*, I, 93.

50   Rosemary O'Day cites examples of schools in England that taught practical skills and had often begun as schools for orphans; *Education and Society 1500-1800* (London & New York: Longman, 1982), pp.183-84. Practical training subsequently formed a significant part of education at Little Gidding. Nicholas employed the women of the household in bookbinding and making of concordances, for example, as well as training his nieces in the various skills of household management. He also requested supplies of hemp and flax from his cousin, Arthur Woodnoth, to be used in providing work for the poor of Gidding and of Bourn; FP 761 (24 Nov 1630).

51   John Edward Sadler, *J. A. Comenius and the Concept of Universal Education*, (London: George Allen and Unwin, 1966) and G. H. Turnbull, Hartlib, Dury and Comenius, ([Liverpool]: University Press of Liverpool), 1947, and Toby Barnard, 'Petty, Sir William (1623–1687)', *Oxford Dictionary of National Biography*, Oxford University Press, 2004; online edn, May 2007 [http://www.oxforddnb.com/view/article/22069, accessed 11 Nov 2010].

52   Blackstone, p.63; also Sharland, p.119.

53   The many surviving prints are reproduced as Ferrar Prints 1-562, http://www.virginacompanyarchives.amdigital.col.uk/Collections/Manuscript. Individual listings give the designer, engraver, publisher, date and subject of each print. Maycock, *NF*, p.210 suggests that Ferrar brought prints back with him for later use but there are certainly later letters from Gidding requesting print purchases: e.g. FP 994 (10 April 1635) in which NF requested Arthur Woodnoth to send sets of illustrations by Adrian Collaerts and Martin de Vos for use in making 'Betty's concordance'.

54   Walton claimed that he acquired Valdes during his travels, but the reliability of this statement is undermined by the accompanying assertion that Nicholas translated it out of Spanish when the title page of the published work said plainly that it had been done from Italian; Walton, 'Herbert' in Herbert, *Works*, p. 379.

55   Mayor, pp.183-84. Peckard also included the story, pp. 46-47.

56   Nicholas's suggestion that Mr. Sheppard would be a more reliable source of funds during his time in Italy than whatever other alternative had been first arranged implied that Nicholas already met him, perhaps in Hamburg; FP 2212 (NF to JF from Venice 5 Feb 1614[NS]).

57   Moryson, *Itinerary*, I, 6. Moryson made the journey from Hamburg to
     Lubeck in a day. For Nicholas to have time actually to see Lubeck he would
     have had to stay over a day or two and then journey back.

58   This absence of any mention of Lutheranism would certainly support Anthony's
     point that Anglicans generally showed little interest in or sympathy for this
     major branch of Protestantism: Anthony Milton, *Catholic and Reformed: The
     Roman and Protestant Churches in English Protestant Thought 1560-1640*,
     (Cambridge: Cambridge University Press, 1995), pp. 384-95 [hereafter Milton,
     Catholic and Reformed]. Nor was there any suggestion that Church of England
     services were an available option in these major trading centres.

59   If he proposed to travel overland, as Moryson did, he would have spent three
     days getting to Magdeburg and a further day and a half from Magdeburg to
     Leipzig; Morison, *Itinerary*, I, 12-13.

60   Jebb's account of the stay in Leipzig is the most detailed; Mayor, pp. 185-86
     and Blackstone, p. 14 n.2. Peckard recounts only the university activities,
     pp. 49-51. On systems of 'artificial memory' see Jonathan D. Spence in *The
     Memory House of Matteo Ricci,* (New York: Penguin, 1985) and Frances
     A. Yates in *The Art of Memory*, (Chicago: University of Chicago Press,
     1966). Since Nicholas by all accounts already had a formidable memory, his
     subsequent capacity must have been extraordinary.

61   FP 2212, s.17. He wrote to his mother of his safe arrival in Venice on 18
     November, adding, however, that he had been held up for six weeks at a point
     only nine days journey from his destination. The delay, perhaps at Trent,
     in any case on the Italian side of the Brenner, resulted from the quarantine
     imposed by the Venetian authorities on all travellers from Germany, where
     plague had been rife. Accounts of his travels mention an episode of quarantine
     coinciding with the forty days of Lent, but that could hardly refer to this
     occasion in October, and suggests that he made another transalpine journey,
     perhaps to Vienna the following February-March.

62   Pp. 52-54.

63   FP 2212, s.17.

64   Stoye, pp. 75, 118, 132. He describes NF as going from Leipzig to Augsburg
     and thence to Padua, though without considering the route he took between the
     two German cities. Certainly it would be difficult to imagine a Rhineland city
     like Strasburg or Speyer could have been part of those visits to neighboring
     courts that he made while based in Leipzig

65   Maurice Lee jr., *Dudley Carleton to John Chamberlain, 1603-1624* (New
     Brunswick, NJ: Rutgers University Press, 1972), p. 150. In this letter from
     Padua dated 4 Nov 1613 Carleton mentioned Trent and Verona as places
     where travelers had been subjected to lengthy quarantine and declared that
     since he had come as Ambassador to Venice (1611) there had never been so
     few English there and that the overall number of students at the university was
     small because of the difficulties of coming out of Germany. One Englishman
     who had arrived and settled in for the winter, however, was John Pory who

subsequently went to Virginia as secretary of the colony; William S. Powell, *John Pory, 1572-1636: The Life and Letters of a Man of Many Parts* (Chapel Hill: University of North Carolina Press, 1977), pp. xiii, 41-42, 74. If Pory and Nicholas met during this time, however, we have no record of it. We know Nicholas had taken himself to Padua by 14 Dec when he wrote from there to his brother John, lamenting that he had not heard from anyone in England in five months; FP 2212, s. 20. Stoye, pp. 77-80 and 87-90, also discusses the popularity of Padua/Venice with visiting Englishmen.

66   FP 2212, s. 20. If he went ahead with this plan, and his biographers certainly claim that he went to Vienna, he might then have served that Lenten quarantine he mentioned in his letter to his mother. He could hardly have done so for the full forty days as alleged or he would not have had time for anything else. The story looks to have conflated two episodes.

67   FP 2213. Easter fell on 30 March (NS) in 1614.

68   Mayor, pp. 189-90. For the medical faculty and course of study as well as the biographies of those Englishmen who studied not only medicine but other subjects as well, including those who did so entirely informally and without any official university status, see Woolfson.

69   There is no indication where he went. He could simply have moved into the countryside to escape the summer heat, as many Italians did, or gone farther afield.

70   Peckard, pp. 59-60. When exactly Garton appeared on the scene is never specified; Nicholas certainly does not mention him in his letter of November 1614.

71   See below, pp. 121-2 and 131-3.

72   FP 56 (11 Nov 1614). The letter was addressed to brother John but the version we have is a copy in his father's hand. A letter from Dudley Carleton to John Chamberlain from Venice in October 1614 reported a great deal of sickness in the area; Lee, *Carleton-Chamberlain*, p. 170.

73   Certainly in later years Ferrar generally opposed bleeding except as a desperate last resort and preferred less drastic measures like rest, diet and appropriate exercise. See below, pp. 150-1.

74   Peckard, p. 58. Peckard attributed this story of Ferrar's aversion to bleeding to Barnabas Oley, who appended it to his edition of George Herbert's *Country Parson*, but went on to add that Ferrar was supposed at the time to have taken a vow of celibacy and proposed to retire, once he had returned to England, to a religious life. Peckard, however, dismissed that story as having insufficient evidence, which certainly seems an appropriate verdict. On Turner's hope to use his Ferrar biography as Tory propaganda in the wake of the Exclusion crises see below, pp. 291-2.

75   Mayor, pp. 191-93 and Peckard, pp. 61-62. Peckard did not include the story about the Swiss guard. Easter fell on 19 April (NS) in 1615.

76   Spain was a much less common destination for touring Englishmen to visit; Stoye, p. 87. Ferrar was said to have included it as part of a larger circle that

would take him from there across the Pyrenees and through France on his
way home to England; Mayor, p. 197; Peckard, p. 73.

77   Peckard, pp. 65-68 and Mayor, pp. 193-94.

78   *Ibid.*, pp. 69-70 and pp. 194-95. For this second journey to Spain Peckard
put him on shipboard in Venice while Mayor returned him to Marseilles first.
Wherever the incident took place, the pirates turned away before actually
attacking, more likely because they had spotted in the distance what looked
a more promising victim than because Ferrar's martial valor had intimidated
them.

79   *Ibid.,* 73-84 and 197-201. The most convincing evidence for the 1617 date
comes from a letter to a 'good cosen' dated 11 October and written by
John Woodnoth from 'Carmincham' in Cheshire. He was the grandson of
Mary Woodnoth Ferrar's brother John, being much the same age as John
and Nicholas Ferrar. He died later in 1617. The writer sends greetings from
his wife and himself (and the younger John was certainly married) to 'your
brother John and his wife'. The letter offered congratulations to the 'good
cosen' on his safe return to England and apologised for not writing sooner.
He blamed his delay on his expectation that the cousin would have come
to Cheshire in the summer just past when the king was visiting the country.
That visit took place in late August 1617, as part of King James's return
journey from Scotland; John Nichols, *The Progresses, Processions, and
Magnificent Festivities of King James the First, His Royal Consort, Family
and Court . . .*, (New York: Burt Franklin, n.d. (first publ. 1828), III, pp. 411-
12.

Further confirmation of the 1617 date comes from the will of Mary Robinson (PCC
88 Meade), who was buried in London on 13 October 1618. If, as seems
probable, the Nicholas Ferrar named by Mary Robinson as her executor was
the returned Nicholas rather than his aging father, he would have had to be
back in London long enough to have become known to her. She had become
part of the family when John Ferrar married her niece Bathsheba Owen. That
marriage, John's second, did not take place till 1615 when Nicholas was
already in Italy.

80   [Edwin Sandys], *Europae Speculum, Or, A View or Survey of the State of
Religion in the Westerne Parts of the World*, (London: By T. Cotes, for Michael
Sparke, 1632), *passim*. An earlier version that Sandys claimed was pirated
appeared in 1605. Moryson also mentions such institutions and societies,
including the Venetian house for orphaned girls; *Itinerary*, I, 184, 256.

81   The Italian title is given in Paul Grendler, *Schooling in Renaissance Italy:
Literacy and Learning, 1300-1600*, (Baltimore & London: Johns Hopkins
University Press, 1989), p. 434. I am indebted to Grendler's volume for
enabling me first to identify Carbone and then to learn about the Schools of
Christian Doctrine. M&W, p.xv, give a Latin title for this work which does not
follow clearly either the Italian or Ferrar's English. See also Mayor, p. 302.

82   Cf. the Jesuits' mission to Naples described in Jennifer D. Selwyn, *A Paradise*

Inhabited by Devils: The Jesuits Civilizing Mission in Early Modern Naples (Ashgate: Institutum Historicum Societatis Iesu, 2004).

83   Mayor, p. xvi.

84   See below, p. 193. On such 'sodalities' that were characteristic of humanist circles in Italy see Daniel A. Crews, *Twilight of the Renaissance: The Life of Juan de Valdes*, (Toronto: University of Toronto Press, 2008), especially Ch. 5, 'The Valdesian Sodality' [hereafter cited as Crews, *Twilight*]. Valdes's followers, most notably Flaminio and Carnesecchi, continued this pattern of informal group life when they joined the household of Cardinal Pole at Viterbo. Pole himself obviously found this pattern congenial and exerted his influence to protect Flaminio from the Inquisition. See Thomas F. Mayer, *Reginald Pole, Prince & Prophet* (Cambridge: Cambridge University Press, 2000), esp Ch.3.

85   His choice of a mercantile career for John probably reflected not only a conventionl wish for a son to follow in his footsteps but also an assessment of his son's strengths and weaknesses. How much it also reflected John's own wishes is unclear, but it was a shrewd judgment for John comes across in his letters as somewhat pedestrian and verbally inept.

86   Ransome, 'John Ferrar' has provided this fact and much of the further information in this account; 17-22.

87   The Ferrar Papers include letters exchanged between the fathers over financial terms of the match. Nicholas had set forth his offer to William Sheppard in a letter of 27 November (FP 34) and he signed a final version drafted by John in January (FP 35). In both these letters he signs himself as 'unknown' or 'unacquainted' with Sheppard, who was not in London but resident on the family's estate at Great Rollright in Oxfordshire. The likely go-between was Timothy Sheppard, probably a younger brother of William, who was indeed in London and who knew John, whom he made an executor of his will in 1612. He would have been the 'Timothy' of whom Mary Ferrar spoke in a letter to John about the negotiations in progress; FP 132 (5 December [1612]).

88   FP 33 (10 June 1612). The Middleton involved could have been either Hugh or Robert and therefore a friend of the elder Ferrars. Mary Ferrar's letter counseling patience (FP 132) is misdated in the online sequence; it is clearly part of the 1612 correspondence about John's marriage.

89   John Stow, *Survey of London* (1633), p. 277. Rev Thomas Ferrar's summary of family letters of 1613 included the brief statement, 'J Ferrars wife ill'; Nicholas's letter to John of 1 May mentioned praying for sister's recovery [Susanna?] and sending love to her 'as to your wife'; FP 2212, ss. 13 & 16.

90   This is the portrait reproduced in E. Cruwys Sharland, *The Story Books of Little Gidding* (London: Seeley and Co., 1899), p. 154 and misidentified as Susanna Collet. It was one of a group of family portraits of Nicholas Sr and Mary, Nicholas Jr and John, the residents of the St Sithes household, hence the probability that it is Bathsheba and little Mary rather than Susanna

Collet.

91 As early as June 1619 he was put on a committee to hear a petition from Captain John Bargrave about his suit in Chancery against the Company's Adventurers in the Joint Stock; Susan Myra Kingsbury, ed., *The Records of the Virginia Company of London* (Washington, DC: US Government Printing Office, 1906-1936), I, p. 223. [Hereafter cited as Kingsbury]

92 For the duties of the company's officials, see Kingsbury, III, pp. 139-44 (a draft of 27 April 1619) and 'Order and Constitutions. . .Anno 1619. And 1620', a pamphlet printed in Force's *Tracts*, III, No. 6.

93 Kingsbury, I, p. 404.

94 *Ibid*, I, p. 583 and II, p. 15.

95 *Ibid.*, I, p. 473.

96 *Ibid.*, II, p. 29. A Deputy could serve only one three-year term.

97 *Ibid.*, I, pp. 387-97. On the sending of the women see David R. Ransome 'Wives for Virginia, 1621', *William & Mary Quarterly*, 3rd ser., Vol. 48, No. 1 (1991), 3-18. On the ultimately unsuccessful efforts to cultivate vineyards and silkworms see Kingsbury, I, pp. 483, 510, 504, 515, 627.

98 Ransome, 'John Ferrar', 20-21.

99 Kingsbury, IV, pp. 290-91. A translation of the *Quo Warranto* writ follows, pp. 358-98.

100 *Ibid.*, I, p. 174.

101 This archive of the company is now in the Ferrar Papers at Magdalene College, Cambridge. Kingsbury published only some 15% of them in her four-volume work cited earlier.

102 Ferrar was the Member for Lymington, Hampshire on the nomination of the Earl of Southampton; 'The Parliamentary Diary of Nicholas Ferrar, 1624', ed. David R. Ransome, *Seventeenth-Century Political and Financial Papers*, Camden Miscellany XXXIII, Camden Fifth Series, Vol. 7, (Cambridge: Cambridge University Press for the Royal Historical Society, 1996), p. 6.

103 Kingsbury, II, p. 539 and Nicholas Ferrar, 'The Parliamentary Papers of Nicholas Ferrar 1624', *Seventeenth-Century Political and Financial Papers: Camden Miscellany XXXII*, ed. David R. Ransome, (Cambridge: Cambridge University Press for the Royal Historical Society,1996), pp. 7- 9, 71-88.

104 A good, concise account of the episode appears in Robert Brenner, *Merchants and Revolution: Commercial Change, Political Conflict, and London's Overseas Traders, 1550-1663* (Cambridge: Cambridge University Press, 1993), pp. 93-102.

105 *Sir Thomas Smith's Misgovernment of the Virginia Company*, ed. with an Introduction by D. R. Ransome, (Cambridge: for the Roxburghe Club, 1990). It was never published though, of course, it could have circulated in manuscript. Ransome in his Introduction (xi-xxii) dates the probable time of writing as July 1624, after the arrival in London the previous month of a declaration from the Virginia Assembly passed in February objecting to the return of the Smith faction to control of the colony. The Mandeville

Commission, entrusted with the task of devising a new government for the colony, was meeting in the summer of 1624 and was loaded with Smith supporters. By the following year, however, both King James and Smith had died, Charles and Buckingham were preoccupied with war against Spain, and the Virginia problem was simply shelved until 1631; Brenner, 102.

106   Kingsbury, III, pp. 519-51.

107   He may not, however, have entirely turned his back on Virginia. In June 1631 he and his brother John were included in a commission, which reported back in November, to propose means for the political and economic development of the colony, including the creation of a new Virginia Company; NA, Co 1/6/14, 30-32, 36, 48, 70, 80-81, and Patent Roll, 7 Charles I, part 20, no. 50. No evidence survives to show that either brother participated, and when a new commission for Virginia was appointed in April 1634, they were not included.

108   R.H. Tawney, *Business & Politics under James I: Lionel Cranfield as Merchant and Minister* (Cambridge: Cambridge University Press, 1958), p. 232.

109   He was not comfortable with either surprises or failures. See below, pp. 145-7 for his later lamentations over his mistakes with John Gabbet and Arthur Woodnoth's nephew Ralph; also his evidently very depressed letter near the end of his life, which the faithful Arthur Woodnoth showed to Dr Winston; FP 1052 (27 April 1637).

110   The prayer of thanksgiving for their deliverance that Nicholas composed and the family recited on the last day of every month at Little Gidding expressed such a view at length; M&W, pp. 60-64.

111   Sheppard had in 1619 joined the Virginia Company and quickly become an active member of its Council; Kingsbury, I, 223, 270, 365, 406, 417; II, 56, 128; III,372, 498; IV, 358-398 (Shepard was one of those named in the *quo warranto* petition.).

112   Lloyds of London provides a modern example of the perils of unlimited liability.

113   The only one who figures extensively in the Papers is one Thomas Barker, who wouldn't settle but took Sheppard to court and eventually to jail. See below, pp. 76-7.

114   FP 513 (22 Nov 1623); Sandys was writing from Northbourne in Kent.

115   He named Mr Keightley, Mr Barber, Mr Wheatley, and Sir John Danvers and was clear that 'ye Knight at Fanchurch' believed the rumor. He thought the one responsible was 'H. H.,' perhaps Sir Humphrey Handford or Hugh Hamersley, both of whom appear to have been friendly with Sir Thomas Smith; see Kingsbury, II, pp. 259-61, 28-29; IV, pp. 80-81, 294.

116   FP 501 (15 Oct 1623) The comment occurred little more than a month before Sandys' letter to John Ferrar (FP 513).

117   FP 587 (30 Jan 1625/6). The letter concludes with a plea that Theophilus pay what he owed to John, a debt of some standing evidently to judge from an earlier letter of 12 Nov 1621 (FP 332) in which Theophilus declared that 'For your money I will promise no more for shame till I performe'. J. It eventually came but considerably later; FP 683 (AW to NF; mid-Aug 1629).

118   FP 2207, f. 9 (21). This was standard procedure as the examples of Cranfield
      and Sir Arthur Ingram illustrate; Menna Prestwich, Cranfield: Politics and
      Profits under the Early Stuarts (Oxford: Clarendon Press, 1966) [hereafter
      cited as Prestwich]; Tawney, Business and Politics; Anthony Upton, Sir
      Arthur Ingram, c. 1565-1642: A Study of the Origins of an English Landed
      Family (Oxford: Oxford University Press, 1961). A broadsheet entitled 'A
      Briefe of the bill exhibited against bankrupts' appeared probably in 1624
      and addressed to Parliament in hopes of tightening legal procedures against
      bankrupts who tried to hide their property and so preserve it.
119   The complicated stages of this sale can be found in the Annesley Mss.
      E6/12/13D/1-25 in the Oxfordshire Record Office The final papers com-
      pleting the sale bear the date 30 May 1625. On the deal with the creditors
      see M&W, p.60; this late and rather opaque account by John does not
      square with his 1626 letter to Theophilus Woodnoth quoted above, p. 17,
      or connect the debt settlement with the purchase of Gidding. Mayor, p. 339
      gives provisions of Mary Ferrar's will and the date of the sale indenture.
          The creditors would have had to have assurance that the money would
      come to them. Cranfield encountered problems when he purchased a
      sequestrated property of Barn Elms privately without guaranteeing access
      for the creditors to the funds; Prestwich, pp. 389-95.
120   The four commissioners in the case were themselves merchants and included
      Ralph Freeman, a Sheriff and Alderman of London, and Maurice Abbott,
      Governor of the East India Company. FP 540 (Sheppard affidavit; 14
      May 1624) & 541 (Ferrar statement; undated but referring to 540). John
      acknowledged that he had perhaps been careless to let pass earlier references
      to him as a 'partner' in this matter when he had in fact no part in it. If,
      however, he should be adjudged liable by a strict definition of partnership,
      then he would insist on full proof by sworn testimony.
121   FP 1257; this much later letter to his son [c. 1655] reiterates his deep and
      continuing sense of obligation and gratitude to his mother and brother for
      bailing him out of this disaster.
122   See below, pp. 234-6 and 246-9.

2

The New Household at Little Gidding:
'United not only in Cohabitation but in Hartes'

1   M&W, 39. The phrase also appears in the 'directions' for collecting
      biographical materials in S Collet Letters, f.4r.
2   M&W, pp. 86-7 and 128, and FP 1064 (After 25 Mar 1637).
3   Froide, Singlewomen, pp. 237-9.
4   John Ferrar in the family home in St Sithes Lane; John Collet at Bourn in
      Cambridgeshire.
5   Rushworth, Historical Collections: The Second Part. . ., London: John

Wright and Richard Chiswell, 1680, p. 178. The comment occurs in the context of his account of King Charles's progress to Scotland in 1633 that took him to the vicinity of Gidding and implies that the king actually came to Gidding whereas he in fact only sent a messenger to borrow the family's gospel Harmony.

6   For example, she took an active part in arranging the initial leases of the Gidding land to local farmers; FP 588 (March [1626].

7   FP 938 undated but probably 1629 from references to the deliverance of cousin Mary Woodnoth and to niece Su[sanna] Collet Mapletoft's state of mind. What the approaches of fire and water were he probably did not feel it necessary to explain.

8   She said as much in an undated letter, the only one we have in her writing; FP 940. In her will of 1628 she left the Little Gidding property entirely to him. John had no legal rights in it while Nicholas lived and would inherit only if he outlived his childless brother; Mayor, p. 339. John cited this provision in a much later quarrel with his wife; FP 1044 (20 Feb 1636/7).

9   FP 665 (26 Feb 1628/9).

10   FP 1257 (c. 1655). The letter explains why JF gives 1/20 of his income from the estate in alms and wants his son to continue this practice when he inherits.

11   FP 1049 (AW to NF, 13 April 1637). Arthur offered this comment as part of his proposal to put up a monument to his aunt.

12   FP 574 (29 June 1625). Whether she herself was at Gidding, in which case she would have been there before Nicholas arrived, or was to relay instructions and materials to John from Bourn is not clear. An arrival before Nicholas would not square with John's later version, in which she could not wait the quarantine month after Nicholas had finally got to Gidding but insisted on riding over to see him only three days after he arrived. That account clearly implies that she had not seen the place before.

13   FP 575 (22 July 1625); Arthur Woodnoth to NF at Gidding.

14   M&W, p.64.

15   *Ibid.*, p. 66; Mayor, p. 224. Before the church was usable the family made the short walk to Steeple Gidding for services and Mary Ferrar paid the rector generously for the help he provided. In later years the Rev. Luke Grose of Great Gidding perhaps provided the morning sermon though this fact is not explicitly stated and his parish was rather more than a short walk away.

16   Blackstone, 244-45 Undated letter including reference to service book and other furnishings. FP 694 (AW to NF, c.16 Nov 1629) about tablets.

17   In January 1627 the nonresident rector, David Stephens at Eton College, had reminded Ferrar of his offer to speak to the Lord Keeper about a prebend for him in exchange for Little Gidding; FP 635. If such an exchange was intended to clear the way for the appointment of a resident rector, the possibility never materialised nor was it mentioned again. Stephens remained the rector and was still at Eton when he wrote in June 1634 a letter of condolence to Ferrar on the death of his mother; FP.942.

18   M&W, p. 101. References to glebe business occur in FP 866 (Sept 1632, when the process started); 918, 937, and 942. One who took up her example was the Rev. Joshua Mapletoft, husband of her granddaughter Susanna Collet Mapletoft, who succeeded in recovering some of the glebe land of his own parish of Margaretting in Essex; FP 949 (NF>JM, 10 Mar 633/4).

19   Edward Wallis, husband of Joyce Collet, was appointed rector in 1648; CCEd, Location ID: 7483 (Little Gidding).

20   King Charles I saw the almshouse during his 1642 visit and it was still functioning when John Jones visited Gidding in 1731; M&W, pp. 87-88 and 140. MWF's almshouse was an example of a type of charity often favoured by widows, one that Amy Erickson attributes to their awareness of the plight of these particularly vulnerable women; *Women and Property in Early Modern England*, (London & New York:Routledge,1993), pp. 202, 211-12.

21   FP 729 (5 July 1630). Bateman had been a close friend of the family since his apprenticeship with Nicholas Senior;. His son Richard was Nicholas's last apprentice, coming to him in 1618. While the surviving letter is a draft or copy not in her own hand but that of Nicholas, it seems unlikely that she would call attention to the writing as she did had she not sent Bateman the original in her own hand. She refers to her 'abillity both of hands and eysight' that the letter will demonstrate to Bateman. The only example of her writing among the Ferrar Papers is an undated letter probably of a later date but with strong and clear writing (FP 940). Other accounts of her remarkable health in Peckard, pp. 241 and 172-73, and Mayor, pp. 63-64, and 64-65 n. 1, which quotes a passage about an eighty-year-old who looked eighteen in *Hygiasticon,* the work on temperance in diet which Nicholas translated and published in 1634, the year of her death.

22   Sharland, pp. li-liii (Feb 1631/2).

23   He inherited substantial property, as his marriage settlement on his son Thomas demonstrated; see below, p. 82. Over the years he corresponded with Ferrar about business matters and clearly appealed to his brother-in-law for financial help, most notably in presenting his accounts to the Countess of Devonshire and her steward Mr Watt in order to secure discharge of a debt of some £ 200; FP 764 (? Jan 1630/1). Ferrar later referred to some failed bargain that Collet had entered into about which Ferrar told his mother there was no point in negotiating with him; FP 797 (17 June 1631).

24   Amy M. Charles, *A Life of George Herbert*, (Ithaca and London: Cornell University Press, 1977), pp. 168-9. [Hereafter cited as Charles, Herbert]

25   FP 633(?1627); other of Arthur's brothers had also been apprenticed to London goldsmiths Charles, Herbert, pp. 168-9

26   Arthur was surely the 'Mr Woodnutt' who attended the extraordinary meeting on 20 October 1623 to consider surrendering the charter: Kingsbury, IV, p. 291. He also composed a history of the Company published posthumously in 1651.

27   FP 575 (22 July 1625).

28   FP 574 (NF to MWF at ?LG/Bourn, 24 June 1625); FP 575 (AW to NF at LG,
      22 July); FP 579 (JCollet to NF in London, 13 Dec). These reconstructions
      of Nicholas's whereabouts, based as they are on the family's letters, can be
      only a rough approximation with considerable periods unaccounted for. They
      do, however, follow closely enough the patterns of the legal and political
      calendar which would have affected Nicholas's affairs.

29   John's letter to Theophilus Woodnoth on 30 January 1626 (FP 587) made
      no specific reference to him but simply said 'they' planned soon to return
      to London. Nicholas certainly went on ahead and wrote to his mother
      from London about the transport of the women of the family to London
      in March; FP 588, 589 (9 & 16 March 1625/6). In FP 588 he mentions
      Nicholas Collet, in London as Arthur Woodnoth's apprentice, as still ill
      with an ague.

30   He had been presented for ordination to William Laud, then Bishop of St.
      David's, by his old college tutor and friend, Augustine Lindsell; M&W,
      p.66.

31   See above, p. 60.

32   FP 562, 559, 561-63.

33   FP 591 (28 April, 2 and 10 May 1626). These were drafts of letters written
      from London but for obvious reasons not properly addressed. John and
      Nicholas must have known, however, where to send them but the family in
      Gidding might or might not have known. He received another letter from
      John Jones a week later (FP 592) telling of another lawsuit also pending, this
      one brought by Swanne and others against Jones, Sheppard, and ? Stubbs.
      The attorney with whom John and Nicholas conferred was not named but the
      cousin Sadd who received the trunk was perhaps the Stephen Sad, who had
      been in the Virginia Company since 1618; Rabb, *Enterprise*, p. 370.

34   FP 596 (Tristram Conyam to NF, 3 Aug 1626). Nicholas had shortly before
      returned to Gidding and Conyam was reporting the sad story to him there
      though he said Sheppard was 'very merry outwards.' Sheppard did himself
      no favor when, instead of taking the opportunity offered to present a careful
      statement to the judge, he launched into a heated denunciation of the decree
      as unreasonable. The Ferrars had at an earlier stage advised him to think
      carefully about his answers to the court. They might not have been surprised
      at this sequel.

35   FP 635 (5 Feb 1627/8) and 640 (17 Apr 1628) letters of Sheppard to NF and
      draft of NF's reply to latter; 650 (13 Nov 1628). Barker in late 1628 was said
      even to have subpoenaed Arthur Woodnoth and others in connection with a
      bill he brought in the Court of Chancery over the Sheppard affair. Thomas
      Collet reported subpoenas but also his failure to discover any actual bill in
      Chancery. Thomas, a recently admitted barrister, was pressed into service
      for such investigations. Sheppard was not successful in shaking off Barker's
      pursuit but by the following February was lamenting that 'they [Barker et.
      al.] have now spit their venom'; FP 663.

36   FP724 (17 May 1630); FP 1070, 884, 891, 980, 984, 1023, 1025, 1028 (10
      Jan1632/3 - 2 Aug 1636). Woodnoth confessed that he had eventually to use a
      variety of people as emissaries so that Sheppard would not guess the source of
      the money. There were also new claims against Timothy Sheppard's will, for
      which John was one of the executors; FP 859 (23 July 1632) and FP 903 (8 July
      1633) concern a belated claim by one Sybil Barber against the estate.
On the antipathy to lawyers and lawsuits, see below, p. 244.
37   FP 602 (JF at LG to NF in London, at house of AW, 21 Nov 1626) and FP 606
      (Maurice Thompson in London to NF at LG, 29 Dec).
38   FP 617 (14 June 1627); He was in London when he annotated a note to
      Arthur Woodnoth from their cousin John Woodnoth, who wrote about a
      longstanding debt to old Nicholas Ferrar, who had never pressed him for
      repayment, and apologetically added that he would gladly repay it but he
      simply hadn't the means.
39   FP 619 (5 July 1627).
40   FP 618 & 621. Ferrar's reply to Su Collet; FP 620
41   FP 626-28, 631. He arranged temporary sanctuary for Richard at the Savoy,
      but that was by no means a lasting solution.
42   Nicholas was made free of the Goldsmiths' Company on 28 March 1634,
      having been apprenticed in Nov 1626; Goldsmiths' Company Records (Foster
      Lane). He clearly was with Woodnoth when on 9 March 1625/6 Nicholas
      Ferrar wrote from London to his mother at Gidding that young Nick was still
      ill with his ague; FP 588.
43   FP 633 [?1627]; The letter is in Arthur's hand though it is not a fair copy;
      on the back are notes in both his and Nicholas's hand. It was a collaborative
      effort that combined Arthur's message and Nicholas's crisper wording.
44   S Collet Letters (November 1628).
45   He went on to become a Bencher on 5 Nov 1652; H A C Sturges (comp)
      , Register of Admissions to the Honourable Society of the Middle Temple.
      .., (London: Butterworth, 1949), Vol. 1, p. 109. Aspiring barristers often
      spent a year or two at university before beginning their legal studies though
      generally without staying to take a degree; Erasmus Ferrar had certainly
      done that. The family papers make no reference to Thomas's following such
      a pattern and there is no evidence to prove that he was the Thomas Collet
      listed in Venn (Part I, Vol I, p.371) as matriculating from Clare in 1616
      and receiving his B.A. in 1619-20. If he were, however, he would have
      been unusual in staying to take a degree. Clare, of course, was his uncle
      Nicholas's college.
46   S Collet Letters (14 Jan 1627/8); the Sheringtons were asking £180 p.a. to
      be settled on the couple while the Collets claimed they could manage no
      more than £120. What the final figure was is not revealed in the surviving
      letters. A subsequent letter from Susanna to Nicholas (FP 508) thanks him
      for letting her and her husband know the terms he had agreed with Mrs
      Sherington but does not specify what those terms were. This document

is incorrectly dated 25 Jan [1626/7] in the Ferrar Papers Finding List; it belongs to early 1628.

47   These included Arthur Woodnoth (25 Jan) and Cosen Stead (21 Jan) and Lady Bodley and Aunt Collet (Feb 1627/8).

48   The Southwark properties settled on Thomas by his father were those inherited by his son John and given to a charity school in Southwark in his will: Will of John Collet of St Andrews, Holborn : PCC Leeds 1713; dated 9 May 1711, with codicil added 12 Nov 1713, proved 26 Nov 1713. FP 645 is the release of Thomas's share of his grandfather's bequest. Susanna Collet wrote of plans to receive the bride at Gidding in July.

49   Tom specially thanked his uncle Nicholas for his kindness to his wife; FP 656 (8 Dec 1628)

50   FP 641, 648, 650 and 656 (25 April, 23 Oct, 13 Nov, and 8 Dec 1628). The marriage must have taken place between 23 Oct and 13 Nov. The correspondence about Bathsheba's letter to Mrs. Sherington is undated but 1629 is the probable date assigned to FP 661. John delivered Nicholas's letter to Mrs. Sherington. Thomas and Martha departed Gidding in Oct 1630; S Collet letters to Aunt Collet, Daughter Collet, and Son Collet (Oct-Nov 1630).

51   His mother, always ready with advice, hastened to remind him of the great obligation they both must feel toward the Browns and most especially to cousin Arthur, a sentiment that Nicholas also expressed in his own letter to Arthur. Susanna also reminded Edward of his promise to continue to learn Psalms and also Proverbs, as he had promised, though his subsequent misadventures showed that a blind hope; S Collet Letters, (Nov 1628). FP 649 (Oct 1628) NF to AW.

52   FP 774 (NF to AW 19 April 1631), 776 (AW to NF 21 April 1631), and 778 (NF to AW 24 April 1631) detail this revealing episode. Ferrar's reaction in a subsequent letter to his mother that there was no point in negotiating further about a failed partnership of Collet's suggests that by that time he had had more than enough of his brother-in-law's business affairs; FP 797 (17 June 1631)

53   S Collet Letters, (26 April 1631) and 2 May 1631).

54   *Ibid.*, (24 July 1631): Edward was supposed to work on improving his handwriting and accounting skills but above all to reform 'his mind & manners'.

55   It was to Bateman that Mary Woodnoth Ferrar had written describing the satisfaction of her new life at Gidding; FP 729 (5 July 1630). See above, pp. 71-2.

56   S Collet Letters, (21 and 28 Oct 1631).

57   FP 830 (14 Jan 1631/2 and 835 (21 Jan 1631/32).

58   FP 762 & 763, probably written c. Jan 1630/1. He composed in Latin these two formal letters in 1630/31 presumably to demonstrate his academic competence.

59   FP 854 (30 April 1632).

60   Venn, Pt I, Vol I, p. 371; FP 1095-6, 1098 (letters between FC and Patrick
      Maxwell at Peterhouse, June-Dec, 1643) place him at Gidding. There were
      two other Collet brothers, Richard and John. John (born 1621) was apprenticed
      to Arthur Woodnoth in 1635, but did not not complete his apprenticeship.
      Richard was older than Ferrar but of his training we have no record. They
      had both emigrated to Virginia and by 1650 had moved to Maryland; see
      Appendix below.

61   Mayor, p. 123. Whether this had anything to do with delicate health is not
      clear.

62   See Craig, C. Leslie, *Nicholas Ferrar Junior*, London: Epworth Press, 1950
      and Monotessaron, 38-9, for Collet's contribution to the later harmonies.

63   FP 649 (Oct 1628)

64   FP 654-56 (1 & 8 Dec 1628).

65   See above, p.83-4.

66   As shock tactics he told Richard that his mother had left him nothing in her
      will, hoping thereby to disabuse him of any false expectations he might have
      entertained on that score FP 678-683 (July-Aug 1629); cf. S Collet Letters,
      (Sept 1629) when Susanna wrote to Nicholas from Margetting and sent love
      to brother Richard, who she hoped was still at Gidding, and also her 'sister',
      Richard's wife. Arthur had been one of the witnesses of Mary Woodnoth's
      will a year earlier. Richard had had in 1620 a legacy from his father's will of
      which his mother, with evident reason, had thought him a poor steward.

67   Evidence of temporary success came in the form of Richard's offer to repay
      Nicholas the £10 he owed him; FP 698 (6 Jan 1629/30).

68   See above, pp. 71-2.

69   Turner, f. 106r. See also below, p. 93.

70   It was one of the points in the king's instructions to his archbishops that he
      wanted information about in each diocese; Kenneth Fincham, ed., 'Annual
      Accounts of the Church of England, 1632-1639', *From the Reformation to
      the Permissive Society*, Melanie Barber and Stephen Taylor with Gabriel
      Sewall, eds., Woodbridge: Boydell Press for Church of England Record
      Society, 2010, pp. 63-149.

71   M&W, 83.

72   To encourage the children they were given the substantial reward of 3d. per
      psalm and 8d. for each New Testament chapter they could recite 'without
      book'; Blackstone, p. 39.

73   Mayor, pp. 40-43.

74   Rastrick (1650-1727) attached immense importance to such reading as
      a means of Christian formation; Andrew Cambers and Michelle Wolfe,
      'Reading, Family Religion, and Evangelical Identity in Late Stuart England',
      Historical Journal, 47, 4 (2004), 875-96. I am grateful to Dr David L. Smith
      for this reference.

75   I am grateful to Trevor Cooper for identifying in a private communication
      (16 Aug 2009) the hymns and songs in the sessions of the Little Academy as

published in Sharland. They included hymns by Richard Verstegan, George Wither and Simon Wastell.

76   Turner. f 106r and f 60r. This vivid image of the mind as a clock needing winding up was quoted by the Patient [probably Anna Collet] in the discussion of reviving the Little Academy in 1632, evidence of the reading of Ferrar's educational 'Instructions' by his nieces; Sharland, pp. 168-70.

77   Peckard, p. 191.

78   On Ralph see below, p. 145; on Danvers' godson see FP 821 (19 Nov 1631).

79   Turner. ff. 55v-61r.

80   *Ibid.*, ff. 117v-119r, 121v-123r. The treatise in virginity only survives in fragmentary form in Turner, ff. 118v-119r abd 121v-123r. It concluded with a comment that the writer [NF} would not counsel any to virginity, it being a gift of God and not attainable by human will alone. The 'Duties' volume is in private hands and I am grateful to its owner for permitting me to examine it. It is written in the same hand that copied substantial portions of the Little Academy's story books and employed a Greek-style 'd' unlike that of the nieces. The scribe was in all likelihood nephew Nicholas although his uncle Nicholas probably composed it for the instruction of the household, with the final section particularly intended for the nieces to prepare them for marriage. Certainly Mary Woodnoth Ferrar expected that her granddaughters would marry and should be trained in housewifery by way of preparation; Sharland, liii.

81   FP 913 (10 Oct 1633). 'Temperance', a later project, was the second of the 'tessara'. Mapletoft had known Nicholas since their days in Cambridge and had become a member of the family by marrying in 1628 Susanna Collet, Nicholas's niece.

82   M&W, p.51.

83   The 150 Psalms and 'Heads' of the Concordance were said over in every month, which would mean that five (or six if not counting Sundays when the whole psalter was recited after evensong; M&W, p. 73) would be read on a given day, a number that fits better with canonical hours but conflicts with comments elsewhere in the biographies that these recitations took place hourly, which would have produced many more sessions than the canonical hours provided. I am grateful to Trevor Cooper for a helpful summary of these conflicting reports: (private communication 28 July 2010).

84   John Cosin's *Devotions* of 1627 based on canonical hours and alleged to have been undertaken at the king's own request after the queen had remarked on the lack of such books of hours in the Church of England, would hardly have allayed such suspicions. Cosin was certainly a Laudian as well as a friend of Ferrar and familiar with the practices of Little Gidding, as was also Francis White, who was said to have relayed the king's request to Cosin: Horton Davies, *Worship and Theology in England, Vol II: From Andrewes to Baxter and Fox*, pp.93-97.

85   The family called them 'concordances', but I have preferred 'harmonies' to

prevent confusion with those concordances that are indexes of biblical words and passages.

86   A detailed study of these harmonies can be found in Dietrich Wuensch, *Evangelienharmonien im Reformationszeitalter: Ein Beitrag zur Geschichte de Leben-Jesu-Darstellungen*, (Berlin & New York: Walter de Gruyter, 1983) [hereafter cited as Wuensch, *Evangelienharmonien*].

87   M&W, pp. 43 and 82.

88   FP 621 (7 July 1627). This timing would corroborate John Ferrar's statement that the 'concordance was a year in making at first'; M&W, p.76.

89   Nicholas explicitly acknowledged Jansen in one of the explanatory 'Advertizements' inserted in the splendid harmony made for Charles I in 1635: British Library, C.23.e.4, f. 4v. This 150-chapter structure had been used in the fifteenth century by Jean Gerson, whom the Rev. Robert Brooks, whose school at Enborne, Berks., Nicholas and his brothers attended, was said to have admired; Mayor, pp. 167-8; also Maycock, p. 11, and Venn, Part 1, Vol. I, p. 229. Jean Buisson, or Rubus, who was also acknowledged as a source in the king's volume and whose work was published in Douai in 1575, used this same 150-chapter structure to which he added an elaborate system of cross-referencing and annotations and a plan whereby his readers could move systematically through the chapters and thus cover the entire story of Christ's life in the course of a week; Wuensch, p. 223. See also *Monotessaron, passim.*

90   M&W, p. 76.

91   Clare's volume of Jansen was his *Commentariorum in suam Concordiam*, a later version with commentary added to the harmony itself. In addition Clare had a copy of Thomas Beaux-Amis' *Commentariorum in evangelicam harmoniam*, which followed the Jansen model. H.M. Adams, *Catalogue of Books printed on the Continent of Europe, 1501-1600, in Cambridge Libraries*, (Cambridge: Cambridge University Press, 1967) I, pp. 580-1, lists copies of works of Jansen printed before 1600 in college libraries [Clare's copy printed 1606]; I, 103 on Beaux-Amis, copies also in St. John's and Emmanuel; I, pp. 160-1 lists various other harmonies in college libraries. Emmanuel had copies not only of Jansen but Gerson, Osiander and Martin Chemnitz: Sargent Bush and Carl J. Rasmussen, *The Library of Emmanuel College, Cambridge, 1584-1637*, (Cambridge: Cambridge University Press, 1986), pp. 75, 169, 67, 65.

92   The only English harmonies,apart from Robert Hill's summary discussed below, that were extant in 1625-6 were a translation of Calvin's harmony of 1555 and a separate translation of his commentary on the Johannine gospel. These were first published in 1584. The two works were subsequently published together in 1610 and constituted a bulky and scholarly tome with much more commentary than actual gospel text and certainly no pictures, a book aimed rather at an academic than a family audience. A second and equally scholarly harmony published in Edinburgh in 1616 was *Lectures*

upon the History of the Passion, Resurrection and Ascension of our Lord Jesus Christ. Beginning at John 18 and 19:16. . .containing a perfect harmonie of all the foure Evangelists. . . Preached by R. Rollocke.

93   Consent of the Foure Evangelists: collected by C. J[ansenius] Englished. To which are added aphorismes, containing the matter of Caluins Institutions. . ., bound with The Contents of Scripture: containing the Sum of euery chapter of the Old & New Testament. . ., London, 1597.

94   For Hill's career and interest in pedagogy see J. F. Merritt's excellent article, 'The Pastoral Tightrope; A Puritan Pedagogue in Jacobean London', in *Politics, Religion and Popularity in Early Stuart Britain*, Thomas Cogswell, Richard Cust and Peter Lake, eds., (Cambridge: Cambridge University Press, 2002), pp.143-161. There is no evidence that Nicholas and Hill knew one another, though their paths could have crossed during the time they both were in London (1617-23).

95   His reaction to Hiud's publication of a harmony would suggest that he was unaware of Hill's earlier work.

96   It was provided with its own fireplace and chimney, painted a restful shade of green, and decorated with edifying 'sentences' supplied by various family members and friends; M&W, pp. 80-81.

97   Perhaps the press supplied by Arthur Woodnoth in 1633; FP 905 (24 July); but was Arthur's a printing press or, more prosaically, a press for clothing? On the 'new kind of printing' see M&W, p. 76.

98   Blackstone, p. 45. Nicholas had arranged for a Cambridge bookbinder's daughter to come to Gidding and teach her skill to the Collet nieces, particularly Mary, the eldest, who became the family's expert. She probably bound the elaborate volume presented to the king, also the later harmony of Kings and Chronicles that Charles requested. She also received requests from others, such as her brother-in-law, Rev. Joshua Mapletoft, to bind psalters and prayer books for use in his parish; FP 991 (18 March 1634/5).

99   Mayor, p. 115.

100 M&W, p. 77.

101 In a letter to Isaac Basire quoted in Mayor, p. 361.

102 She, with her uncle John, was in charge of hearing the 'Psalm-Children's' recitations and of supplying the 'balsams' and other medicines to the neighbours..

103 Anna, who never married, remained at Gidding until her death in the winter of 1638-39..

104 We do not have baptismal records for the older Collet children so cannot be precise about the sequence except that Mary was the eldest. Joyce (bapt 1615) would have been old enough to join in soon after the family got to Gidding as would her elder sister Elizabeth, but Judith (bapt. 1624) would clearly not have been a proper participant for some years nor would her cousin Virginia Ferrar, John's daughter, who was born in 1627 or Ann and Mary Mapletoft, Su's stepdaughter and daughter who spent significant time at Gidding after 1635.

105 M&W, p. 76.

106 See David Ransome's Appendix on the birth order of the Collet children.

107 On the bookbinding lessons see M&W, p. 83. On MCF's expertise **see** Chap 6 on Harmonies as well as FP 991 (18 Mar 1634/5).

108 In 'Directions for biographer', M&W, p. 39.

109 Anna, who had occasion explicitly to articulate her view, hastened to add that her choice implied no denigration of marriage in general; FP 802, 809, 816, and 817 (July-Oct 1631). Neither of the nieces nor Nicholas ever made any more generalised claim, as Catholicism did, for the superior sanctity of virginity. Indeed, we have no record to suggest that they ever made any public comment on this matter. All the younger Collet daughters married and their grandmother and mother, as well as their Uncle Nicholas, insisted that all the girls, including Mary and Anna, take their turn at running the household as preparation for managing households of their own.

110 M&W, p. 58.

111 On his deathbed Ferrar was said to have specially encouraged Mary and Anna to persevere in their choice of celibacy that they had made with his advice and assistance; M&W, p. 117.

112 See below, p. 110-12 on Anna's response to Arthur Woodnoth's desire to marry her.

113 Mayor, p. 278. A rather harsher reaction by Williams, Gidding's diocesan, conflicts with this account, 105n. Bishop John Williams, despite a strong initial negative reaction to Anna and Mary's embrace of celibacy cited in Hacket's *Scrinia Reserata*, p. 105n. was said to have ultimately come round to saying that he would support the nieces in their intention; M&W, p. 108.

114 Turner, ff 118v, 121v-123r

115 Sharland, pp. 168-70.

116 There was in the 'Directions' to his biographer a note that he was ever mindful of religious monasteries, a point to which I shall return in the final chapter; Turner, f. 135. M&W did not include this note in their published version of the 'Directions'.

117 M&W, p. 132.

118 FP 797 (17 June 1631). He had further economising plans for remaking existing garments for the other children. Mary and Anna would probably have found his views on fashion and inward unity more acceptable than would their younger and less dedicated sisters.

119 Nicholas drafted letters to Susanna for her sisters and in one case her Uncle John to send; we shall consider the significance of these later. I have based my count of letters on the finding list in FP.

120 Her grandfather in his will spoke of having brought her up from childhood; Mayor, p. 342.

121 FP.861 (25 July 1632). Mary's letter, to which this was a reply, addressed Nicholas as 'Father of my soule, faithfull freinde −' ; FP.860 (23 July), Elsewhere Nicholas referred to Mary as having become his 'sister' while

Anna was his 'daughter;' FP.675 (NF to AC, 18 June 1629). The contrast in tone is notable even when both nieces address him as 'father.'

122   Anna's letter of 10 June 1626 in FP 594; Susanna's of 27 July 1627 in FP 618.

123   FP 601 (13 Nov 1626).

124   FP 675. This letter had been preceded by one in January asking 'may I Tytell you my tender Father'; FP 660.

125   FP 676 (18 June 1629).

126   John's letter to his mother in February (FP 665) refers not only to 'my Neice Sister Moll' [Mary] but also 'my neice Sister Hester'. We have no letters between Nicholas and either Hester or Margaret during this period, hence cannot compare their relationships with those of Anna and Mary to their uncles. Su, being by this time a married woman and in any case no longer resident at Gidding, was apparently not included in this change of status.

127   Certainly she signed herself 'Mary Farrar' in the Bodleian gospel harmony dated December 1631. Other letters of 1629 and 1630 [FP 674, 687, and 700] are unsigned and drafted in Nicholas's hand though attributed to Mary and in one case Anna and Hester as well so that it is unclear how Mary styled herself during that time. An earlier letter to her from her brother Thomas [FP 641 (25 April 1628)] addresses her as 'my dearly beloved sister Mary Collet'. The assumption of the 'Ferrar' surname would thus appear to have happened in 1629-30.

128   FP 788 (1 June). Not all Anna's letters were written to Nicholas when he was absent, viz. her early 'confessional' letter on what sounds to have been a household matter.

129   His visit had been cut short by a letter from Sir John Danvers requesting his prompt return to London so that he could undertake a business trip for Sir John; FP 808 (14 Sept 1631).

130   FP 809 (22 Sep 1631). Ferrar's endorsement on the letter explains the route and timing by which he received Anna's letter.

131   FP 816 (Mary Collet Ferrar to Nicholas, 18 Oct 1631).

132   FP 817 (22 Oct 1631).

133   See above, pp. 83-4.

134   S Collet Letters, August 1629.

135   She referred to him as 'Mr. Sa' or 'Mr La' or so the later transcript of her letters copied the original. 'Mr Sa' could conceivably have been Stephen Sad, the cousin of Thomas Sheppard to whom the Ferrars delivered Sheppard's 'great trunke'. 'Mr La' could be the Mr Lamb who wrote to Susanna that he should marry her kinswoman, Lady Smart. Susanna clearly thought him a most unsuitable match and wrote to Lady Smart asking her version of the situation. She entirely approved of Nicholas's refusal of 'Mr La/Sa's request to send also for Hester, who was then away at Margaretting, apparently so that he could take his choice.

136   Her much later letter to Basil Berridge, when she was in effect driven out

of Gidding in 1658, emphasised the financial sacrifice this represented; FP 1320 (23 April 1658). Her uncles struggled to find ways to raise the funds she was entitled to and expressed gratitude for her financial assistance in the dark days after 1624; FP 573 (17 June 1625), FP 699 (15 Jan 1629/30) in which Nicholas proposed that Mary have a £20 annuity rather than the £50 p.a. for 10 years which her grandmother had included in her will, which of course had not yet come into effect, to cover the original £500 legacy from her grandfather. There was a further renegotiation in May 1631connected to the restoration of the glebe lands; Archives of Clare College, Cambridge, Safe A: 3/17. Mary Woodnoth Ferrar's will of 1628 is summarised in Mayor, p. 339.

137   As the daughter and granddaughter of formidable women she had lived with examples of their successful marriages; she had on the other hand witnessed the turbulent marriage of that other redoubtable woman in the household, Bathsheba Ferrar.

138   M&W, pp. 71, 84, 87.

139   Sharland, pp. 163-4 and 178-81.

140   FP 911 (3 Oct 1633), Su Mapletoft to [MCF]. Whether Arthur's niece, who was never named, actually appeared is unclear though Arthur's nephew Ralph had just arrived at Gidding when Susanna Collet, writing to AW (July 1628) about Ralph, reported that although Mary was ill, she would do her best if the niece came. Letter quoted in Mayor, pp. 310-15.

141   M&W, pp. 77-79; FP 972 (11 Dec 1634) and 991 (18 Mar 1635).

142   Blackstone, pp. 31 and 35.

143   FP 618 (2 July 1627; Su C to NF); his reply FP 620 (5 July). Su's letter travelled very quickly to Nicholas in London though she had made oral confession of her mistake earlier. Nicholas clearly believed that written statements carried much greater weight than merely oral ones.

144   FP 638 (3 Mar 1627/8).

145   S Collet Letters (24 Nov and ?Dec 1628).

146   *Ibid.*, (24 Nov 1628).

147   FP 652 (18 Nov 1628). Nicholas often drafted letter for members of the family, including his mother's message to Robert Bateman; see above, p. 71. This practice apparently roused some objection in later years for Susanna Collet explicitly expressed her approval at a later date in response to what she termed 'some speeches' (evidently critical) about this practice; S Collet Letters (undated but probably between February and April 1634).

148   FP 687 (21 Sep 1629), again in Nicholas's hand, though it speaks of 'the departure of our most deare & honored mother' as would have been appropriate for Mary to write.

149   FP 657 (22 Dec 1628) and 668 (16 Mar 1628/9) as well as one of effusive thanks to Joshua for his loving and comforting letters, 685 (Aug 1629) from Anna; FP 669 (29 Mar 1629) from Hester.

150   FP 698 (6 Jan 1629/30).

151 FP 697 (Jan 1629/30); ostensibly from Uncle John, this letter actually quotes from Woodnoth's letter and must therefore have been written after his of the 6th had reached Gidding. Mary's letter was sent somewhat later; FP 700 (18 Jan 1629/30).

152 FP 706 J Mapletoft to A Woodnoth reporting Su's illness (2 Feb 1629/30) and FP 710 S Collet to NF (1 Mar 1629/30).

153 FP 747 (12 Oct 1630).

3

Enlarging the Community: The 'Web of Friendship'

1 FP 751 (27 Oct 1630).

2 FP 722 (10 May 1630).

3 Joshua Mapletoft began his letters to Nicholas with the simple salutation 'Frend'.

4 FP 698 (6 Jan 1629/30).

5 *Ibid.*

6 Kingsbury IV, p. 291.

7 Sean Kelsey, 'Danvers, Sir John (1584/5-1655)', *Oxford Dictionary of National Biography*, Oxford University Press, 2004 [accessed 21 Oct 2004: http://www.oxforddnb.com/view/article/7135].

8 M&W, p. 67. Though Sir Edwin continued to write to John Ferrar on business matters, he on his deathbed in 1629 charged his wife always to seek Nicholas's advice. She did indeed follow his advice as the Ferrar Papers testify; *e.g.* FP 783 (23 May 1631), FP 798 (22 June 1631), FP 818 (25 Oct 1631).

9 An isolated remark in an early Ferrar biography (M&W, p.107) and an enigmatic comment in Woodnoth's report to Nicholas of his discussions with Herbert in October, 1631 (FP 813), have been taken as evidence that Woodnoth proposed to serve God by becoming a minister. On the contrary the correspondence as a whole gives no support to the claim that Woodnoth contemplated taking holy orders either as the alternative to his craft or as an adjunct to Danvers' service. Royal opposition to chaplains in non-noble households would also have militated against this option. Woodnoth's choices, as I hope the ensuing discussion will demonstrate, were to remain a goldsmith, work entirely for Danvers, or somehow combine both tasks.

10 FP 703 (*c.* 27 Jan 1629/30).

11 Susanna Collet mentions Ned's master's dissatisfaction in a letter to Nicholas Collet; S Collet Letters (11 Jan 169/30). It is hard to imagine that if she knew it, Woodnoth did not. See above, pp. 83-6 on the family's problems with Ned.

12 FP 712 (*c.* 1 Mar 1629/30).

13 FP 714 (9 Mar 1629/30). Ned's 'friends' whom Ferrar thought should find this offer attractive were of course John and Susanna Collet. Whether or not

Ferrar had cleared this proposal with them is unclear, but the idea was never put to the test and Ned's subsequent behaviour killed the idea if it had ever been entertained seriously.

14 FP 718 (12 April 1630).

15 FP 719 (19 April 1630).

16 FP 720 (3 May 1630).

17 FP 731 (26 July 1630).

18 FP 732 (2 Aug 1630).

19 See below, pp. 145-6.

20 FP 738 (?18 Aug 1630).

21 FP 748 (19 Oct 1630) and FP 749, (Margaret Woodnoth to Mary Woodnoth Ferrar, 19 Oct 1630) and FP 744(4 Oct 1630). This work was perhaps the plan devised by Ferrar and George Herbert, in which Woodnoth did indeed become involved, to raise funds and renovate the church at Leighton Bromswold. Unfortunately for us, as is so often the case in these letters, the correspondents felt no need to clarify their references so that we cannot be certain what this 'work' was.

22 FP 751 (27 Oct 1630).

23 FP 753 (5 Nov 1630): this letter refers to another written hastily the previous week. Richard Ferrar in a letter of 3 Nov (FP 752) mistakenly claimed that Woodnoth had gone to Gidding the previous week without letting him know; Woodnoth was in fact with Sir John Danvers in Chelsea.

24 FP 754 (8 Nov 1630).

25 FP 755 (9 Nov 1630).

26 FP 758 (24 Nov 1630); there is no suggestion that he had concerted this response with Nicholas.

27 Cf. Edward Lenton, who was dying for an invitation to dinner but was instead politely but firmly escorted to his horse by Nicholas and seen on his way; Mayor, p. xxxv.

28 Mayor, pp. 89-93.

29 On Gabbet, see below, p. 145-6.

30 FP 761 (14 Dec 1630).

31 FP 815 (13 Oct 1631). Herbert's reply on this point was discouragingly ambiguous unlike his unequivocal view that Woodnoth should stick with Danvers. This was by no means the first time Woodnoth had inclined to marriage. In January 1619 Ferrar had written his brother William that Woodnoth wanted to make one 'N. G.' his wife; FP 99. Why his proposal failed we do not know; certainly Ferrar expressed the hope that N.G. would accept Woodnoth. He was said to have approached Anna earlier, in 1627, though reference to that episode only came in Mary's letter to Ferrar in October, 1631.

32 She had reiterated that wish in July when she thanked her 'Most Honnored Parents and dearest Frends' for agreeing to her wish to live a virgin and providing for her an estate; FP 802 ([?] Jul [1631].

33 See above, pp. 110-2.

34 His original letter dated 19 Nov 1631 is in the Ferrar Papers (FP 821). The
    boy's mother was Frances Herbert, sister of George and wife of Sir John
    Browne; Charles, *Herbert*, p.57.

35 FP 815 (13 Oct 1631). The business trip for Danvers that had called
    Woodnoth away from Gidding, evidently took him to Wiltshire though he
    had returned to London by the time he wrote this letter to Ferrar. He had also
    taken with him a gospel harmony that he presented to Herbert as a gift from
    the Collet nieces.

36 Mary's and Anna's letters to their uncle were dated 18 and 22 October.

37 FP 814 ([4 or 5 Oct 1631).

38 FP 827 (1 Dec 1631). That seems a more likely topic than the more positive
    one of Leighton Bromswold.

39 FP 832 (16 Jan 1631/2 and 839 (9 Feb 1631/2). The directions most probably
    pertained not to Woodnoth's employment with Danvers but rather to the
    fund-raising and management of the Leighton Bromswold restoration, a
    work in which Herbert, the Ferrars, and Woodnoth all collaborated and took
    particular satisfaction. John Ferrar, who was in charge of the actual building,
    reported that in July 1632 there were eighteen masons and labourers at work
    with ten carpenters coming in the following week FP 862. Ferrar perhaps
    broached this subject to Woodnoth in October 1630; FP 748.

40 FP 844 (15 Mar 1631/2); the scriptural reference is to the Epistle of James
    1:6-8.

41 FP 890; the date wrongly assigned in the FP Finding List, *c.* 18 Mar 1632/3, is a
    year too late, but the close correspondence of this letter to Woodnoth's (FP 844)
    shows it to have been a direct answer to Woodnoth's letter of 15 Mar 1631/2.

42 That Woodnoth would provide for Danvers 'temporal benefits' reinforces the
    argument that ordination was not part of Woodnoth's plans.

43 In a subsequent letter Woodnoth talked of his plan to spend Easter at Gidding;
    FP 846 (25 Mar 1631/2) but it is not clear that he actually did so.

44 FP 815 (13 Oct 1631). It is embedded in his account to Ferrar of his visit to
    Herbert at Bemerton.

45 FP 733 (4 Aug 1630).

46 Susanna Collet in a letter to Su Mapletoft, (S Collet Letters, 4 Oct 1630)
    reported that Dorothy, who obviously had remained at Gidding, was still
    afflicted with a quartan ague. Dorothy was perhaps 'Mr Stroothers sister',
    one of the two kitchen maids, referred to in Ferrar's letter to his brother
    Richard (FP 922 16 Dec 1633). The other was Mary Woodnoth, perhaps
    Woodnoth's niece; she may have come with his nephew Ralph in 1628 or
    later; S Collet Letters (July 1628). The Ferrars evidently employed friends
    and family rather than locals in the household.

47 Ferrar took comfort from the fact that Gabbet was Sir John's responsibility
    so that Woodnoth was at least not out of pocket over the affair, FP 735 (12
    Aug 1630), 737 (16 Aug 1630); Gabbet either was not sent away at that point
    or subsequently returned for he was at Gidding in the following June when

Sir John Danvers arranged to send him off with a Herbert stepson on a ship bound for Italy and Ferrar wrote his mother urgently to send Gabbet up to London immediately; FP 793 (8 June 1631). Gabbet must indeed have been difficult for Ferrar wrote the next week to his mother about the relief she must feel to be rid of him; FP 797 (17 June 1631).

48   FP 734 (9 Aug 1630).

49   FP 735 (12 Aug 1630).

50   Mall probably went to Gidding in 1631 when Susanna was very ill after the birth of her son John. Mary Collet Ferrar had, of course, been largely brought up in her grandmother's house. After Mapletoft's death in 1635 Susanna took their two sons John and Peter, as well as Mapeltoft's daughter Ann by his first marriage, to join their sister at Gidding.

51   FP 810 (29 Sept 1631); in the hand of John Ferrar.

52   FP 820 (15 Nov 1631). What that project might have been is impossible to identify with certainty. It could have involved the Little Academy or a publishable gospel harmony or the possibility of night vigils, even perhaps a very tentative form of temperate diet. Other early examples of his correspondence with his sisters-in-law are: FP 685 (*c.* Aug 1629), 707 (*c.* 8 Feb 1629/30), 828 (5 Dec 1631).

53   She had persisted in eating foods hard to digest, such as saltfish, 'rootes' and cheese and thus weakened had caught a cold during her Christmas Eve vigil. It had left her 'discomposed rather than sick for almost a weeke'.

54   FP 923 (13 Jan 1633/34), NF to JM. On the battles between John and Bathsheba Ferrar, see below, pp. 225-7 and 234-6; for Richard Ferrar see FP 922 (16 Dec 1633), NF and MWF to Richard F. On the difficulties over *The Temple* see Daniel Doerksen, 'Nicholas Ferrar, Arthur Woodnoth, and the Publication of George Herbert's *The Temple*, 1633', *George Herbert Journal* 3 (1979-80), 22-44 [hereafter cited as Doerksen, 'Temple'].

55   FP 924 (30 Jan 1633/4).

56   See below, Chap. 5.

57   FP 923 (13 Jan 1633/4).

58   See above, p. 122.

59   FP 949 (6 Aug 1634). The 'spare dyett' was that prescribed by Cornaro and subsequently by Lessius and will be discussed in detail in Chap. 5.

60   Ferrar's translation of Lessius's *Hygiasticon* had appeared at the end of January according to Robert Mapletoft's letter to Ferrar cited earlier (FP 924). Chapter 5 deals at length with the family's missionary hopes for their example of temperance.

61   FP 952, 953, 955 (3, 10, 25 Sep 1634).

62   FP 956 (9 Oct 1634); this letter from Arthur Woodnoth to Nicholas Ferrar gives thanks for Mapletoft's recovery, adding that 'the greatness of the danger magnifies the riches of God's grace'.

63   FP 957 (16 Oct 1634); He requested them also to give him help with some liturgical particulars in that connection. Monthly communion was, of course,

the practice at Little Gidding also.

64 FP 959 (29 Oct 1634).

65 On these promises that Mapletoft and his wife made, and the reservations that had held him back initially, see below, pp. 221-2 and 224-5. For Ferrar such promises clearly constituted vows, comparable in his eyes to baptismal vows that imposed a 'common obligation' on all Christians..

66 FP 971 (undated but presumably before 27 Nov when Robert endorsed his brother's letter to the Ferrars cited below, (FP 965), with the information that he was now in London with Joshua.)

67 See below, pp.219-20.

68 FP 970 (6 Dec 1634; AW to [NF]); 978 (8 Jan 1634/5; JM to NF); 983 (5 Feb 1634/5; AW to [NF]).

69 FP 988 and 990 (988, pair of letters undated but before 12 Mar 1634/5; 990 to Woodnoth also undated). He cautions Woodnoth against bloodletting as a treatment, advising him first to give rest, diet and exercise a chance to do their restorative work.

70 FP 989 (12 Mar 1634/5).

71 Letters about binding psalmbooks, FP 991(18 Mar 1634/5) and FP 997 (9 June 1635); about monthly communion, FP 997; FP 999 (14 July 1635) informs Ferrar about the Lindsell bequest.

72 FP 1002 (5 Aug 1635).

73 R. Newcourt, *Repertorium Ecclesiasticum Parochiale Londinense*, II (1710), p. 656 [Wickford]. His death came before 10 September and his will (PCC 96 Sadler) was proved on 18 September 1635. Robert was his executor.

74 On Woodnoth's account of Mapletoft's estate, FP 970 (6 Dec 1634). Mapletoft's letters after his recovery are FP 991 to Mary Collet Ferrar (18 Mar 1634/5); 997 to 'dearest brethren' at Gidding (9 June 1635); 998 to Nicholas Ferrar (24 June 1635); 1002 to NF (5 Aug 1635); Nicholas's letter to Robert is FP 1004 (2 Nov 1635).

75 FP 722 (10 May 1630).

76 Turner, f.44.v. What happened to the letters, which the family lent to Turner, is unclear; they are not to be found in the Ferrar Papers.

77 Lessius, Leonard, *Hygiasticon: Or, The Right course of Preserving Life and Health unto Extream old Age*, [Cambridge]: Roger Daniel, 1634. [translated by Nicholas Ferrar]. See Chap 4, pp. 162ff. on the Ferrar/Herbert collaboration.

78 The prayer for Herbert is quoted from Peckard in Blackstone, p. 79. Duncon's visits to the dying Herbert are in Walton's 'Life', Herbert, Works, pp. 375-6 and 380.

79 On the Martha Sherington episode see above, p. 82-3.

80 For these later episodes see below, pp. 233-6 and 246-9.

81 The manuscript volume entitled 'Duties of Man and Woman' with its additional section on 'Duties Peculiar to Woman' made this point very forcefully with many scriptural citations.

82 FP 1056 (*c.* Jun 1637).

4

Voluntarism and the Wider Mission:
'A Light upon a Hill could not be hid'

1   M&W, p. 39. The phrase occurs in the Directions to the Historian.
2   I have adopted the term from Mark Goldie's article, 'Voluntary Anglicans', *The Historical Journal*, 46, 4 (2003), especially pp. 989-90, and will consider this later development in the final chapter, 'Nicholas Posthumous'.
3   Arch. A.d.3. A table of contents was added in a later hand. For a more detailed discussion of the volume see my article, 'Monotessaron: the Harmonies of Little Gidding', *The Seventeenth Century*, XX (Spring 2005), pp. 27-9. [hereafter cited as 'Monotessaron'].
4   See above, pp. 101-2. The Herbert volume has not survived.
5   This is the volume that King Charles borrowed in 1633 and annotated. It is now in the Houghton Library at Harvard.
6   These links pointed the reader to the next verses of a given gospel passage when the main text had switched to material from a different gospel. Some of the handwritten lines extended well beyond the ruled margins of the text itself, indeed to the edge of the page. In a few cases, including the last line on the final page ('At Litle Gidding'), a letter or two is missing or truncated, evidence that the pages had been cropped at some point. The sheets at the beginning (title page and table of contents in later hand) and end are mostly blank and are a different paper from the numbered pages 1-293.
7   FP 832 (16 Jan 1631/2).
8   *The Storie of Stories: or the Life of Christ, according to the foure holy Evangelists; with a harmony of them . . .*, London: M. Flesher, 1632. [Hereafter Hiud, Storie].
9   Presumably one of the several court chaplains who knew the Ferrars would have alerted them to this publication; there is no evidence that it was Haywood.
10   The 1629 edition was in folio; later ones which Thomas Buck produced with Roger Daniel were in quarto; Herbert, *Historical Catalogue,* pp. 158-60, 167, 172, 175-6, 179-80. On the battles over publishing rights see P.M. Handover, *Printing in London from 1476 to Modern Times*, (Cambridge, MA: Harvard University Press, 1960), pp.54-60.
11   'The Duties Common to Man and Woman' spoke of 'Those Precepts of Loue . . . that bid us . . . to studie to be quiet, doing our own busines & working with our own hands. I Thes: 4.11'.
12   Letters describe the fund-raising as well as the execution of the work at Leighton: e.g. FP 744 (4 Oct 1630), FP 832 (16 Jan 1631/2 and FP 839 (9 Feb 1631/2 and FP 862 (July 1632). On *The Temple* see below, pp. 176-7.
13   FP 722 (Ferrar to Arthur Woodnoth, 10 May 1630).
14   Herbert in an undated letter to Ferrar expressed his thanks for 'the heart that God has given you and yours, to pious works'; Herbert, Works, p. 299.
15   For the complete passage see above, pp. 161-2.

16   M&W, p. 92 .

17   Turner, f.88.r and f.109.r.

18   M&W, pp. 92-3. Edward Lenton mentioned the vigils and the 'nuns' of Gidding in his account of his visit, probably in 1633, and recorded Ferrar's corrections of his views on these points; *ibid.*, pp. 129-30. His letter was later published in distorted and vitriolic form as *The Arminian Nunnery* (1641).

19   M&W, p. 92. One who would have had no qualms about saying 'no' was John's wife Bathsheba. Perhaps Ferrar's remarks were at least in part a conciliatory gesture to her.

20   On Mapletoft see FP 959 (29 Oct 1634) and 959 (29 Oct 1634); on Woodnoth FP 890 (18 Mar 1631/2); see also the discussion of the binding nature of commitment to a project or promise incorporated in 'The Winding Sheet' in Blackstone, pp. 109-10.

21   Miss Carter, his nineteenth-century biographer, thus characterised his approach in a passage quoted in E. Mansfield Forbes, 'Nicholas Ferrar: America and Little Gidding', *Clare College, 1326-1926*, (Cambridge: Printed for the College at the University Press, 1930), Vol. II, p. 576 [hereafter cited as Forbes].

22   Bodleian Library, Oxford, Ms. Rawl.lett. 27.c [John Jones to Thomas Hearne, from Abbots Ripton] April 1.1731, f.4.r. The book, when Jones heard about it, was in the possession of Edward Ferrar, an attorney in Huntingdon. Many of Turner's notes suggest that he saw this volume.

23   M&W, pp. 43-4.

24   Turner, f.65.r. This passage Turner might well have seen in Ferrar's spiritual diary. Ferrar also recited daily Psalm 71, a practice he began during an illness of his mother; *Ibid.,* f.70.r.

25   See below, p. 194-5. .

26   A letter from its translator, Richard Drake, to John Ferrar (FP 1126; 18 Oct 1648) suggests the two had known each other for some time. Drake quoted the price of the book in quires; perhaps John had thoughts of purchasing some for binding, as he later did with *Eikon Basilike*.

27   Herbert's phrase in 'Superliminare', 1.4, in Herbert, Works, p. 22.

28   Turner, f.126v. The French books presumably included de Sales, though it had been translated into English, but could have included others as well. It is not clear whether the 'meditations' were part of his spiritual diary or were written for the instruction of his nephews as described in M&W, p. 91.

29   Herbert to Edmund Duncon quoted in Walton's *Life of Herbert*, Herbert, Works, p. 380.

30   Helen Wilcox, 'Entering *The Temple*: women, reading, and devotion in seventeenth-century England', in *Religion, Literature, and Politics in Post-Reformation England*, Donna B. Hamilton and Richard Strier, eds., Cambridge: Cambridge University Press, 1996, p. 195,

31   Daniel W. Doerksen, 'Nicholas Ferrar, Arthur Woodnoth, and the Publication of George Herbert's The Temple, 1633', *George Herbert Journal*, 3 (1979-80), 22-44. Mapletoft's letter: FP 913 (10 Oct 1633).

32   S Collet Letters (February 1633/4).

33   This introductory passage to 'The Winding Sheet' is printed in Blackstone, pp. 101-5.

34   George Hunston Williams, *The Radical Reformation*, 3rd ed. revised and expanded, (Kirksville, MO: Sixteenth Century Journal Publishers, *c.* 1992), p. 829. [Hereafter cited as Williams, *Radical Reformation*.]

35   For a biography that presents Valdes not only as a religious figure but also a courtier in Rome and Naples see Crews, *Twilight*. See also Massimo Firpo, translated by John Tedeschi, 'The Italian Reformation and Juan de Valdes', *Sixteenth Century Journal*, Vol. 27, No. 2 (Summer 1996), 353-64; [hereafter cited as Firpo, 'Valdes'] and Elisabeth G. Gleason's review of *Lo Evangelio di San Matteo*, Carlo Ossola, ed., in *The Sixteenth Century Journal*, Vol. 19, No.3 (Autumn, 1988), 515-6. Indeed several of Valdes's associates in Naples turned Protestant and spent time in England, most notably Ochino and Peter Martyr.

36   Lindsell's copy, now in the Bodleian library at Oxford, bears an inscription on the flyleaf in Nicholas Ferrar's own hand: 'This Booke was the Right Reverend Father in God['s] Austin Lord Bishop of Hereford'. In addition the book bears on its front cover 'AVG. LINDSEL' stamped in gold letters. The past tense of the first inscription suggests that Ferrar acquired it along with other books on Lindsell's death (1634). Beneath Ferrar's inscription on the flyleaf is written in another hand, but not that of his brother John, 'Given to the Publique Library in Oxford, by Mr John Farrar of Huntingdonshire, September 8. 1642'. Mayor, p. 376, noted that the book was in the Bodleian. Why John Ferrar donated the volume to Oxford is unknown. I am indebted to David Ransome for the information about Bodley's copy, as well as the Spanish copy donated by one of the Duncons (personal communication 19 Feb 2006).

37   Marginalia in Herbert's commentary state that the notes (on Considerations 37 and 65) are those of the French translator, which suggest that he had seen the latter at some point, but when is not clear. Herbert had not spent any time in Italy though he was said to know some Italian. He would, however, have likely been more fluent in French. When he translated Cornaro's book on temperance, he used a Latin version rather than the original Italian; Herbert, *Works*, p. 304.

38   For a more detailed and very helpful exposition of Valdes's theology see Crews,*Twilight*., esp. Chaps. 5 and 6.

39   Milton, *Catholic and Reformed*), esp. Ch. 7.

40   Consideration XVIII, pp.41-43.

41   Williams, *Radical Reformation*, pp. 824-6.

42   Consideration XC, pp. 237.

43   Crews, *Twilight*, p. 145.

44   Comment on Consideration 11.

45   FP 995 (1635).

46   Mayor, pp. 59-63.

47   Barry Collett, 'A Long and Troubled Pilgrimage: the Correspondence of Marguerite D'Angouleme and Vittoria Colonna', *Studies in Reformed*

Theology and History, New Series, No. 6, (Princeton: Princeton Theological Seminary, 2000), 88 [hereafter cited as Collett, 'Pilgrimage']. This low-profile, avoidance approach to controversy was the essence of Valdes's 'Nicodemite' position; see Firpo, 'Valdes', 353-64. Williams also refers to Valdes as a 'Nicodemite'; *Radical Reformation*, p. 827.

48   Pp. 15-17 and 36-43 (on communion). This volume Ferrar presumably prepared for the instruction of members of the household.

49   Barnabas Oley in his prefatory life of Herbert that accompanies *Herbert's Remains Or, Sundry Pieces of that Sweet Singer of the Themple, Mr George Herbert, sometime Orator of the University of Cambridg*, (London: Timothy Garthwait, 1652), sig.b.v. mentioned the rejection of Carbone's book [hereafter Oley, Remains]. Also on Carbone see Mayor, p. 302.

50   Jackson's statement comes between a table of contents that is a list of the 110 Considerations and Herbert's commentary. Oley in *Remains*, sig. [a.9]-b.5, grouped Jackson with Ferrar and Herbert as three exemplary clergymen at a time when many of their contemporaries were failing in their duty.

51   Barnabas Oley, 'Out of the Life of Mr G Herbert', in *Herbert's Remains, Or, Sundry Pieces of that Sweet Singer of The Temple, Mr George Herbert*, London: Timothy Garthwait, 1652, sig. [b 8r].

52   Ferrar's enthusiasm for Valdes seems almost an anomaly in one whom Arthur Woodnoth once accused of putting too much value on set forms of prayer; FP 908 (22 Aug 1633).

53   John M. Adrian has elucidated this point in his article, 'George Herbert, parish 'dexterity', and the Local Modification of Laudianism', *The Seventeenth Century*, 24 (Spring 2009), 26-51.

54   See above, p. 161-2. It would also embody that 'mean' that Herbert called the praise and glofy of the British Church; Herbert, Works, pp. 106-7.

55   Trevor Cooper in '"As Wise as Serpents": the Form and Setting of Public Worship at Little Gidding in the 1630s', in *Worship and the Parish Church in Earrly Modern Britain*, Alec Ryrie and Natalie Mears, eds., (Ashgate, forthcoming 2012) claims that Little Gidding's twin pulpits were in all likelihood the first example in England although after the Restoration John Cosin, Bishop of Durham (who had knowledge of Gidding), introduced such an arrangement at Bishop Auckland In a letter to the Diocesan Architectural Comm of Ely (14 May 2009) Cooper discusses the arrangement at Leighton Bromswold (p. 4).

56   On Flaminio and the Valdes circle in Reginald Pole's Viterbo see Williams, *Radical Reformation*, pp. 832-4.

57   *The Benefite of Christs Death, or the glorious Riches of Gods free Grace . . .*, London: Lucas Harison and George Bishop, 1573, Preface.

58   Margaret Collet married as her second husband Thomas Posthumous Legat; see Appendix.

59   See in addition to the preface itself the article by M.E. Overell, 'Arthur Golding's Translation of the "Beneficio di Cristo"', *Notes and Queries*, 223 (October 1978), 424-6.

60   For a stimulating discussion of this concept of the Spirit's combining individual and collective action see Collett, 'Pilgrimage', pp.44-88.

61   George Herbert's phrase; see above, p. 14.

62   Lady Margaret Hoby, for example, in her diary describes sitting with her women, listening to and discussing readings and sermons; Meads., D.M., ed., *The Diary of Lady Margaret Hoby, 1599-1605*, (London: Routledge, 1930), passim.

63   A record of these conversations, originally published in 1628-29 as *Entretiens spirituals*, was translated later into English; Jean Pierre Camus, *The Spirit of St. Francis de Sales*, (London: Longmans, Green & Co, 1893). John Ferrar cited de Sales in one of the Academy discussions, 'On the Austere Life'; Williams, p. 297. In 1636, Isaac Basire wrote to his wife that he was sending her a copy of de Sales's *Introduction to the Devout Life* that had been bound by the 'devout virgins' of Little Gidding; see Mayor, p. 243n and Hilton Kelliher, 'Crashaw at Cambridge,' in *New Perspectives on the Life and Art of Richard Crashaw*, ed. John R. Roberts (Columbia: University of Missouri Press, 1990), pp. 186-87.

64   John North, *The Ambassadors' Secret*, (London: Hambledon and London, 2002), pp. 16-17. I am indebted to David Ransome for this reference. Blackstone on this point is careful to disclaim any direct connection with the Cambridge Platonists (pp. 98-9) and makes no reference to earlier examples of households that resembled Academies, e.g. Erasmus's on the household of Sir Thomas More.

65   Sharland, p. iii.

66   One of the sources of historical stories was Jacques-Auguste de Thou, or 'Thuanus' as members of the group called him. His *History of His Times*, first published in England in 1615, was not translated into English from its original Latin until the 18th century. Since we have no evidence that the nieces studied Latin, they would have needed a translator to tell them de Thou's stories; Samuel Kinser, *The Works of Jacques-Auguste de Thou*, Hague, 1966 gives a detailed account of the publication and translations of the *History*.

67   FP 788 (1 June 1631); this letter to Anna Collet suggests the sense of partnership in learning he sought to convey.

68   They had presumably, in accordance with Ferrar's 'Duties Common to Man & Woman' (p. 13) made their calling and election sure.

69   Sharland, pp. 1-2.

70   See above, pp. 96-7.

71   Blackstone, 111-12. In explaining the reason for taking different names in the later revival of the Academy in 1634 or 1635, the writer (?Ferrar) admitted that this original plan had not worked as the group had hoped but had instead encouraged complacency. The original cast of names with Sharland's identification appears in Sharland, xliv. Mary Collet was the exception, being dubbed the Chief in recognition of her leadership in the group. Williams (p. xiv) offers a variant set of identifications for the nieces. See also Jessica Martin, *Walton's Lives: Conformist Commemorations and the Rise of Biography*, Oxford: Oxford University Press, 2001, pp. 123-4.

72 S Collet Letters (5 Oct 1629).

73 *Ibid.*, Dec 1634 and June 1635.

74 On Ferrar's later negative verdict on the effect of the nicknames, see below, p. 241-2.

75 FP 674 (1 June 1629).

76 Williams, pp. 136-43. Elizabeth as the older of the two might have been likelier to be wishing to make this move.

77 The musicality of the Ferrars is apparent in these songs, which included selections from George Withers, Richard Verstegan, perhaps from a poem by Francis Quarles set to music and even a passage from Foxe. I am grateful to Trevor Cooper for this information: (private communication 28 July 2010).

78 FP 765 (15 Feb 1631). Ferrar could be just as rigorous with Woodnoth himself, as also later with Joshua Mapletoft, and Woodnoth could on rare occasions reciprocate as in FP 908 (22 Aug 1633).

79 Sharland, p. 2. Those of 'neerest Blood' were identified as the Founder, the Guardian, and the Visitor, who would have been their grandmother and two uncles. Their mother did not become an active participant until a later session.

80 Williams, pp. 51-2

81 Sharland, pp. 164-65

82 *Ibid.*, p. 11.

83 Sharland, pp. 19-20

84 Sharland, pp. li-liii.

85 A letter from Ferrar to Arthur Woodnoth (FP 838 6 Feb 1631/2) that accompanied the book forbade Arthur to show the book to anyone else though he could read it if he wished.

86 FP 863. As with much of the correspondence there was no explicit statement of what the 'design' was though Ferrar referred to the opposition and great difficulties that Mary Collet Ferrar must expect as she endeavored to launch it.

87 Sharland, p. 2. Certainly the first organisation of the Academy was described in the storybook's record as a 'great Attempt' without precedents.

5

Temperance and Tensions: 'Frayltie & Fears'

1 Williams, 171. The speaker is Mary Collet Ferrar.

2 *Ibid.*, 179. She wanted the group to agree to discuss temperance specifically as a means of increasing grace in their souls. Unwillingness to subscribe to this proposal could then become a reprehensible lack of desire for increased grace. For the context of this comment see below, pp. 214-5.

3 M&W, p. 105.

4 *Ibid.*, p. 100; Butler's advice quoted in Peckard, p. 26; Even that remedy presently failed, leaving foreign travel as the best remaining, and in Ferrar's case successful, hope

5   Amy Charles suggests that he made the translation during his convalescence; *Herbert*, p. 130.
6   Herbert, *Works*, pp. 234-5 (on diet) and 229-31 (on physick). Herbert's definition of an appropriate amount to eat and drink was very similar to that of Ferrar's quoted above.
7   They were hardly alone in this view. There were numerous volumes published in the 16th and early 17th centuries on temperate diet and its medical as well as spiritual benefits: e.g. Sir John Harrington, *The Englishman's Doctor, Or, The Schoole of Salerne* (1617), Henry Butter, *Dyetts Dry Dinner* (1599) and Christopher Langton, *An Introduction into Physicke* (1550). As the Physicke Fellow at Clare Nicholas might well have known of many of these.
8   T.S., 'Publisher to Reader' in *Hygiasticon*
9   What constituted an 'ounce' and what measure Cornaro himself used was nowhere elaborated though Ferrar had spent enough time in Italy to be familiar with its measures.
10 'A Treatise of Temperance & Sobriety' in Herbert, *Works*. Pp. 304-15.
11 *Hygiasticon*, pp. 44-46. Ferrar's translation also included the Herbert translation of Cornaro.
12 *Ibid.*, pp. 114-5. Ferrar as we have seen (pp. 138-9) was also a keen advocate of exercise.
13 For comparison inmates of St. Bartholomew's Hospital in London in 1686 received daily sixteen ounces of solid food (bread, cheese, butter) plus an unspecified amount of 'milk pottage' and three pints of beer; J. C., Drummond, and Anne Wilbraham, *The Englishman's Food: A History of Five Centuries of English Diet*, London: Jonathan Cape, 1939, p. 562. Other existing seventeenth-century menus were mostly either for sailors and soldiers, definitely not sedentary and intellectual occupations, or for great households and special occasions and consequently not appropriate comparisons. Nor would be a late sixteenth-century menu for inmates of the Bury St. Edmunds House of Correction, who were clearly kept to a harsh working routine; Jane O'Hara-May, *Elizabethan Dyetary of Health*, (Lawrence, KS: Coronado Press, 1977), p. 180.
14 Sharland, p. 156-63; given Ferrar's tendencies to caution and indirection and his later account prefacing *The Winding Sheet* of another effort to revive the Academy, there had probably been considerable preparatory discussion among the more sympathetic family members before the sort of 'confessional' meeting that took place on St. Luke's Day.
15 *Ibid.*, p. 156.
16 *Ibid.*, pp 163-5. The title of 'Mother' rather than the 'Chief', as she had been earlier, provides another interesting example of the family's readiness to reconfigure its relationships. In recognition of her new role as 'Mother' her own mother Susanna presented to Mary her own siblings to become her 'children'; *ibid.*, p. 179.
17 See above, p. 204.
18 *Ibid.*, p. 176. I shall hereafter identify participants by their real names and

assume that Cheerful is Hester and Affectionate is Margaret. See above, pp, 199-201.

19   *Ibid.*, pp. 159-60.

20   *Ibid.*, pp. 230-9.

21   Ibid., p. 177. The speaker here is Susanna Collet, the Moderator.

22   *Ibid.*, p. 179.

23   *Ibid*, p. 180.

24   *Ibid.,* pp. 191-2; another indicator of Nicholas's Socratic teaching methods. Turner's notes contain a reference to 'Dialogues in ye Platoniqe way, a thing of great skill to draw ye knowledge of ye Truth from anothers Ignorance' though it is not clear if this is Turner's own comment or one he copied from a Ferrar meditation; Turner, f. 62r.

25   Williams, pp.192-315.

26   *Ibid.*, p. 225.

27   Ferrar told Arthur Woodnoth of this agreement in a letter of 17 Dec 1632; FP 879.

28   St Francis de, Sales in *An Introduction to the Devout Life*, New York: Doubleday Image, 1989 [first published 1613]), pp. 411-12 [hereafter cited as de Sales] elaborates this point; John Ferrar mentions reading 'Divine & Learned Sallis' on the subject of slanders and backbiting; Williams, 297.

29   Williams, pp.264-306.

30   FP 884 (10 Jan 1632/3); letter to NF.

31   Williams,, p. 172.

32   *Ibid.*, p. 187.

33   See below, pp. 221-2.

34   Quoted in Margaret Aston, 'Moving Pictures: Foxe's Martyrs and Little Gidding' *Agent of Change:Print Culture Studies after Elizabeth L. Eisenstein*, edited by Sabrina Alcorn Baron, Eric N. Lindquist, and Eleanor F. Shevlin, (Amherst and Boston: University of Massachusetts Press in association with The Center for the Book, Library of Congress, Washington, D.C., 2007), p. 96. [Hereafter cited as Aston, 'Moving Pictures'].

35   Sharland, pp. 246-9.

36   FP 879 (17 Dec 1632).

37   See above, p. 156.

38   de Sales, pp. 64-104.

39   FP 882 (22 Dec 1632)

40   FP 884, 886, 891.

41   FP 884 (10 Jan 1632/3). Joshua's letter does not survive in the Ferrar Papers so that we can only speculate as to its contents.

42   FP 911.

43   FP 913 (10 Oct 1633).

44   FP 913 and 914 (Oct 1633). In March 1634 she confirmed that she was indeed pregnant (FP 930) and Joshua wrote of her not being in the best of health (FP 935 6 May 1634). Peter Mapletoft was born in June.

45   See below, p. 225-6. Ferrar was undoubtedly the T.S. to whom the preface was attributed.
46   FP 928 (10 March 1633/34).
47   FP 930 (25 Mar 1634).
48   FP 931 (29 Mar 1634).
49   FP 932 (30 Mar 1634).
50   See above, pp. 152-59.
51   Sig. 4v.
52   See below, p. 273-4.
53   See above, p. 221.
54   FP 923 (13 Jan 1633/4). .
55   Peckard, pp. 240-45. Certainly Bathsheba in the spring of 1637 thought it was about to be the death of him, attributing Nicholas's illness to the starvation that was his Lessius diet; see below, p. 279.
56   Blackstone, pp. 101-2.
57   This account of the relation of faith and works echoes Nicholas's translation of Valdes; see above, p. 183-4.
58   For the entire passage see above. p. 177.
59   *Ibid.*, p. 106.
60   S Collet Letters, The letter is undated; John Ferrar III, the copyist, has placed it between one dated Feb 1633/4 and another dated April of that year.
61   See above, p. 207.
62   Aston, 'Moving Pictures', pp. 94-100.
63   FP 940.
64   Peckard, pp. 240-45 reports Mary Ferrar's view of her son's austeriries.
65   Perhaps preparing *Hygiasticon* for the press or litigation related to restoration of the glebe lands for which see FP 963, 970.
66   FP 903, 916.
67   FP 916,917,919 and 920 (all in December) concern Herbert's book; see also, p. 141. FP 910 (26 Sept 1633), FP 915 (22 Nov 1633) concern Bathsheba.
68   See above, pp. 82-3. Bathsheba's letter to Mrs. Sherrington and its unpleasant consequences might well have been what prompted John to intercept and monitor her subsequent correspondence.
69   FP 797 (NF to MWF, 17 June 1631).
70   S Collet Letters, SC to 'Sister Farrar' from Margaretting, July 1631.
71   FP 818 (Lady Sandys to NF, 25 Oct 1631).
72   FP 910 (26 Sept 1633) and 915 (22 Nov 1633).
73   FP 923 (13 Jan1633/4). See also above, p. 225-6. The work presumably involved finishing Lessius and sending it off for printing. Its preface is dated 7 Dec 1633. Robert Mapletoft then wrote that Lessius would be finished sometime on 31 January; FP 925 (30 Jan 1633/4).
74   Blackstone, p. 107.
75   She had been its 'Founder' and acknowledged as its motive force in Mary and Anna's letter to her that accompanied the book recording its first sessions:

Sharland, pp. li-iii. For her distress at these later problems is recounted in
Blackstone, p. 107.

76   *Ibid,* p. 107. Bathsheba had complained bitterly (see above, p. 236) about
intrusions into her and John's bedroom. Others who might have felt their
'liberty of carnal Affections' encroached upon were Hester and Margaret
who were approaching marriage by 1635 and perhaps resented a revived
Little Academy as an instrument of spiritual pressure. Their views might in
turn have influenced their younger sisters.

77   *Ibid,* pp. 108-9.

78   When her mother wrote to her in December 1634, she was simply 'my
daughter Hester' and Susanna was worried about whether Hester could
adjust to life with less money. By June 1635 she had become 'my daughter
Kestian'; S Collet Letters.

79   *Ibid.,* (June 1635) Susanna mad clear her opposition to cousin marriages in this
letter to Hester. The marriage was licensed in London on 11 April 1636.

80   Susanna (in London) to Nicholas, FP 1006 (6 Jan 1635/6); Nicholas to
Susanna, FP 1009 (11 Jan 1635/6). He added that if she/they did not want
him to have this frank talk with Ramsay, they should keep him away from
Nicholas. It is not clear what information Nicholas might supply that he
thought would put Ramsay off: perhaps something in John Collet's finances,
which in the Edward Collet case, had not impressed Nicholas. It seems highly
unlikely that the Ferrar finances were the problem since they were good
enough to provide a settlement shortly thereafter. The financial settlement
after the marriage was duly witnessed by parents and sisters; FP: 1012 (25
Mar 1636) and 1015 (7 April 1636).

81   S Collet Letters; after the letter to Hester the last five letters date from the
winter of 1645/6. FP 1006 (SC to NF).

82   Blackstone, p. 110. He might have needed (or wanted) to attend to his
various business affairs including the various marriage negotiations but also
the management of his Southwark properties. We can only ascertain that he
was in London in the early part of 1639 but at Gidding in February 1641 and
again in October 1642; FP 1076, 1077 and 1078 (London) and FP 1090 and
1093 (Gidding). Susanna might or might not have been with him on those
occasions.

83   She, like her parents, might have absented herself from Gidding for substantial
periods orj equally likely, the final session had finished before the autumn of
1635.

84   Blackstone, p. 111, does not attempt to decide which of the characters was
Anna and which Mary. The basis of my choice I shall indicate later.

85   *Ibid.,* p. 110.

86   *Ibid.,* pp. 109-11.

87   *Ibid.,* p. 121. Camden's book was originally published in Latin and not
translated into English until 1695.

88   *Ibid,* pp. 115-21.

89   *Ibid.*, p. 129.

90   *Ibid.*, pp. 170-1 and 189-91.

91   *Ibid.*, pp. 184-5.

92   FP 995, also printed in Blackstone, 292-95. Blackstone dates Nicholas's letters describing the confrontation in 1636 but Ransome in 1635. If young John was born in 1631, which Ransome now thinks more likely, the 1636 date would be more plausible.

93   How clearly her hostility was centred on Nicholas is suggested by the fact that once he was dead and John became head of the household, there is no more evidence of dramas of this sort, at least in the Ferrar Papers.

94   'Duties' includes a final section on 'The Duties Peculiar to Women,' duties which essentially of obedience to men. This response sounds as if he feared that John lacked the courage to defend his God-given rights. Nicholas, a strong believer in order and structure, attached particular importance to what he, like St. Paul, saw as a divinely ordained and gender-based hierarchy of authority, though he was obviously within that framework ready to seek consent and accommodation.

95   FP 1044 (20 Feb 1636/7). Mayor's paraphrase of Mary Ferrar's 1628 will hints that this bequest to Nicholas was for his lifetime only; he must therefore have in turn bequeathed it to John though his will does not survive; p. 339.

6

Harmonies Royal: 'Rarities in their Kind'

1   John Ferrar in a letter to Isaac Basire quoted in Mayor, p. 361.

2   FP 852 (19 April 1632).

3   Phrases quoted in Mayor, p. 115

4   Whether Cosin and White actually visited Gidding in person is unclear for no specific records other than references in letters survives. White was an old family connection whom Nicholas's father was said to have brought to London as a lecturer. As Bishop of Ely from 1631 till his death in 1638 he would have been within range of Gidding; he was also a close associate of Cosin in the Durham House group. On these two men see Timothy Wadkins, 'White, Francis (1563/4-1638)', *Oxford Dictionary of National Biography*, Oxford University Press, 2004 [hereafter ODNB; accessed 19 October 2004: http://www.oxforddnb.com/view/article/29239] and Anthony Milton, 'Cosin, John (1595-1672)', *ibid.*, [accessed 18 October 2004: . . ./article/29239]. Cosin, who by 1633 had become a royal chaplain, was with Laud for the presentation of the king's harmony in 1636: see below, p. 257-8. Williams was certainly a visitor on several occasions; M&W, pp. 101-2.

5   FP 815 (AW to NF 13 Oct 1631). Woodnoth reported delivering 'my Cosens [Mary Collet Ferrar's] Concordance' to Herbert and recounted a visit to

Wilton in this same letter. That would not have been the only opportunity for Bemerton is very near to Wilton.

6   M&W, p. 20, which cites as supporting evidence a passage from Rushworth's *Collections*, Part 2, p. 147. Identification of Charles's companions as associates from Nicholas's London days is, however, inaccurate. The Southampton of those London days died in 1624, the Hamilton in early 1625, and the Pembroke in 1630. The successors to Southampton and Hamilton were in 1633 very young. Only the new Pembroke (brother Philip, also Earl of Montgomery, b. 1584) might have known Nicholas in London but that past acquaintance would not have been as likely a source of information about Little Gidding and the harmonies as the friendship with George Herbert.

7   His comments were relayed to the family by the messenger who returned the borrowed book; M&W, p.77.

8   Opponents of this revival of pictures in bibles regarded them, when they appeared in 'the Bishop of Canterburies' Bibles', as idolatrous and further evidence of Archbishop Laud's popish tendencies. On the protests both in England and particularly in Scotland against these 'Laudian' bibles, see George Henderson, 'Bible Illustration in the Age of Laud', *Transactions of the Cambridge Bibliographical Society*, VIII, No. 2 (1982), 173-216 [hereafter Henderson, 'Bible Illustration'], *passim*.

9   Aston, 'Moving Pictures', esp. p. 101. I am indebted to Margaret Aston for illuminating discussion of the Little Gidding harmonies' combination of text and pictures and the different audience to which it iwas addressed.

10   The acknowledgment of Jansen and Buisson came in the 'Advertizement' that prefaced the royal harmony. I have discussed in greater detail the features of these harmonies and Ferrar's use of them in Monotessaron, 22-52.

11   FP 950 and 951; Robert Mapletoft and John Tabor to NF (22 Aug 1634). Only Nicholas's letter of disappointment in 1632 suggests his ownership of a copy of Hiud.

12   FP 1000 (16 July 1635); Mapletoft reported finding Perpinian set forth by [Daniel] Heinsius, which he assumed was the same work also found by Wallis at St. John's, and gave Nicholas a brief description of Perpinian's method. He also reported he had only two more colleges to search. The British Library Printed Catalogue, p. 959, lists a harmony by Guidone de Perpiniano entitled *Quatuor Unum. Hoc est Concordia Evangelica . . .* published in Cologne in 1631 (some three hundred years after his death) in a collection of his works.

13   BL C.23.e.4. On 12 May 1636 Nicholas (FP 1016) instructed Arthur Woodnoth about delivery of the harmony. Replying (FP 1017, undated but clearly an answer to 1016) Arthur reported its delivery. He had seen the book and was sure that God would accept what in it was right and pardon anything else because of the devotion and humility which its invention and execution showed. It seems a rather surprising comment on so elaborate a piece of workmanship. For Laud's and Cosin's presence at the presentation see M&W, p. 79.

14   John Ferrar in his 1641 letter to Isaac Basire said that the king's book had
      cost the family £100; Mayor, p. 361.
15   The illustrations included only a few collage-style pictures and those very
      simple. This technique the family would develop much more elaborately in
      later works. Only one roundel had been coloured, a depiction of the scourging
      of Christ.
16   'To wch [texts] are added Sundry Pictures expressing Either the Facts
      Themselves or their Types & Figures Or other matters appertaining thereunto'.
      This statement became standard in subsequent title pages.
17   For example, Ch. 28 in the 'Order' is entitled 'Simons Wives Mother & all
      Diseased' while in the text it is 'Peters Wives Mother & other Sick Folk'.
18   This phrase had served as the entire title of the Bodleian volume.
19   BL C.23.e.2.
20   Hatfield House, Cecil Papers 341.
21   Into the text but not into the table of contents was inserted a new Chapter
      29, 'The Leaper Cleansed', which included most of the old Chapter 44. The
      original Chapter 29, entitled 'The Reproofe of Three' then became the textual
      Chapter 30. Yet the remaining material from the old Chapter 44 continued
      under the same title, 'The Leaper Cleansed', numbered in the Contents as 43
      though it would in the text have been 44 as before.
22   The pencilled corrections in the Cotsen harmony would appear to be
      nineteenth century additions, probably by their new owner, Arthur (Troyte)
      Acland. In the Collet harmony, however, four pages are devoted to the
      chapter lists, the first of which (f.6v.) is headed in Nicholas's hand 'The
      Table of Contents of this Book'. There are three columns of chapters,
      which are printed but cut into columns and pasted in, with 'Page' or 'Pages'
      written above and to the right of the printed columns and the appropriate
      numbers filled in, also by hand. The third column includes the problematical
      Chapter 29 and that difficulty is got round by pasting in the listed chapters
      through 28, then adding in smaller type, Chapter 29, 'The Leper Cleansed',
      and continuing the list using separate cutout bits pasted together instead
      of a continuous column. That pasted pattern continues on the remaining
      pages. The next page (f.7r.) has its manuscript heading and page numbers
      in John Ferrar's hand, while the two remaining pages have no heading
      but only page listings. Within the text itself the printed chapter headings
      and numbers are also cut and pasted in at the appropriate divisions. The
      Hatfield harmony resorted to a similar manipulation to deal with the altered
      chapters in both table of contents and chapter headings.
23   Sean Kelsey, 'Wharton, Philip, fourth Baron Wharton (1613-1696), ODNB
      [http://www.oxforddnb.com/view/article/29170, accessed 9 May 2006].
24   Mayor, p. 361. John included this information as part of his larger plea
      to Basire to solicit other orders among the higher clergy. Lord Wharton's
      volume has vanished.
25   A seal attached to the inside cover is identified as the 'Book Stamp of the great

Sir Robert Cotton who died 1631 / used also by his grandson Sir John Cotton, Bart. who died 1702'. Although these Cottons of Conington were described as near neighbours of the Ferrars, other Cottons were even nearer neighbours at Steeple Gidding. But the surviving evidence fails to reveal which branch of the family acquired it first and whether they bought it or received it as a neighbourly gift, however, the surviving evidence fails to reveal. In the 18th century the senior branch of the Cottons removed from Conington to Steeple Gidding and in that way had taken possession of the harmony. The volume descended from Cottons to Bowdlers to Acland-Troytes in whose possession it remained until 1997 when Cotsen purchased it and placed it at Princeton. On the sale see Sotheby's Catalogue #7775 (11 December 1997).

26 FP 1320 (23 Aug 1658). After a brief sojourn in Holland with her uncle John and his children in 1643-5, she had lived at Gidding until after the deaths of her uncle and her mother in 1657.

27 Davenport, 'Bindings', proposes the 1636 date; 143-4. Henderson's claim ('Bible Illustration', 202 n. 7) that MCF gave it to her sister Hester, who then passed it to her daughter Elizabeth, ignores the John Collet bookplate as well as the fact that Hester was in all likelihood dead before 1680, for Mary's will does not mention her but does leave a legacy to Elizabeth.

28 Mayor, pp. 136-7.

29 Young James wanted his book soon and Nicholas assured him it would be done 'with all good speed', a promise the more plausible if he had known there was an available copy ready for finishing. By 1704 the Cecils possessed it as it bears the bookplate of 'James Cecil, Earl of Salisbury 1704', [f.3v.].

30 Interpolations in the Table of Contents in her father's distinctive hand, however, suggest a considerable role for him in its creation.

31 f.67r. Either of two possible Thomas Jermyns who could have acquired the harmony: Sir Thomas Jermyn (1573-1644/5), a courtier and soldier, or his son Thomas (d. 1659) a Groom of the Bedchamber (1638) to Prince Charles. Did he see the royal harmonies, perhaps even attend the presentation to the prince of his polyglot *Monotessaron* in 1640 and decide to acquire a simpler one for himself?

32 Diarmaid MacCulloch, 'Jermyn, Sir Thomas (bap. 1573, d/ 1644/5), ODNB [http://www.oxforddnb.com/view/article/37601, accessed 6 May 2006].

Sir Thomas Hervey was the son of Suzan, sister to Sir Thomas Jermyn, and her husband Sir William Hervey. J. E. Acland., *Little Gidding and its Inmates in the Time of King Charles I, with an Account of the Harmonies. . .*, London: SPCK, 1903., pp. 194 and 201-2 cites the marriage of Thomas Hervey and Isabella May, and their names appear in the harmony at the foot of f. 4. Jermyn wills can be found in S. H .A. H. Hervey, ed, *Rushbrook Parish Registers 1567 to 1850, with Jermyn and Davers Annals (Suffolk Green Books)*, Woodbridge, 1903, pp. 155-6. I am grateful to David Ransome for much of this information on the Jermyn-Hervey connection and the provenance of the Ickworth harmony.

33   The Heming volume bears on its title page the initials S M. Is later descent makes it all but certain that this was Solomon Mapletoft, who was certainly at Little Gidding in 1641 when he was one of the signers of the Protestation; Granville Proby, 'The Protestation Returns for Huntingdonshire', *Transactions of the Cambridgeshire and Huntingdonshire Archaeological Society*, vol. V pp.289-368 (Ely, 1937), p. 323. He later married Judith Collet; it was perhaps a wedding gift.

34   FP 1016 (NF to AW 12 May 1636) and 1017 (AW to NF [mid-May 1636]). The book was dated 1635 on its title page.

35   M&W, p. 79. Impressed with the title page, and perhaps the 'Advertizement', which he was said to have perused when he had first received the gospel harmony, he was essentially asking for a similar treatment of these historical books. The volume he had borrowed in 1633 had had no such elaborate system though one could with an effort have read an individual gospel by following the appropriate letter through the text.

36   See above, pp. 238-9.

37   FP 1057.

38   MS. Royal Appendix 65.

39   Barnabas Oley in his 'To the Reader' prefacing the 1671 edition of George Herbert's *The Country Parson*, [p.5].

40   Brit Library C.23.e.3. The volume bore no date but could hardly have been earlier than Kings and Chronicles.

41   Cited in Kevin Sharpe, *The Personal Rule of Charles I*, (New Haven: Yale University Press, 1992), p.281n.

42   Henderson, 'Bible Illustration', 174-5.

43   Mayor, p. 149, gives JF's account of what he called the 'Seventh Work', which was the second Pentateuch harmony. He there said that the work had been 'contrived' in NF's lifetime and a draft version made, and that a similar volume had been given to Laud in NF's lifetime, though the great second version was not 'fully contrived' till later as gift for Prince Charles. Laud's volume dated 1640 could not, unless the date is wrong, have been given in NF's lifetime. While the unbound work in Magdalene [FP 1852] includes a title page dated 1641, the text pages are sufficiently rough to qualify as a 'draught version'.

44   Oxford, St. John's College Library, Ms. 262, title page. I am grateful to Catherine Hilliard, Librarian at St. John's, for enabling me to examine this harmony and for supplying information relating to it. Loose sheets in the front of the volume as well as the Library's 'Supplementary Catalogue of MSS.', pp.18-9, discuss the documentation of Laud's acquisition of and later presentation of the book to his college. Since Laud would hardly have been in a position after 1641 to receive such a gift, it would be more likely to have been part of the presentation by nephew Nicholas of polyglot volumes to the king and Prince of Wales at Easter 1640. See C. Leslie Craig, *Nicholas Ferrar Junior*, (London: Epworth Press, 1950), pp.48-53 x. [Hereafter cited as Craig, *NFJr*].

45 Ms. 262, p. 29.

46 Craig, *NFJr*, pp. 26. There is no record of such a request, however, though if he did not, why did the family make it on such a lavish scale?

47 Though deprived of the help of his son Nicholas, who died shortly after the 1640 presentation, JF was negotiating with Robert Peake for bibles and prints in April, 1641, notably texts of Genesis, a map of the land of Canaan, and pictures of the 'utensils in the sanctuary' needed for this second Pentateuch; FP 1091.

48 Mayor, pp. 150-3. The volume is now in the Royal Library, Windsor.

49 *The Eternal Truth of Scriptures* and his *Of the Harmonical Parallel between the predictions or types and the Evangelical Relations. . . .* There was also an excerpt from a work by John Jackson, *Ecclesiastes. The Worthy Churchman described by the polishing of the twelve stones in the high-priests pectorall* (1628).

50 Jackson, *Eternal Truth*, Ch XII & XIII, pp.186-218. There was considerable interest in the fate of the Jews in England at this time particularly as it related to the timing of the apocalypse. For an extended discussion of this topic see David S. Katz, *Philo-Semitism and the Readmission of the Jews to England, 1603-1655* (Oxford: Clarendon Press, 1982).

51 Ickworth and Heming, both dated 1640.

52 This volume is owned by Lord Normanton to whom I am indebted for permission to examine it. He and his secretary, Mrs. Valerie Garner, were most generous in their welcome to Somerley, for which I offer my grateful thanks. For John Ferrar's account of the book's creation, see Mayor, pp. 123-4.

53 The letters from 'A' through 'P' were needed to indicate every possible combination of sources, from a single gospel to two, then three and finally episodes related by all four gospels. For an episode related in only one gospel, of course, no 'Composition' was needed.

54 Pp. 65-66.

55 Young Nicholas had also armed himself with a 'proufe book' of the Gospel of John with each of its twenty-two chapters in a different language to show the king that he really understood these languages; Craig, *NFJr*, pp. 28-40. Craig presumably based his account on John Ferrar's story in Mayor, pp. 129-33, in which young Nicholas offered the king two large books with their title pages indicating the scope of the two projects. What, if anything, further they had by way of a start on the work is unclear, but the king himself talked of them as yet to be finished. The 'proufe book' is now in the archives of Clare College, Cambridge.

56 Mayor, pp. 359-60. The two letters are quoted in full, pp.359-62.

57 Craig, *NFJr*, Chs. 2 and 3.

58 *Ibid.*, p. 38.

59 Peter N. Miller, 'The "Antiquarianization" of Biblical Scholarship and the London Polyglot Bible (1653-57)', *Journal of the History of Ideas*, 62:3, pp. 463-82, discusses this movement and Archbishop Laud's leading role

in it, *e.g.* his founding of a chair in Arabic at Oxford. I am grateful to Karen and Joel Kupperman for bringing the article to my attention. Laud also gave Oriental and Greek books to the Bodleian and obtained a royal letter to the Turkey Company ordering that every one of its ships returning from the Levant should bring back one Persian or Arabic ms; Graham Parry, *The Golden Age Restor'd: The Culture of the Stuart Court, 1603-42*, New York: St. Martin's Press, 1981 [paperback, 1985], p. 251. John Ferrar certainly knew of this polyglot scholarship when he inquired of Isaac Basire whether the French polyglot bible was yet available in London; Mayor, p.359.

7

Nicholas Posthumous

1   Arthur Woodnoth, who had himself been ill in the spring of 1637, wrote to Ferrar in April a report of his consultations with three London physicians about Ferrar's symptoms. The doctors concurred that 'melancholy' was the most obvious source of his poor health; FP 1052.

2   FP 1056 (c. June 1637); Blackstone, p. 289 reprints the letter but dates it wrongly to 1636. John Ferrar commented that his wife was wrong to say Nicholas could no longer speak.

3   M&W, p. 108. A letter from Woodnoth (2 Oct 1637) refers to Ferrar's journey from which he had by then returned to Gidding. It has no comment on Ferrar's health though he would be dead within two months.

4   *Ibid.*, p. 111.

5   *Ibid.*, p. 118.

6   *Ibid.*, pp. 109-10.

7   Christopher W. Brooks, 'Hetley , Sir Thomas (*c.*1570–1637)', *Oxford Dictionary of National Biography*, Oxford University Press, Sept 2004; online edn, Jan 2008 [http://www.oxforddnb.com/view/article/70494, accessed 27 Oct 2009]. On the date of Lenton's visit see Appendix, p. 325.

8   Local gossip at a noble household about crosses in the church's east window echoed Lenton's suspicions about crosses and candles, bows and genuflections that were probably not wholly dispelled despite the refutation supplied by one of the guests at that gathering. M&W, Materials, 103-4

9   Both of these print runs are said to be second editions though EEBO shows no first edition. If this was a deliberate device on Ferrar's part, it is hard to see what purpose it would serve. The 1636 edition was called the third.

10   This new edition had been preceded two years earlier by another book, also a translation from Italian, entitled *Medicina Statistica*, that also applied, though in a rather different manner, weight and measure to questions of diet. This volume was advertised on the flyleaf of *The Temperate Man* and its Italian author, Santorio Santorio (1561-1636), had been a professor at Padua during the time Ferrar studied there.

11   Mark Goldie, 'Voluntary Anglicans', *The Historical Journal*, 46 4 (2003), 977-90 [hereafter cited as Goldie, 'Anglicans']. On the process that effected this change see Alexamdra Walsham, *Charitable Hatred: Tolerance and Intolerance in England, 1500-1700*, (Manchester and New York, Manchester University Press, 2006).

12   Richard Busby of Westminster School wrote to Isaac Basire (27 July 1647) that John Ferrar was back at 'Gidden' with his family at the same time that Timothy Thurscross was back in Yorkshire and Robert Mapletoft had a 'good living' [no place given]; Basire, Isaac, *The Correspondence of Isaac Basire D.D. . . .*, London: John Murray, 1831, p. 62.

13   Elizabeth R. Clarke, 'Oley, Barnabas (*bap.* 1602,*d.*1686)', *ODNB* http://www.oxforddnb.com/view/article/20704, accessed 27 Jan 2007] [this article hereafter cited as Clarke, 'Oley'].

14   Turner, ff. 135-130. The 'Directions' are dated 20 July 1655 at Little Gidding. They are, with the exception of the statement about monasteries quoted on p. 291, in a hand identical with that of the writer of the Ferrar material in the Almack Ms., Cambridge University Library, Add Ms 4484 [hereafter cited as Almack] and also in S Collet Letters. See also M&W, pp. 13-14.

15   Surviving members of this 'Web of Friendship' included, besides Oley, Robert Mapletoft, Peter Gunning, Timothy Thurscross and Edmund Duncon.

16   E. Mansfield Forbes, 'Nicholas Ferrar: America and Little Gidding', *Clare College, 1326-1926*, (Cambridge: Printed for the College at the University Press, 1930), Vol. II, pp. 380-1, 482n. [hereafter cited as Forbes]. Little Gidding would hardly have been the only model for Oley; for a clergyman to take in students to prepare them for further education was hardly uncommon; the Ferrar brothers had attended such a school in the household of the Rev. Robert Brooks at Enborne, Berks., M&W, p. 44.

17   Perhaps because, as he acknowledged in the preface to the third volume of his edition of Thomas Jackson's works (1657), God had made clear to him that he lacked the ability to produce original work; Clarke, 'Oley'.

18   For this family drama see letters FP 1284, 1285, 1306 and 1320 between John Ferrar, Ann Brooke Ferrar, Mary Collet Ferrar and John Ferrar Jr [with a draft reply from Berridge].

19   She made her £500 legacy from her grandfather available to her uncles in the financial straits of 1624-5; FP 573 (17 June 1625). They subsequently offered her an annuity by way of compensation; FP 699 (15 Jan 1629/30), and another (May 1631) in lieu of rights surrendered to enable her grandmother to restorate the glebe lands of Little Gidding; Clare College Archives, Safe A: 3/17. She was also elected 'Chief' of the Little Academy to take her grandmother's place; Sharland, p. 179; was the chief bookbinder for the harmonies and other books the family compiled; M&W, 77-79; FP 972 (11 Dec 1634) and 991 (18 Mar 1635); and had dieted so strenuously as to make herself ill after Christmas 1633; FP 923 (13 Jan 1633/4).

20   FP 861 (25 July 1632),

21   PCC Wills, 11/364, 1680, f. 143.

22   Kenneth W. Stevenson, 'Gunning, Peter (1614-1684)', ODNB, [http://oxforddnb.com/view/article/11748, accessed 27 Jan 2007].

23   Basire, *Correspondence,* p. 262. Cf. Busby's letter of 1647 to Basire with news of John Ferrar, Thurscross and Robert Mapletoft; p. 284.

24   See above, pp. 263 and 277. Isaac Basire presented to his wife in 1636 a copy of de Sales' *Introduction to the Divine Life,* that he said had been bound by the 'virgins of Little Gidding'; Mayor, p. 243n.

25   See Elsie Elizabeth Duncan-Jones's article, 'Who was the Recipient of Crashaw's Leyden Letter?', *New Perspectives on the Life and Art of Richard Crashaw,* John R. Roberts, ed., (Columbia, MO and London: University of Missouri Press, 1990), pp. 174-79. At the end of the letter Crashaw says that his 'mother' [Mary Collet Ferrar] asks to be remembered to him [Beaumont] and in his prayers with an 'affection worthee of her self'. The text of the letter appears in Richard Crashaw, *The Poems English Latin and Greek of Richard Crashaw,* L.C. Martin, ed., (Oxford: Clarendon Press, 1957), pp. xxvii-xxxi.

26   FP 1191 and 1192 (*c.* 1650) and 1235 (?1653).

27   On Beaumont's importance in the Restoration Church see Nicholas Tyacke, 'Arminianism and the theology of the Restoration Church' in his *Aspects of English Protestantism, c. 1530-1700,* (Manchester and New York: Manchester University Press, 2001), esp. pp. 328-34.

28   Letter dated 6 May 1670, Basire, *Correspondence,* p. 285. Basire's son was among the younger Fellows of the college and in 1674 Turner wrote to Basire asking him to delay his son's return to college because of a plot to remove Turner from the Mastership, a request that Gunning seconded; *Ibid.,* 305-8.

29   The original biographical materials apparently stayed at Gidding where Turner used or copied them although John Jones, describing in 1731 records he had seen in family possession, reported that the family claimed not to know what had become of materials Turner had used; Bodleian Library, Oxford, Ms. Rawl. lett. 27.c. (Jones to Thomas Hearne) [hereafter Jones, Rawl.lett]. See below, pp. 295-7, on Mary Collet Ferrar's possession of family mss. She kept the Story Books till her death; in her will she bequeathed them to her nephew John Collet, son of her brother Thomas; see below, pp. 309.

30   Turner's biography only survives in later and partial transcripts which did ultimately find their way into print, notably in the Jebb 'Life' published in Mayor, and in an abridged form in *The Christian Magazine* of 1761 as well as other transcripts by Nonjurors discussed below; M&W, pp. 6-7 gives a helpful summary of this complicated cluster of manuscripts.

31   Turner, f. 125v. A note in the manuscript reminded him to ask Ken for information about a particular French saint. I have not been able to identify this saint, whom Turner described as retiring to Mt. Libanus; presumably Turner thought his example relevant to Ferrar.

32   Thomas Hearne in 1730 applied the term 'Protestant Nunnery' to Little Gidding, a move the more striking in light of the earlier pejorative application of 'nunnery' in 1641; in *Thomae Caii . . . Vindiciae antiuitatis AcademiaeOxoniesis contra Joannem Caium. . . .* Oxonii, e theatro Sheldoniano, (1730), Vol II, pp. 684-794 and 812-15. [Hereafter cited as *Thomae Caii*].

33   The hand is definitely not John Ferrar's nor is it identical with that of the rest of the 'Directions'. It is almost certainly Turner's and occurs in Turner as well as in Almack and S Collet Letters.

34   Turner, f. 125v, where Turner says that 'Some few such familys w[ou]]d be a greater Bulwarke to [th]e Natio[n] [tha]n if England were walled w[I]th brass. The papists would be afraid to Vie w[I]th such men.'

35   Mark Goldie, 'Danby, the Bishops and the Whigs', in Tim Harris, Paul Seaward and Mark Goldie, eds.,*The Politics of Religion in Restoration England*, (Oxford: Basil Blackwell, 1990), pp. 89-99.

36   Turner. There is no further documentation of such a contact. Dodwell's letter is pasted to the inside front cover of the ms. volume. Many of Turner's notes in fact look like his efforts to plan the work so as to implement the points he and Dodwell discussed.

37   FP 1049 (13 April 1637) letter from Paul Glisson to NF about Thurscross's decision; other related letters FP 1045 and 1060. The surname is variously spelled and I am using the form in which it appears in Part I,, Vol 4, p.239.

38   John T. Young, 'Worthington, John (*bap.* 1618, *d.* 1671)', *ODNB* [http://www.oxforddnb.com/view/article/29992, accessed 11 Nov 2006] [hereafter cited as Young, 'Worthington'].

39   *The Diary and Correspondence of Dr. John Worthington*, James Crossley Esq, ed., (The Chetham Society, 1847), Vol. 1, pp. 219-20 [hereafter cited as Worthington, *Diary*].

40   For a wide-ranging discussion of this important topic see Peter Clark, *British Clubs and Societies c.1580-1800: the Origins of an Associational World*, (Oxford: Clarendon Press, 2000).

41   [Richard Allestree], *The Causes of the Decay of Christian Piety* (London: R. Norton for T. Garthwait, 1667), p. 434.

42   Worthington's correspondence with Hartlib contained numerous references to plans for Christian societies; e.g. Worthington, *Diary*, I, 156, 164, 211.

43   FP 1189 (1652). Hartlib knew of Nicholas Ferrar's ms. treatise on education [probably Carbone], which he said was in Sir John Danvers' possession; Ephemerides 1640 Part 3 Hartlib, [30/4/53-54A], *The Hartlib Papers* 2nd edition (Sheffield, HROnline, 2002).

44   Worthington lamented to his friend, Dr Ingelo, after he had left Cheshire that while he still thought such societies highly desirable, he had begun to believe that 'they are very precious and rare and hard to meet with'; *Diary*, 1, p. 233 (10 June 1667). Ingelo had a strong nonconformist background, having started a Presbyterian but become an Independent minister in 1644. He would consequently have firsthand experience of voluntary religious

societies; Ian William McLellan, 'Ingelo, Nathaniel (1620/21–1683)', ODNB [http://www.oxforddnb.com/view/article/14385, accessed 9 Nov 2010].

45   She is identified in a note as Mary Collet Ferrar and the manuscripts probably the five folio volumes of 'Lives, Characters, Histories, and Tales . . .' that she had herself bound. *Diary,* 2, 1, p. 231. They were not the work of Nicholas Ferrar, as Peter Peckard had declared, but were taken from Thomas Fuller's *Holy State* at some time after its first publication in 1642; on this derivation from Fuller, see John Eglington Bailey, *The Life of Thomas Fuller, D. D. . . .,* (London and Manchester, 1874), pp. 228-30. These were not the only manuscripts she possessed.

46   In noting that Ferrar had been called a papist and a puritan Turner added that 'halfe of each (as Dʳ Wickham sed of Mʳ Thirscross, make upp a whole good Xian)'; Turner, f. 126v and f.124v.

47   JW to Dr Ingelo (4 June 1670) in *Diary,* 2.2, pp. 337-9. Worthington must have seen a much more extensive and varied a collection of papers than he had described in 1667 in order to make such observations about what editing them would require. He could have seen them while he was in London as the rector of St. Benet Fink in 1665-6 or perhaps when he came to Hackney in 1669; Young, 'Worthington'. The papers Mary bequeathed to her nephew John Collet included not only the Fuller transcripts but also Little Academy dialogues.

48   Whether he got the original papers from Mary Collet Ferrar or Thurscross or he had copies made, he clearly had in his possession a substantial portion of them, at least some of which his son inherited and passed on to Thomas Hearne for publication. For John Worthington Jr's extensive correspondence with Hearne see *Remarks and Collections of Thomas Hearne,* Vol IX and X, H. E. Salter, ed., , Oxford Historical Society vols, LXV and LXVII, Oxford: Clarendon Press, 1914-15, vol IX, pp. 297-8, 3012, 303-4, 305,309-10, 313; vol X, pp 235, 253, 266-7, 275-7, 314, 339, 349-51, 3390, 441, 459 [hereafter cited as Hearne, *Remarks*]. He had earlier supplied Hearne with the material printed in *Thomae Caii.*

49   See Sharland, pp. 1-2 giving the Little Academy's covenant by which they formed themselves originally and the call for a renewal of such promises in the group's revival, pp. 154-6. Blackstone's account of the final revival includes the text of the most elaborate such covenant; pp. 110-12.

50   Hearne, *Thomae Caii,* II, pp. 724, 713, 783-94.

51   Quoted in Mayor, pp. 344-48; the quoted passage is on p. 344. Hacket's picture, which included the erroneous claim that all the members of the family were single, emphasises how much the family fasted and prayed. He certainly portrays them as a community, indeed a quite monastic one. He died in 1670, but his book, *Scrinia Reserata,* was published only in 1693.

52   I have relied on the following sources for general information about the societies and their organisation: W. R. Ward, 'Horneck, Anthony (1641–1697)', *ODNB* [http://www.oxforddnb.com/view/article/13801, accessed 19 Oct

2006] [hereafter cited as Ward, 'Horneck'], Richard Kidder, *The Life of the Reverend Anthony Horneck, D.D., Late Preacher at the Savoy*, (London: B. Aylmer, 1698), and Josiah Woodward, *An Account of the Rise and Progress of the Religious Societies in the City of London, &c. And of the Endeavours for Reformation of Manners Which have been Made Therein*, 2nd ed., (London: J.D., 1698) [hereafter cited as Woodward, *Societies*].

53   These 'Orders', printed in Woodward, *Societies*, pp. 120-30, included a declaration of membership in the Church of England yet of charity to Dissenters of 'good conversation', attendance at weekly meetings at which there were to be no disputes, contribution to a common fund for charitable uses, avoiding alehouses, taverns and 'Play-Houses', praying daily and taking communion once a month at least, and in general avoiding wickedness and doing good to others.

54   London: Benj. Tooke, p. 81. The title could, of course, be intended to link this work with George Herbert's *Country Parson*, which had been republished by Oley in 1671. If, as reported, Oley had forsworn attempting original work of his own, he would not be the author however much he approved of the call for 'societies'.

55   Quoted in Ward, 'Horneck'. Gidding had been accused by earlier 'puritans and dissenters' not of being a separatist conventicle but rather as an 'Arminian nunnery', part of Laud's plan to restore England to popery.

56   Woodward, *Societies*. pp. 53-5. The account justifies the societies and refutes such criticisms of them. During the turbulent years of James II's reign they protected themselves from suspicion by calling themselves 'clubs' rather than 'societies' and meeting in pubs rather than private houses; p. 42.

57   John Spurr, 'The Church, the societies and the moral revolution of 1688', *The Church of England c. 1689-c.1833: From Toleration to Tractariansim*, John Walsh, Colin Haydon and Stephen Taylor, eds., Cambridge: Cambridge University Press, 1993, pp. 137-8, 140. [Hereafter Spurr, 'Church, Societies, Revolution'].

58   John Spurr, 'Fowler, Edward (1631/2–1714)', *ODNB,* online edn, Oct 2005 [http://www.oxforddnb.com/view/article/10007, accessed 27 Jan 2007] [hereafter cited as Spurr, 'Fowler'].

59   Mark Goldie and John Spurr, 'Politics and the Restoration Parish: Edward Fowler and the Struggle for St Giles Cripplegate', *English Historical Review*, 109 (June 1994), esp. 579-85.

60   The group was led by Edward Stephens, who also called for the establishment of a house that would be a 'Seminary of Piety and Vertue' for single women in *The more excellent way; or, A proposal of a compleat work of charity*, (London? : s.n., 1696) p. 2. See also John Spurr, *The Restoration Church of England, 1646-1689*, New Haven and London: Yale University Press, 1991, pp. 132ff, 139-40 [hereafter cited as Spurr, *Restoration CofE*].

61   W. O. B. Allen and Edmund McClure, *Two Hundred Years: The History of the Society for Promoting Christian Knowledge, 1698-1898*, London: SPCK,

1898, p. 21 [hereafter Allen & McClure]. He was not, however, among those active members whose names appeared regularly among those present at the Society's regular meetings; *A Chapter in English Church History: being The Minutes of the Society for Promoting Christian Knowledge for the Years 1698-1704*, Edmund McClure, ed., (London: SPCK, 1888) [hereafter cited as McClure, *Chapter*].

62   Fowler with his Nonconformist ties was both keener and better prepared than many to see the societies in an ecumenical light. His example needs to be balanced against Jeremy Gregory's cautionary comments on the limitations to 'common pastoral aims' when estimating the impact and function of the various societies in uniting people in a common work of 'reformation'; 'The Making of a Protestant Nation: 'Success' and 'Failure' in England's Long Reformation', *England's Long Reformation*, Nicholas Tyacke, ed., (London: University College, London, Press, 1998), pp. 307-33, esp. pp. 320-4.

63   Worthington's wife was the daughter of Benjamin Whichcote, the Cambridge Platonist. There was a Whichcote-Ferrar connection in a later decade;John Ferrar III brought home with him from Cambridge to Gidding in 1679 or 1680 a 'Mr Whichcott' to whom John's sister Ann sent her service; FP 1447.

64   Grigg referred to him as 'my brother Fowler' when she asked Locke to present her affection and service to him; E S De Beer, *The Correspondence of John Locke*, (Oxford: Oxford University Press, 1976-82), Vol, 2,) [hereafter cited as De Beer, *Correspondence*], Vol 2, #555, p. 214, July 1680 and #606 ,p. 336, 1 Jan 1681. The editor of Worthington's *Diary*, however, noted that while they obviously knew each other there is no evidence they were related; p. 214. Though Fowler as Worthington's executor was to have overall charge of the worldly needs of his children, Worthington on his deathbed had asked Grigg to take his children into her care so as to provide them 'the best earliest impressions of religion'; *Diary*, 2.2, p. 379, letter of 26 July 1691 to Worthington's son John. Grigg received a 10/- ring in Mary Collet Ferrar's will and had earlier received a copy of Eikon Basilike which she mistakenly claimed had been bound by her friend; Mayor, p. 396, On her mistaken identification see G. D. Hobson, *Bindings in Cambridge Libraries*, (Cambridge: Cambridge University Press, 1929) p. 122. Turner for his part had got Grigg's son Will a place at Jesus College, Cambridge; letter to Locke in De Beer, *Correspondence*, Vol 2, #820 (April 1685), p. 715. Ken sent to 'Mrs. Gregge' an undated letter that internal evidence points to a date shortly after his deprivation; Thomas Ken, *The Prose Works of the Right Rev. Father in God, Thomas Ken*, James Thomas Round, ed., London: J.G. & F. Rivington, 1838, pp. 42-3.

65   Patrick Wallis, 'Mapletoft, John (1631-1721)', ODNB [accessed 19 Oct 2004: http://www.oxforddnb.com/view/article/18018] The choice of Westminster for John and his cousin Hugh was hardly surprising since Robert knew Richard Busby; see above, p.284.

66   John much later added a tribute to his 'much honoured aunt Mary' to a letter

in his possession that his aunts Mary and Anna had written to his mother in 1631; Mayor, p. 301. John went to Westminster as a King's Scholar and four years later matriculated at Trinity. Robert also sent another nephew, Hugh, son of Robert's brother Solomon, to Westminster and then to Trinity. G. F. Russell Barker and Alan H. Stenning, eds., *The Record of Old Westminsters*, (London: Chiswick Press, 1928), II, p. 619.

67   FP 1054 (20 June 1637) Mapletoft explained to Nicholas Ferrar what Thurscross offered and why he did not want to accept.

68   Mayor, pp 144-6. That Frank knew young Nicholas, who had rarely left Gidding, suggests that Frank, like Robert Mapletoft, had spent time there.

69   Edmund Venables, 'Mapletoft, Robert (1609-1677)', rev.S. L. Sadler, *ODNB* [accessed 19 Oct 2004: http://www.oxforddnb.com/view/article/18019]

70   FP 1186-7 (c. 1650). He also supplied information about turtles (FP 1185, *c.* 1650) and a flowery letter to his cousin Virginia that expressed hope that he would see her at Stourbridge Fair (FP 1178, 26 Aug 1650). He later offered his cousin John Ferrar II medical advice (FP 1379, 7 Sep 1669) and several years later asked his cousin to repay him money he had borrowed (FP 1405, 8 Feb 1674/5).

71   Locke reported to his absent friend how he and Collet proposed to bring pressure to bear on someone who owed Mapletoft money. JL (Exeter House) to JM (with Countess of Northumberland in France) 19 Oct 1672 and 14 Feb 1672/3, De Beer, *Correspondence*, Vol 1, pp. 371 & 378.

72   Roger Morrice reported the Lord Chancellor's displeasure at what he saw as a rushed election of Mapletoft before he could intervene and described Mapletoft as 'a Whig or at best a trimmer / and whether [Whig or trimmer] was the verier rogue no man knew.' , Mark Goldie et al, eds, *The Entring Book of Roger Morrice (1677-1691)*, (Woodbridge: Boydell & Brewer in Association with the Parliamentary History Yearbook, 2007), Vol III, p. 93: Saturday, 30 Jan 1685/6. I am grateful to Tim Harris for this reference.

73   Mapletoft would not have been likely to follow his friend quite so far along this contractual path. For the later development of this idea by one who explicitly acknowledged his admiration for Little Gidding and called his own organizations 'societies', see Frederick Dreyer, 'A 'Religious Society under Heaven': John Wesley and the Identity of Methodism', *Journal of British Studies*, 25 (Jan 1986). especially p. 82.

74   Spurr, 'Church, Societies, Revolution', p. 134.

75   Woodward, *Societies*, p. 214

76   Charles Frederick Secretan, *Memoirs of the Life and Times of the Pious Robert Nelson*, (London: John Murray, 1860). p. 90. [Hereafter cited as Secretan, *Nelson*] The two men had known each other since at least 1679 when Mapletoft had sponsored Nelson's election to the Royal Society.

77   In his *An Address to Persons of Quality and Estate* quoted in [J.F.M. Carter], *Undercurrents of Church Life in the Eighteenth Century*, T.T. Carter, ed., London: Longmans, 1899, pp. 30-1. Calls for such homes or 'colleges',

including one for girls to be run by suitably grave and pious virgins and widows, had appeared earlier in works by Edward Chamberlayne, a friend of Timothy Thurscross and Isaac Basire: *England's Wants* (1667) and *An Academy* (1671) the latter appealing not to Gidding but to continental models.

78   For more detailed accounts of these schools see W.M. Jacob, 'The Eye of His Master: Children and Charity Schools', *The Church and Childhood: Studies in Church History*, 31, R. N. Swanson, ed., (Oxford: Blackwell for the Eccelesiastical History Society, 1994), pp. 363-77, and M. G. Jones, *The Charity School Movement: A Study of Eighteenth Century Puritanism in Action*,(London: Frank Cass, 1964).

79   Will of John Collet of St Andrews, Holborn : PCC Leeds 1713; dated 9 May 1711, with codicil added 12 Nov 1713, proved 26 Nov 1713. [Hereafter Will of John Collet] Mapletoft's own contributions to charity schools are recorded in McClure, *Chapter*, pp. 5, 6, and 11.

80   Mayor, p. 302.

81   McClure, *Chapter*, pp. 81, 303, 304, 305. The Rev. Thomas Ferrar, Mapletoft's second cousin, rector of Little Gidding and resident with his brother John in the family house, was presumably among that unenthusiastic group; John Mapletoft never mentioned him in this or any other connection I have discovered. Both Thomas Ferrar and Hugh Mapletoft, however, at different times were said to have wanted to write Nicholas Ferrar's biography; Ms. Rawl. Lett. 27.c (Rev. John Jones to Thomas Hearne, 1 April 1731).

82   See above, p. 17. As late as 1636 Nicholas was arranging support for 'my Indian' then in London: FP 1014 (2 April).

83   *The Rich Man's Bounty, the True Measure of His Wisdom*, (London: Brabazon Aylmer, 1695), p. 23.

84   These items are documented in J.B. Mayor's inventory of Ferrar materials, pp. 293-4.

85   For the movements of this volume around the family see above, p. 264-5. Elizabeth Kestian received from John Collet not only the concordance but the Gidding story books, and the writings and translations of their uncle Nicholas Ferrar. On these see the next footnote.

86   Mayor, pp. 301-3, listed these papers, which followed the movements of the harmonies (previous footnote) and added that the list had been annotated by Francis Peck, an eighteenth-century biographer of Nicholas Ferrar who had also seen Turner's biography and materials. This Middle Hill MS 9527 is now at Clare College, Cambridge.

87   The collection includes proverbs in Italian, French, Spanish and 'British/ Welsh' as well as English, with translations as needed. Nicholas Ferrar was not the only collector of such sayings; George Herbert had earlier produced a collection of 'Outlandish Proverbs'.

88   *A Perswasive to the Conscientious Frequenting the Daily Publick Prayers of the Church of England*, London: Walter Kettilby, 1687. He reiterated this point subsequently in *A Sermon Preach'd at the Church of St. Mary le Bow*,

to the *Societies for Reformation of Manners*, (London: B. Aylmer, 1700), esp. pp.11ff.

89   Secretan, *Nelson,* p. 7.

90   Sir George Wheler, *The Protestant Monastery, or Christian Oeconimicks*, (London, 1698). Hearne of course would subsequently print Gidding material under the title 'Protestant Nunnery'.

91   Goldie, 'Anglicans', 990; W. M., Jacob, *Lay People and Religion in the Early Eighteenth Century*, Cambridge: Cambridge University Press, 1996, esp. pp. 77-91.

92   [J.F.M. Carter], *Undercurrents of Church Life in the Eighteenth Century*, T.T. Carter, ed., London: Longmans, 1899, p. 221.

93   *Ibid.*, p. 13.

Conclusion

1   Turner, ff. 54v – 55r.
2   *Ibid.*, f.61v.
3   *Ibid.*, ff. 73v – 74r.
4   See above, pp. 145-6.
5   Turner, ff. 83r and 84r.
6   See above, p. 144.
7   Turner, ff. 60r and 61r.
8   *Ibid.*, f. 63r.
9   See above, p. 243.
10   See above, p. 248 (Bathsheba), p. 247 (John), p. 239 (Margaret), and pp. 118-9 (Susanna).
11   Turner, ff. 61v and 62r.
12   Jeremiah 6:16.
13   M&W, pp. 113-4.

Appendix: The Ferrar and Collet Families

1   Mayor, p. 380.
2   M&W, p. 115
3   FP 818 (25 Oct [1631].
4   FP 712.
5   By the 1680s Peg was living with her niece Betty Kestian, Hester's daughter. The latter kept a school in Westminster. The registers of St James, Piccadilly record the burials of two widows: of Ann Alsop in 1686, and of Margaret [BLANK] in 1692. It is possible that Margaret [BLANK] was Peg Legatt, a suggestion made just that much more plausible if the Ann Alsop who died in 1686 was her second husband's niece, the daughter of Joshua Mapletoft and his first wife Margaret Legatt.

WOODNOTHS and FERRARS mentioned in the text

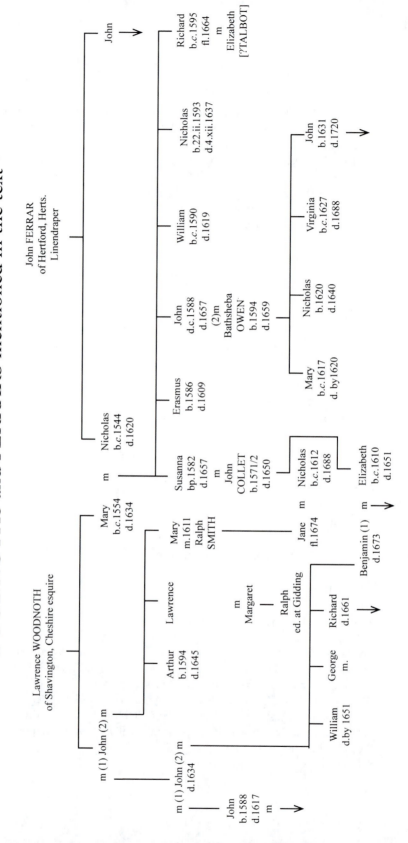

The COLLET Children

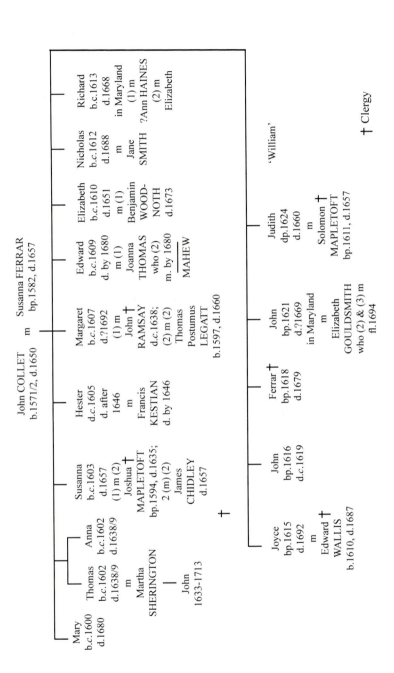

John COLLET   m   Susanna FERRAR
b.1571/2, d.1650   bp.1582, d.1657

Mary
b.c.1600
d.1680

Thomas
b.c.1602
d.1638/9
m
Martha
SHERINGTON

Anna
b.c.1602
d.1638/9

John
1633-1713

Susanna
b.c.1603
d.1657
(1) m (2)
Joshua †
MAPLETOFT
bp.1594, d.1635;
2 (m) (2)
James
CHIDLEY
d.1657

Hester
d.c.1605
d. after
1646
m
Francis
KESTIAN
d. by 1646

Margaret
b.c.1607
d.?1692
(1) m
John †
RAMSAY
d.c.1638;
(2) m (2)
Thomas
Postumus
LEGATT
b.1597, d.1660

Edward
b.c.1609
d. by 1680
m (1)
Joanna
THOMAS
who (2)
m. by 1680
MAHEW

Elizabeth
b.c.1610
d.1651
m (1)
Benjamin
WOOD-
NOTH
d.1673

Nicholas
b.c.1612
d.1688
m
Jane
SMITH

Richard
b.c.1613
d.1668
in Maryland
(1) m
?Ann HAINES
(2) m
Elizabeth

Joyce
bp.1615
d.1692
m
Edward †
WALLIS
b.1610, 1687

John
bp.1616
d.c.1619

Ferrar †
bp.1618
d.1679

John
bp.1621
d.?1669
in Maryland
m
Elizabeth
GOULDSMITH
who (2) & (3) m
fl.1694

Judith
dp.1624
d.1660
m
Solomon †
MAPLETOFT
bp.1611, d.1657

'William'

† Clergy

The MAPLETOFT Connection

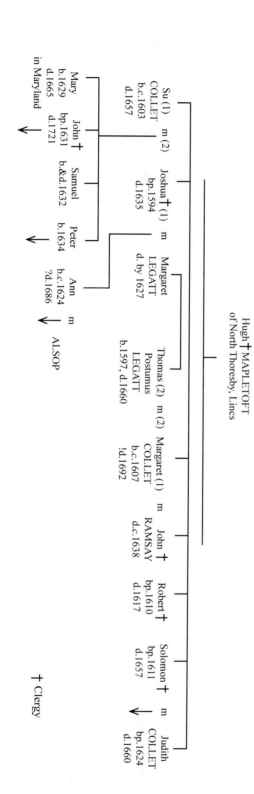

Hugh ✝ MAPLETOFT
of North Thoresby, Lincs

Su (1)
COLLET
b.c.1603
d.1657

m (2)

Joshua ✝ (1)
bp..1594
d.1635

m

Margaret
LEGATT
d. by 1627

Thomas (2)
Postumus
LEGATT
b.1597, d.1660

m (2)

Margaret (1)
COLLET
b.c.1607
!d.1692

m

John ✝
RAMSAY
d.c.1638

Robert ✝
bp.1610
d.1617

Solomon ✝
bp.1611
d.1657

m

Judith
COLLET
bp.1624
d.1660

←

Mary
b.1629
d.1665
in Maryland

John ✝
bp.1631
d.1721

←

Samuel
b.&d.1632

Peter
b.1634

←

Ann
b.c.1624
?d.1686

m

ALSOP

←

✝ Clergy

BIBLIOGRAPHY

PRIMARY SOURCES

MANUSCRIPTS

Cosin Letterbook. 1B. 164 (Francis Turner to Isaac Basire, 30 September 1674), John Cosin Library, Durham University.

John Ferrar's account of Little Gidding Harmonies, Lambeth Palace Library, Ms. 251.

The Ferrar Papers, 1590-1790, David R. Ransome, ed, [in microform] Wakefield, Eng: Microform Academic Publishers, 1992, and [online] *The Virginia Company Archives*, Marlborough, Wilts: Adam Matthew Publications, 2005. The original papers are in the Old Library, Magdalene College, Cambridge.

[Nicholas Ferrar], 'Duties Common to Man and Woman' with concluding section on 'Duties Peculiar to Woman', Ms volume in private possession.

Bodleian Library, Oxford

Ms. Rawlinson. [K] Letters [Jones/Hearne]. 27.c (15585) and 15.99.

Notebook of Francis Turner; Ms. Rawlinson. D. 2.

Letters of Susanna Collet (copied by John Ferrar III); Ms. Top. Hunts. e.1.

University Library, Cambridge

Ms. Additional 4484 (Almack)

Ms. Mm.i.46 (Baker Manuscripts, vol. 35)

Dr Williams's Library, London

Mss. Jones. B.22, [John Jones] 'Delamira: Advancement of Religion and Philosophy'

Mss. Jones. B.87 'Account of Gidding &c'

Ms. Jones, B.101, 'Autobiography of the Reverend John Jones'

Oxfordshire Records Office

Annesley Mss: E6/12/13D/1-25

BIBLICAL HARMONIES
Of the Four Gospels

Houghton Library, Harvard University (c. 1630) A 1275.5.

Bodleian Library, Oxford (1631) Arch.A.d.3.

British Library: the Royal Harmony made for King Charles I (1635) C.23.e.4.
the harmony that had belonged to the Collet family (1637) C.23.e.2.

Cotsen Library, Princeton University (1635).

Hatfield House, the harmony belonging to Lord Salisbury (1637) Cecil Papers 341.

Somerley, the harmony belonging to Lord Normanton (1640).

Ickworth, the harmony belonging earlier to the Hervey family and now to the National Trust (1640).

Private possession: the harmony belonging earlier to the Heming family (1640).

Of Other Biblical Texts

British Library: the harmony of Kings and Chronicles made at the request of Charles I (1637) a volume of Acts and Revelation that is not in fact a harmony of those books but simply an illustrated version, made for the king probably c. 1638.

St John's College, Oxford, Pentateuch harmony presented to Archbishop Laud (1640).

Royal Library, Windsor, Pentateuch harmony made for Prince Charles (1642).

Ferrar Papers: a partial plan for the harmony of Kings and Chronicles (FP 1057) and a bundle of materials for another Pentateuch harmony (FP 1892a).

PRINTED BOOKS

The Anglican Canons 1529-1947, Bray, Gerald, ed., Church of England Record Society, Vol. 6, Woodbridge: Boydell Press, 1998.

'Annual Accounts of the Church of England, 1632-1639', Fincham, Kenneth, ed., in *From the Reformation to the Permissive Society*, Melanie Barber and Stephen Taylor with Gabriel Sewall, eds., Woodbridge: Boydell Press for Church of England Record Society, 2010, pp. 63-149.

Basire, Isaac, *The Correspondence of Isaac Basire D.D. . . .*, London: John Murray, 1831.

Richard Bernard, *Iosvahs Godly Resolution. . . touching houshold gouernment for well ordering a familie*, London: Iohn Legatt, 1612

Boswell, James, *The Life of Samuel Johnson L.L.D.*, New York: Modern Library, n.d. (originally published 1791).

Burton, Robert, *The Anatomy of Melancholy*, A.R. Shilleto, ed., London: George Bell, 1903.

Calvin, John, *A Harmonie Upon the Three Evangelistes Matthewe, Marke, and Luke, with the Commentaries of M. John Calvine: Faithfully translated out of Latine into English by E. P. [Eusebius Paget] Whereunto is also added a Commentarie upon the Evangelist S. John, by the same authour. [transl. by Christopher Fetherstone, student in divinitie]*, London: Thom[as] Adams, 1610.

Cawdrey, D[aniel], *Family Reformation Promoted*, London: Printed by T.G. for John Wright, 1656.

Certain Sermons Appointed by the Queen's Majesty to be Declared and Read by all Parsons, Vicars, and Curates. Every Sunday and Holiday in Their Churches: . . .for the Better Understanding of the Simple People. . . According [to]. . . Book of Common Prayers, 1574, Cambridge: John Parker, 1850. [Homilies]

[Chamberlayne, Edward], *An Academy or Colledge: Wherein Young Ladies and Gentlewomen May at a very moderate Expence be duly instructed in the true Protestant Religion, and in all Vertuous Qualities that may adorn that Sex: . . .*, [London] In the Savoy: Tho. Newcomb, 1671.

[Chamberlayne, Edward], *Englands Wants: Or Several Proposals probably beneficial for England, Humbly offered to the Consideration of all Good Patriots in both Houses of Parliament by a true lover of his Country*. 2nd ed. (1st in 1667), London: Jo. Martyn, 1668.

Clarke, Samuel, *The lives of sundry eminent persons in this later age in two parts : I. of divines, II. of nobility and gentry of both sexes*, London: Thomas Simmons, 1683.

Clarke, Samuel, *A collection of the lives of ten eminent divines famous in their generations for learning, prudence, piety, and painfulness in the work of the ministry*, London: Printed for William Miller. . ., 1662.

Conferences and Combination Lectures in the Elizabethan Church: Dedham and Bury St Edminds, 1582-1590. Patrick Collinson, John Craig, Brent Usher, eds, Woodbridge: Boydell Press for Church of England Record Society, 2003.

Conversations at Little Gidding: 'On the Retirement of Charles V' 'On the Austere Life', A. M. Williams, ed., Cambridge: Cambridge University Press, 1970.

Coryat, Thomas, *Coryat's Crudities*, Glasgow: Maclehose, 1905 (first published 1617).

Cosin, John, *A Collection of Private Devotions*, P. G. Stanwood, ed., Oxford: Clarendon Press, 1967. First published London: R. Young, 1627.

Crashaw, Richard, *The Poems English Latin and Greek of Richard Crashaw*, L. C. Martin, ed., Oxford: Clarendon Press, 1957.

The Diaries of Lady Anne Clifford, D. J. H. Clifford, ed., 3 vols. Stroud: Sutton, 1992-96.

The Diary of Lady Margaret Hoby 1599-1605, D. M. Meads, ed., London: G. Routledge & Sons, 1930.

Dod, Iohn and Robert Cleuer, *A Godly Forme of Houshold Gouernment*, London: Printed by the Asssignes of Thomas Man, for Iohn Clarke, 1630.

[Duncon, John], *The Returnes of Spiritual Comfort and Grief in a Devout Soul* [Lettice, Lady Falkland], London: Richard Royston, 1648.

The Entring Book of Roger Morrice (1677-1691), Mark Goldie *et al*, eds, Woodbridge: Boydell & Brewer in Association with the Parliamentary History Yearbook, 6 vols., 2007.

[Fell, John], *The Life of the most Learned, Reverend and Pious Dr H. Hammond*, London: John Flesher, 1661.

[Ferrar, Nicholas], 'Sir Thomas Smith's Misgovernment of the Virginia Company', David R. Ransome, ed., Cambridge: Roxburghe Club, 1990.

Ferrar, Nicholas, 'The Parliamentary Diary of Nicholas Ferrar, 1624', David R. Ransome, ed., *Seventeenth-Century Political and Financial Papers: Camden Miscellany XXXII* (Fifth Series, Vol 7), Cambridge: Cambridge University Press for the Royal Historical Society, 1996, pp. 1-104.

The Ferrar Papers, B. Blackstone, ed., Cambridge: Cambridge University Press, 1938.

The Ferrar Papers, 1590-1790, David R. Ransome, ed. [in microform, Wakefield, Eng: Microform Academic Publishers, 1992, and online, Marlborough, Wilts: Adam Matthew Publications, 2005, *The Virginia Company Archives*].

Fletcher, Mary [Mary de la Flechere*]*, *A Letter to Mons. H. L. De la Flechere, . . . On the Death of his Brother, the Reverencd John William De la Flechere, . . .* London: R. Hindmarsh, 1786.

G.[ainsford], T.[homas], *The Rich Cabinet Furnished with Varietie of Excellent descriptions. . .*, London: Printed by I[ohn] B[eale] for Roger Iackson, 1616.

Gouge, William, *Of Domesticall Dvties*, London: Printed by Iohn Haviland for William Bladen, 1622.

Harbot[tle] Grimston, *A Christian New-Years Gift: or Exhortations to the Chief Duties of a Christian*, n.p.: Roger Daniel, 1644.

Hacket, John, *Scrinia Reserata*.

Hearne, Thomas, *Remarks and Collections of Thomas Hearne* , ed. by C. E. Doble, D.W. Rannie, and H.E. Salter, 11 Vols., Oxford: Oxford Historical Society Publications, 1885-1921. Vols. 10 & 11.

Hearne, Thomas, ed., *Thomae Caii . . .Vindiciae antiuitatis AcademiaeOxoniesis contra Joannem Caium. . . .* Oxonii, e theatro Sheldoniano, 1730, 2 vols.

Herbert, George, *The Complete English Works*, Anne Pasternak Slater, ed., London: Everyman, 1995

Hill, Robert, *The Contents of Scripture: containing the sum of every Booke and chapter of the old and new Testament. . .*, London: A. Islip for R Jackson, 1596.

Hinde, William, *A Faithfull Remonstrance of the Holy Life and Happy Death, of Iohn Bruen of Bruen-Stapleford, in the County of Chester, Esquire,* London: Printed by R. B. for Philemon Stephens, and Christopher Meredith, 1645.

Hiud, Johan, *The Storie of Stories: or the Life of Christ, according to the foure holy Evangelists; with a harmony of them. . .*, London: M. Flesher, 1632.

I.[ansen], C.[ornelius], *The Consent of the foure Euangelists: Or, The Life of Christ: Collected by C. I. And placed before his Harmony. . .*, London: Adam Islip for R Jackson, 1596.

Jackson, Thomas, *The Eternall Truth of Scriptures*, London: W. Stansby, 1613.

Ken, Thomas, *The Prose Works of the Right Rev. Father in God, Thomas Ken*, James Thomas Round, ed., London: J.G. & F. Rivington, 1838.

LeClerc, John, *The Harmony of the Evangelists*, London: Sam. Buckley, 1701.

Lessius, Leonard, *Hygiasticon: Or, The Right course of Preserving Life and Health unto Extream old Age*, [Cambridge]: Roger Daniel, 1634 [translated by Nicholas Ferrar].

The Letters of John Chamberlain, Norman Egbert McClure, ed., Philadelphia: American Philosophical Society, 1939.

Materials for the Life of Nicholas Ferrar, Lynette R Muir and John White, eds., Leeds: The Leeds Philosophical and Literary Society Ltd, 1996.

Mapletoft, John, *A Perswasive to the Conscientious Frequenting the Daily Publick Prayers of the Church of England*, London: Walter Kettilby, 1687.

Mapletoft, John, *A Sermon Preach'd at the Church of St. Mary le Bow, to the Societies for Reformation of Manners*, London: B. Aylmer, 1700.

Mapletoft, John, *The Principles and Duties of the Christian Religion, Consider'd & Explain'd; In order to Retrieve and Promote the Christian Life, or that Holiness, without which no man shall see the Lord*, London: Joseph Downing, 1710.

Mapletoft, John, *The Rich Man's Bounty, the True Measure of His Wisdom*, London: Brabazon Aylmer, 1695.[sermon preached before Lord Mayor and Aldermen of London, 27 Mar 1695; includes report on all charities under charge of City, e.g. Christ's Hospital]

Mapletoft, John], *Select Proverbs, Italian, Spanish, French, English, Scotish [sic], British, &c. Chiefly Moral. The Foreign Languages Done into English*, London: J.H. for Philip Monckton, 1707.

Masters, Robert, 1713-1798. *Memoirs of the life and writings of the late Rev. Thomas Baker, B.D. of St John's College in Cambridge,. . .*, Cambridge: J. Archdeacon, 1784.

Newcourt, R., *Repertorium Ecclesiasticum Parochiale Londinense*, II (1710).

Nicholas Ferrar: Two Lives by his Brother John and by Dr Jebb, Mayor, J. E. B., ed., Cambridge: Cambridge University Press, 1855.

Oley, Barnabas, *Herbert's Remains, Or, Sundry Pieces of that Sweet Singer of The Temple, Mr George Herbert*, London: Timothy Garthwait, 1652.

Peckard, Peter, *Memoirs of the Life of Mr Nicholas Ferrar*, Cambridge: J. Archdeacon, 1790.

Perkins, William, *Christian Oeconomie, or, A short survey of the right manner of erecting and ordering a familie according to the Scriptures*, London: Felix Kyngston, 1609.

The Register of St. Lawrence Jewry and St. Mary Magdalen Milk Street London, Part II (1677-1812), Publications of the Harleian Society, LXXI, London: 1941

Rollocke, R., *Lectures upon the History of the Passion, Resurrection and Ascension of our Lord Jesus Christ. Beginning at John 18 and 19:16 . . . containing a perfect harmonie of all the foure Evangelists. . . Preached by R. Rollocke*, Edinburgh, 1616.

Rushworth, John, *Historical Collections: The Second Part. . .*, London: John

Wright and Richard Chiswell, 1680.

Sales, St Francis de, *An Introduction to the Devout Life*, New York: Doubleday Image, 1989 [first published 1613].

Sales, St Francois de, *Oeuvres*, Paris: Gallimard, 1969.

[Sandys, Edwin], *Europae Speculum, Or, A View or Survey of the State of Religion in the Westerne Parts of the World*, London: By T. Cotes, for Michael Sparke, 1632.

Speed, John, *The Theatre of the Empire of Great Britaine...*, London: [J. Dawson], 1627.

The Story Books of Little Gidding, E. Cruwys Sharland, ed., London: Seeley and Co., 1899.

Thomas Taylor, *The Pilgrims Profession. Or a Sermon Preached at the Funerall of M^{ris} Mary Gunter*, London: Printed by I.D. for Io: Bartlet, 1622.

Valdes, Juan de, 'Evangelical Catholicism as represented by Juan de Valdes', in *Spiritual and Anabaptist Writers*, Angel M. Mergal ed., Library of Christian Classics, Philadelphia: Westminster Press, 1957, pp. 297-394..

Valdesso, John [Juan de Valdes], *The Hundred and Ten considerations of Signior John Valdesso: Treating of those things which are most profitable, most necessary, and most perfect in our Christian Profession. Written in Spanish, Brought out of Italy by Vergerius, and first set forth in Italian at Basel . . . Afterward translated into French and published at Lions in 1565 and again in Paris 1566. . . Now translated out of Italian copy into English with notes*, Oxford: Leonard Lichfield, 1638.

Valdes' Two Catechisms: The 'Dialogue on Christian Doctrine' and the 'Christian Instruction for Children', Jose C. Nieto and Translators William B. and Carol D. Jones, eds., [Lawrence, KS]: Coronado Press, 1981.

Wheler, Sir George, *The Protestant Monastery, or Christian Oeconimicks*, 1698

W[oodnoth], A[rthur], 'A Short Collection of the Most Remarkable Passages from the Originall to the Dissolution of the Virginia Company', *Copy of a Petition from the Governor and Company of the Sommer Islands with Annexed Papers, presented to the Right Honorable The Council of State July the 19th 1651*, London: Edward Husband, 1651.

Worthington, John, *The Diary and Correspondence of Dr. John Worthington*, James Crossley, ed., [Manchester] Printed for the Chetham Society, 2 vols in 3, 1847-86.

SECONDARY SOURCES

Acland, J. E., *Little Gidding and its Inmates in the Time of King Charles I, with an Account of the Harmonies...*, London: SPCK, 1903.

Amussen, S. D., *An Ordered Society: Gender and Class in Early Modern England*, Oxford: Oxford University Press, 1988.

Aston, Margaret and Elizabeth Ingram, 'The Iconography of the Acts and Monuments', in *John Foxe and the English Reformation*, David Loades, ed.,

Aldershot: Scolar Press, 1997, pp. 66-142.

Aston, Margaret, 'Bibles to Ballads: Some Pictorial Migrations in the Reformation', in *Christianity and Community in the West: Essays for John Bossy*, Simon Ditchfield, ed., Aldershot & Burlington, VT: Ashgate, 2001, pp. 106-30.

Aston, Margaret, 'Bishops, Seals, Mitres', in *Life and Thought in the Northern Church, c. 1100-c.1700: Essays in Honour of Claire Cross*, Diana Wood, ed., Studies in Church History, Subsidia 12, Bury St. Edmunds: Boydell and Brewer, 1999, pp. 183-226.

Aston, Margaret, 'The *Bishops' Bible* Illustrations', in *The Church and the Arts*, ed. Diana Wood, Oxford: Blackwell for the Ecclesiastical History Society, 1992, pp. 267–85

Aston, Margaret, *England's Iconoclasts: Vol I, Laws against Images*, Oxford: Clarendon Press, 1988.

Aston, Margaret, 'Imageless Devotion: What kind of an ideal?', in *Pragmatic Utopias: Ideals and Communities, 1200-1630*, Rosemary Horrox and Sarah Rees Jones, eds, Cambridge: Cambridge University Press, 2001, pp.188-203.

Aston, Margaret, 'Lap Books and Lectern Books: The Revelatory Book in the Reformation', in *The Church and the Book*, R. N. Swanson, ed., Studies in Church History, 38, Woodbridge: Boydell Press for The Ecclesiastical History Society, 2004,.pp. 163-89.

Aston, Margaret, 'Moving Pictures: Foxe's Martyrs and Little Gidding' in *Agent of Change:Print Culture Studies after Elizabeth L. Eisenstein*, edited by Sabrina Alcorn Baron, Eric N. Lindquist, and Eleanor F. Shevlin, Amherst and Boston: University of Massachusetts Press in association with The Center for the Book, Library of Congress, Washington, D.C., 2007

Aston, Margaret, 'Puritans and Iconoclasm, 1560-1660', in *The Culture of English Puritanism, 1560-1700*, Christopher Durston and Jacqueline Eales, eds., New York: St Martin's Press, 1996.

Ayres, Paul and David Selwyn, eds., *Thomas Cranmer: Churchman and Scholar*, Woodbridge: Boydell Press, 1999 (first published 1993).

Baker, Derek, ed., *Religious Motivation: Biographical and Sociological Problems for the Church Historian,* Oxford: Basil Blackwell, 1978.

Baker, J. H., ed., *Legal Records and the Historian: Papers Presented to the Cambridge Legal History Conference*, London: Royal Historical Society, 1978.

Baker, J. H., *The Legal Profession and the Common Law: Historical Essays*, London: Hambledon Press, 1986.

Barnard, Toby, 'Petty, Sir William (1623–1687)', *Oxford Dictionary of National Biography*, Oxford University Press, 2004; online edn, May 2007 [http://www.oxforddnb.com/view/article/22069, accessed 11 Nov 2010] 'Petty, Sir William (1623–1687)', *Oxford Dictionary of National Biography*, Oxford University Press, 2004; online edn, May 2007 [http://www.oxforddnb.com/view/article/22069, accessed 11 Nov 2010]

Beaver, Daniel C., *Parish Communities and Religious Conflict in the Vale of Gloucester, 1590-1690*, Cambridge, MA and London: Harvard University

Press, 1998.

Beier, Lucinda McCray, *Sufferers and Healers: The Experience of Illness in Seventeenth Century England*, London: Routledge & Kegan Paul, 1987.

Belladonna, Rita, 'Aristotle, Machiavelli, and Religious Dissimulation: Bartolomeo Carli Piccolomini's *Trattati Nove Della Prudenza*', in *Peter Martyr Vermigli and Italian Reform*, Joseph C. McLelland, ed., Waterloo, ON: Wilfrid Laurier University Press, 1980, pp. 29-42.

Benedict, Philip, *Christ's Churches Purely Reformed: A Social History of Calvinism*, New Haven and London: Yale University Press, 2002.

Blaisdell, Charmarie J., 'Calvin's and Loyola's Letter to Women: Politics and Spiritual Counsel in the Sixteenth Century', in *Calviniana: Ideas and Influence of Jean Calvin*, Robert V. Schnucker, ed., Kirksville, Mo: Sixteenth Century Essays & Studies, 1988, pp. 235-54.

Bossy, John, 'Blood and Baptism: Kinship, Community and Christianity in Western Europe from the Fourteenth to the Seventeenth Centuries' in *Sanctity and Secularity: The Church and the World,* Derek Baker, ed., Studies in Church History, 10, Oxford: Blackwell for the Ecclesiastical History Society, 1973, pp.129-43.

Bremer, Francis , *Congregational Communion: Clerical Friendship in the Anglo-American Puritan Community 1610-1692*, Boston, 1994.

Bremer, Francis J. *John Winthrop: America's Forgotten Founding Father*, Oxford: Oxford University Press, 2003.

Bremer, Francis J., 'To Live Exemplary Lives: Puritans and Puritan Communities as Lofty Lights,' *The Seventeenth Century*, VII (Spring, 1992), 27-39.

Brenner, Robert, *Merchants and Revolution: Commercial Change, Political Conflict, and London's Overseas Traders, 1550-1663*, Cambridge: Cambridge University Press, 1993.

Bullock, F.W. , *Voluntary Religious Societies, 1520-1799*, St Leonards on Sea, Budd & Gillatt, 1963.

Bush, Sargent and Carl J. Rasmussen, *The Library of Emmanuel College, Cambridge, 1584-1637*, Cambridge: Cambridge University Press, 1986.

Cabot, Nancy G., 'The Illustrations of the First Little Gidding Concordance', *Harvard Librarty Bulletin*, III (1949), 139-43.

Cambers, Andrew and Michelle Wolfe, 'Reading, Family Religion, and Evangelical Identity in Late Stuart England', *Historical Journal*, 47, 4 (2004), 875-96.

Cameron, Euan, 'For Reasoned Faith or Embattled Creed: Religion for the People in Early Modern Europe', in *Transactions of the Royal Historical Society*, Sixth Series, VIII (1998), pp. 165-87.

Cameron, Euan, 'The "Godly Community" in the Theory and Practice of the European Reformation', in *Voluntary Religion*, W.J. Sheils and Diana Wood, eds., Studies in Church History 23, [Oxford]: Basil Blackwell for the Ecclesiastical History Society, 1986, pp. 131-53.

Cameron, Euan, *The European Reformation*, Oxford: Clarendon Press, 1991.

Camus, Jean Pierre, *The Spirit of St. Francis de Sales*, London: Longmans, Green & Co, 1893.

Carlton, Charles et al, eds., *State, Sovereigns and Society: Essays in Honour of A. J. Slavin*, New York: St Martin's Press, 1998.

Carter, J.F.M, *Life and Work of the Rev. T.T. Carter*, London: Longmans, Green, 1911.

[Carter, J.F.M.], *Undercurrents of Church Life in the Eighteenth Century*, T.T. Carter, ed., London: Longmans, 1899. [said to be by author of *Nicholas Ferrar* and *Life of John Kettlewell*]

[Carter, J.F.M.] Carter, T.T., ed., *Nicholas Ferrar: His Household & His Friends*, London: Longmans, 1893.

Charles, Amy M., *A Life of George Herbert*, Ithaca & London: Cornell University Press, 1977.

Chavasse, R. A., 'Humanism in Exile: Celio Secondo Curione's Learned Women Friends and Exempla for Elizabeth I', in *Protestants, Property, Puritans: Godly People Revisited,* Sybil Milliner Jack, Bernadette A. Masters, Patrick Collinson eds, Nedlands: Australian and New Zealand Association for Medieval and Modern Studies, 1996, pp. 165-85.

Cheney, C. R., ed., *Handbook of Dates for Students of English History*, London: Royal Historical Society, 1945.

Chojnacka, Monica, 'Singlewomen in Early Modern Venice: Communities and Opportunities', in *Singlewomen in the European Past, 1250-1800,* Judith M. Bennett and Amy M. Froide, eds., Philadelphia: University of Pennsylvania Press, 1999, pp. 217-31.

Chojnacka, Monica, 'Women, Charity and Community in Early Modern Venice: The Casa Delle Zitelle', *Renaissance Quarterly*, 51 (Spring 1998), 68-91.

Christopher Wordsworth, 'Nicholas Ferrar', *Ecclesiastical Biography* (London: Rivington, 1818), Vol. 4, pp. 73

Clanchy, Michael, 'Images of Ladies with Prayer Books: What do they Signify?', in *The Church and the Book*, R. N. Swanson, ed., Studies in Church History, 38, Woodbridge: Boydell Press for The Ecclesiastical History Society, 2004, pp. 106-22.

Clark, Peter, *British Clubs and Societies, 1580-1800: The Origins of an Associational World*, Oxford: Clarendon Press, 2000.

Claydon, Tony, 'The Sermon, the "public sphere" and the political culture of late seventeenth-century England', in *The English Sermon Revised: Religion, Literature and History 1600-1750*, Lori Anne Ferrell and Peter McCullough, eds., Manchester and New York: Manchester University Press, 2000, pp. 208-34.

Collett, Henry, *Little Gidding and Its Founder: An Account of the Religious Community Established by Nicholas Ferrar in the XVIIth Century*, London: SPCK, 1925.

Collinson, Patrick, *The Elizabethan Puritan Movement*, Berkeley & Los Angeles: University of California Press, 1967.

Collinson, Patrick, *Godly People: Essays on English Protestantism and Puritanism,*

London: Hambledon Press, 1983.

Collinson, Patrick, 'One of Us? William Camden and the Making of History', *Transactions of the Royal Historical Society*, Sixth Series, VIII (1998), 139-63.

Collinson, Patrick, Puritanism and the poor', in *Pragmatic Utopias: Ideals and Communities, 1200-1630*, Rosemary Horrox and Sarah Rees Jones, eds, Cambridge: Cambridge University Press, 2001, pp. 242-258.

Collinson, Patrick, *The Religion of Protestants: The Church in English Society 1559-1625* (Ford Lectures 1979), Oxford: Clarendon Press, 1st printed 1982, paperback 1984, esp. Ch 6 'Voluntary Religion: Its Forms and Tendencies', pp. 242-283.

Collinson, Patrick, 'The Shearmen's Tree and the Preacher: the Strange Death of Merry England in Shrewsbury and Beyond', in *The Reformation in English Towns, 1500-1640*, Patrick Collinson and John Craig, eds.,New York: St Martin's, 1998, pp. 205-20.

Collinson, Patrick, 'What's in a Name? Dudley Fenner and the Peculiarities of Puritan Nomenclature', in Kenneth Fincham and Peter Lake, eds, *Religious Politics in Post-Reformation England: Essays in Honour of Nicholas Tyacke*, Woodbridge: Boydell Press, 2006, pp.113-27.

Cooper, Trevor, '"As Wise as Serpents": the Form and Setting of Public Worship at Little Gidding in the 1630s', in *Worship and the Parish Church in Earrly Modern Britain*, Alec Ryrie and Natalie Mears, eds., Ashgate, forthcoming 2012.

Costin, W.C. and J. Steven Watson, *The Law and Working of the Constitution: Do cuments 1660-1783*, Vol. 1, London: Adam and Charles Black, 1952.

Craig, C. Leslie, 'The Earliest Little Gidding Concordance', *Harvard Library Bulletin*, 1 (1947), 311-31.

Craig, C. Leslie, *Nicholas Ferrar Junior*, London: Epworth Press, 1950.

Crawford, Patricia, 'Public Duty, Conscience, and Women in Early Modern England', in *Public Duty and Private Conscience in Seventeenth-Century England*, John Morrill, Paul Slack and D. Woolf, eds., Oxford: Oxford University Press, 1993.

Crawford, Patricia, *Women and Religion in England, 1500-1720*, London and New York: Routledge, 1993.

Cressy, David and Lori Anne Ferrell, eds, *Religion and Society in Early Modern England: A Sourcebook*, London & New York, Routledge, 1996.

Cressy, David, *Birth, Marriage & Death: Ritual, Religion, and the Life-Cycle in Tudor and Stuart England*, Oxford & New York: Oxford University Press, 1997.

Crews, Daniel A., *Twilight of the Renaissance: The Life of Juan de Valdes*, Toronto, Buffalo, London: University of Toronto Press, 2008.

Cross, Claire, 'Realising a utopian dream: the transformation of the clergy in the diocese of York, 1500-1630', in *Pragmatic Utopias: Ideals and Communities, 1200-1630*, Rosemary Horrox and Sarah Rees Jones, eds, Cambridge: Cambridge University Press, 2001, pp. 259-276

Curtis, T. C. and W. A. Speck, 'The Societies for Reformation of Manners: A Case

Study in the Theory and Practice of Moral Reform', *Literature and History*, 3 (1976), 45-64.

Curtis, Mark H., *Oxford and Cambridge in Transition, 1558-1642*, Oxford: Clarendon Press, 1959.

Cust, Richard and Ann Hughes, eds., *Conflict in Early Stuart England: Studies in Religion and Politics 1603-1642,* London & New York: Longman, 1989

Dabhoiwala, Faramerz, 'The Construction of Honour, Reputation and Status in Late ', Seventeenth- and Early Eighteenth-Century England', *in Transactions of the Royal Historical Society*, Sixth Series, VI (1996), pp. 201- 13.

Davies, Horton, *Worship and Theology in England: Vol I: From Cranmer to Hooker 1534-1603, Vol II: From Andrewes to Baxter and Fox 1603-1690*, Grand Rapids, MI & Cambridge, UK: William Eerdmans, 1996.

Davies, Julian, *The Caroline Captivity of the Church: Charles I and the Remoulding of Anglicanism, 1625-1641*, Oxford: Clarendon Press, 1992.

Davis, J. C., 'Against Formality: One Aspect of the English Revolution', in *Transactions of the Royal Historical Society*, Sixth Series, III (London, 1993), pp. 265-88.

Davis, Natalie Zemon and Arlette Farge, eds. *A History of Women in the West: Vol 3: Renaissance and Enlightenment Paradoxes*, Cambridge, MA: Harvard University Press, 1993.

De Beer, E. S., *The Correspondence of John Locke*, 8 vols, Oxford: Oxford University Press, 1976-82.

DeMolen, Richard L., ed., *Religious Orders of the Catholic Reformation*, New York: Fordham University Press, 1994.

Deursen, A. T. van, *Plain Lives in a Golden Age*, Cambridge: Cambridge University Press, 1991.

Diefendorf, Barbara B., *From Penitence to Charity: Pious Women and the Catholic Reformation in Paris,* Oxford: Oxford University Press, 1994.

Dodd, A. H., 'Mr Myddelton the Merchant of Tower Street', in *Elizabethan Government and Society*, S T Bindoff, J Hurstfield and C H Williams, eds., London: Athlone Press, 1961, pp. 249-72.

Doerksen, Daniel W., *Conforming to the Word: Herbert, Donne, and the English Church before Laud,* Lewisburg, PA: Bucknell University Press and London: Associated University Presses, 1997.

Dreyer, Frederick, 'A "Religious Society under Heaven": John Wesley and the Identity of Methodism', *Journal of British Studies*, 25 (Jan 1986), 62-83.

Drummond, J. C., and Anne Wilbraham, *The Englishman's Food: A History of Five Centuries of English Diet*, London: Jonathan Cape, 1939.

Duffy, Eamon, *'Correspondance Fraternelle*; the SPCK, the SPG and the Churches of Switzerland in the War of the Spanish Succession', in *Reform and Reformation: England and the Continent, c. 1500-c. 1750,* Studies in Church History: Subsidia 2, Derek Baker, ed., Oxford: Blackwell for the Ecclesiastical History Society, 1979, 251-80.

Duffy, Eamon, 'The Godly and the Multitude in Stuart England', *The Seventeenth*

Century, I (January 1986), 31-55.

Duncan-Jones, Elsie Elizabeth, 'Who was the Recipient of Crashaw's Leyden Letter?', in *New Perspectives on the Life and Art of Richard Crashaw*, John R. Roberts, ed., Columbia, MO and London: University of Missouri Press, pp. 174-79.

Eales, Jacqueline and Christopher Durston, eds., *The Culture of English Puritanism 1560-1700*, New York: St Martin's Press, 1996.

Eales, Jacqueline, 'Provincial Preaching and Allegiance in the First English Civil War, 1640-46', in *Politics, Religion and Popularity in Early Stuart Britain: Essays in Honour of Conrad Russell*, Thomas Cogswell, Richard Cust, and Peter Lake, eds., Cambridge: Cambridge University Press, 2002, pp. 185-207.

Eales, Jacqueline, 'Gender Construction in Early Modern England and the Conduct Books of William Whately (1538-1639)', in *Gender and Christian Religion*, R. N. Swanson, ed., Woodbridge: Boydell Press, 1998, pp. 163-74.

Ehrenberg, Richard, *Hamburg und England im Zeitalter der Koenigin Elisabeth*, Jena: Gustav Fischer Verlag, 1896.

Erb, Peter C., ed., *Pietists: Selected Writings*, New York, Ramsey, Toronto: Paulist Press, 1983. (Classics of Western Spirituality)

Erickson, Amy Louise, *Women and Property in Early Modern England*, London & New York: Routledge, 1993.

Evans, Joan, *A History of the Society of Antiquaries*, Oxford: Oxford University Press for the Society of Antiquaries, 1956.

Evans, R. J. W., *Rudolf II and His World*, London: Thames and Hudson, 1997.

Fildes, Valerie, *Breasts, Bottles and Babies: A History of Infant Feeding*, Edinburgh: Edinburgh University Press, 1985.

Fincham, Kenneth, ed., *The Early Stuart Church: 1603-1640*, Stanford: Standord University Press, 1993.

Fincham, Kenneth, 'Material Evidence: The Religious Legacy of the Interregnum at St George Tombland, Norwich', in *Religious Politics in Post-Reformation England: Essays in Honour of Nicholas Tyacke*, Kenneth Fincham and Peter Lake, eds, Woodbridge: Boydell Press, 2006, pp. 224-40.

Fincham, Kenneth, *Prelate as Pastor: The Episcopate of James I*, Oxford: Clarendon Press, 1990.

Fincham, Kenneth and Nicholas Tyacke, *Altars Restored: the Changing Face of English Religious Worship, 1547-c.1700*, Oxford: Oxford University Press, 2007.

Firpo, Massimo, 'Lorenzo Lotto and the Reformation in Venice', in *Heresy, Culture, and Religion in Early Modern Italy: Contexts and Contestations*, Ronald Delph, Michelle M. Fontaine, and John Jeffries Martin, eds., Sixteenth Century Essays & Studies 76: Truman State University Press, 2006, pp. 21-36.

Firpo, Massimo, (John Tedeschi, translator), 'The Italian Reformation and Juan de Valdes', *Sixteenth Century Journal*, Vol. 27, No. 2 (Summer 1996), 353-64.

Fitzpatrick, Edward A., ed., *St. Ignatius and the Ratio Studiorum*, New York and London: McGraw-Hill, 1933.

Fletcher, 'Anthony, 'Beyond the Church: Women's Spiritual Experience at Home and in the Community, 1600-1900', in *Gender and Christian Religion*, R. N. Swanson, ed., Woodbridge: Boydell Press for the Ecclesiastical History Society, 1998, pp. 187-204.

Fletcher, Anthony, 'Prescription and Practice: Protestantism and the Upbringing of Children, 1560-1700', *The Church and Childhood*, Diana Wood, ed., Studies in Church History, 31, Oxford: Blackwell for Ecclesiastical History Society, 1994, pp. 325-46.

Fletcher, Anthony, *Gender, Six and Subordination in England 1500-1800*, New Haven: Yale University Press, 1995.

Fletcher, John M., and James K. McConica, 'A Sixteenth-Century Inventory of the Library of Corpus Christi College, Cambridge', *Transactions of the Cambridge Bibliographical Society*, 3 (1959-63), 187-99.

Fletcher, Mary, *The Life of Mrs. Mary Fletcher. . .,* compiled by Henry Moore, 3rd ed., London: Thomas Cordeux, 1818.

Fontaine, Michelle M., 'Making Heresy Marginal in Modena', in *Heresy, Culture, and Religion in Early Modern Italy: Contexts and Contestations*, Ronald Delph, Michelle M. Fontaine, John Jeffries Martin, eds., Sixteenth Century Essays & Studies 76: Truman State University Press, 2006, pp., 37-51.

Foot, Miriam, *The History of Bookbinding as a Mirror of Society*, London: British Library, 1998.

Forbes, E. Mansfield, 'Nicholas Ferrar: America and Little Gidding', *Clare College, 1326-1926*, Vol II, Cambridge: Cambridge University Press, 1930, pp. 391-585.

Foster, Andrew, 'Church Policies of the 1630s', in *Conflict in Early Stuart England: Studies in Religion and Politics 1603-1642,* Richard Cust and Ann Hughes, eds., London & New York: Longmans, 1989, pp. 193-217.

Fowler, Thomas, *The History of Corpus Christi College*, Oxford: Clarendon Press, 1893.

Franits, Wayne E., *Paragons of Virtue: Women and Domesticity in Seventeenth Century Dutch Art*, Cambridge: Cambridge University Press, 1993.

Fraser, Antonia, *The Weaker Vessel*, New York: Vintage, Random House, 1985.

French, Roger and Andrew Wear, eds., *The Medical Revolution of the Seventeenth Century*, Cambridge and New York: Cambridge University Press, 1989.

Froide, Amy, *Never Married: Singlewomen in Early Modern England*, Oxford: Oxford University Press, 2005.

Froide, Amy M., 'Marital Status as a Category of Difference: Singlewomen and Widows in Early Modern England', in *Singlewomen in the European Past, 1250-1800,* Judith M. Bennett and Amy M. Froide, eds., Philadelphia: University of Pennsylvania Press, 1999, pp. 236-69.

Frye, Susan and Karen Robertson, eds., *Maids and Mistresses, Cousins and Queens: Women's Alliances in Early Modern England*, New York & Oxford: Oxford University Press, 1999.

Gleason, Elisabeth G. , review of *Lo Evangelio di San Matteo*, ed. Carlo Ossola, in *The Sixteenth Century Journal*, Vol. 19, No. 3 (Autumn, 1988), 515-6

Goldie, Mark, 'Danby, the Bishops and the Whigs', in *The Politics of Religion in Restoration England*, Tim Harris, Paul Seaward and Mark Goldie, eds., Oxford: Basil Blackwell, 1990, pp. 75-106.

Goldie, Mark and John Spurr, 'Politics and the Restoration Parish: Edward Fowler and the Struggle for St Giles Cripplegate', *English Historical Review*, 109 (June 1994), 572-596.

Gough, J. W., *Sir Hugh Myddelton, Entrepreneur and Engineer*, Oxford: Clarendon Press, 1964.

Grassby, Richard, *Kinship and Capitalism: Marriage, Family, and Business in the English-Speaking World, 1580-1740*, Cambridge: Cambridge University Press and Woodrow Wilson Center Press, 2001.

Green, I[an] M. , *The Re-Establishment of the Church of England 1660-1663*, Oxford: Oxford University Press, 1978. 120:3.c.95.5

Green, Ian *The Christian's ABC: Catechisms and Catechizing in England c. 1530-1740*, Oxford: Clarendon Press, 1996. 127:8. c.95.2

Green, Ian, *Print and Protestantism in Early Modern England*, Oxford: Oxford University Press, 2000.

Green, I[an], 'For Children in Yeeres and Children in Understanding: the Emergence of the English Catechism', *Journal of Ecclesiastical History*, 37 (1986), 397-425.

Gregory, Jeremy, 'Gender and the Clerical Profession in England, 1660-1850', in *Gender and Christian Religion*, R. N. Swanson, ed., Woodbridge: Boydell Press, 1998, pp. 235-72.

Gregory, Jeremy, *Restoration, Reformation and Reform, 1660-1828:Archbishops of Canterbuty and Their Diocese*, Oxford: Clarendon Press, 2000.

Grendler, Paul, 'The Circulation of Protestant Books in Italy', in *Peter Martyr Vermigli and Italian Reform*, Joseph C. McLelland, ed., Waterloo, ON: Wilfrid Laurier University Press, 1980, pp.5-16.

Guibbory, Achsah, *Ceremony and community from Herbert to Milton: Literature, Religion, and Cultural C onflict in Seventeenth-century England*, Cambridge: Cambridge University Press, 1998.

Haigh, Christopher, *The Plain Man's Pathways to Heaven: Kinds of Christianity in Post-Reformation England, 1570-1640*, Oxford: Oxford University Press, 2007.

Hall, Basil, 'Cranmer, the Eucharist, and the Foreign Divines in the Reign of Edward VI', in *Thomas Cranmer: Churchman and Scholar*, Paul Ayres and David Selwyn, eds., Woodbridge: Boydell Press for the Ecclesiasical History Society, 1999, pp. 227-8.

Hambrick-Stowe, Charles E., *The Practice of Piety: Puritan Devotional Disciplines in Seventeenth-Century New England*, Chapel Hill: University of North Carolina Press for Institute of Early American History and Culture, 1982.

Hamilton, William, *The Exemplary Life and Character of James Bonnell, Esq; Late Accomptant General of Ireland*, London: F. and C. Rivington, 1807.

Hannay, Margaret P., *Silent but for the Word: Tudor Women as Patrons, Translators and Writers of Religious Works*, Kent, OH: Kent State University Press, 1985.

Harrington, Joel, *Reordering Marriage and Society in Reformation Germany*,

Cambridge: Cambridge University Press, 1995.

Harris, Tim, 'Lives, Liberties and Estates'; Rhetorics of Liberty in the Reign of Charles II', in *The Politics of Religion in Restoration England*, Tim Harris, Paul Seaward and Mark Goldie, eds., Oxford: Basil Blackwell, 1990, pp. 217-42.

Harris, Tim, *Restoration: Charles II and His Kingdoms, 1660-1685*, London and New York: Penguin, 2005.

Harris, Tim, *Revolution: The Great Crisis of the British Monarchy, 1685-1720*, London and New York: Penguin, 2006.

Hart, A. Tindal, *The Life and Times of John Sharp, Archbishop of York*, London: SPCK, 1949.

Heal, Felicity, 'Reputation and Honour in Court and Country: Lady Elizabeth Russell and Sir Thomas Hoby', in *Transactions of the Royal Historical Society*, Sixth Series, VI (1996), pp. 161-78.

Heal, Felicity, *Reformation in England and Ireland*, Oxford: Oxford University Press, 2005.

Heal, Felicity and Clive Holmes, *The Gentry in England and Wales, 1500-1700*, Stanford: Stanford University Press, 1994.

Henderson, George, 'Bible Illustration in the Age of Laud', in *Studies in English Bible Illustration,* London: Pindar Press, 1985, pp. 254-85.

Hennessy, George, *Novum Repertorium Ecclesiasticum Parochiale Londoniense*, or London Diocesan Clergy Succession from the Earliest Times to the Year 1893, London: S. Sonnenschein, 1898.

Herbert, A. S., *Historical Datalogue of Printed Editions of the English Bible 1525-1961*, London & New York, British and Foreign Bible Society & American Bible Society, 1968.

Herzog, Frederick, *European Pietism Reviewed*, San Jose, CA: Pickwick, 2003.

Highley, Christopher and John N. King, eds., *John Foxe and His World*, Aldershot & Burlington, VT: Ashgate, 2002.

Hobson, G. D. *Bindings in Cambridge Libraries*, Cambridge: Cambridge University Press, 1929.

Hole, C[hristina], *The English Housewife in the Seventeenth Century*, London: Chatto and Windus, 1953.

Houlbrooke, Ralph A., *The English Family 1450-1700*, London and New York: Longmans, 1984.

Hsia, R. Po-chia, *The World of Catholic Renewal: 1540-1770*, Cambridge: Cambridge University Press, 1998.

Hufton, Olwen, 'The Widow' Mite and Other Strategies: Funding the Catholic Reformation', *Transactions of the Royal Historical Society*, Sixth Series, VIII (1998), pp. 117-37.

Hufton, Olwen, *The Prospect Before Her: A History of Women in Western Europe*, Vol 1 (1500-1800), New York: Knopf, 1996.

Hull, S. W., *Chaste, Silent and Obedient: English Books for Women 1435-1640*, San Marino, CA: Huntingdon Library, 1982.

Hunter, Lynnette and Sarah Hatton, eds., *Women, Science and Medicine 1500-*

1700, Stroud: Sutton, 1997.

Hurst, Clive, ed., *Catalogue of the Wren Library of Lincoln Cathedral: Books Printed before 1801*, Cambridge: Cambridge University Press, 1982.

Jacob, W. M., *Lay People and Religion in the Early Eighteenth Century*, Cambridge: Cambridge University Press, 1996.

Jones, M. G., *The Charity School Movement: A Study of Eighteenth Century Puritanism in Action*, London: Frank Cass, 1964.

Katz, David S., *Philo-Semitism and the Readmission of the Jews to England, 1603-1655*, Oxford: Clarendon Press, 1982.

Kelliher, Hilton, 'Crashaw at Cambridge', in *New Perspectives on the Life and Art of Richard Crashaw*, John R. Roberts, ed., Columbia, MO and London: University of Missouri Press, 1990, pp. 180-214.

Kendrick, T. D., *British Antiquity*, London: Methuen, 1950.

Kingsbury, Susan Myra, ed., *The Records of the Virginia Company of London*, 4 vols., Washington, DC: US Government Printing Office, 1906-36.

Kinser, Samuel, *The Works of Jacques-August de Thou*, The Hague: Martinus Nijhoff, 1966.

Knox, R. Buick , 'The social teaching of Archbishop Williams', in *Popular Belief and Practice*, G. J. Cuming and Derek Baker, eds., Studies in Church History, 8, Cambridge: Cambridge University Press, 1972, pp. 179-86.

Komensky, Jan Amos, *The Analytic Didactic of Comenius*, Chicago: University of Chicago Press, 1953.

Kuemin, Beat, 'Voluntary Religion and Reformation Change in Eight Urban Parishes,' in *The Reformation in English Towns, 1500-1640*, Patrick Collinson and John Craig, eds.,New York: St Martin's, 1998, pp. 175-89.

Lake, Peter, 'Anti-Puritanism: The Structure of a Prejudice', in *Religious Politics in Post-Reformation England: Essays in Honour of Nicholas Tyacke*, Kenneth Fincham and Peter Lake, eds,, Woodbridge: Boydell Press, 2006, pp. 80-97.

Lake, Peter, 'Feminine Piety and Personal Potency', *The Seventeenth Century*, II (1987), 143-65.

Lake, Peter, ''Joseph Hall, Robert Skinner and the rhetoric of moderation at the early Stuart Court', in *The English Sermon Revised: Religion, Literature and History 1600-1750*, Lori Anne Ferrell and Peter McCullough, eds., Manchester and New York: Manchester University Press, 2000, pp. 167-85.

Lake, Peter, 'Lancelot Andrewes, John Buckeridge, and Avant-Garde Conformity at the Court of James I', in Linda Levy Peck, ed., *The Mental World of the Jacobean Court*, (Cambridge: Cambridge University Press, 1991), pp. 113-33.

Laurence, Anne, *Women in England, 1500-1760*, London: Weidenfeld and Nicolson, 1994.

Lee, Jr., Maurice, *Great Britain's Solomon: James VI and I in His Three Kingdoms*, Urbana, IL: University of Illinois Press, 1990.

Leedham-Green, E.,S., *Books in Cambridge Inventories: Book-Lists from Vice-Chancellor's Court Probate Inventories in the Tudor and Stuart Periods*, Cambridge: Cambridge University Press, 1986.

Legg, J. Wickham, *English Church Life from the Restoration to the Tractarian Movement Considered in Some of its Neglected or Forgotten Features*, London: Longmans, 1914.

Levy, F. J., 'The Making of *Camden's Britannia*', *Bulletin d'Humanisme et Renaissance*, 26 (1964), 70-97.

Lewalski, Barbara Kiefer, *Protestant Poetics and the Seventeenth-Century Religious Lyric*, Princeton: Princeton University Press, 1979.

Lewalski, Barbara Kiefer, *Writing Women in Jacobean England*, Cambridge, MA: Harvard University Press, 1993.

Liebowitz, Ruth P., 'Virgins in the Service of Christ: The Dispute over an Active Apostolate for Women during the Counter-Reformation', in *Women of Spirit: Female Leadership in the Jewish and Christian Traditions*, Rosemary Ruether and Eleanor McLaughlin, eds., New York: Simon and Schuster, 1979, pp. 131-52.

Lindberg, Carter, ed., *The Pietist Theologians*, Oxford: Blackwell Publishing, 2005.

Loftis, J., *The Memoirs of Anne Lady Halkett and Ann Lady Fanshaw*, Oxford: Oxford University Press, 1979.

Logan, Oliver, 'Counter-Reformatory Theories of Upbringing in Italy', in *The Church and Childhood*, Diana Wood, ed., Studies in Church History, 31, Blackwell for Ecclesiastical History Society, 1994, pp. 275-84.

Longfellow, Erica, *Women and Religious Writing in Early Modern England*, Cambridge: Cambridge University Press, 2004.

Luborsky, Ruth Samson and Elizabeth Morley Ingram, *A Guide to English Illustrated Books, 1536-1603: Medieval & Renaissance Texts & Studies 166*, Tempe, AZ: Arizona State University, 1998.

Lynch, Katherine A., *Individuals, Families, and Communities in Europe, 1200-1800*, Cambridge: Cambridge University Press, 2003.

MacCulloch, Diarmaid, 'The Latitude of the Church of England', in *Religious Politics in Post-Reformation England: Essays in Honour of Nicholas Tyacke*, Kenneth Fincham and Peter Lake, eds,, Woodbridge: Boydell Press, 2006, pp. 41-59.

MacCulloch, Diarmaid, *Reformation*, London: Penguin, 2004 (first published 2003)

MacCulloch, Diarmaid, *Thomas Cranmer: A Life*: New Haven & London: Yale University Press, 1996.

Maltby, Judith, *Prayer Book and People in Elizabethan and Early Stuart England*, Cambridge: Cambridge University Press, 1998.

Marius, Richard, *Thomas More*, New York: Vintage Books, 1985.

Marshall, Sherrin, ed., *Women in Reformation and Counter Reformation Europe. Private and Public Worlds*, Bloomington: University of Indiana Press, 1989.

Martin, Jessica, *Walton's Lives: Conformist Commemorations and the Rise of Biography*, Oxford: Oxford University Press, 2001.

Martz, Louis L., *The Poetry of Meditation: A Study in English Religious Literature of the Seventeenth Century*, New Haven & London: Yale University Press, 1969.

Matar, N. I., '"Alone in our Eden": A Puritan Utopia in Restoration England', *The Seventeenth Century*, II (1987), 189-98.

Maycock, A. L., *Nicholas Ferrar of Little Gidding*, Grand Rapids, MI: William B. Eerdmans, 1980 [first published 1938].

Mayer, Thomas, *Cardinal Pole in European Context: A Via Media in the Reformation*, Aldershot & Burlington, VT: Ashgate, 2000.

Mayer, Thomas, *Reginald Pole, Prince & Prophet*, Cambridge: Cambridge University Press, 2000.

McCullough, Peter E., *Sermons at Court: Politics and religion in Elizabethan and Jacobean preaching*, Cambridge: Cambridge University Press, 1998.

McLellan, Ian William, 'Ingelo, Nathaniel (1620/21–1683)', *Oxford Dictionary of National Biography*, Oxford University Press, 2004; online edn, Jan 2008 [http://www.oxforddnb.com/view/article/14385, accessed 9 Nov 2010]

McNair, Philip M. J., 'Peter Martyr in England', in *Peter Martyr Vermigli and Italian Reform*, Joseph C. McLelland, ed., Waterloo, ON: Wilfrid Laurier University Press, 1980, pp. 85-106.

Mendelson, Sara and Patricia Crawford, eds, *Women in Early Modern England, 1550-1720*, Oxford: Clarendon Press, 1998.

Mendelson, Sara Heller, *The Mental World of Stuart Women: Three Studies*, Amherst: University of Massachusetts Press, 1987.

Merrill, T. F., ed., *William Perkins 1558-1602: English Puritanist*, Nieuwkoop: B. de Graaf, 1966.

Merritt, J. F., 'The Pastoral Tightrope: A Puritan Pedagogue in Jacobean London', in *Politics, Religion and Popularity in Early Stuart Britain: Essays in Honour of Conrad Russell*, Thomas Cogswell, Richard Cust and Peter Lake eds, Cambridge: Cambridge University Press, 2002, pp. 143-61.

Michels, Georg Bernhard, *At War with the Church: Religious Dissent in Seventeenth-Century Russia*, Stanford: Stanford University Press, 1999.

Milham, Mary Ella, ed., *Platina, On Right Pleasure and Good Health*, Tempe, AZ: Medieval and Renaissance Texts and Studies, 1998.

Milton, Anthony, '"Anglicanism by Stealth": The Career and Influence of John Overall', in *Religious Politics in Post-Reformation England: Essays in Honour of Nicholas Tyacke*, Kenneth Fincham and Peter Lake, eds,, Woodbridge: Boydell Press, 2006, pp. 159-76.

Milton, Anthony, ed., *The British Delegation and the Synod of Dort (1618-1619)*, Woodbridge: Boydell Press for the Church of England Record Society, 2005.

Milton, Anthony, *Catholic and Reformed: The Roman and Protestant Churches in English Protestant Thought, 16600-1640*, Cambridge: Cambridge University Press,1995.

Milton, Anthony, 'The Creation of Laudianism: a new approach', in *Politics, Religion and Popularity in Early Stuart Britain: Essays in Honour of Conrad Russell*, Thomas Cogswell, Richard Cust and Peter Lake, eds, Cambridge:

Cambridge University Press, 2002, pp. 162-84.

Milton, Anthony, *Laudian and Royalist Polemic in Seventeenth-century England: The Career and Writings of Peter Heylyn*, Manchester and New York: Manchester University Press, 2007.

Milton, Anthony, '"The Unchanged Peacemaker"?' in *Samuel Hartlib and Universal Reformation: Studies in Intellectual Communication*, Mark Greengrass *et al.*, eds.,Cambridge and New York: Cambridge University Press, 1994, pp. 95-117.

Moody, Joanna, *The Private Life of an Elizabethan Lady: The Diary of Lady Margaret Hoby, 1599-1605*, Stroud: Sutton, 1998.

Moore, Susan Hardman, 'New England's Reformation: 'We shall be as a Citty upon a Hill, the Eies of all People are upon Us', in *Religious Politics in Post-Reformation England: Essays in Honour of Nicholas Tyacke*, Kenneth Fincham, and Peter Lake, eds, Woodbridge: Boydell Press, 2006, pp. 143-58.

Moore, Susan Hardman, 'Sexing the Soul: Gender and the Rhetoric of Puritan Piety', in *Gender and Christian Religion*, R. N. Swanson, ed., Studies in Church History, 34, Woodbridge: Boydell Press for the Ecclesiastical History Society, 1998, pp. 175-86.

Moryson, Fynes, *An Itinerary Containing His Ten Years Travell*, Glasgow: James Maclehose and Sons, 1908.

Mullett, Michael M., *The Catholic Reformation*, London & New York, Routledge, 1999.

Mumm, Susan, ed.,*All Saints Sisters of the Poor: An Anglican Sisterhood in the Nineteenth Century*, Woodbridge: Boydell Press for Church of England Record Society, 2001.

Mumm, Susan, *Stolen Daughters, Virgin Mothers: Anglican Sisterhoods in Victorian Britain*, London and New York: Leicester University Press, 1999.

Murphy, Paul V., ''Rumors of Heresy in Mantua', in *Heresy, Culture, and Religion in Early Modern Italy: Contexts and Contestations*, Ronald Delph, Michelle M. Fontaine, John Jeffries Martin, eds.Sixteenth Century Essays & Studies 76: Truman State University Press, 2006, pp. 53-67.

Newcome, William, *An English Harmony of the Four Evangelists, Generally Disposed after the Manner of the Greek of William Newcome, Archbishop of Armagh*, Philadelphia: Kibmer and Conrad, 1809.

Nichols, John, *The Progresses, Processions, and Magnificent Festivities of King James the First, His Royal Consort, Family and Court*, New York: Burt Franklin, n.d. (first published 1828).

Nieto, Jose C., *Juan de Valdes and the Origins of the Spanish and Italian Reformation*, Geneva: Librairie Droz, 1970.

Nixon, Howard M. and Miriam M. Foot, *The History of Decorated Bookbinding in England*, Oxford: Clarendon Press, 1992

Novarr, David, *The Making of Walton's Lives*, Ithaca: Cornell University Press, 1958.

O'Day, Rosemary, *Education and Society 1500-1800*, London & New York:

Longman, 1982.

O'Day, Rosemary, *The English Clergy: The Emergence and Consolidation of a Profession, 1558-1642*, Leicester: Leicester University Press, 1979.

O'Hara-May, Jane, *Elizabethan Dyetary of Health*, Lawrence, KS: Coronado Press, 1977.

Ogg, David, *England in the Reign of Charles II*, 2 vols., Oxford: Clarendon Press, 1955.

Overell, M. E., 'Arthur Golding's Translation of the "Beneficio di Cristo"', *Notes and Queries*, 223 (October 1978), 424-6.

Overell, M.A., 'Bernardino Ochino's Books and English Religious Opinion: 1547-80', in *The Church and the Book*, R. N. Swanson, ed., Studies in Church History, 38, Woodbridge: Boydell Press for The Ecclesiastical History Society, 2004. pp.201-211.

The Oxford Guide to The Book of Common Prayer, Charles Hefling and Cynthia Shattuck, eds., Oxford: Oxford University Press, 2006.

Packer, John W., *The Transformation of Anglicanism 1643-1660, with special reference to Henry Hammond*, Manchester: Manchester University Press, 1969.

Page, William, Granville Proby and S. Inskip Ladds, eds., *The Victoria History of the County of Huntingdon*, London: St Catherine Press for the Institute of Historical Research, University of London, 1926-1936.

Parker, Geoffrey, *The Thirty Years' War*, London & New York: Routledge & Kegan Paul, 1984.

Parry, Graham, *The Arts of the Anglican Counter-Reformation: Glory, Laud and Honour*, Woodbridge: Boydell, 2006.

Patterson, Mary Hampson, *Domesticating the Reformation: Protestant Best Sellers, Private Devotion, and the Revolution of English Piety*, Madison & Teaneck, NJ: Fairleigh Dickinson University Press, 2007.

Patterson, William B., *King James VI and I and the Reunion of Christendom*, Cambridge: Cambridge University Press, 1997.

Pepper, Robert., ed., *Four Tudor Books on Education*, Gainesville, FL; Scholars' Facsimiles & Reprints, 1966.

Pettegree, Andrew, *Reformation and the Culture of Persuasion*, Cambridge: Cambridge University Press, 2005.

Pettit, Norman, *The Heart Prepared: Grace and Conversion in Puritan Spiritual Life*, New Haven and London: Yale University Press, 1966.

Phelps, William Lyon, ed., *Matthew Merian's Illustrated Bible*, New York: William Morrow & Company, 1933.

Piggott, Stuart, 'William Camden and the *Britannia*', *Proceedings of the British Academy*, xxxvii (1951), 199-217.

Pinchbeck, Ivy and M Hewitt, *Children in English Society*, London: Routledge & K Paul, 1969.

Pollard, A. W. and G. R. Redgrave, *A Short-Title Catalogue of Books Printed in England, Scotland and Ireland . . . 1475-1640*, 2nd ed. revised, W. A. Jackson, F. S. Ferguson, Katharine F. Pantzer, eds., London: Bibliographical Society, 1986.

Pollock, Linda, *With Faith and Physic: The Life of a Tudor Gentlewoman, Lady*

Grace Mildmay, 1552-1620, London: Collins and Brown, 1993.

Popkin, Richard, 'Hartlib, Dury and the Jews', in *Samuel Hartlib and Universal Reformation: Studies in Intellectual Communication*, Mark Greengrass *et al, eds.,* Cambridge and New York: Cambridge University Press, 1994, pp. 118-136.

Porter, Roy, *The Greatest Benefit to Mankind: A Medical History of Humanity*, New York & London: Norton, 1997.

Powell, William S., *John Pory, 1572-1636; The Life and Letters of a Man of Many Parts*, Chapel Hill: University of North Carolina Press, 1977.

Powers-Beck, Jeffrey, *Writing the Flesh: The Herbert Family Dialogue*, Pittsburgh: Duquesne University Press, 1998.

Prestwich, Menna, *Cranfield: Politics and Profits under the Early Stuarts*, Oxford: Clarendon Press, 1966.

Prior, Charles W. A., *Defining the Jacobean Church: The Politics of Religious Controversy, 1603-1625*, Cambridge: Cambridge University Press, 2005.

Proby, Granville, 'The Protestation Returns for Huntingdonshire', *Transactions of the Cambridgeshire and Huntingdonshire Archaeological Society*, vol. V pp.289-368 [Ely, 1937].

Questier, Michael, *Conversion, Politics and Religion in England, 1580-1625*, Cambridge: Cambridge University Press, 1996.

Rabb, Theodore K, *Enterprise & Empire: Merchant and Gentry Investment in the Expansion of England, 1575-1630*, Cambridge, MA: Harvard University Press, 1967.

Rabb, Theodore K, *Jacobean Gentleman: Sir Edwin Sandys, 1561-1629*, Princeton: Princeton University Press, 1998.

Ransome, D. R., 'John Ferrar of Little Gidding', *Records of Huntingdonshire*, Vol 3, No 8 (2000), 16-29.

Joyce Ransome 'Prelude to Piety: Nicholas Ferrar's Grand Tour', *The Seventeenth Century*, 18 (Spring 2003), 1-24.

Joyce Ransome, 'Little Gidding in 1796', *Records of Huntingdonshire*, 3 (2001-2), 13-28.

Joyce Ransome, 'Monotessaron: The Harmonies of Little Gidding', *The Seventeenth Century*, 20 (Spring 2005), 22-52.

Joyce Ransome, '"Voluntary Anglicanism": The Contribution of Little Gidding', *The Seventeenth Century*, 24 (Spring 2009), 52-73

Joyce Ransome, 'George Herbert, Nicholas Ferrar and the "Pious Works" of Little Gidding', *George Herbert Journal*, 31 (2007-08), 1-19.

Rapley, Elizabeth, *The Devotes: Women and Church in Seventeenth-Century France*, Montreal & Kingston, London, Paris: McGill-Queen's University Press, 1990.

Roper, Lyndal, *The Holy Household: Women and Morals in Reformation Augsburg*, Oxford: Clarendon Press, 1989.

Rose, Craig, 'Providence, Protestant Union and Godly Reformation in the 1690s', *Transactiions of the Royal Historical Society*, Sixth Series, III (London, 1993), pp. 151-169.

Rosser, Gervase, 'Parochial Conformity and Voluntary Religion in Late Medieval

England', in *Transactions of the Royal Historical Society*, Sixth Series, I (London, 1991), pp. 173-89.

Ruigh, Robert E, *The Parliament of 1624: Politics and Foreign Policy*, Cambridge, MA: Harvard University Press, 1971.

Russell, P. A., *Lay Theology in the Reformation*, Cambridge: Cambridge University Press, 1986.

Rutman, Darret B., *Winsthrop's Boston: A Portrait of a Puritan Town, 1630-1649*, Chapel Hill, NC: University of North Carolina Press for the Institute of Early American History and Culture, 1965

Ryrie, Alec, ed., *Palgrave Advances in the European Reformations*, Basingstoke: Palgrave MacMillan, 2006.

Sadler, John Edward, *J. A. Comenius and the Concept of Universal Education*, London: George Allen and Unwin, 1966.

Salmon, J. H. M., 'Seneca and Tacitus in Jacobean England', in *The Mental World of the Jacobean Court*, Linda Levy Peck, ed., Cambridge: Cambridge University Press, 1991, pp. 169-88.

Santosuossso, Antonio, 'Religion *More Veneto* and the Trial of Pier Paolo Vergerio', in *Peter Martyr Vermigli and Italian Reform*, Joseph C. McClelland, ed., Waterloo, ON: Wilfrid Laurier University Press, 1980, pp. 43-52.

Saunders, Jason Leweis, *Justus Lipsius*, New York: Liberal Arts Press, 1955.

Schoenfeldt, Michael, *Bodies and Selves in Early Modern England: Physiology and Inwardness in Spenser, Shakespeare, Herbert and Milton*, Cambridge: Cambridge University Press, 2000.

Scott, Jonathan, 'England's Troubles: Exhuming the Popish Plot', in *The Politics of Religion in Restoration England*, Tim Harris, Paul Seaward and Mark Goldie, eds., Oxford: Basil Blackwell, 1990, pp. 107-32.

Scott, Jonathan, *England's Troubles*, Cambridge & New York: Cambridge University Press, 2001.

Scribner, Bob, Roy Porter and Mikulas Teich eds., *The Reformation in National Context*, Cambridge: Cambridge University Press, 1994.

Scribner, R. W., *For the Sake of Simple Folk: Popular Propaganda for the German Reformation,* Oxford: Clarendon Press, 1994.

Scribner, Robert W, 'Ritual and Reformation', in *The German People and the Reformation,* R. Po-Chia Hsia, ed., Ithaca & London: Cornell University Press, 1988, pp. 122-44.

Searle, Arthur, ed., *Barrington Family Letters, 1628-32*, London: Royal Historical Society for Camden Society, 1983.

Seaver, Paul S., 'Laud and the Livery Companies', in *State, Sovereigns and Society: Essays in Honour of A. J. Slavin*, Charles Carlton, *et al*, eds., New York: St Martin's Press, 1998, pp. 219-34.

Seaver, Paul S., *The Puritan Lectureships: The Politics of Religious Dissent, 1560-1662*, Stanford: Stanford University Press, 1970.

Seaver, Paul, *Wallington's World: A Puritan Artisan in Seventeenth-Century London*, Stanford: Stanford University Press, 1985.

Seaward, Paul, 'Gilbert Sheldon, the London Vestries, and the Defence of the Church', in Harris, Tim, Paul Seaward and Mark Goldie, eds.,*The Politics of Religion in Restoration England*, Oxford: Basil Blackwell, 1990, pp. 49-74.

Secretan, Charles Frederick, *Memoirs of the Life and Times of the Pious Robert Nelson*, London: John Murray, 1860.

Sellin, Paul R., *Daniel Heinsius and Stuart England*, Leiden & London: Leiden University Press, Oxford University Press, 1968.

Selwyn, Jennifer D., *A Paradise Inhabited by Devils: The Jesuits Civilizing Mission in Early Modern Naples*, Ashgate: Institutum Historicum Societatis Iesu, 2004.

Shagan, Ethan, 'The Battle for Indifference in Elizabethan England', in *Moderate Voices in the European Reformation*, Luc Racaut, and Alec Ryrie, eds, Aldershot: Ashgate, 2005, 122-44.

Sharpe, Kevin, *The Personal Rule of Charles I*, New Haven: Yale University Press, 1992.

Sharpe, Kevin, *Sir Robert Cotton, 1586-1631: History and Politics in Early Modern England*, Oxford: Oxford University Press, 1979.

Sherman, William H., *John Dee: The Politics of Reading and Writing in the English Renaissance*, Amherst, MA: University of Massachusetts Press, 1995.

Sherrard, Philip, 'The Desanctification of Nature', in *Sanctity and Secularity: The Church and the World*, Derek Baker, ed., Studies in Church History, 10, Oxford: Blackwell for the Ecclesiastical History Society, 1973, pp. 1-20.

Sherwood, Terry G., *Herbert's Prayerful Art*, Toronto: University of Toronto Press, 1989.

Shirley, Evelyn Philip, *Stemmata Shirleiana:or the Annals of the Shirley Family, Lords of Nether Etindon in the County of Warwick, and of Shirley in the County of Derby*, 2nd edition, Westminster: Nichols and Sons, 1873.

Sim, Alison, *The Tudor Housewife*, Stroud: Sutton, 1996.

Slater, M., *Family Life in the Seventeenth Century: The Verneys of Claydon House*, London and Boston: Routledge, 1984,

Smith, David L., 'Catholic, Anglican or Puritan? Edward Sackville, Fourth Earl of Dorset and the Ambiguities of Religion in Early Stuart England', in *Transactions of the Royal Historical Society*, Sixth Series, II (London, 1992), pp. 105-24.

Spence, Jonathan D., *The Memory Palace of Matteo Ricci*, New York: Penguin, 1985.

Spinks, Bryan D., *Sacraments, Ceremonies and the Stuart Divines: Sacramental Theology and Liturgy in England and Scotland, 1603-62*, Aldershot and Burlington, VT: Ashgate, 2002.

Spurr, John, 'The Church, the societies and the moral revolution of 1688', in *The Church of England c. 1689-c.1833: From Toleration to Tractariansim*, John Walsh, Colin Haydon and Stephen Taylor, eds., Cambridge: Cambridge University Press, 1993, pp. 127-42.

Spurr, John, *The Restoration Church of England, 1646-1689*, New Haven and London: Yale University Press, 1991.

Spurr, John, '"Virtue, Religion and Government": the Anglican Uses of Providence', in Tim Harris, Paul Seaward and Mark Goldie, eds.,*The Politics of Religion in Restoration England*, Oxford: Basil Blackwell, 1990, pp. 29-48

Staves, Susan, *Married Women's Separate Property in England, 1660-1833*, Cambridge, MA: Harvard University Press, 1990.

Stoye, John, *English Travellers Abroad, 1604-1667,* Revised Edition, New Haven and London: Yale University Press, 1989.

Strachan, Michael, *The Life and Adventures of Thomas Coryate*, London: Oxford University Press, 1962.

Strauss, Gerald, *Luther's House of Learning*, Baltimore & London: Johns Hopkins University Press, 1978.

Sturges, H. A. C. (comp), *Register of Admissions to the Honourable Society of the Middle Temple, from the fifteenth century to the year 1944, I (1501-1781),* London: Butterworth, 1949.

Symonds, Richard, *Alternative Saints: The Post-Reformation British People Commemorated by the Church of England*, New York: St. Martin's, 1988.

Tadmor, Naomi, *Family and Friends in Eighteenth-Century England: Household, Kinship, and Patronage*, Cambridge: Cambridge University Press, 2001.

Tawney, R. H., *Business and Politics under James I: Lionel Cranfield as Merchant and Minister*, Cambridge: Cambridge University Press, 1958.

Todd, Margot, ed., *Reformation to Revolution: Politics and Religion in Early Modern England*, London & New York: Routledge, 1995.

Turnbull, G. H., *Hartlib, Dury and Comenius*, [Liverpool]: University Press of Liverpool, 1947.

Tyacke, Nicholas, *Anti-Calvinists: The Rise of English Arminianism, c. 1590-1640*, Oxford: Clarendon Press, 1987.

Tyacke, Nicholas, *Aspects of English Protestantism, c. 1530-1700*, Manchester and New York: Manchester University Press, 2001.

Tyler, J. Jeffrey, *Lord of the Sacred City: The Episcopus Exclusus in Late Medieval and Early Modern Germany*, Studies in Medieval and Reformation Thought, LXXII, Heiko Oberman, ed.,Leiden, Boston, Cologne: Brill, 1999.

Upton, Anthony F., *Sir Arthur Ingram, c. 1565-1642: A Study of the Origins of an English Landed Family*, Oxford: Oxford University Press, 1961.

Vendler, Helen, *The Poetry of George Herbert*, Cambridge & London: Cambridge University Press, 1975.

Venn, John and J. A. Venn, *Alumni Cantabrigiensis*, Cambridge: Cambridge University Press, 1922-54.

Vicinus, Martha, *Independent Women: Work and Community for Single Women, 1850-1920*, Chicago and London: University of Chicago Press, 1985.

Vieth, Jr., Gene Edward, *Reformation Spirituality: The Religion of George Herbert*, Lewisburg, PA, London & Toronto: Bucknell University Press and Associated University Presses, 1985.

Wabuda, Susan, 'Triple Deckers and Eagle Lecterns: Church Furniture for the Book in Late Medieval and Early Modern England', in *The Church and the Book*, R.N. Swanson, ed., Studies in Church History, 38, Woodbridge: Boydell Press for The Ecclesiastical History Society, 2004, pp. 143.

Wabuda, Susan, 'The Woman with the Rock: the Controversy on women and

Bible reading', in *Belief and Practice in Reformation England. A Tribute to Patrick Collinson from his Students*, Susan Wabuda and Caroline Litzenberger, eds., Aldershot: Ashgate, 1998, pp.40-59.

Wadkins, Timothy, 'White, Francis (1563/4-1638)', *Oxford Dictionary of National Biography*, Oxford University Press, 2004 [accessed 19 Oct 2004: http://www.oxforddnb.com/view/article/29239]

Wallas, Ada, *Before the Bluestockings*, Folcroft Library Editions, 1977 (first published London: George Allen & Unwin, 1929).

Walsham, Alexandra, *Charitable Hatred: Tolerance and Intolerance in England, 1500-1700*, Manchester and New York, Manchester University Press, 2006.

Walsham, Alexandra, *Church Papists: Catholicism, Conformity and Confessional Polemic in Early Modern England*, Woodbridge: Boydell Press for Royal Historical Society, 2nd ed. 1999.

Walsham, Alexandra, 'The Parochial Roots of Laudianism Revisited: Catholics, Anti-Calvinists and "Parish Anglicans" in Early Stuart England', *Journal of Ecclesiastical History*, Vol 49, No 4 (October 1998), 620-51.

Walsham, Alexandra, *Providence in Early Modern England*, Oxford: Oxford University Press, 1999.

Watson, Andrew G., *The Library of Sir Simonds D'Ewes*, London: Trustees of the British Museum, 1966.

Webster, Tom, *Godly Clergy in Early Stuart England: The Caroline Puritan Movement, 1620-1643*, Cambridge: Cambridge University Press, 1997.

Wiesner, Merry E. and Joan Skocir, *Convents Confront the Reformation: Catholic and Protestant Nuns in Germany*, Milwaukee: Marquette University Press, 1996.

Wiesner, Merry E., 'Having Her Own Smoke: Employment and Independence for Singlewomen in Germany, 1400-1750', in Judith M. Bennett and Amy M. Froide, eds., *Singlewomen in the European Past, 1250-1800*, Philadelphia: University of Pennsylvania Press, 1999, pp. 192-216.

Wilcox, Helen, 'Entering *The Temple*: women, reading, and devotion in seventeenth-century England', in *Religion, Literature, and Politics in Post-Reformation England*, Donna B. Hamilton and Richard Strier, eds., Cambridge: Cambridge University Press, 1996, pp. 187-207.

Wilcox, Helen, '"You that Indeared are to Pietie": Herbert and Seventeenth_Century Women', in Jonathan. F. S. Post and Sidney Gottlieb, eds., *George Herbert in the Nineties: Reflections and Reassessments*, Fairfield, CT: George Herbert Journal Special Studies and Monographs, 1995, pp. 201-14.

Wing, Donald, ed., *Short-Title Catalogue of Books Printed in England, Scotland, Ireland, Wales, and British North America, 1641-1700*, 4 vols., New York: Modern Language Association of America, 1998.

Woolfson, Jonathan, *Padua and the Tudors*, New York: Penguin, 1985.

Wrightson, Keith, *English Society 1580-1680*, London: Hutchison, 1982.

Yates, Frances A., *The Art of Memory*, Chicago: University of Chicago Press, 1966.

Yates, Frances, *The Occult Philosophy in the Elizabethan Age*, London & New York: Routledge, Classics, 2001 (first published 1979).

Index

model for later religious societies,
185
nicknames, 129–30
nicknames in reconstituted group, 154
purposes, 128–29
revived and reconstituted 1634/5,
154–56
socratic dialogue, 127, 138
'storying' as Christmas cheer, 132, 140
Story Books, 14
temperance debate, 137
Little Gidding
almshouse, 54
as community, 19
as 'Protestant Monastery', 192
church, 53–54
contemporary critics, 176
estate management, 50
household Life
daily devotions, 64–65
education, 66
music, 65
readings, 65
influence as example, 22, 191
links to Nonjurors, 181
preserving the legacy, 176–78
purchase 1624, 47
remembered as 'religious society'.
See Thurscross, Timothy and
Worthington, John
Locke, John
friend of Dr John Mapletoft, 188

Mapletoft, Dr John, 22, 167
active in Society for Propogating
Gospel, 190
at Gidding and Westminster
School, 187
circle of friends, 188
education, 188
family papers held by, 190
influence of Gidding, 190
in Royal Society and Gresham
College, 188

promotes Charity Schools, 189
voluntary societies, 188–90
Mapletoft, Joshua, 15, 21, 164
death, 105
illness and temperance, 101
illness as sign from God, 102
marriage to Susanna Collet, 77
on The Temple, 116
Mapletoft, Robert, 80, 163
his temperance diet, 143
in Restoration church, 187–88
Mapletoft, Solomon, 167
Mapletoft, Susanna Collet, 133
final revival of Little Academy, 154
relationship to Nicholas, 78
Maycock, Alan, 13, 14
Middleton, Hugh, 26
Middleton, Robert, 26, 57
Middleton, Thomas, 26, 29, 30

Neile, Richard, 27
Nelson, Robert, 189
Night vigils, 22, 161

Oley, Barnabas, 80, 144
and Ferrar biography, 178
knows Mary Collet Ferrar, 179

Palsgrave. *See* Elector Palatine
Peckard, Peter, 14
Pembroke, Earl of, 160
Ralegh, Sir Walter, 26

Ramsay, John (husband of Margaret
Collet), 80
Religious Societies, 185–86
procedures and purposes, 185

Sales, St Francis de, 127
Sandys, Sir Edwin, 29, 38, 42, 43, 82
bankruptcy threat, 46
Scot, Robert, Master of Clare Hall, 32
Sheldon, Gilbert, 188
Sheppard, Thomas, 34, 41, 42, 46, 48, 56
lawsuit against, 57–58
Sherington, Martha (wife of Thomas
Collet), 60